Quality Tourism Experiences

165101

Quality Tourism Experiences

Gayle Jennings
Norma Polovitz Nickerson

ELSEVIER
BUTTERWORTH
HEINEMANN

Amsterdam • Boston • Heidelberg • London • New York • Oxford
Paris • San Diego • San Francisco • Singapore • Sydney • Tokyo

Elsevier Butterworth–Heinemann
30 Corporate Drive, Suite 400, Burlington, MA 01803, USA
Linacre House, Jordan Hill, Oxford OX2 8DP, UK

Library of Congress Cataloging-in-Publication Data
Jennings, Gayle, 1955-
  Quality tourism experiences / Gayle Jennings and Norma Polovitz Nickerson.— 1st ed.
    p. cm.
  Includes bibliographical references and index.
  ISBN 0-7506-7811-9 (alk. paper)
  1. Tourism. 2. Quality (Aesthetics) I. Nickerson, Norma Polovitz. II. Title.
  G155.A1J46 2005
  910—dc22   2005012669

British Library Cataloguing-in-Publication Data
A catalogue record for this book is available from the British Library.

ISBN 13: 978-0-7506-7811-7
ISBN 10: 0-7506-7811-9

For information on all Elsevier Butterworth–Heinemann publications
visit our Web site at www.books.elsevier.com

Working together to grow
libraries in developing countries

www.elsevier.com | www.bookaid.org | www.sabre.org

ELSEVIER   BOOK AID
             International   Sabre Foundation

Printed in the United States of America
05 06 07 08 09 10   10 9 8 7 6 5 4 3 2 1

Contents

List of Figures   xi

List of Tables   xiii

Preface   xv

Acknowledgments   xvii

About the Contributors   xix

Chapter 1: Perspectives on Quality Tourism Experiences: An Introduction   1
Gayle Jennings

Theoretical Research Paradigms Informing This Book   2
Dominant Theoretical Concepts, Frameworks, and Themes in the Book   4
State of Knowledge: Quality Tourism Experiences   4
  Tourism and Tourist Experiences   8
  Quality Tourism Experiences and Sustainability   10
  Quality Tourism Experiences and Authenticity   11
Various Potential Stakeholder Groups Associated with the (Re)Presentation
  of Quality Tourism Experiences   11
Conclusion   13
References   15

Section One: Social Construction of Quality Tourism Experiences   23

Chapter 2: State of Knowledge: Mass Media and Its Relationship to Perceptions of Quality   25
Sue Beeton, Heather E. Bowen, and Carla Almeida Santos

Social Construction   27
Social Construction through Mass Media   29
  Social Construction, Mass Media, and Their Relationship to Tourism   30

The Rise of International Travel as an Aspect of Mass Entertainment   30
Mediascapes   32
Tourism Imaging and Mass-Mediated Social Construction   33
The Social Construction of Quality Tourism Experiences through
     Mass Media   34
Implications   35
References   35

Chapter 3: Constructing Quality, Constructing Reality   38
Heather E. Bowen and Carla Almeida Santos

Constructing Quality, Constructing Reality   38
Why Television?   40
     The Travel Channel's *World's Best*   41
Methodology   42
Constructed Notions of Quality Tourism: Travel Channel   44
     High Level of Service   45
     Seclusion and Solitude   45
     Beautiful and Pristine, Yet Ordered and Controlled   46
     Unique or Superlative Feature or Activity   47
     Fine Dining   48
     Well-Appointed Rooms   48
     Expensive and Therefore Exclusive   48
     European Superiority   49
Constructed Notions of Quality Tourism: *The Australian*   49
Discussion   51
References   53

Section Two: Mediating Meaning   55

**Chapter 4: Mediating Meaning: Perspectives on Brokering
Quality Tourist Experiences**   57
Gayle Jennings and Betty Weiler

Purpose, Focus, and Definitions   57
State of Knowledge   60
     Types of Brokers   60
     Brokering of What?   65
Theoretical Lenses   68
     Factors That Influence the Tourist's Need or Desire for Mediators
       or Brokers   68
Discussion   70
     Mediation, Tourist Typologies, and the Tourist Experience   70
Implications   72
     When and How Does Mediation Contribute to or Enhance
       the Quality of the Tourist Experience?   73
     Toward a Specific Research Agenda   74
References   75

Section Three: Interpretation of Meaning and Place — 79

Chapter 5: Connecting Experiences to Quality: Understanding the Meanings Behind Visitors' Experiences — 81
Kathleen Andereck, Kelly S. Bricker, Deborah Kerstetter, and Norma Polovitz Nickerson

Experience — 82
  Experience in a Recreational or Travel Context — 82
  Experience as Understood Through Different Methodological Lenses — 83
The Arizona Experience — 84
  Pull Factors — 85
  The Social Component — 87
  Support and Customer Service Components — 87
The Montana Experience — 88
  Environment — 88
  Activities — 88
  Western Frontier — 89
  Spirituality — 90
California and the River Running Experience — 90
  Recreational-Environmental — 90
  Human-Recreation — 92
  Heritage-Environmental — 92
Discussion — 93
  Creating Quality Experiences — 95
References — 96

Chapter 6: Saravanua ni vanua: Exploring Sense of Place in the Rural Highlands of Fiji — 99
Kelly S. Bricker and Deborah Kerstetter

Sense of Place — 99
Vanua: Place and Its Meaning in Fiji — 101
Tourism Development — 101
Tourism Development in Fiji — 102
  Tourism Development in Serua and Namosi Provinces — 102
Village Residents and Their *Vanua* — 103
  Constructing the Data — 103
    Phase I – Sense of Place as Described by Village Residents — 103
    Phase II – Residents' Level of Agreement with Sense of Place Statements — 104
Discussion — 107
References — 109

Section Four: Quality of Life and Interpretation of Quality Tourism Experiences — 113

Chapter 7: Linking Quality Tourism Experiences, Residents' Quality of Life, and Quality Experiences for Tourists — 115
Barbara A. Carmichael

Role of Local Residents in Quality Tourism Experiences — 116
Perceived Impacts of Tourism — 117

Resident Attitudes Toward Tourism   118
  Theory Development   119
  Advances in Methods: Measurement, Scales, and Modeling   124
Resident Attitudes and Their Link with Resident Behaviors and
  Coping Strategies   126
Resident Coping Strategies and the Link with Tourism Experiences and
  Tourist Behaviors   127
Chapter Implications   129
References   131

Chapter 8: Tourism and Quality of Life   136
Kathleen Andereck and Claudia Jurowski

Quality-of-Life Measures   136
Quality-of-Life Dimensions   137
Tourism and Resident Quality-of-Life Studies   138
  Economic Aspects of Resident Quality of Life   139
  Sociocultural Aspects of Resident Quality of Life   140
  Environmental Aspects of Resident Quality of Life   140
  Predictors of Residents' Perceptions of Tourism   141
Arizona Residents   142
  Measurement   143
  Data Analysis   143
  Results   145
  Discussion   149
Implications   150
References   152

**Section Five: Political-Economic Construction of Quality
Tourism Experiences**   155

**Chapter 9: Introduction to Political-Economic Construction
of Quality Tourism Experiences**   159
Margaret J. Daniels and Lori Pennington-Gray

Tourism as an 'Industry'   159
Tourism and Economic Development   161
Tourism as an Export: Economic Base Theory   161
The Distributional Effects of Economic Development   163
Case Study: No Growth Policy in Alachua County   165
Justification and Goals   168
References   169

Chapter 10: Quality Tourism Development and Planning   171
Kelly S. Bricker, Margaret J. Daniels, and Barbara A. Carmichael

Development and Tourism   171
  Addressing Tourism Development   173

A Meta-Analysis of Current Research in Tourism and Environment
  Relationships Relative to Biodiversity Hotspots   174
  Representation of Biodiversity Hotspots and Countries   177
    Constituency Building   178
    Economic Benefits   180
  Funding for Conservation?   182
    Process and Planning   182
    Land Tenure and Ownership   182
    Mismanagement and Distribution of Funds   182
    Access to Visitors and Visitor Dollars   183
  Discussion   183
Case Study: Native Americans in Southeast Connecticut—Contested
  Spaces and Tourism Developments   184
  Contested Landscapes – Historical Background   184
  Changing Power Relations   185
  Boundaries, Land Annexation, and Infrastructure—Contested Spaces   186
  Quality of Life and Sustainability—Perceived Impacts and
    Social Representations   187
Implications   189
References   189

Chapter 11: The Distribution of Tourism Benefits   192
Claudia Jurowski, Margaret J. Daniels, and Lori Pennington-Gray

Efficiency and Equity   193
Social Exchange Theory   195
Case Study: Daytona Beach, Florida   197
Implications   204
References   205

**Chapter 12: Political-Economic Construction of Quality
Tourism Experiences**   208
Lori Pennington-Gray and Barbara A. Carmichael

Model of Tourism Planning and Development   208
  Sustainability and Tourism Planning: The Three Tenets of Sustainability 209
  Social Equity at the Core of Decision Making   211
  Revised Model of Tourism Planning and Development   211
Case Study #1: Government Labeling of a Quality Tourism Experience:
  An Example from Ontario, Canada: Is the Process Democratic?   212
Case Study #2: Political-Economic Construction of Quality Tourism
  Experiences in a Medium-Sized County in Florida: How to Do It Right 218
  Social Equity in Alachua County Tourism Planning   219
  Economic Vitality in Alachua County Tourism Planning   220
  Ecological Integrity in Alachua County Tourism Planning   220
Implications   220
References   222

Section Six: Towards a Conclusion 225

Chapter 13: Some Reflections on Quality Tourism Experiences 227
Norma Polovitz Nickerson

Influences on Quality Tourism Experiences 228
The Traveler 229
The Product 230
Local Population 232
Future Directions 233

Appendix 237

Index 245

List of Figures

1.1	Emblematic usage of the term quality tourism experiences	5
1.2	The travel experience [Killion (1992) after Clawson (1963)]	9
1.3	The three phases of the vacation experience (Craig-Smith and French, 1994)	9
1.4	Research agenda for quality tourism researchers	14
7.1	Linkages between quality of life experiences for local residents and tourists	116
7.2	Factors influencing quality of life for residents and quality experiences of tourists within a tourism context	130
9.1	Systems representation of travel and tourism (Adapted from Crompton, 1999)	160
9.2	Map of north-central Florida and Alachua County	165
9.3	Vision for tourism in Alachua County	168
11.1	Support variables	202
11.2	Predictor variables	202
12.1	Model of tourism planning and development (Middleton and Hawkins, 1998)	209
12.2	Sustainability model from Flint and Danner (2001)	210
12.3	A model for quality tourism experiences	212
12.4	Framework used in the premier ranking destination measurement process	215
13.1	Various influences on quality tourism experiences	228

List of Tables

1.1	Overview of trends in academic literature	7
1.2	Overview of some of the themes involved in the study of authenticity and tourism experiences	12
3.1	World's best episodes	43
4.1	Examples of mediators and brokers associated with the tourist experience	62
4.2	Model of tourist settings based on Cohen (1979)	70
5.1	Arizona travel experience categories	85
5.2	A Montana vacation – the meaning behind the experience	89
5.3	The California River experience	91–92
6.1	Place meaning statements	104
6.2	Level of agreement with statements that describe the village (i.e., place)	105
6.3	Differences in place meaning between residents of Nakavika and Nabukelevu	106
8.1	Means for QOL indicators	144
8.2	Factor analysis of TQOL domains	145–146
8.3	Final regression models	148
9.1	Short-run household distributional effects of state and local economic development policies	164
9.2	Goals for sustainable Alachua county	166–167
10.1	Biodiversity hotspot areas represented by case studies	177
10.2	Does tourism promote constituency building to promote conservation? (From Bricker et al., in press)	179
10.3	Does tourism provide local people with alternatives to exploiting conservation areas? (From Bricker et al., in press)	181

10.4	Changes in resident responses to quality of life variables over time	188
10.5	Changes in resident attitudes toward the Mashentucket Pequot tribe over time	188
11.1	Means of cost benefit variables for three groups	200
11.2	Results of t-test comparison of means	201
11.3	Regression statistics	203
12.1	Dimensions for a premier ranked tourism destination	214
12.2	Criteria and measures used in assessing element K: managing within carrying capacities	216

Preface

The genesis of this book, *Quality Tourism Experiences,* has its roots in a number of conversations, which occurred in different places, at different times, and with different researchers around the world until the intent of those conversations coalesced into a focused conversation at the 2002 Travel and Tourism Research Association (TTRA) conference. A number of us who have contributed to this book thought it would be a generative and creative experience to hold a research retreat involving researchers with similarly placed interests to plan a collaborative research agenda and produce a series of research outputs, one of which would be the publication of this book. Other research outputs included conference papers, conference posters, and a conference panel session, all related to *Quality Tourism Experiences.*

Through our various networks, a group of thirteen researchers was able to come together at a nominated time and place. The time was 10-13 June 2003 and the place was the delightful and idyllic "Montana Island Lodge," a small island conference center in Western Montana, USA, connected to The University of Montana. The researchers, in alphabetical order, were: Kathleen Andereck, Arizona State University, USA; Sue Beeton, LaTrobe University, Australia; Heather E. Bowen, University of New Hampshire, USA; Kelly S. Bricker, West Virginia University, USA; Barbara A. Carmichael, Wilfrid Laurier University, Canada; Margaret J. Daniels, George Mason University, USA; Gayle Jennings, Griffith University, Australia; Claudia Jurowski, Northern Arizona University, USA; Deborah Kerstetter, Penn State University, USA; Norma Polovitz Nickerson, The University of Montana, USA; Lori Pennington-Gray, University of Florida, USA; Carla Almeida Santos, University of Illinois-Champaign, USA; and Betty Weiler, Monash University, Australia.

During the course of the 4-day retreat we worked long and hard hours into the night. We dialogued and synthesized our shared interests related to the notion of *Quality Tourism Experiences.* As a group, we scoped our research agenda and we framed the overall structure and content of the book as well as the sections and chapter foci. We collaborated across disciplinary boundaries, theoretical paradigms and methodologies, areas of interest, and geographical spaces. We commenced writing chapters. We identified and assigned internal and external review processes to match the rigor of the writing process with the rigor of our research processes.

In the course of our research and writing, we discovered that our unifying feature was the knowledge that there can be no one definition of quality tourism experiences and that through this book we would celebrate the multiplicity of phenomena associated with a term such as quality tourism experiences. We also realised that in this book we would not be able to cover the diversity that is quality tourism experiences. And, because of that, we do not profess that this is a definitive representation of all that constitutes quality tourism experiences. There are additional representations and interpretations. Subsequently, we hope that others from differing backgrounds, disciplines, contexts, spaces, and times will also add their voices and their texts to the consideration of quality tourism experiences.

Gayle Jennings
Norma Polovitz Nickerson
February 2005

Acknowledgments

Firstly, the contributors to *Quality Tourism Experiences* would like to thank the participants who engaged in the research work which has been reported in this book; without their cooperation our research would not have been able to be undertaken. Subsequently, we acknowledge their substantive contribution to the generation of knowledge in this area of tourism research.

Secondly, all of the contributors wish to acknowledge and thank all our respective families, friends, colleagues, and institutions for their support throughout the process of generating this book, *Quality Tourism Experiences.* Such a network of support is important and sustains both our personal and working lives.

Thirdly, we would like to thank Jane Fisher, the Director, as well as the staff of the "Montana Island Lodge"; we express our appreciation for your catering to our needs and for the care and support provided to us all during the research retreat and writing workshop.

Fourthly, thank you to the Institute for Tourism and Recreation Research, College of Forestry and Conservation, The University of Montana, for assistance with return transportation between the airport and the "Montana Island Lodge."

Fifthly, thank you to the Faculty of Business and Law, Central Queensland University, in 2003, especially the Dean, Professor Kevin Fagg, and the Interim Dean, Associate Professor Les Killion, for their support of this project in its initial phases. Thanks also to Dr. Ross Rynehart, Director of *Change Australia,* for financial and infrastructure support for this project.

Sixthly, thank you Heather E. Bowen, the University of New Hampshire, for assistance in the preparation of the WebCT site developed for the project, and Claudia Jurowski and Tim Foster, Northern Arizona University, for the design, maintenance, and hosting of the WebCT site to facilitate project discussions and archiving of project materials.

Seventhly, our sincere thanks to Lee-Anne Maher, Nicole Hartley, and Helen Lobegeier for their substantive assistance with the final preparation of the manuscript.

Eighthly, to Sally North and Jane Macdonald, Elsevier, thank you for your faith in and encouragement of the project, Dennis McGonagle, Anne McGee, Brandy Lilly, Linda Hah, and Jack Pitts thank you for your contributions to the publication and production process, as well as all other staff at Elsevier involved in the production of *Quality Tourism Experiences*.

Finally, to the contributing authors, thank you for being part of this journey in search of quality tourism experiences.

About the Contributors

Kathleen Andereck, PhD, Arizona State University, USA

Kathleen Andereck is a Professor in the Department of Recreation and Tourism Management at Arizona State University at the West campus. Her area of study focuses on recreation and tourism experiences as they relate to visitors, community residents, and tourism/recreation managers. Much of her research has been focused on exploring the nature of tourists' behavior and on the factors that influence that behavior.

Sue Beeton, PhD, LaTrobe University, Australia

Dr. Sue Beeton is Senior Lecturer in Tourism at LaTrobe University, Australia, where she has specialized in tourism and services marketing, community tourism and rural tourism. Her research has revolved around protected area management and community and adventure tourism experiences, which in turn has led to her current focus on film-induced tourism. Her publications include a book *Film-Induced Tourism* as well as *Ecotourism: A Practical Guide for Rural Communities* which has also been published in Japanese.

Heather E. Bowen, PhD, University of New Hampshire, USA

Heather E. Bowen is a Senior Lecturer in the School of Health and Human Services at the University of New Hampshire, USA. Her research includes investigation into the use of human images in tourism magazine advertising and study of the influence of hostel travel on cross-cultural understanding and world peace.

Kelly S. Bricker, PhD, West Virginia University, USA

Kelly S. Bricker is a Senior Social Scientist for Devine, Tarbell and Associates and Affiliate Professor in Recreation, Parks, and Tourism Resources at West Virginia University and Colorado State University. She completed her PhD research with The Pennsylvania State University, where she specialized in Outdoor Recreation and Nature-based Tourism within the program of Recreation, Parks, and Tourism Management. She has special research and teaching interest in sustainable tourism development, natural resource management, and sense of place.

Barbara A. Carmichael, PhD, Wilfrid Laurier University, Canada

Dr. Barbara A. Carmichael is an Associate Professor in the Department of Geography and Environmental Studies and the Associate Director of NEXT Research Centre in the School of Business at Wilfrid Laurier University, Waterloo, Ontario, Canada. She has an MBA from Durham University Business School, United Kingdom, and a PhD from the University of Victoria, British Columbia. Her research interests are in skier choice behavior, special events, casino impacts, market segmentation and resident attitudes toward tourism.

Margaret J. Daniels, PhD, George Mason University, USA

Margaret (Maggie) Daniels is an Assistant Professor of tourism and events management in the School of Recreation, Health and Tourism at George Mason University. Her research interests center on tourism and event economics, tourism planning and policy, visitor motivations, and tourism for individuals with specialized needs.

Gayle Jennings, PhD, Griffith University, Australia

Gayle Jennings is an Associate Professor in Tourism. Her research interests include theoretical paradigms informing research processes, research methodologies, tourism education at the tertiary level, impacts of tourism, tourism and development studies, policy and planning, special interest tourism, marine and national park tourism, rural tourism, adventure tourism, and sport tourism.

Claudia Jurowski, PhD, Northern Arizona University, USA

Claudia Jurowski is a Professor in the School of Hotel and Restaurant Management at Northern Arizona University, where she teaches international courses on hospitality and tourism. Her research is focused on sustainable tourism management, environmental issues related to tourism, and resident attitudes toward tourism development.

Deborah Kerstetter, PhD, Penn State University, USA

Dr. Deborah Kerstetter is an Associate Professor in Recreation, Park and Tourism Management at Penn State University. Her research has primarily focused on issues related to tourism behavior, particularly in heritage and cultural contexts. More recently she has adopted a life course perspective to understanding tourism behavior, especially among women.

Norma Polovitz Nickerson, PhD, The University of Montana, USA

Norma Polovitz Nickerson, PhD, directs the Institute for Tourism and Recreation Research in the College of Forestry and Conservation at The University of Montana. Her research is mostly focused within the state of Montana on nonresident and resident travel and recreation characteristics, economic impacts, market segments, and travel patterns.

Lori Pennington-Gray, PhD, University of Florida, USA

Lori Pennington-Gray's current position is Assistant Professor. Her primary research interest falls under the umbrella of tourism marketing. Primarily she is interested in destination management. She focuses on both the supply-side of the destination (including policy, decision-making, and marketing strategies) as well as the demand-side for the destination (*i.e.*, consumer behavior).

Carla Almeida Santos, PhD, University of Illinois at Urbana-Champaign, USA

Carla Almeida Santos is an Assistant Professor in the Department of Recreation, Sport, and Tourism at University of Illinois at Urbana-Champaign, USA. Her research seeks to elucidate the forces that shape and organize tourism narratives and their use by tourists. Within this framework she explores two general issues: (1) the narrative(s) that constitute the key set of references used by producers and promoters of tourism, and (2) the ways in which readers/tourists play with and against those narratives.

Betty Weiler, PhD, Monash University, Australia

Dr. Betty Weiler is Professor of Tourism at Monash University, Melbourne, Australia. As Director of the Monash Tourism Research Unit, Betty undertakes and supervises a wide range of projects in the broad area of visitor services and tourist experience management. Betty is known for her applied research focus in strategic communication and is currently working with a number of industry partners, including state tourism authorities, protected area management agencies, and major nature-based and heritage tourism attractions.

1

Perspectives on Quality Tourism Experiences: An Introduction

Gayle Jennings

What is a quality tourism experience? At first glance, this would seem to be an easy question to answer, especially given the plethora of tourism literature, which is permeated with references and commentaries in regard to "quality" and "tourism experiences," let alone "quality tourism experiences." However, within the multiplicity of references, an inherent deception is masked, for the answer to "What is a quality tourism experience?" is not so easy. The body of tourism literature resonates with influences from various disciplinary fields and studies, of differing perspectives, standpoints, and theoretical predilections, as well as audience expectations. Further, the development of tourism at local, regional, and national levels has resulted in the appearance of "tourism reflexivity": "the set of disciplines, procedures and criteria that enable each (and every?) place to monitor, evaluate and develop its tourism potential within the emerging patterns of global tourism" (Urry, 2002, p. 141). Such reflexivity has not always resulted in consistent or standardized practices. This is not surprising, given the elusive and unpredictable nature of the phenomenon of tourism itself with all its complexity and multiplicity of interactions, settings, and participants—particularly in the first half of the twenty-first century compared to, for example, the mid-twentieth century.

The passage of time also adds to the difficulty of providing a definitive answer to "What is a quality tourism experience?" This is because the phenomenon of tourism has a temporal nature—what was "quality" yesterday may not be so today and what is a "tourism experience" tomorrow may not have been so 10 years ago. Subsequently, quality tourism experiences need to be interpreted within specific contexts and by specific "actors" as well as reflect the temporality of the settings in which they were constructed. Moreover, returning to the tourism literature, the meaning of "quality tourism experiences" is often assumed as tacit knowledge—

that is, it is taken-for-granted knowledge (see Schutz, 1967). And such knowledge is constantly being reframed, reconstructed, and reinterpreted (see Ryan, 1997). At best chance, we may be able to pin down a number of unifying themes, but a definitive answer remains continually out of reach.

Having introduced the indefinite nature of quality tourism experiences, the purpose of this book needs to be stated. The book explores a number of perspectives and representations of quality tourism experiences in order to emphasize the nebulous nature of what is often assumed as a taken-for-granted concept called quality tourism experience(s). In doing so, the purpose of the book becomes twofold. First is the representation of multiple perspectives of quality tourism perspectives. Second, in the pursuit of those perspectives, the book aims to serve as a model of a collaborative effort among tourism scholars from varying disciplinary backgrounds and settings, who together negotiated the structure, style, and intent of the book.

As a consequence of its twofold purpose, the book draws on a number of theoretical research paradigms—postpositivism, social constructivism, critical theory paradigm, and postmodern paradigm—to inform its discourse. Each of these has differing positions in regard to ontology (world-view), epistemology (relationship between knower and that which is to be known), methodology (quantitative, qualitative, and mixed), and axiology (value free or value embedded). As background for readers who may be unfamiliar with a number of these paradigms, each is briefly discussed in turn.

Following this brief discussion of theoretical research paradigms, an overview of the dominant theoretical concepts, frameworks, and themes evident in the various chapters is presented. This overview is then counterpointed against the multiple perspectives inherent in tourism-related literature in regard to quality tourism experiences in the section titled State of Knowledge: Quality Tourism Experiences. Two additional sections have been included in this chapter as a result of the reviewing process. Several reviewers made commentary in regard to sustainability and authenticity issues related to quality tourism experiences. Their commentaries are addressed in the two related sections: Quality Tourism Experiences and Sustainability and Quality Tourism Experiences and Authenticity. Having mentioned previously the various actors associated with quality tourism experiences, the penultimate section addresses various potential stakeholder groups associated with the (re)presentation of quality tourism experiences. The final section provides the reader with a reiteration of the book's intent.

Theoretical Research Paradigms Informing This Book

Postpositivism considers that there is a single "reality," although postpositivists acknowledge that this is imperfectly and probabilistically determined (Robson, 2002). The epistemological position is objective; however, postpositivists also acknowledge that the knowledge and experiences of the researcher may influence results despite attempts at objectivity, and such biases are acknowledged. Methodologically, postpositivism is primarily predicated on quantitative methods, albeit that mixed methods are utilized with a continuing emphasis on internal and external validity as well as reliability. The axiology of postpositivism is propositional, intrinsic, and objective, although the influence of researchers and any subsequent bias in research design is acknowledged. A related tradition of postpositivism is critical realism, which is based on the work of Bhasker (1978, 1982, 1990) and Harré (1981, 1986). Bhasker (1986) purports that critical realism should have an emancipatory role (axiology). This paradigm tends to inform Chapters Five, Seven, and Eight, and is applied variously in Chapters Six (second phase of the reported study) and Ten (case study example).

Social constructivism has an ontological position that acknowledges the multiple realities of the people (sometimes called actors) participating in the research. Consequently, the ontological position of social constructivism with its multiple realities is contrary to postpositivists who perceive a "reality." The epistemological position of social constructivism is a subjective and value-laden one. Moreover, researchers utilize primarily a qualitative methodology and engage in an intrinsic, instrumental, and transactional axiology. This paradigm informs Chapters Two, Three, and Four, as well as in Chapters Ten and Twelve.

Critical theory paradigm adopts an ontological position that the social world is constrained by rules, although these rules can be changed. Its epistemological perspective is halfway between subjectivism and objectivism. Axiologically, this paradigm should lead to transformational change, as the aim of research in this paradigm is to alter the social circumstances of those being studied. In general, a qualitative research methodology is applied. The work reported in Chapters Six, Nine, Ten, Eleven, and Twelve is predicated on this paradigm.

The *postmodern paradigm* disputes grand theory and views the world (its onto-logical perspective) as being constructed of multiple realities and that no one real-ity has favor over another. A central tenet is the deconstruction of the surface features of phenomena in order to expose underlying core realities. A variety of methods are used, which are generically derived from a qualitative methodology. Axiologically, the postmodern paradigm is propositional, transactional, instru-mental, and intrinsic in its values and ethical stance. This paradigm partially informs the writing of Chapters One, Two, and Four.

Prior to moving on to the dominant theoretical concepts, frameworks, and themes used in *Quality Tourism Experiences,* a note regarding the writing style needs to be made. As readers may be aware, each of the paradigms mentioned here may require a different writing style. To provide some consistency for readers, each chapter, including this chapter, follows the following organizational structure. Each chapter begins with a state of purpose(s), then outlines the state of knowl-edge of the related literature and the methodological/theoretical lens applied. Models and/or frameworks are then presented that inform the writing, followed by research examples and reflections of the implications of each chapter to the further consideration of quality tourism experiences. (See Appendix for research sum-maries of latter.)

Rather than prescriptively use a homogeneous style of writing, those authors writing from a social constructivist perspective use the active first-person voice, whereas those authors operating within a critical realist perspective use the third-person voice. This decision was made to ensure that the writers would be able to remain true to the paradigm informing their work and to simultaneously demon-strate that collaborative works do not have to be homogenized and that differences in style may be celebrated and recognized.

Dominant Theoretical Concepts, Frameworks, and Themes in the Book

The dominant theoretical concepts, frameworks, and themes in *Quality Tourism Experiences* are fivefold in nature. The overlying theoretical concept is the social construction of meaning—in this case, the social construction of meaning for quality tourism experiences. This theoretical concept is specifically introduced in Chapter One, elaborated in Chapter Two, and further extended in Chapters Three and Four. It also resonates variously in the remaining Chapters Five through Twelve. The second theoretical concept cluster is the mediation of meaning and/or meaning making and their related and potential linkages to quality tourism experiences. This concept cluster is explored in Chapters Three, Four, and Five. The interpretation of meaning and place, the third conceptual organizer, appears in Chapters Five and Six. Elements of this conceptual organizer reverberate in Chapters Seven, Eight, and Ten in regard to tourism interfaces with resident communities and their quality of life. This fourth concept, the social construction of quality of life and its relationship to quality tourism experiences, is the particular focus of Chapters Seven and Eight. Further references are made in regard to quality of life in Chapters Ten and Eleven. The final dominant theoretical framework applied in this book is the political construction of quality tourism experiences, and this informs Chapters Nine, Ten, Eleven, and Twelve.

Various sub-themes, concepts, and theories are also applied throughout the book, the main ones being semiotics (Chapter Three), cultural studies (Chapter Three), communication theory (Chapters Two, Three, and Four), symbolic interaction (Chapter Three), heuristics (Chapter Four), the politics of representation (Chapters Three, Four, and Ten), social representations theory (Chapter Seven), social exchange theory (Chapters Seven, Eleven, and Twelve), and political economic theory (Chapters Nine through Twelve). Other sub-themes and concepts include traveler typologies (Chapter Four), cultural brokering (Chapter Four), personal construct theory (Chapter Five), motivation theories (Chapter Five), space and place theories (Chapter Six), and life cycle theory (Chapter Seven). Tourism as a panacea is explored in Chapter Six, while development theory (Chapters Six, Nine, Ten, and Eleven), resident impacts (Chapters Six, Seven, and Eight), quality-of-life measures (Chapters Seven, Eight, and Eleven), and tourism planning concepts are explained and utilized (Chapters Six, Nine, Ten, and Twelve). Dependency theory resonates in Chapter Six, and power is discussed in Chapters Six and Ten. The economic base theory appears in Chapter Nine, and social exchange theory is presented in Chapter Eleven. Other additional sub-themes are variously explored; the reader is referred to the Index for further assistance in locating those.

Having identified the dominant theoretical concepts, frameworks, and themes, as well as the various subthemes, concepts, and theories, the chapter now draws on tourism literature, directly focused on quality tourism experiences, to provide an overview of the state of knowledge in regard to quality tourism experiences at the time of writing this chapter.

State of Knowledge: Quality Tourism Experiences

Earlier in this chapter, it was reported that "quality tourism experiences" is a widely used phrase in tourism and tourism-related texts and is associated with a diversity of meanings and usage. As was intimated, these meanings are ascribed implicitly, explicitly, and tacitly by industry/business, government agencies, tourists, communities, and academics. To establish the diversity of its use and the meanings reflected in its application, two studies were undertaken. The first was a study of publicly available and widely distributed documents sourced from government and quasi-government sites, tourism associations/organizations, as well as tourism consultant sites. This study utilized web-based content analysis and was conducted during the period from September 2003 to April 2004 using Google as a search engine. The first study (as did the second study) considered much of the advice by Ó Dochartaigh (2002) in regard to Internet research. As previously stated, it is interesting to note that the term *quality tourism experiences,* while frequently used, tends not to be explicitly defined in any way, particularly in the public arena. Implicit in the use of the phrase, again, was the assumption by writers that the phrase was understood (that is, meaning was embedded within the words themselves and in the context of their usage—the social construction of meaning). Moreover, the phrase tends to be further qualified with adjectives such as *high, good,* and *higher.* Figure 1.1 provides emblematic examples of such usage.

BALTIC 21: Series No 7/98: Agenda 21 – Baltic Sea Region Tourism
"Social goal: to promote **quality tourism experiences** between visitors and the local population and to promote favourable [sic] social outcomes of tourism"
[www.ee/baltic21/publicat/R7-2.htm]
"Delivering high **quality tourism experiences** to Queensland visitors"
[www.dtrft.qld.gov.au/tourism/documents/Strategy-1.pdf]
"Develop and promote high **quality tourism experiences**"
[www.culture.gov.uk/pdf/8385cdtdcmsp48p57.pdf]
"Québec has considerable potential in terms of **quality tourism experiences**"
[www.tourisme.gouv.qc.ca/mto/publications/pdf/admin/politdev_a.pdf]
"We need to develop a range of high-**quality tourism experiences** targeted to the needs of different markets."
[www.joehockey.com/sptenyrplantou.php]
"The task on hand for the tourism industry and the government is to convert its strengths into marketable, easy to access, good **quality tourism experiences**."
[www.expresshotelierandcaterer.com/20020624/cover1.shtml]
"Tourists are becoming more interested in higher **quality tourism experiences**"
[www.unece/env/europe/kiev/tourism.e.pdf]
"High **quality tourism experiences** are a result of the visitor's interaction with employees, other tourists, the setting or environment, and the host community."
[www.extension.umn.edu/distribution/resourcesand tourism/components/6184g.html]
"So at every opportunity we should encourage high **quality tourism experiences**, which bring satisfaction and enrichment to visitors and a greater appreciation."
[www.nationaltrust.gov.gy/trustnewsd.html]
"Arts and cultural activities can be related to **quality tourism experiences** that provide the benefits of economic activity to the local community."
[www.bmcc.nsw.gov.au/index.cfm?L1=1&L2=636]
"Trends indicate that tourists are becoming increasingly interested in higher **quality tourism experiences** with particular interest in cultural, historic, and natural sites."
[www.coastalguide.org/trends/tourism.html]

Figure 1.1 Emblematic usage of the term *quality tourism experiences.*

This content analysis of public sources indicated that quality tourism experiences were associated with one or more of the following:

■ Interaction between host and guest based on tourist and community perspectives
■ The classification of type of tourism product, particularly perspectives from the tourism industry and government sector
■ Market differentiation and development; tourist perspectives
■ The notion of an integrated system as well as benefits from an economic perspective

Still further, the phrase was used to argue for

■ Positive social impacts
■ Economic benefits
■ Environmental protection
■ Government policy formulation
■ Discrimination between tourism products and sustainability issues

The second study focused on academic source documents in order to determine the usage of "quality tourism experiences" within those sources. Again, the method used was content analysis. The content analysis search term used was *quality tourism experiences*. It was used as an open search term—that is, the term *quality tourism experiences* was used rather than the closed term of *"quality tourism experiences"*. This study was conducted between September 2003 and April 2004 via the Proquest (approximately 4,000 newspapers and periodicals), Ingenta (130 journals by Blackwell Science), and WebSPIRS database search engines. The designated search period in each of these electronic databases was 1988-2004, and only scholarly articles were identified. The search included titles, keywords, and abstracts. It is recognized that this study was a sample, as other database search engines are available on the Internet. However, the intent of the study was to determine a snapshot of quality tourism experiences and it was deemed through conversations with disciplinary-specific librarians (expert opinion) that these three search engines together would provide that information.

To summarize the foci of the academic articles, the following discourses were inductively identified:

■ The importance of quality tourism products for quality tourism experiences
■ The quality of tourism experiences and satisfaction
■ Quality tourism experiences and the management of tourist experiences and associated environmental issues
■ Degradation of environments in different locations (marine, cities, terrestrial, and heritage sites)
■ Consequences for quality tourism products

To a lesser degree, the following themes were also found:

■ Quality tourism experiences and reputation
■ Sustainability and quality tourism experiences
■ Quality tourism experiences and host-guest interactions
■ Quality of life
■ Quality and profitability
■ Modes of experience
■ Place and identity
■ Quality of tourism experiences and motivation (See Table 1-1)

Table 1.1 Overview of trends in academic literature related to quality tourism experiences as well as examples of representative academic articles
(References listed in reverse chronological order)

Trend Topic	Examples of Representative Academic Articles
Importance of quality products for quality tourism experiences	Onome (2003); Weber and Roehl (1999); Laws (1998); Murphy (1997); Vaughan and Russell (1982)
Quality tourism experiences and satisfaction	Yuksel and Yuksel (2001); Laws (1998); Murphy (1997); Chadee and Mattson (1996); Uysal, McDonald, and Martin (1994)
Quality tourism experiences and management of tourist experiences and associated environmental issues, degradation of environments in different locations (marine, cities, terrestrial, and heritage sites) and consequences for quality tourism products	Bhat (2003); Lawson, Manning, Valliere, and Wang (2003); Boyd (2002); Font (2002); Schneider (2002); Bauer and Chan (2001); Harborne, Afzal, and Andrews (2001); Ross and Wall (1999); Mak and Moncur (1998); Murphy (1997); Ayala (1996); Moscardo (1996); Weiler and Davis (1993); Laws (1991); Vaughan and Russell (1982); Smith, Webster et al. (1976)
Service delivery and quality	Warden, Liu, Huang, and Lee (2003); Lennon and Harris (2002); O'Neill, Palmer, and Charters (2002); Ryan (2002); King (2001); Lennon and Graham (2001); Yuksel and Yuksel (2001); Gyimothy (2000); O'Neill, Williams, MacCarthy, and Groves (2000); Ekdahl, Gustafsson, and Edvardsson (1999); Weber and Roehl (1999); Laws (1998); Kandampully and Duddy (1997); Chadee and Mattson (1996); Turco and Riley (1996); Larsen and Rapp (1993); Braithewaite (1992); Bitner (1990); Sheldon and Fox (1988)
Quality tourism experiences and reputation	Keane (1996)
Sustainability and quality tourism experiences	Boyd (2002); Font (2002); Ross and Wall (1999); Cooper and Morpheth (1998); Moscardo (1996)
Quality tourism experiences and host-guest relations	Perdue, Long, and Yang (1999); Cooper and (1998); Timothy and Wall (1997); Howell (1994)
Quality of life	Neal, Sirgy, and Uysal (1999); Perdue, Long, and Yang (1999); Howell (1994)
Quality and profitability	Ayala (1996); Braithewaite (1992)
Modes of experience	Ryan (1997, 2002); Urry (1990, 2002); Lengkeek (2001); Cohen (1972, 1979, 1988)
Place and identity	Campbell (2003); Bricker and Kerstetter (2002); Schneider (2002)
Quality tourism experiences and motivation	Onome (2003); MacCannell (2002); Ryan (1997); Uysal, McDonald, and Martin (1994)

Similarly, quality was associated with different meanings and was used in a variety of contexts within tourism literature. For example, quality was associated with service quality, quality assurance/auditing and control, perceptions of quality at an individual/business/community level (that is, stakeholder level), and in regard to product and market differentiation.

As can be seen from Table 1-1 in this second study, the phrase *quality tourism experiences* tended to be associated with the key focuses of quality and product, quality and satisfaction, and quality and environmental issues.

Both of the studies, undertaken in order to ascertain the state of knowledge, demonstrate that which Urry (2002) posits—specifically, that *quality* is a contested term, and, as this book proposes, so too are the terms *tourism experience(s)* and *tourist experience(s)*. This view, explicitly articulated in Chapters Two, Four, Five, and Seven, emphasizes that a multiplicity of interpretations can be ascribed to quality tourism experiences as well as quality tourist experiences (see Chapter Four). Specifically, in Chapter Two, Beeton, Bowen, and Santos outline the nature of the social construction of reality, drawing on the works of Schutz (1962) and Goffman (1974). Then in Chapter Three, Bowen and Santos comment on the shift from quality being defined by consumer criteria to mass media–mediated definitions and constructions. In Chapter Four, Jennings and Weiler proffer a generic definition of quality tourist experiences as a self-defined term that requires the listener or reader to inquire of the specific meaning from the user. Alternately, in Chapter Five, Andereck, Bricker, Kerstetter, and Nickerson highlight the use of "experiences" as associated with "optimal" or "flow" experiences (Csikzentmihalyi, 1988) and advance a warning found in the critique of research by Stewart (1998) regarding attempts to explain leisure experiences via singular frames that do not endure the test of time or representativeness. Again, to reiterate, this book sets out to affirm that there is not just one definition of *quality,* but multiple definitions and interpretations.

Having discussed the findings of the two studies used to overview the public and academic literature on quality tourism experiences as well as counterpointing this with the intentions of the book, the next section will consider the term *tourist/tourism experience* in isolation from *quality,* as these two terms are also variously used in the literature.

Tourism and Tourist Experiences

Within the scholarly literature, a number of tourism sources use the term *tourism experience,* implicitly or tacitly, but several writers have attempted to chronologically and temporally define the related term *tourist experience* in particular. Specifically, the generic term *tourist experience* is defined by Killion (1992) using the Clawson (1963) recreation experience model in terms of the "planning" phase, the "travel to" phase, the "on-site activities" phase, the "return travel" phase, and the "recollection" phase (see Figure 1.2). Killion presents the experience as a circular model, whereas Clawson represents the experience as a linear model with specific beginning and end points.

A further variation of Killion's model takes into account the fact that the various phases may replicate the entire travel experience, particularly when multidestination travel is undertaken by tourists (Jennings, 1997). Another more simplistic model is provided by Craig-Smith and French (1994), which sees the experience as three linear phases with previous experiences informing future experiences: anticipatory phase, experiential phase, and reflective phase (see Figure 1.3).

These four models reflect some similarity as well as differences in their representation and connectivity between phases. An earlier model, by Erik Cohen

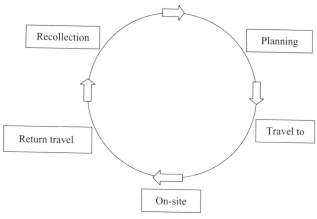

Figure 1.2   The travel experience [Killion (1992) after Clawson (1963)].

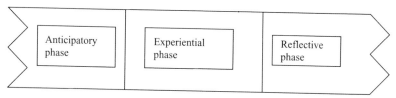

Figure 1.3   The three phases of the vacation experience (Craig-Smith and French, 1994).

(1979), refers to "modes of experience." Each of these examples of models demonstrates again that there are different perspectives on defining the temporal nature of tourism/tourist experiences.

Similarly, within this book the writers provide an even wider array of interpretations beyond the temporal dimension of the tourist experience. For example, in Chapter Two, Beeton, Bowen, and Santos, as do Jennings and Weiler in Chapter Four, introduce the notion of the *tourist gaze* (Urry, 1990, 2002) in regard to the tourist experience. Urry's work iterates that "there is no single tourist gaze as such. It varies by society, by social group and by historical period" (2002, p. 1). In Chapter Five, Andereck, Bricker, Kerstetter, and Nickerson report a historical framework for understanding tourists' experiences as reported by Borrie and Birzell (2001). This framework includes using methods associated with satisfaction, benefits, experiences, and meanings to achieve an understanding of tourists' experiences. Additional deconstructions of the meaning of tourism experience may be classified by social, environmental, and activities components of the overall experience. Furthermore, the authors of Chapter Five also make linkages to the work of Pine and Gilmore (1999) and the latter's coinage of the "experience economy." Specifically, Pine and Gilmore advocate that the western world is operating in the experience economy rather than earlier economic base organizers of commodities, goods, and then services. Like Jennings and Weiler, Andereck, Bricker, Kerstetter, and Nickerson explicitly note that experiences may have both positive and negative consequences regardless of their intention toward quality and that this is associated with the multiple interpretations of quality associated with temporal, social, cultural, political, and environmental cues. This point is reiterated in Chapter Seven by Carmichael, and in Chapter Eight, by Andereck and Jurowski.

Quality Tourism Experiences and Sustainability

Given the emphasis in the tourism literature on tourism and sustainability, the position adopted in this book toward the issue of sustainability requires some discussion. Are quality tourism experiences and issues of sustainability mutually inclusive? On the one hand, it can be convenient and valid to associate quality tourism experiences with the term *sustainability,* as in the following quotes:

The researcher believes the BR [World Biosphere Reserve] designation has strong potential as a way to enhance the tourism profile of a region as well as encourage partnerships between agencies, departments and tourism operators that will stimulate more sustainable practices, while encouraging high-**quality tourism experiences**." *[www.escarpment.org/ leading_edge/LE99/le99_s6/deSalaberry.pdf]*

First, there is a wish to remain small while offering high **quality, sustainable tourism experiences.** (Ryan, 1998)

Sustaining quality in tourism destinations can be described as seeking to maintain a destination's reputation. . . . The task of building reputation will necessitate some investment which implies that, in equilibrium, high **quality tourism experience** will sell for a premium about its cost of production. (Keane, 1996)

To adopt such a focus might assume that *quality* and *sustainability* are synonymous. This is not always the case, as perceived high-quality experiences may in fact be unsustainable For example, a five-star resort experience in a developing nation may place pressure on the allocation of local level resources—water, for instance—and subsequent challenges to the sustainability of indigenous ways of life. To focus only on sustainability would remove the emphasis from an examination of the phrase *quality tourism experiences* in regard to the multiple contexts in which it is applied, as demonstrated in the preceding discussion. Within this book, sustainability is considered, albeit in the context of quality tourism experiences and the related social, political, cultural, and environmental contexts in which it occurs, and with due regard to stakeholder groups.

The theme of sustainability identified in the literature (see Table 1.1) also pervades the writings of the authors of Chapters Six, Ten, and Twelve, which make linkages between quality and sustainability. In particular, in Chapter Eleven, Jurowski, Daniels, and Pennington-Gray note the importance of sustainability for quality tourism experiences for tourists and residents. Bricker and Kerstetter present a similar perspective in Chapter Six. Elsewhere in Chapter Ten, Bricker, Daniels, and Carmichael relate decision making to the short- and long-term consequences of tourism development for the sustainability of local residents' quality of life. Finally, in Chapter Twelve, three tenets of sustainability reported by Flint and Danner (2001)—ecologic integrity, social equity, and economic vitality—are investigated by Pennington-Gray and Carmichael and linked back to quality tourism experiences.

The reader is asked to remember that sustainability is not the dominant organizer for the presentation and discussions of the chapters in this book. Quality tourism experiences assume this role, and sustainability is either a second- or third-level discussant. Moreover, there are a substantive number of currently published books that address sustainability issues and use sustainability as the driver for the organization of textual discussion. This book does not attempt to locate itself as another competitor within the "sustainability and tourism" market segment; instead, it serves to locate within a new niche that focuses on quality tourism experiences as the textual organizer.

Quality Tourism Experiences and Authenticity

Within this book, quality tourism experiences have sometimes been synonymously linked to authentic tourism experiences. The representation of "authentic" tourist experiences can also affect the tourist's, the community's, and the industry's interpretation of an authentic/quality experience. The multiple theoretical approaches that have been used to study "authenticity" in regard to tourism are outlined in Table 1-2. This literature has parallels with the notion of "quality" tourist experiences when used to imply "authentic" tourist experiences.

However, as noted in Table 1-2, although literature has tried to definitively define *authentic* tourist experiences, this has proved to be a relatively futile activity, as the definition of *authentic,* like *quality,* is determined by the tourists and indeed the community, tourism industry, and other stakeholders and is embedded in their own (re)constructions—all essentially and probably different. Postmodern writings have also served to remind us that use of terms such as *authentic* and, in the context of this chapter and book, *quality* is problematic. As Baudrillard (1990, p. 155) commented, "We are presently living with a minimum of real sociality and a maximum of simulation," tourism being one such "simulacrum." More importantly, tourism enables the tourist to consume the "signs" (Baudrillard, 1981) of tourism, and these signs acquire greater exchange value than the authenticity or quality of the experience itself—a point that is intimated in Chapter Three by Bowen and Santos.

Consequently, authenticity is variously discussed in *Quality Tourism Experiences* by Beeton, Bowen, and Santos in Chapter Two; Jennings and Weiler in Chapter Four; Andereck, Bricker, Kerstetter, and Nickerson in Chapter Five; Bricker and Kerstetter in Chapter Six; and Bricker, Daniels, and Carmichael in Chapter Ten.

Various Potential Stakeholder Groups Associated with the (Re)Presentation of Quality Tourism Experiences

As is evident in Chapters Four (Jennings and Weiler), Six (Bricker and Kerstetter), Nine (Daniels and Pennington-Gray) and Ten (Bricker, Daniels, and Carmichael), the mediation of various stakeholders in the process of producing and representing quality tourism experiences can have particular ramifications for the representation of place, space, and peoples' identities. At times, these representations serve to generate dialogue regarding the mismatch between marketing bodies' representations and the lived experiences of residents with whom tourists engage, and they attempt to make sense of the disparity between marketing representations and the

Table 1.2   Overview of some of the themes involved in the study of authenticity and tourism experiences as well as examples of representative academic articles
(References listed in reverse chronological order)

Thematic Focus of the Literature	*Examples of Representative Academic Articles*
Discussion of cultural, ethnic, and heritage tourism and authenticity as a means to sustain authentic cultural and heritage practices, mores as well as settings, societies and (sub)cultures	Brooke, 2001; French, 1997; Francaviglia, 1995
Linkage of tourism with the erosion of the authentic; for example, in questing for authentic experiences, tourists serve to erode cultures as a result of touristic encounters	Fainstein and Stokes, 1998; Amador, 1997; Boynton, 1997; Dilworth, 1996; Francaviglia, 1995; Wang and Godbey, 1994
The demonstration effect also contributes to a loss of authenticity	Boynton, 1997; Bell, 1992
Cultural commodification and appropriation and expectations of authenticity	Jamison, 1999; Fainstein and Stokes, 1998; Amador, 1997; Tucker in Abram, Waldren, and MacLeod, 1997; Francaviglia, 1995
Authenticity in regard to the politics of representation, identity, and touristic encounters	Aggarwal, 2000; Adams, 1999; McCabe, 1998; Abram, Waldren, and MacLeod (1997); Richter, 1997; Rogers, 1996; White and Lindstrom, 1995
Authenticity and a sense of place	Lew, 1989
Tourism, authenticity, and imperialism	Boynton, 1997
Authenticity in relation to market segmentation, particularly tourist types who quest for authentic experiences	Kastenholz, Davis, and Paul, 1999; Hana, 1996; Littrell, Baizerman, Kean, Gahring et al., 1994
Authenticity and service quality	Augustyn and Ho, 1998
Authenticity and postmodern concepts such as the tourists' gazes	Jamison, 1999; Fainstein and Stokes, 1998; Koshar, 1998; Abram, Waldren, and MacLeod, 1997; Rojek and Urry, 1997; Thorns, 1997; Dilworth, 1996; Urry, 1990
Tourism and authentic experiences of the "other"	van den Berghe, 1994
Mediated or staged authenticity	Holyfield, 1999; Jamison, 1999; Arnould, Price, and Tierney, 1998; Adams, 1997; Buck, 1978
The search for authenticity	Lyons, 1997; Dann, 1996; Graburn, 1989; Cohen, 1988; MacCannell, 1976
Models of authenticity, such as references to MacCannell	Hollinshead, 1998; Koshar, 1998; McCabe, 1998; Adams, 1997; Amador, 1997; Lyons, 1997; Wang and Godbey, 1994

Source: Jennings and Stehlik (2001)

representations offered by residents. The residents tend to provide an authentic representation, as in grounded in everyday life experiences, rather than a mythologized or manufactured representation.

This mismatch between marketing bodies and residents provides a space in which the tourist may contest not only the reality of her or his tourist experience but also its quality in relation to mismatch of expectations. Literature is punctuated with examples of such mismatches. For example, Ooi (2002) examines the role of respective tourism boards in constructing the identity of Copenhagen and Singapore's tourism products, and the rebranding of city identities in relation to resident involvement or noninvolvement in decision making. Henderson (2001) discusses issues associated with Hong Kong and conflicts in regard to representation, identity, and decolonization. Silk (2002) reports on the use of the 1989 Kuala Lumpur Commonwealth Games by power groups to reshape the (re)presentation of Malay peoples and the commodification of place to draw global capital. Other similar examples of tourism marketing bodies brokering and (re)constructing place images for capital gain are the "mythification" of Scotland (Hughes, 1992), the commodification of Santa Claus to market Lapland (Pretes, 1995), the construction of "place meanings" for the Daintree and Cape Tribulation areas in Far Northern Queensland, Australia (Young, 1999), and the commodification of culture resulting in residents living a representational life akin to "theme park actors" as a result of UNESCO World Heritage Listings (Honggang, 2003) and requirements of "authenticity." The film industry has also contributed to the Ballykissangelization of Ireland (among other films) and the (re)presentation of "tourist-friendly images" that mismatch with Irish identity but fulfill "economic pragmatism" (Barton, 2000). Borgenson and Schroeder (2002) iterate the role of marketing in the construction of identity using Hawaii as a case study in which the identity of the various Hawaiian peoples is stylized and reflective of colonial attitudes. The power of the marketing and promotional media and their roles in mediating and (re)constructing quality tourism experiences is examined more fully in Chapter Three (Bowen and Santos). Important connections to decision making and power holders in regard to representations is further explored in Chapter Six (Bricker and Kerstetter).

Within *Quality Tourism Experiences*, key stakeholders in tourism are also considered: providers, government, tourists, communities, and their points of interphase. The book also recognizes that the same people may be role players in different stakeholder groups. However, by nature of assuming a specific stakeholder role, people will also adopt the mores/codes of practice of that stakeholder role. It is noted that various contexts can also overlap—for example, government can also be part of the provider sector as can community also be part of tourist stakeholder groups. Essentially, the *Quality Tourism Experiences* chapters reflect the interconnectedness of the various contexts and the stakeholders within the phenomenon of tourism as they occur in the contexts being studied.

Conclusion

To summarize, the use of the phrase *quality tourism experiences* in this book is not adopted in a nomothetic manner but rather one associated with multiple interpretations and meanings. The title demonstrates the plurality of the subject area—*Quality Tourism Experiences*. As is already evident, the premise of the authors is that there is not just one definition of *quality tourism experiences*. The book reifies current practice by presenting differing representations and interpretations of quality and quality tourism experiences. The book's overarching tenet is that *quality* is a socially constructed term, as is the term *tourism experiences*. In the course of their writings, the authors investigate who is/are doing the constructing. The book examines the role of the mass media, the role of travel providers, the role of host communities, the role of tourists, and the role of government at all its levels in regard to this meaning-making process associated with understanding quality tourism experiences.

In adopting such an approach, understanding of the meaning making and (re)construction and (re)interpretation of quality tourism experiences is grounded in the everyday experiences of the relevant "actors." Such knowledge generation is associated with the sociology of knowledge, a perspective that purports that

> the sociology of knowledge must first of all concern itself with what people "know" as "reality" in their everyday, non- or pre-theoretical lives. In other words, common-sense "knowledge" rather than "ideas" must be the central focus for the sociology of knowledge. It is precisely this "knowledge" that constitutes the fabric of meanings without which no society could exist. (Berger and Luckmann, 1981, p. 27)

Further, the book also demonstrates that multiple theoretical lenses are required in order to move toward an understanding of the phenomenon of quality tourism experiences across its various contexts. *Quality Tourism Experiences* draws together writers from different backgrounds and interdisciplinary interests and research methodologies. As a consequence, the book provides a model of the way researchers can work together to illuminate an area and to provide multiple representations and interpretations of that area. Moreover, the book demonstrates intradisciplinary, transdisciplinary, and interdisciplinary approaches and collaborations. Based on this experience, it is suggested that, when considering various research agenda, researchers need to adopt more integrated and collaborative enterprises. Some of the tenets of such research are listed in Figure 1.4.

Finally, and to reiterate the key focus of this book, there is no one definition of *quality tourism experience.* The book demonstrates a range of quality tourism experiences and their interpretation and construction across numerous sectors involved in tourism: tourist attractions, hospitality, transportation, government departments, host communities, and more. The book also emphasizes that quality tourism experiences are constructed as a result of interaction between tourists, host communities and their residents, tourism providers, government bodies, and environmental settings—and that all of these constructions and interpretations have cultural and temporal contexts.

Tourism researchers need to engage in and/or utilize:

- Holistic research
- Suite of research paradigms
- Quantitative, qualitative, indigenous methodologies and mixed methods
- Emic and etic approaches
- Interdisciplinary research projects (and multidisciplinary approaches)
- Team-skilled projects
- Studies across spaces
- Collaborations

Source: Jennings (2003)

Figure 1.4   Research agenda for quality tourism researchers.

References

Abram, S., Waldren, J., and D. MacLeod (Eds.). (1997). *Tourists and Tourism: Identifying People and Places.* Oxford: Berg.

Adams, K. (1997). Ethnic tourism and the renegotiation of tradition in Tana Toraja (Sulawesi, Indonesia). *Ethnology*, **36** (4), 309-320.

Adams, K. (1999). Tourists and tourism: Identifying with people and places. *American Anthropologist*, **101** (4), 868ff.

Aggarwal, R. (2000). Points of departure: Feminist locations and the politics of travel in India. *Feminist Studies*, **26** (3), 535-562.

Amador, L.M.G. (1997). Ethnic, cultura and eco-tourism. *The American Behavioral Scientist*, **40** (7), 936-943.

Arnould, E., Price, L., and P. Tierney. (1998). Communicative staging of the wilderness servicescape. *The Service Industries Journal*, **18** (3), 90-115.

Augustyn, M., and S. Ho. (1998). Service quality and tourism. *Journal of Travel Research*, **37** (1), 71-75.

Ayala, H. (1996). Resort ecotourism: A paradigm for the 21st century. *The Cornell Hotel and Restaurant Administration Quarterly,* **37** (5), 54-61.

Baltic 21 Tourism Group. (1998). BALTIC 21: Series No 7/98: Agenda 21 – Baltic Sea Region Tourism. Downloaded 18 August 2003. [*www.ee/baltic21/publicat/R7-2.htm*]

Barton, R. (2000). The Ballykissangelization of Ireland. *Historical Journal of Film, Radio, and Television*, **20** (3), 413-427.

Baudrillard, J. (1981). *For a Critique of the Political Economy.* (B Singer, Trans.) Introduction by C. Levin. St Louis: Telos Press.

Baudrillard, J. (1990). *Seduction.* (B singer, Trans.) London: Macmillan.

Bauer, T.G., and A. Chan. (2001). Does the environment matter? Experiences, attitudes, and revisit intentions of international visitors to Hong Kong. *Pacific Tourism Review*, **5** (1), 75-82.

Bell, C. (1992). Bali: How to maintain a fragile resort. *Cornell Hotel and Restaurant Administration Quarterly*, **33** (5), 28ff.

Berger P.L., and T. Luckmann. (1981). *The Social Construction of Reality.* Harmondsworth: Penguin Books.

Bhasker, R. (1978). *A realist theory of science* (2nd ed.). Brighton: Harvester.

Bhasker, R. (1982). Emergence, explanation and emancipation. In P. Secord (Ed.), *Explaining Social Behaviour: Consciousness, Behaviour and Social Structure.* Beverly Hills, CA: Sage.

Bhasker, R. (1986). *Scientific Realism and Human Emancipation.* London: Verso.

Bhasker, R. (Ed.). (1990). *Harré and His Critics.* Oxford: Blackwell.

Bhat, M.G. (2003). Application of non-market valuation to the Florida Keys Marine Reserve Management. *Journal of Environmental Management*, **67** (4), 315.

Bitner, M.J. (1990). Evaluating service encounters: The effects of physical surroundings and employee responses. *Journal of Marketing*, **54** (2), 69ff (14 pp).

Blue Mountains City Council. (n.d.) Revitalising Katoomba: Improving recreational, cultura and urban open space facilities. Downloaded 18 August 2003. [*www.bmcc.nsw.gov.au/index.cfm?L1=1&L2=636*].

Borgeson, J.L., and J.E. Schroeder. (2002). Ethical issues of global marketing: Avoiding bad faith in visual representation. *European Journal of Marketing*, **36** (5/6), 570 (25 pp).

Borrie W.T., and R. Birzell. (2001). Approaches to measuring quality of the wilderness experience. In W.A. Freimund and D.N. Cole (Eds.), *Visitor Use and Density and Wilderness Experience: Processings 2001, June 1-3.* Missoula, MT, Proc RMRS-P-20 (pp. 29-38). Ogden, UT: US Department of Agriculture, Forest Service, Rocky Mountain Research Station.

Boyd, S. (2002). Cultural and heritage tourism in Canada: Opportunities, principles and challenges. *Tourism and Hospitality Research,* **3** (3), 211ff (23 pp).

Boynton, G. (1997). The search for authenticity. *The Nation,* **265** (10), 18-20.

Braithewaite, R. (1992). Value-chain assessment of the travel experience. *Cornell Hotel and Restaurant Administration Quarterly,* **33** (5), 41ff (9 pp).

Bricker, K.S., and D.L. Kerstetter. (2002). An interpretation of special place meanings: Whitewater recreationists attach to the South Fork of the American River. *Tourism Geographies,* **4** (4), 396-425.

Brooke, J. (2001, January). In the far north, fabled dogs come bounding back. *New York Times,* Late Edition (East Coast), p. A4.

Buck, R. (1978). Boundary maintenance revisited: Tourism experience in an Old Order Amish community. *Rural Sociology,* 221-234.

Campbell, C. (2003). Our dear north country: Regional identity and national meaning in Ontario's Georgian Bay. *Journal of Canadian Studies,* **37** (4), 68ff (25 pp).

Chadee, D.D., and J. Mattson. (1996). An assessment of customer satisfaction in tourism. *The Service Industries Journal,* **16** (3), 305ff (16 pp).

Clawson, M. (1963). *Land and water for recreation: Opportunities, problems and policies.* Chicago: Rand McNally.

Cohen, E. (1972). Toward a sociology of international tourism. *Social Research,* **39,** 164-182

Cohen, E. (1979). A phenomenology of tourist experiences. *Sociology,* **13,** 179-201.

Cohen, E. (1988). Traditions in the qualitative sociology of tourism. *Annals of Tourism Research,* Special Issue, **15,** 29-46.

Cooper, C., and N. Morpheth. (1998). The impact of tourism on residential experience in central-eastern Europe: The development of a new legitimation crisis in the Czech Republic. *Urban Studies,* **35** (12), 2253ff (23 pp).

Craig-Smith, S., and C. French. (1994). *Learning to live with tourism,* Melbourne: Pitman.

Csikzentmihalyi, M. (1988). The future of flow. In M. Csikzentmihalyi and I. Csikzentmihalyi (Eds.), *Optimal Experience: Psychological Studies of Flow in Consciousness* (pp. 365-383). Cambridge: Cambridge University Press.

Dann, G.M.S. (1996). *The Language of Tourism: A Sociolinguistic Perspective.* Wallingford, England: CAB International.

Department of Culture, Media and Sport. (1998). Promoting Efficiency and competitiveness. Department of Culture, Media and Sport. Downloaded 18 August 2003. [*www.culture.gov.uk/pdf/8385cdtdcmsp48p57.pdf*].

De Salaberry, N., and D.G. Reed. (n.d.). Tourism in Ontario's Niagara Escarpment Biosphere Reserve. Leading Edge'99. Downloaded 18 August 2003. [*www.escarpment. org/leading_edge/LE99/le99_s6/deSalaberry.pdf*].

Dilworth, L. (1996). *Imagining Indians in the Southwest: Persistent Visions of a Primitive Past.* Washington, DC: Smithsonian Institution Press.

Ekdahl, F., Gustafsson, A., and B. Edvardsson. (1999). Customer-oriented service development at SAS. *Managing Service Quality,* **9** (6), 403.

European Union for Coastal Conservation. (1999). Tourism and recreation. Downloaded 18 August 2003. [*www.coastalguide.org/trends/tourism.html*].

Fainstein, S., and R. Stokes. (1998). Spaces for play: The impacts of entertainment development on New York City. *Economic Development Quarterly*, **12** (2), 150-165.

Flint, W.R., and M.J.E. Danner. (2001). The Nexus of sustainability and social equity: Virginia's Eastern Shore (USA) as a local example of global issues. *International Journal of Economic Development, 3* (2), 1-30.

Font, X. (2002). Environmental certification in tourism and hospitality: Progress, process and prospects. *Tourism Management, 5* (1), 75-82.

Francaviglia, D. (1995). Branson, Missouri: Regional identity and the emergence of a popular culture community. *Journal of American Culture, 18* (2), 57ff.

French, H. (1997, June 15-18). Tourism impacts in Canada: Aboriginal tourism. Paper presented at the 28th Annual TTRA Conference. Norfolk, VA.

Goffman, E. (1974). *Frame Analysis: An Essay on the Organization of Experience.* New York: Harper and Row.

Graburn, N.H. (1989). Tourism: The sacred journey. In V. Smith (Ed.), *Hosts and Guests: The Anthropology of Tourism* (pp. 17-31). Philadelphia: University of Pennsylvania Press.

Gyimothy, S. (2000). Odysseys: Analysing service journeys from the customer's perspective. *Managing Service Quality, 10* (6), 389.

Hana, A. (1996). Resort ecotourism: A paradigm for the 21st century. *Cornell Hotel and Restaurant Administration Quarterly, 37* (5), 46ff.

Harborne, A.R., Afzal, D.C., and M.J. Andrews. (2001). Honduras: Caribbean Coast. *Marine Pollution Bulletin, 42* (12), 1221-1235.

Harré, R. (1981). The positive-empiricist approach and its alternative. In P. Reason and J. Rowan (Eds.), *Human Inquiry: A Sourcebook of New Paradigm Research.* Chichester: Wiley.

Harré, R. (1986). *Varieties of Realism: A Rationale for the Natural Sciences.* Oxford: Blackwell.

Henderson, J. (2001). Heritage, identity and tourism in Hong Kong. *International Journal of Heritage Studies, 7* (3), 2.

Hockey, J. (2002, May 2). Growth Strategy for Tourism. Delivering on the Promise: A Ten-Year Growth Strategy for Tourism. ATEC Symposium, Adelaide. Downloaded 18 August 2003. [*www.joehockey.com/sptenyrplantou.php*].

Hollinshead, K. (1998). Tourism, hybridity, and ambiguity: The relevance of bhabha's "third space" cultures. *Journal of Leisure Research, 30* (1), 121-156.

Holyfield, L. (1999). Manufacturing adventure: The buying and selling of emotions. *Journal of Contemporary Ethnography, 28* (1), 3-32.

Honggang, X. (2003). Managing the side effects of cultural tourism development – The case of Zhouzhuang. *Systems Analysis Modeling Simulation, 43* (2), 188-202.

Howell, B.J. (1994). Weighing the risks and rewards of involvement in cultural conservation and heritage tourism. *Human Organization, 53*, 150.

Hughes, G. (1992). Tourism and the geographical imagination. *Leisure Studies, 11*, 31-42.

Jamison, D. (1999). Masks without meaning: Notes on the processes of production, consumption, and exchange of the first world-third world tourism. *Journal of Macromarketing, 19* (1), 8-19.

Jennings, G.R. (1997). The travel experience of cruisers. In M. Oppermann (Ed.), *Pacific Rim 2000: Issues, Interrelations, Inhibitors* pp. 94-105). London: CAB International.

Jennings, G.R., and D. Stehlik. (2001, June 10-13). Mediated authenticity: The perspectives of farm tourism providers. 2001: A tourism odyssey. TTRA 32nd Annual Conference Proceedings (pp. 84-92), Fort Meyers, FL.

Jennings, J.R. (2003, June 15-18). Tourism Research: theoretical Paradigms and Accountability. Targeted Research: The Gateway to Accountability. TTRA 34th Annual Conference Proceedings. St. Louis, MO.

Kandampully, J., and R. Duddy. (1997). Shotover to quality: The world's most exciting jet boat ride. *Managing Service Quality*, 7 (5), 221.

Kastenholz, E., Davis, D., and G. Paul. (1999). Segmenting tourism in rural areas: The case of north and central Portugal. *Journal of Travel Research*, **37** (4), 353-363.

Keane, M.J. (1996). Sustaining quality in tourism destinations: An economic model with an application. *Applied Economics*, **28** (12), 1545.

Killion, G.L. (1992). *Understanding tourism*. Study Guide. Rockhampton: Central Queensland University.

King, T. (2001). Inflight catering. *Tourism and Hospitality Research*, **3** (2), 181ff (4 pp).

Koshar, R. (1998). What ought to be seen: Tourists' guidebooks and national identities in modern Germany and Europe. *Journal of Contemporary History*, **33** (3), 323-340.

Lakshmkan, V. (2002). Hospitality—Karnataka's New Favourite. *Express Hotelier and Caterer*, Mumbai, India: Indian Express Group, p. 1. Downloaded 18 August 2003. [*www.expresscomputeronline.com/cgi-bin/ecprint/MasterPFP.cgi?doc*].

Larsen, S., and L. Rapp. (1993). Creating the service driven cruise line. *International Journal of Contemporary Hospitality Management*, **5** (1), IVff (3 pp).

Laws, E. (1991). *Tourism Marketing: Service and Quality Management Perspectives*. Cheltenham, UK: Stanley Thornes.

Laws, E. (1998). Conceptualizing visitor satisfaction management in heritage settings: An exploratory blueprinting analysis of Leeds Castle, Kent. *Tourism Management*, **19** (6), 545-554.

Lawson, S.R., Manning, R.E., Valliere, W.A., and B. Wang. (2003). Proactive monitoring and adaptive management of social carrying capacity in Arches National Park: An application of computer simulation modelling. *Journal of Environmental Management*, **68** (3), 305.

Lengkeek, J. (2001). Leisure experience and imagination: Rethinking Cohen's modes of tourism experience. *International Sociology*, **16** (2), 173-184.

Lennon, J.J., and M. Graham. (2001). Commercial development and competitive environments: The museum sector in Scotland. *International Journal of Tourism Research*, **3** (4), 265-281.

Lennon, R., and J. Harris. (2002). Customer service on the Web: A cross-industry investigation. *Journal of Targeting, Measurement and Analysis for Marketing*, **10** (4), 325ff (14 pp).

Lew, A. (1989). Authenticity and sense of place in the tourism development experience of older retail districts. *Journal of Travel Research*, **27** (4), 15-22.

Littrell, M.A., Baizerman, S., Kean, R., Gahring, S., et al. (1994). Souvenirs and tourism styles. *Journal of Travel Research*, 33(1), 3ff.

Lyons, P. (1997). Pacific scholarship, literary criticism, and touristic desire: The spectre of A. Grove Day. *Boundary 2*, **24** (2), 47-78.

MacCannell, D. (1976). *The tourist, a new theory of the leisure class*. New York: Schocken Books.

MacCannell, D. (2002). The ego factor in tourism. *Journal of Consumer Research*, **29** (1), 146ff (6 pp).

Mak, J., and E.T. Moncur. (1998). Political economy of protecting unique recreational resources: Hanauma Bay, Hawaii. *Ambio*, **27** (3), 217.

McCabe, S. (1998). Contesting home: Tourism, memory, and identity in Sackville, New Brunswick. *Canadian Geographer*, **42** (3), 231-245.

Moscardo, G. (1996). Mindful visitors–Heritage and tourism. *Annals of Tourism Research*, **23** (2), 376-397.

Murphy, P.E. (1997). *Quality Management in Urban Tourism*. International Western Geographical Series. Chichester, UK: Wiley and Sons.

National Trust of Guyana. (2002, December). National Trust of Guyana Newsletter, Volume 1.4. Georgetown, South Africa, National Trust of Guyana. Downloaded 18 August 2003. [*www.nationaltrust.gov.gy/trustnewsd.html*].

Neal, J., Sirgy, M.J., and M. Uysal. (1999). The role of satisfaction with leisure travel/tourism services and experience in satisfaction with leisure life and overall life. *Journal of Business Research*, **44** (3), 153ff (11 pp).

Norman, W. (1993). Q & A about Rural Tourism Development. University of Minnesota Extension Service. Downloaded 18 August 2003. [*www.extension. umn.edu/distribution/resourcesand tourism/components/6184g.html*].

Ó Dochartaigh, N. (2002). *The Internet Research Handbook: A Practical Guide for Students and Researchers in the Social Sciences*. London: Sage.

O'Neill, M., Palmer, A., and S. Charters. (2002). Wine production as a service experience—The effects of service quality on wine sales. *The Journal of Services Marketing*, **16** (4), 342.

O'Neill, M., Williams, P., MacCarthy, M., and R. Groves. (2000). Diving into service quality—The dive tour operator perspective. *Managing Service Quality*, **10** (3), 131.

Onome, D.A. (2003). Destination environment quality and tourists' spatial behaviour in Nigeria: A case study of third world tropical Africa. *The International Journal of Tourism Research*, **22**, 1-15.

Ooi, C-S. (2002). *Cultural tourism and tourism cultures: The business of mediating experiences in Copenhagen and Singapore*. Copenhagen: Copenhagen Business School Press.

Perdue, R.R., Long, P.T., and Y.S. Yang. (1999). Boomtown tourism and resident quality of life—A Colorado case study. *Journal of Business Research*, **44** (3), 165-177.

Pine II, J., and J. Gilmore. (1999). *The Experience Economy: Work Is Theatre & Every Business Is a Stage*. Boston: Harvard Business School Press.

Pretes, M. (1995). Postmodern tourism: The Santa Claus Industry. *Annals of Tourism Research*, **22**, 1-15.

Queensland Department of Tourism, Racing and Fair Trading. (2002). Tourism in the Smart State: Progress report 2001-2002 and future directions. Brisbane: Queensland Department of Tourism, Racing and Fair Trading. Downloaded 18 April 2004. [*www.dtrft.qld.gov.au/tourism/documents/Strategy-1.pdf*].

Richter, L. (1997). The politics of heritage tourism: Emerging issues for the New Millennium. Paper presented at the 5th Biennial Meeting of the International Academy for the Study of Tourism, Melaka, Malaysia.

Robson, C. (2002). *Real World Research: A Resource for Social Scientists and Practitioner-Researchers* (2nd ed.). Oxford: Blackwell.

Rogers, M. (1996). Beyond authenticity: Conservation, tourism, and the politics of representation in the Ecuadorian Amazon. *Identities*, **3**, 73-125.

Rojek, C., and J. Urry (Eds.). (1997). *Touring Cultures: Transformation of Travel and Theory*. London: Routledge.

Ross, S., and G. Wall. (1999). Evaluating ecotourism: The case of North Sulawesi, Indonesia – The impact of regionalization. *Tourism Management*, **20** (6), 673-682.

Ryan, C. (Ed.). (1997). *The tourist experience: An introduction*. London: Cassell.

Ryan, C. (1998). Dolphins, canoes and "marae"—Ecotourism products in New Zealand. In E. Laws, B. Faulkner, and G. Moscardo (Eds.), *Embracing and Managing Change in Tourism: International Case Studies* (pp. 285-306). London: Routledge.

Ryan, C. (Ed.). (2002). *The Tourist Experience: An Introduction* (2nd ed.). London: Thomson Learning.

Schneider, R. (2002, September-October). P'town Agonistes. *The Gay and Lesbian Review Worldwide*, **9** (5), 4.

Schutz, A. (1962). *Collected Papers: The Problem of Social Reality*. M. Natanson (Ed.). Boston: Hague.

Schutz, A. (1967). *The Phenomenology of the Social World*. (G. Walsh and F. Lehnert, Trans.). Chicago: Northwestern University Press.

Sheldon, P., and M. Fox. (1988). The role of foodservice in vacation choice and experience: A cross-cultural analysis. *Journal of Travel Research*, **27** (2), 9ff (7 pp).

Silk, M. (2002). Bangsa Malaysia: Global sport, the city and the mediated refurbishment of local identities. *Media, Culture and Society*, **24** (6), 775 (20 pp).

Smith, V. (Ed.). (1989). *Hosts and Guests: The Anthropology of Tourism* (2nd ed.). Philadelphia: University of Pennsylvania Press.

Smith, V.K., and D.B. Webster et al. (1976). The management of wilderness areas—A simulation model. *Decision Sciences*, **7** (3), 524.

Stewart, W. (1998). Leisure as multiphase experiences: Challenging traditions. *Journal of Leisure Research*, **30** (4), 391-400.

Thorns, D. (1997). The global meets the local: Tourism and the representation of the New Zealand City. *Urban Affairs Review*, **33** (2) 189-208.

Timothy, D.J., and G. Wall. (1997). Selling to tourists: Indonesian street vendors. *Annals of Tourism Research*, **24** (2), 322-340.

Tourisme Quebec (1997/8? n.d.). Selling Quebec to the world. Downloaded 18 August 2003. [*www.tourisme.gouv.qc.ca/mto/publications/pdf/admin/politdev_a.pdf*].

Turco, D.M., and R.W. Riley. (1996). Choice factors and alternative activities for riverboat gamblers. *Journal of Travel Research*, **34** (3), 24ff (6 pp).

United Nations Economic Commission for Europe. (n.d.). Technical Report Kiev Tourism. Downloaded 18 August 2003. [*www.unece/env/europe/kiev/tourism.e.pdf*].

Urry, J. (1990). *The Tourist Gaze: Leisure and Travel in Contemporary Societies*. London: Sage.

Urry, J. (2002). *The Tourist Gaze: Leisure and Travel in Contemporary Societies* (2nd ed.). London: Sage.

Uysal, M., McDonald, C.D., and B.S. Martin. (1994). Australian visitors to US national parks and natural areas. *International Journal of Contemporary Hospitality Management*, **6** (3), 18ff (7 pp).

Van den Berghe, P. (1994). *The Quest for the Other: Ethnic Tourism in San Cristobal, Mexico*. Seattle: University of Washington Press.

Vaughan, W.J., and C.S. Russell. (1982). Valuing a fishing day: An application of a systematic varying parameter model. *Land Economics*, **58** (4), 450ff (14 pp).

Wang, P., and G. Godbey. (1994). A normative approach to tourism growth to the year 2000. *Journal of Travel Research*, **33** (1), 33ff.

Warden, C.A., Liu, T-C., Huang C-T., and C-H. Lee. (2003). Service failures away from home: Benefits in intercultural service encounters. *International Journal of Service Industry Management*, **14** (3/4), 436.

Weber, K., and W.S. Roehl. (1999). Profiling people searching for the purchasing travel products on the World Wide Web. *Journal of Travel Research*, **37** (3), 291ff (8 pp).

Weiler, B., and D. Davis. (1993). An exploratory investigation into the roles of the nature-based tour leader. *Tourism Management*, 91-98.

White, G., and L. Lindstrom. (1995). Anthropology's new cargo: Future horizons. *Ethnology*, **34** (3), 201ff.

Young, M. (1999). The social construction of tourist places. *Australian Geographer*, **30,** (3), 373ff [*http://gateway.proquest.com/openurl?ctx_ver=z39.88-2003&res_id= xri:pqd&rft_val_fmt=:kev:mtx:journal&genre=article&rft_id=xri:pqd:did=00000 0048843266&svc_dat=xri:pqil:fmt=html&req_dat=xri:pqil:pq_cintid=20863*].

Yuksel, A., and F. Yuksel. (2001). Comparative performance analysis: Tourists' perceptions of Turkey relative to other tourist destinations. *Journal of Vacation Marketing*, **7** (4), 333-355.

I

Social Construction of Quality Tourism Experiences

The social construction of meaning is a central theoretical premise in *Quality Tourism Experiences*. It purports that meaning making and sensemaking is a continuous engagement between "social actors" involving continuous construction and reconstruction of meanings and/or interpretations of meaning. As a consequence, and as already alluded to in Chapter One, a set or emphatic definition of "quality tourism experiences" is problematic and contestable due to the subjective, individualized and collective interpretations that emanate from life experiences, social engagements and the mediation of meaning within social interactions. The mediation of social interactions can occur during real time exchanges, that is face-to-face, vicariously, as well as virtually assisted or via the mass media. Additionally, with regard to this book, "social actors" participating in those interactions and mediations include tourists, tourism industry personnel, government staff, residents, and other interested stakeholders as well as employees, management, and shareholders in mass media sectors.

As noted in Chapter One, the social construction of meaning specifically informs the writings of the two chapters in this Section, Chapters Two and Three and, in addition, Section Two, Chapter Four. It also variously permeates the writings of all the remaining chapters. In addition to the premise—social construction of meaning, Chapters Two and Three are also informed by social constructivism, while elements of postmodern perspectives are apparent in Chapter Two. Moreover, both chapters reflect elements of communication theory, and Chapter Three is further influenced by semiotics, cultural studies, symbolic interaction, and the politics of representation.

Within Chapter Two, Sue Beeton, Heather E. Bowen, and Carla Almeida Santos provide readers with a background to the theoretical concept "social construction of meaning." The chapter also highlights the significant role that the mass media has in influencing the social construction of meaning within contemporary societies and especially for tourism and the notion of quality tourism experiences. It considers mass entertainment and mediascapes in relation to tourism and the mass–mediated social construction of tourism imaging. The chapter concludes with considerations and implications of the nature of the social construction of quality tourism experiences through the mass media.

In Chapter Three, Heather E. Bowen and Carla Almeida Santos extend the consideration of the role of the mass media in the social construction of quality tourism experiences. The authors elaborate on the mass media's role in constructing and broadcasting interpretations of quality which then become absorbed by audiences and readerships and thereby societies at large. Subsequently, the mass media is represented as having a significant role in interpreting and constructing quality and as a consequence in constructing "reality." To exemplify and demonstrate this, the authors draw on research conducted within the medium of television and newsprint media. Based on their research into "quality tourism experiences," the authors comment that "quality tourism experiences" as constructed by the mass media may result in the social construction of an experience that is well beyond the reach of many travellers and tourists.

2

State of Knowledge: Mass Media and Its Relationship to Perceptions of Quality

Sue Beeton
Heather E. Bowen
Carla Almeida Santos

Since the early days of travel for pleasure and recreation, the mass media has influenced people's decisions on where to go, where to stay, and what to do by providing images and information that can serve to define notions of "quality" in tourism experiences. Media that is geared toward mass audiences influence them by assigning certain meanings to places, particularly regarding notions of romance, danger, or adventure, influencing the audience's response to the appeal (or revulsion) of those places. In the nineteenth into the twentieth centuries such media included literature, poetry, song, paintings, railway and steamship posters, as well as photographs and postcards (Tooke and Baker, 1996; Davidson and Spearritt, 2000). In addition, the newspapers and radio of the twentieth century provided a more immediate, and at times authoritative, group of media, particularly in terms of news and current affairs (Nielsen, 2001; Santos, 2004). More recently, television and film have become the predominant forms of media for accessing the mass population, and they play a significant role in influencing travel as well as notions of what constitutes a "quality experience" (Cohen, 1986; Riley, 1994; Tooke and Baker, 1996; Bowen, 2002; Beeton, 2000, 2001).

Although media's influences, such as those just noted, are well documented, it can be argued that it is individual social interactions that influence a culture more than the mass media. This is evident when we consider the influence of "word-of-mouth" promotion; however, this chapter is primarily concerned with the more consciously structured elements of the mass media. Other chapters in the book focus on the additional social interaction elements, particularly Chapter Four, which considers the formal and informal personal mediation of tourism experiences. Nevertheless, the rise of the influence of mass media has been contemporaneous with the rise in mass tourism. This was predicated by the development of economical forms of travel that can transport large numbers of people over great distances in little time, particularly since the development of the jet aircraft in the 1970s (Goeldner et al., 2000). The "tourist gaze," as introduced by Urry (1990) through which the tourist objectifies and interprets the tourist experience, is becoming more and more mediated, with the mass media providing much of the gazing framework and meaning for the individual as well as mass tourists. As Jansson (2002, p. 431) observes, "The tourist gaze has become more and more intertwined with the consumption of media images."

The exponential growth in tourism and globalization has been met by the mass media through the development of travel-specific media products that mold the public's perception of quality tourism experiences. These products include travel sections in the daily press (local and international), specialized publications such as travel guides and magazines, as well as free-to-air, cable, and satellite television travel programs, including an entire niche cable channel dedicated to travel, the Travel Channel.

Because the work in this text comes predominantly from a western cultural viewpoint, it is pertinent to understand the perspectives of "looking," "seeing," and "knowing" in western culture. When we look back to the influential European Grand Tours of the seventeenth and eighteenth centuries, they were highly visual, with young lords studying at museums and art galleries, often returning with their own artistic renditions of the sights (Davidson and Spearritt, 2000). The nineteenth-century developments in photography brought visual representation and leisure into a collaborative relationship that continues today. Visual representations in the form of postcards and travel posters also became ways in which travelers viewed their experiences and passed them on to others (Davidson and Spearritt, 2000). These early mass-mediated forms of knowing through seeing and looking have supported and affirmed the western travel and tourism experience over the centuries, leading to many postmodern discourses regarding the tourist gaze (Urry, 1990), authenticity (MacCannell, 1973; Eco, 1983), and the quest for the new.

However, even within western hegemony, there are cultural differences, particularly in the framework and manner in which various cultures view themselves. For example, nonindigenous Australians have traditionally viewed themselves from the gaze of others, such as the colonial British Empire of the eighteenth and nineteenth centuries, the visiting American soldiers during WWII, the postwar migrants of the 1950s, the nation's Asian neighbors in the 1970s, and the international sports fans in the late twentieth and early twenty-first century. A high majority of Australians continue to refer to successful people in terms of how they are viewed "overseas," often using the terms "as good as in England/France/America" (Beeton, in press). In part, this is due to the origins of colonial Australia, where the country's early settlers did not necessarily choose to come, and constantly longed to return to a homeland that was superior to everything they experienced in such a foreign land (which became known as the "cultural cringe"). In the United States, where the nation's foundations were more constructive, the framing gaze tends to be from other Americans, with the local media reflecting, influencing, and promoting U.S.

views and values that tend to be aimed back at them, underpinning a domestic construct of being "American" (Santos, 2004).

These differences can be seen in many of the popular/mass media productions from each country, and although some elements are transferable between the cultures, the perspective of each gaze is subjective, yet pervasive. While acknowledging these differences, in this chapter we take a broader, more globalized view of the media's interpretation of a quality tourism experience, even though it is from a western hegemonic perspective. One justification for this is that the major tourist-generating regions still tend to be the "developed" westernized cultures such as Australia, North America, the United Kingdom, and Europe (Hall and Page, 1999; Leiper, 2002). Even Japan, a major Asian tourist-generating region, is highly westernized in its approaches to tourism and mass media. Further justification for this approach is a pragmatic one, in that the authors come from western U.S. and Australian backgrounds, which inform this work.

This section of the book considers elements specific to the role that the mass media play in defining and socially constructing quality tourism experiences. In order to have such a discussion, some background on the literature in the field of social construction and mass media follows. We then build on the notion of the construction of meaning by the mass media by considering the concepts in relation to tourism.

Social Construction

Peter Berger and Thomas Luckmann's 1966 publication, *The Social Construction of Reality*, described the notion of "social construction." In what can be seen as an adjunct to the concept of social constructionism, Thomas Kuhn (1962) introduced the notion of "paradigm shifts," which he considered in overall terms of knowledge, not specifically as social construction. He argued that science functions under a mutually agreed upon paradigm about how the world works. Using the example of science, Kuhn claimed that when experiments do not show evidence that concurs with the mutually agreed scientific paradigm, a new theory—one that better explains the evidence and is accepted by the scientific community—is put forth. This process of knowledge development can also be referred to as the *social construction of reality* by the scientific community—a reality framed by their mutually agreed upon paradigm or that is congruent with the beliefs of the scientific community. For Kuhn, reality is understood as a socially generated and a linguistically maintained entity.

At the same time, Schutz (1962) also acknowledged the fact that reality is a socially constructed phenomenon, but, unlike Kuhn, he chose to focus on the way people create "realities" in everyday life. Schutz claimed that people have a "stock of knowledge . . . of social collections and artifacts, including cultural objects" (p. 81). The term "stock of knowledge" bears a close resemblance to Kuhn's paradigm example in that humans or members of a given community have a collection of information in their minds that helps them understand the world—a template of sorts that is used to make sense of world issues. According to Schutz, one's stock of knowledge represents his or her reality and it is often interpreted as the objective facts, or as described by Washburn (1992, p. 55), it "is understood by people in a commonsense fashion as reality itself." For Schutz, the stock of knowledge that is available to each individual is acquired through the process of socialization. He further mentioned that the process of socialization aids in the interpretation of the unknown, providing a point of reference and orientation to the world through the use of "typifications." The use of the term *typifications* is used in this instance as synonymous to standardizations that, for instance, the media use as short-cuts to describe and understand destinations and hosts. These standardizations then represent "reality," which, with time, may seem "natural" to the producers and the receivers who use them to interpret their everyday experiences (Washburn, 1992). Schutz posits that individuals of a given social group understand each other because they share the common stock of knowledge as well as the common language of typifications, which are used to make sense of objects and events.

Renowned sociologist Erving Goffman also contributed to the understanding of the social construction of reality. Like his predecessors, Goffman (1974) agrees that world objects and events have no inherent meaning other than the one assigned through human action in a given social context. According to Goffman, once individuals acquire the meanings through the socialization process, they do not reflect on them or question the social force that formed them. It is precisely this point that provides the media with the power to portray reality through the use of standardizations. The media help construct and maintain social reality because the audience receives the information unquestioningly and files it away as reality (Surette, 1992). These standardizations, however, are mere representations of reality and are not only culturally framed but also historically based. Thus, it is crucial to examine and understand the agencies that disseminate these ideas. In fact, as was purported by Rorty (1979, p. 170), "we understand knowledge when we understand the social justification of belief, and thus have no need to view it as accuracy of representation."

In reference to "reality," Anderson (1990) considers that it is not a fixed entity, supporting the social constructionist notion of "multiple realities" (Berger and Luckmann, 1966). Essentially, this is similar to the Kuhnian approach, with reality being created and re-created by society in an attempt to understand the world. Through the use of stories, individuals explain the world around them, with such stories being merely a representation of "reality" (Anderson, 1990). These stories are neither accurate nor complete. In fact, humans rarely have an unmediated contact with reality, and what they have and know is socially constructed, or mediated by their society. Therefore, the set of beliefs on which "reality" is based justify what is accepted as good and moral in any given society. Anderson believes that individuals remain faithful to these beliefs due to the punitive consequence of deviating from them. In a similar vein, the media capitalize on these beliefs through the use of standardizations, rarely venturing far from them for fear of causing public cynicism and/or apathy (Bennett, 1996).

So why, one may ask, do we unquestionably bear these standardizations or social realities? The reason, according to Searle (1995), is because the structure of social reality is invisible: "[We] use cars, bathtubs, houses, money, restaurants, and schools without reflecting on the special features of their ontology and without being aware that they have a special ontology" (p. 4). In a similar manner, we perceive standardizations as a simplified way of describing complex objects and events in the world. These representations seem natural to us because of the process of socialization; we have been socialized to think that way. Emphasizing this point, Searle posits that "social reality is created by us for our purposes and seems as readily intelligible to us as those purposes themselves" (p. 4). It is only after we remove ourselves from the social force (for example, media portrayals) that we are able to see the creator of these representations (Searle, 1995).

Social Construction through Mass Media

It is important at this stage to define our use of the term *mass media*. The term relates not only to television and newspapers, but also to videos and digital video disks (DVDs), the Internet, radio, some books and magazines – that is, all forms of media that can reach a mass audience. However, these forms are merely the tools used to get the media stories and social constructs across. As noted previously, there are forms of tourism mediation other than the mass media that come directly from tourism participants and brokers, such as the word-of-mouth representations from other tourists, tour guides, employees, and so on, which is discussed in more depth in Chapter Four. In this section we are considering primarily visual and written forms of nonfiction media as presented through television and newspapers—namely, a travel series presented on cable television and travel editorial columns in a national newspaper. This focus is reflected in this review of the state of knowledge of the social construction of quality tourism experiences.

The application of the concept of a socially constructed reality to media analysis has enabled media researchers such as Vhang and colleagues (1998) and McQuail (1994) to explore the relevance of social constructionism to our omnipresent-media society. The mass media have been shown to construct social reality in their portrayal of powerful standardized symbols (for example, a "native" dressed in costume), actors (such as a "native" performing a traditional dance), and meanings (for example, legitimizing the social role of "natives" to limited stereotypical roles) (McQuail, 1994). In essence, the media extract unique aspects of a given society, community, or individual, and use that as the basis on which to explain all social phenomena associated with that society or community. Unfortunately, such media standardizations or social realities may create barriers, which obfuscate rather than facilitate communication among societal groups. The media thus play not only a reporting role but also a defining role, establishing their audience's sense of reality; prescribing society's accepted norms, behaviors, and boundaries.

Littlejohn (1991) recognizes this link between media and social construction, maintaining that the world is socially constructed by interconnected patterns of human behavior that are communicated (and known) through language and semiotics, as in the mass media. Markwell (2001) recognizes this link as extending to tourism, noting that the visual and textual forms of popular culture, which includes nonfiction media such as television travel programs and newspaper travel sections, influence tourists' ideas and beliefs.

The literature tends to position social constructionism as one body of work, but there are some differences in understanding and use of the term. According to Abercrombie and colleagues (2000), the concept of "social constructionism" has been applied in broad general terms as well as specifically. When applied generally, explanations are given in terms of overall social description instead of individual characteristics. When used more specifically, social construction refers to the process of people actively constructing their social world, rather than having it imposed on them. Hacking (1999) also proposes that constructionism exists in a variety of forms: historical constructionism, which seeks to identify how particular issues have developed over time; reformist constructionism, which seeks to improve (or qualify) some aspects of a particular issue even if it is not possible to undo its social construction; and unmasking constructionism, which seeks to expose social functions in order to undermine their authority.

The notion that the media socially construct reality has been linked to much of the research on mass media, including television (Lang and Lang, 1984; DeFleur and Ball-Rokeach, 1989; Lipschultz and Hilt, 2002). Dann (1996) has argued that the media actively construct certain images and notions of destinations for popular consumption, supporting the premise that the mass media are a key driver of social construction, not the individual. This view is also espoused by Lipschultz and Hilt (2002), who argue that portrayals of certain incidents construct a social reality in which groups as well as individuals operate. Surette (1992) also considers this to be the case, linking the media's social construction with that of the consumer's (viewer or reader), as described earlier.

Fürsich (2002) contends that the media shape a view of other cultures through media textualization in terms of representational politics. Whereas we are considering a similar scenario, we are specifically concerned with the construction and potential shaping of notions of "quality" rather than simply representations of tourism. The assumptions underpinning this interest are that the mass media does influence people's construction of various realities and tend to drive (or at the very least, reflect) their wants, needs, and desires, particularly in terms of travel. This relationship is discussed next.

Social Construction, Mass Media, and Their Relationship to Tourism

Tourism destinations and businesses extensively use imaging techniques to create the desire to experience their products and visit their regions. The mass media are the primary means used to disseminate and reinforce such images. However, it is not merely those directly involved in touristic exchange who create the images from which potential visitors construct meaning. Many mass media productions are not controlled by the actual tourism interests but by the medium itself. Butler (1999) supports Surette's (1992) previously noted view, considering it in terms of the increasing significance of the media in relation to tourism:

A significant emerging trend in tourism is the role of the media in the popularization and development of destinations. The media now have the ability to transform even an event with little sightseeing appeal into a major attraction if it so desires. Such is the power of the media to influence public taste and fashion, both directly and indirectly, that it seems impossible now, for example, to envisage an America's Cup Yachting Competition as anything other than a major tourist attraction, primarily because of media attention. (Butler, 1999, p. 102)

The Rise of International Travel as an Aspect of Mass Entertainment

Many scholars credit the rise of domestic and international travel to increased standards of living and greater leisure time that eventuated over the second half of the twentieth century, after the period of postwar reconstruction in most developed countries. For example, Williams and Shaw (1995) see the increase in income, coupled with an increase in available leisure time, as having led to growing demand for relaxation and vacation destinations. They conclude that it is these factors that have contributed to growth in the tourism sector. Murphy (1982) adds that although increases in income and leisure time do not necessarily result in a growing tourism sector, they do lead to the increase of individual leisure options. According to Murphy, the goals of travelers can be seen as physical (relaxation), cultural (learning), social (visiting family), and fantasy. It is this fantasy goal to which Krippendorf (1986, p. 131) refers when explaining that people "do not feel at ease where they are, where they work and where they live. They need to escape from the burdens of their normal life." For this reason, Urry (1990) argues that the preferences of individuals, along with the social construction of tourism consumption, have had as much of an impact on the increase of tourism as the acknowledged tourism drivers of increased income and leisure time.

Scholars agree that people's overall decisions to travel are contingent on locality, activity preferences, past experiences, and their desire to use tourism as a status reference (Williams and Shaw, 1995). The "right" resort says much about the patron, and, while in the past it was the upper classes (traditionally royalty and aristocracy, followed by the *nouveau riche*) who once defined these "right" places and activities, today it is travel editors and marketers who make those determinations.

Morgan and Pritchard (1998) claim that cultural meanings born from tourism processes possess a breadth of symbolism that is wider than the actual consumption of tourism products and the places themselves. Identities are created according to the dominant value systems and meanings. "Just as tourism sites are associated with 'particular values, historical events and feelings,' so values, feelings and events are used to promote such sites, reinforcing the dominant ideologies" (Morgan and Pritchard, 1998, p. 3). Mass-mediated travel narratives that describe tourism experiences are highly selective, highlighting the beautiful and exotic (Santos, 2004) and proposing notions and expectations of quality (as demonstrated in the next chapter). Rowe (1993) argues that these narratives are part of the sociocultural, economic, and political relations that form our society. Also, the increase in international travel generates audience interest in travel-related information, with potential travelers turning to mass-mediated travel narratives for travel guidance. However, gleaning information by travelers is not the sole use of mass-mediated travel narratives. With the increasing desire for travel experiences, those who cannot afford to travel often turn to these narratives for the purpose of entertainment, fantasy, and daydreaming, as well as at times to experience a sense of superiority ("Our beaches are better").

Santos (2004, p. 122) presents the well-supported notion that the mass media's tourism discourse "negotiates tourism experiences for the general public by promoting ways of directing the tourists' gaze, . . . [transforming it] into leisure consumerism for the masses." This concept is amply illustrated in Chapter Three, where the strength of the themes promoted through the discourses in travel programs is analyzed. Morgan and Pritchard (1998) look at this mass mediation of tourism from the perspective of tourism image construction, arguing that a place's image-makers (such as destination marketers) draw on a frame of reference provided by the media, which in turn is based on certain values and assumptions that have been made by the aforementioned media.

Mediascapes

Linking together the various elements of tourism, imaging, and media, Jansson (2002) describes three different "scapes": landscapes, socioscapes, and mediascapes. *Landscapes* are the physical elements of an experience, such as the scenery or condition of the natural and built environments, whereas *socioscapes* refer to spaces that are turned into places for social interaction, such as shops, beaches, and even airports. Jansson (2002) conceptualizes *mediascapes* as the complete range of mediated texts in our lives, including media such as postcards and advertisements as well as television programs. The pervasiveness of these mediascapes makes it difficult to separate the representations from that which they represent (so-called reality).

Preceding Jansson's work by some years, Lang and Lang's 1984 work underpins this notion of mediascapes as a powerful and distinct concept. When studying the influence of television news in constructing and reinforcing social meaning, they note that "television emphasises close-up views creating a sense of familiarity with distant people and places . . . [and] television pictures seem authentic to viewers" (p. 26). When looking at the effect of television news, Tuchman (1978, p. 12) goes so far as to claim that "the act of making news is the act of constructing reality itself rather than a picture of reality."

A further element of mediascapes and the role that the mass media play in tourism is that they are experienced before, during, and after the actual landscapes and socioscapes (Jansson, 2002). That is, the media are a pervasive element of the entire touristic experience, from anticipation to action and, finally, to reflection and analysis. Consequently, the media construct a social reality that is more pervasive and exists far longer than initial image-developing anticipatory stages. As Jansson argues,

Paradoxically, it seems, the more organized tourism gets, the more mediatized it becomes – and the more it is turned into simulation . . . . [T]ourism catalogues, travel magazines and Internet sites are not only simulations of reality, they are simulations of already simulated environments – the more or less standardized tourist resorts. (pp. 438-439)

In addition, it is increasingly being recognized that tourism has many ramifications and consequences from political, social, and environmental aspects. One example of this phenomenon is the power of mass-mediated messages to create collective images of what a destination and its people are supposed to look like, what accommodations they should provide, and how they should treat the tourists, who, of course, are economic saviors with pockets full of cash and expectations to boot. Löfgren (1999) articulates this relationship, which is illustrated in the next chapter.

The travel sections of the daily papers burst with fantasies about one's next vacation, promising everything from a magical vacation package, invitations to the "fine art of overindulgence," "truly genuine experiences," perfect adventures, holidays you'll never forget, getaways, and escape routes. Simultaneously moving in a physical terrain and in fantasylands or mediaworlds, we create *vacationscapes*. Personal memories mix with collective images (Löfgren, 1999, p. 2).

In the following section we examine this notion that the mass media constructs social realities that influence the entire touristic experience. Identifying such mass-mediated social constructs is the primary theme of the next chapter.

Tourism Imaging and Mass-Mediated Social Construction

Since the beginning of the twentieth century, promoters have utilized the power of mass-mediated messages to market tourism. Most often, they have enrolled the expertise of advertisers in order to create images, dreams, fantasies, and senses of nostalgia. Although much has been written about the nostalgic images of tourism advertising, its messages, and ideologies (O'Barr, 1994), we have failed to analyze travel narratives as socially constructed notions of quality tourism experiences. The premise for such a discussion ought to be the selected sets of expectations that these narratives promote. We will not embark on a discussion of the literature on expectations since this elaboration would go beyond the scope of this study, but we do recognize expectations as a necessary element to the overall discussion. As Gnoth (1999) explained,

The way we obtain new knowledge depends on what we already know, so expectations are often reconfigured recollections of things we have already experienced. [Expectations are] forward-directed, tentative attitudes containing a more or less definite element of knowledge about an object (for example, tourism experiences, destinations, objectives, etc.). They contain an emotional charge expressing the intensity of the drive with which the behavior, in reaction to the drive, is executed. (p. 264)

The expectations and motivations driving people to travel for leisure or pleasure are complex and necessitate an area of separate study. However, a simple model can be used here to illustrate the position of nonfiction mass media in tourism motivation. Dann (1977) divided tourism motivational forces into two categories: the push and pull factors. *Push factors* are those that enable a person to travel, such as having the time and money to undertake a journey, or those that may create a desire to get away from "normal" life, such as boredom or stress. The *pull factors* are those that encourage the potential traveler to choose a specific destination, activity, or product, such as its romantic appeal, heritage elements, perceived safety, and so on, depending on the individual's wants and needs. Underpinning the push and pull factors is the crucial element of *access,* which includes considerations of transport and availability. In this chapter we are considering the pull factors that primarily influence destination (and) image in terms of "quality," which is the predominant role of the travel media.

Jansson's (2002) notion of landscapes, socioscapes, and mediascapes can be incorporated into this simple conceptual model. As noted earlier, mediascapes exist concurrently with the other "scapes," bringing various media texts into a significant part of the model. Jansson separates mediascapes into three basic categories based on the traveler's desired outcomes or approach to the experience—namely, symbiotic, antagonistic, and contextual. The *symbiotic* traveler is searching for "authenticity," avoiding the created "spectacular" in preference for the ordinary. According to Jansson, this traveler tends to utilize the mediascapes found in documentaries, photography, and everyday life. The antagonistic traveler is looking for more adventurous and spectacular experiences and uses tourism brochures and popular travel programs as the primary mediascape or source of information and construction. The third category is the *contextual* traveler, who focuses more on a particular practice or activity that is not site-specific, such as a wine tasting or golf trip, utilizing the broader mediascapes of sports programs, movies, cooking magazines, and the like (Jansson, 2002).

33

The significance of imaging in tourism has been noted throughout the chapter, yet the images that mass media engage to construct our realities are also criticized as being too simplistic. According to Chen and Starosta (1998), media such as television and newspaper contribute to certain images of "others" (people and places, socioscapes, and landscapes) by portraying them in such a generalized manner as to create oversimplified concepts. Such concepts and images can be adopted by potential tourists, affecting their decisions as to where to travel, their interaction and relationships with others once at a destination, and their perceptions of enjoyment, fulfillment, and participation in a "quality" experience (Chen and Starosta, 1998; Bowen, 2002). The very act of writing an article or filming a program about a tourist destination produces and circulates a particular cultural commodity, which is in turn interpreted and analyzed by the reader. What is presented may become the main image and expectation, particularly if the reader/viewer has no previous notion of the destination.

Consequently, travel writers and producers are what Cohen (1986) and Dann (1996) refer to as "cultural brokers," relying on frames or organizing narratives established by what they consider to be the audience's cultural or political mores to confirm and legitimize their mass-mediated representations of their subjects. (The concept of cultural brokering is taken up in Chapter Four.) Using such established, familiar frames to present the exotic "other" assists the reader/viewer to understand the piece but can result in a certain level of homogenization and repetitiveness in mass travel reporting (Bowen, 2002; Santos, 2004). At the very least, this may raise false expectations or incorrect and potentially dangerous assumptions.

The Social Construction of Quality Tourism Experiences through Mass Media

Apart from advertising images, the relationship between mass-mediated messages and tourism has been occasionally addressed in mainstream tourism or communications studies research (Santos, 2004). However, this relationship is significant and is supported by Jansson (2002, p. 439), who contends that "mediated images are thus becoming the 'originals' against which experiences of simulated landscapes and socioscapes are measured." We also maintain that this relationship is considerable, and the next chapter discusses nonfiction travel representations from two forms of mass media—newspaper and television—to demonstrate the social construction of quality tourism by such media.

We have outlined the notion of social construction and mass media's powerful role in constructing tourism and now take these notions into the field of assessing tourism experiences in terms of quality. In any study of quality it is important to question and come to a position as to what is actually being referred to by such an amorphous term.

In this book various ways of looking at and defining *quality* are introduced, discussed, and examined. In this section we are not defining quality ourselves, but searching for the meaning(s) that the mass media present to its audience. One way that the media present quality is in terms of another highly contested notion—that of *authenticity*. As Jansson (2002, p. 439) notes, "The authenticity of a tourist destination may be defined in terms of how well it meets the customer's own ideas of what the particular destination is about." As he considers such ideas to be informed (and formed) by the media, Jansson refers to this highly mass-mediated form of authenticity as "symbolic authenticity." Although there are undeniable connections between authenticity and quality within the socially constructed notion of tourism, the notion of mass-mediated quality tourism is examined, not through the authenticity discourse, but through a contextual semiotic analysis of manifest and latent content of various media presentations in the next chapter.

As established earlier, with its power to construct and represent images, themes, and social and political realities, the presentation of travel writing in print media and television often blurs the margins between fact and fiction (Santos, 2004). So, by studying two forms of nonfiction media presented on television and in news-paper, we identify various interpretations and social constructions of quality as presented by that media.

In the following chapter, two forms of media are analyzed and discussed. These include a series of "World's Best" tourist phenomena presented by a television travel program, broadcast on the specialist cable television channel, the Travel Channel, and an Australian newspaper travel section. While it is possible that these two different media and creators could represent "quality" in vastly divergent terms, the results point to a convergence of such constructs, particularly with the western hegemonic paradigm, in spite of some cultural contextual differences. The results outlined in Chapter Three are particularly interesting when considered in relation to the discourse on forms of mediating meaning in Chapter Four.

Implications

The implications of bringing the social construction and media theories into the realm of tourism are significant. Through applying these theories we are providing another way in which to view social construction in terms of tourism and mass media. This opens up possibilities for improved in-depth research into tourist moti-vation, examining the expectations of quality and satisfaction by not only intro-ducing theories and models from other disciplines but also developing new models and theories specific to tourism.

References

Abercrombie, N., Hill, S., and Turner, B.S. (2000). *The Penguin Dictionary of Sociology* (4th ed.). Middlesex, England: Penguin Books.

Anderson, W.T. (1990). *Reality Isn't What It Used to Be: Theatrical Politics, Ready to Wear Religion, Global Myths, Primitive Chic and Other Wonders of the Postmodern World*. San Francisco: Harper and Row.

Beeton, S. (2000). It's a wrap! What happens after the film crew leaves? An examina-tion of community responses to film-induced tourism. *TTRA National Conference— Lights! Camera! Action!* Burbank, CA: TTRA National Conference, pp. 127-136.

Beeton, S. (2001). Smiling for the camera: The influence of film audiences on a budget tourism destination. *Tourism, Culture and Communication*, **3** (1), 15-26.

Beeton, S. (in press). Rural tourism in Australia–Has the gaze altered? Tracking rural images through film and tourism promotion. *International Journal of Tourism Research—Special Issue: Rural Tourism*.

Bennett, W.L. (1996). *News: The Politics of Illusion*. White Plains, NY: Longman.

Berger, P., and T. Luckmann. (1966). *The Social Construction of Reality*. Garden City, NY: Anchor Books.

Bowen, H.E. (2002). Images of women in tourism magazine advertising: A content analysis of *Travel* & Leisure magazine from 1969 to 1999. *Dissertation Abstracts* (UMI No. 3060773).

Butler, R.W. (1999). Understanding tourism. In: E. L. Jackson and T. L. Burton (Eds.), *Leisure Studies: Prospects for the Twenty-First Century* (pp. 97-118). State College, PA: Venture Publishing.

Chen, G., and W.J. Starosta. (1998). *Foundations of Intercultural Communication*. Boston: Allyn and Bacon.

Cohen, J. (1986). Promotion of overseas tourism through media fiction. *Tourism Services and Marketing: Advances in Theory and Practice: Proceedings of the Special Conference on Tourism Services* (pp. 229-237). Cleveland, OH.

Dann, G. (1977). Anomie, ego-enhancement and tourism. *Annals of Tourism Research*, **4** (4), 184-194.

Dann, G. (1996). *The Language of Tourism: A Sociolinguistic Perspective*. Oxford: CABI.

Davidson, J., and P. Spearritt. (2000). *Holiday Business. Tourism in Australia Since 1870*. Melbourne: Melbourne University Press.

DeFleur, M.L., and S. Ball-Rokeach. (1989). *Theories of Mass Communication* (5th ed.). New York: Longman.

Eco, U. (1983). *Travels in Hyperreality*. San Diego: Harcourt Brace Jovanovich.

Feighey, W. (2003). Negative research? Developing the visual in tourism research. *Current Issues in Tourism*, **6** (1), 76-85.

Fürsich, E. (2002). Packaging culture: The potential and limitations of travel programs on global television. *Communication Quarterly*, Spring, **50** (2), 204-226.

Gnoth, J. (1999). Tourism expectation formation: The case of camper-van tourists in New Zealand. In A. Pizam and Y. Mansfeld. (Eds.), *Consumer Behavior in Travel and Tourism* (pp. 245-264). New York: Haworth Press.

Goeldner, C.R., Ritchie, J.R.B. and McIntosh, R.W. (2000). *Tourism—Principles, Practices, Philosophies* (8th ed.). New York: John Wiley and Sons.

Goffman, E. (1974). *Frame Analysis: An Essay on the Organization of Experience*. New York: Harper and Row.

Hacking, I. (1999). *The Social Construction of What?* Cambridge, MA: Harvard University Press.

Hall, C.M., and S.J. Page. (1999). *The Geography of Tourism and Recreation: Environment, Place and Space*. London: Routledge.

Hall, S. (1997). The work of representation. In S. Hall (Ed.), *Representation: Cultural Representations and Signifying Practices* (pp. 13-74). London: Sage.

Jansson, A. (2002). Spatial phantasmagoria: The mediatization of tourism experience. *European Journal of Communication,* **17** (4), 429-433.

Krippendorf, J. (1986). The new tourist turning point for leisure and travel. *Tourism Management*, **7,** 131-135.

Kuhn, T. (1962). *The Structure of Scientific Revolution* (2nd ed.). Chicago: University of Chicago Press.

Lang, G.E., and K. Lang. (1984). *Politics and Television Reviewed*. Beverly Hills: Sage.

Leiper, N. (2002). *Tourism Management* (2nd ed.). Melbourne: Pearson Education.

Lipschultz, J.H., and M.L. Hilt. (2002). *Crime and Local Television News: Dramatic, Breaking, and Live from the Scene*. Mahwah, NJ: Lawrence Earlbaum.

Littlejohn, S. (1991). *Theories of Human Communication*. Belmont, CA: Wadsworth.

Löfgren, O. (1999). *On Holiday: A History of Vacationing*. Berkeley, CA: University of California Press.

MacCannell, D. (1973). Staged authenticity: Arrangements of social space in tourism settings. *American Journal of Sociology*, **79** (3), 357-361.

Markwell, K. (2001). An intimate rendezvous with nature? Mediating the tourist-nature experience at three tourist sites in Borneo. *Tourist Studies*, **1** (1), 39-57.

McQuail, D. (1994). *Mass Communication Theory, an Introduction* (3rd ed.). London: Sage.

Morgan, N., and A. Pritchard. (1998). *Tourism Promotion and Power: Creating Images, Creating Identities*. Chichester, England: John Wiley and Sons.

Murphy, P. (1982). Perceptions and attitudes of decision making groups in tourism centers. *Journal of Travel Research*, **21**, 8-12.

Nielsen, C. (2001). *Tourism and the Media: Tourist Decision Making, Information and Communication*. Melbourne: Hospitality Press.

O'Barr, W.M. (1994). *Culture and the Ad: Exploring Otherness in the Worlds of Advertising*. Boulder, CO: Westview Press.

Riley, R.W. (1994). Movie-induced tourism. In A.V. Seaton (Ed.), *Tourism: The State of the Art* (pp. 453-458). West Sussex, England: John Wiley and Sons.

Rorty, R. (1989). *Contingency, Irony, and Solidarity*. New York: Cambridge University Press.

Rowe, D. (1993). Leisure, tourism and "Australianness," *Media, Culture and Society*, **15**, 253-269.

Santos, C. (2004). Framing Portugal: Representational dynamics. *Annals of Tourism Research*, **31** (1), 122-138.

Searle, J.R. (1995). *The Construction of Social Reality*. New York: The Free Press.

Schutz, A. (1962). In M Natanson (Ed.), *Collected papers: The problem of social reality*. Boston: Hague.

Surette, R. (1992). *Media, Crime and Criminal Justice, Images and Realities*. Pacific Grove, CA: Brooks/Cole.

Tooke, N., and M. Baker. (1996). Seeing is believing: The effect of film on visitor numbers to screened locations. *Tourism Management*, **17** (2), 87-94.

Tuchman, G. (1978). *Making News*. New York: The Free Press.

Urry, J. (1990). *The Tourist Gaze: Leisure and Travel in Contemporary Societies*. London: Sage.

Vhang, T., Wang, J., and C. Chen. (1998). The social construction of international imagery in the post-Cold War era: A comparative analysis of U.S. and Chinese national TV news. *Journal of Broadcasting and Electronic Media*, **42**, 277-296.

Washburn, P.C. (1992). *Broadcasting Propaganda: International Radio Broadcasting and the Construction of Political Reality*. Westport, CT: Greenwood.

Williams, A., and G. Shaw. (1995). *Tourism and Economic Development: Western European Experiences*. West Sussex, England: John Wiley and Sons.

3

Constructing Quality, Constructing Reality

Heather E. Bowen
Carla Almeida Santos

Constructing Quality, Constructing Reality

Audio, visual, and written media establish representations that serve to construct particular notions of excellence and significance concerning tourism experiences. These notions of excellence and significance, identified in this chapter as notions of "quality," are shared among popular cultural products providing references that shape and legitimize tourist expectations. That is to say, travel media serve to negotiate notions of quality tourism experiences for the general public by promoting images that help define and direct tourist expectations. In order to assure resonance with their audiences, travel media rely on previously established representations (Bowen, 2002; Santos, 2004), and, in so doing, notions of quality tourism experiences are recycled or reconstructed on a continuing basis. As a result of this process, although seeking to provide accounts of tourism experiences in unique and exciting destinations, travel media provide accounts that contribute to homogeneous notions of quality tourism. The result of this homogenization is visible in such mass-mediated cultural products as the Travel Channel programming and newspaper travel sections, both of which are growing in popularity.

Construction of notions of quality tourism experiences through Travel Channel programming and newspaper travel sections is of particular concern because the editors of these media are not obligated by traditional rules of journalism that require neutrality; rather, they are free to productively encourage readers to visit destinations. However, their position as experts lends validity to their opinion about tourism products that, as service products, consumers cannot try out in advance. Tourists therefore must rely on the opinion of experts, including travel media representatives, when making purchase decisions.

Relying on previously established and socially accepted representations (Santos, 2004), travel editors construct expectations and experiences. Therefore, by examining mass-mediated approaches to tourism, we are able to identify what is socially regarded as relevant and important in a tourism experience. This allows for discussion about the manner in which notions of quality tourism experiences introduced by mass media come to be taken for granted and accepted as natural, and are therefore rarely questioned. Furthermore, as it would seem to be in the best interest of travel editors to support and praise the benefits of an international travel experience, they become active in turning both the Travel Channel and newspaper travel sections into marketing tools used to guide tourists toward destinations. Stabler (1990, p. 140) stated, "[T]ransmission of information from supply (destination) through the marketing of tourism and media, previous experience and opinions of other consumers, combined with motivations and socio-economic characteristics form perceptions, the image of tourism and tourist destinations." Mass-mediated messages, such as the ones found in both the Travel Channel programming and newspaper travel sections, function as references for tourists. Considering this referencing function, their sociopolitical role must not be undermined (Santos, 2004).

In the past, the individual consumer has been used as the measurement for studies into quality tourism experiences (Gnoth, 1999; Sussmann and Unel, 1999). Quality, therefore, has been defined almost exclusively in terms of the demands and wishes of the consumer. This paradigm centers the truth as existing with the consumer and proposes that a progressively greater consumption of goods is beneficial. In this chapter, however, we argue that notions of quality tourism experiences must be investigated from a mass-mediated perspective, allowing us to understand how the construction of quality occurs in the first place. As noted in the previous chapter, social construction of reality asserts that we make sense of what occurs around us, based on what information we access. Determination of quality in tourism experiences will be produced, processed, and stored according to the information provided to us in a variety of mass-mediated images of tourism.

Building on the literature outlined in Chapter Two, we propose that a social constructivist perspective provides insight into mass-mediated travel narratives by questioning the representations utilized to promote notions of what constitutes quality tourism experiences. Maintaining that notions of quality tourism experiences are developed within a dominant cultural system and not given to objective or value-neutral depiction (Santos, 2004), this chapter takes a critical stance seeking to discuss the social origins of what is commonly seen as a "natural" rather than human creation. By documenting the approaches to the promotion of tourism in the social construction of tourism experiences, we identify some of the travel media characteristics that contribute to representations of quality tourism experiences. As Chapter Two introduced social constructionism within the overall context of tourism and mass-mediated messages, that discussion is continued here within the context of cable television programming and newspaper travel sections.

Two forms of mass media through which quality tourism experiences are socially constructed will be discussed. Specifically, we look in depth at how the Travel Channel's *World's Best* series, produced by cable television giant, U.S. based Discovery Communications, has defined quality tourism. Episodes of *World's Best* were viewed as an audio and visual representation of elements and participants in the tourism system, selected by editors of the Travel Channel to signify superlative-quality tourism experiences. Additionally, the chapter looks at how quality tourism experiences are described through editorial commentaries in the travel section of Australia's national newspaper, *The Australian*. These editorial commentaries communicate interpretations of tourism events that are designed to influence others. Framed as the expert opinion of a tourism professional, these commentaries provide a strong basis for an exploration that centers on the examination of how reality is socially constructed as a product of mass communication.

Grounded in cultural studies, and with social constructionist perspectives, this analysis found quality tourism to be defined by personal service, seclusion and solitude, pristine beauty, unique characteristics, fine dining, and luxurious accommodations, all of which are expensive to purchase. Each of these characteristics is expounded upon in a detailed description of our results. An explanation of the methods by which we arrived at these results is then followed by a discussion about their meanings and the implications of media construction of quality tourism experiences.

Why Television?

According to Lash (1988) and Emmison and Smith (2000), the postmodern times we live in can be characterized by a turn from the literary to the visual. Images have replaced texts as the dominant cultural form. Potter (2001) points out,

We all live in two worlds: the real world and the media world. The real world is where we come in direct contact with other people, locations, and events. Most of us feel that the real world is too limited, that is, we cannot get all the experiences and information we want from just the real world. In order to get those experiences and information, we journey into the media world . . . . We are continually entering the media world to get experiences and information we cannot get very well in our real lives. When we find these experiences, we bring them back onto our real lives. We are constantly crossing the border between the real world and the media world. (p. vii)

Most people are not present for significant world, national, or local events. Most have never seen, in person, the national leader of their country, the governor of their local state, or even the mayor of their city. We rely on the media to make these people real to us, to bring us images of the world in which we are meant to live and to help us define the behavior we are to employ to interact with this world in a way that will bring about the effects and experiences we desire. With advancement in technology, the world in which we are impacted, and with which we have the ability to interact, on a daily basis, has grown much larger than one with which we can physically engage. We have grown accustomed to employing various forms of media to enable us to make sense of a world much larger than that with which we can personally and physically interact. In the twenty-first century, we do this easily for business, education, social networking, recreation, and entertainment. It would not be unusual for someone to see a destination on television, research and book a trip to that destination on the Internet, and then purchase a guidebook to inform them about what to do in that place. This then delimits the experiences the tourist can have in a particular location because guidebooks and other media focus on destination and attractions that have already been marked for tourism. Sites are prequalified as worth seeing and destinations worth visiting based on the notions of quality tourism experiences that continually circulate and recirculate, construct and reconstruct, through the mass media.

For [Stuart] Hall the extraordinary power of the news photograph lies in its ability to obscure its own ideological dimensions by appearing as a "literal visual-transcription of the real world" (Hall, 1973, p. 214). Selection and framing decisions made by photographers and editors are ignored (the newspaper might have printed, for example, a picture of a demonstrator being hit by the police) and so we tend to read such photographs as a truthful document of what really happened, ignoring the possibility of other interpretations of the event" (Emmison and Smith, 2000, p. 48).

Pictorial images that have been widely distributed in the public sphere, such as those published in newspapers and magazines or broadcast on network and cable television, "are not only an indicator of shared beliefs and ideology, but are also presumed to have considerable influence in shaping them" (Emmison and Smith, 2000, p. 63). An illustrative example can be taken from the realm of advertising. According to means-end-chain theory, advertisers create advertisements for their products based on which product attributes they believe will reinforce the beliefs and personal values of their target audience (Shimp, 1997). To do this, advertisements create the meaning of product attributes to be desirable to their target audience. The images in tourism advertisements can thus be seen as a window into beliefs and personal values of the (potential) tourist audience, while the ads are at the same time shaping them. "Ultimately advertising works in a circular movement which once set in motion is self-perpetuating" (Williamson, 1978/1995, p. 13). A similar argument can be made for the circular influence of the images in documentary-style travel programming, such as Travel Channel's *World's Best*.

The Travel Channel's *World's Best*

World's Best is a travel documentary program on U.S.-based Discovery Communications' Travel Channel, a cable television station dedicated to travel and tourism programming, primarily for a U.S. audience. Individual episodes focus on different aspects of the tourism system, such as beach resorts, built wonders, or fast-food stops. Each one is structured into a top-10 list, such as the "top-10 pleasure palaces," or a best-of list, such as the "best cruises by individual category, including fastest cruise and best activities cruise." Although all episodes fall under the series title *World's Best*, the focus may be more narrow, and include only regional destinations, such as American beach resorts or European castles. The television episodes are produced by independent production companies and not necessarily shown in chronological order of completion. They air during prime time and are then re-aired later in the evening and/or later that same week.

The discussion in this chapter will focus on the content of three episodes of *World's Best*: *World's Best Cruise Ships*, *America's Best Beach Resorts*, and *World's Best Pleasure Palaces*. In July 2003, *World's Best Cruise Ships* (Michael Hoff Productions, Inc., 2002) aired on July 1, at 8:00 p.m. and at 11:00 p.m., and on July 6 at 6:00 p.m.; *America's Best Beach Resorts* (KAOS Entertainment, 2000) aired on July 11 at 8:00 p.m. and at 11:00 p.m., and on July 13 at 6:00 p.m.; and *World's Best Pleasure Palaces* (Termite Art Productions, 2000) aired on July 30 at 8:00 p.m. and at 11:00 p.m.

Each of these episodes is hosted by a single commentator, presumably an affiliate of the Travel Channel, whose voice is heard throughout the program. For all three episodes, the commentator is a male who never actually appears himself but remains an omniscient voice. In the case of *World's Best Cruises*, a second *female* commentator actually appears and introduces herself at the outset and then reappears between each of the cruises presented. Throughout the travel documentary, employed hosts, tourists, and, in some cases, travel industry professionals are pictured as talking heads giving their own commentary. While their elaborations or testimonials are being given, the image changes from the speaker to the characteristic or aspect of the beach resort/cruise/pleasure palace to which they are referring. The pictures and words of the staff, most often a male manager or director, and of the tourists and industry professionals are edited into the program in such a way as to give credibility to the selection for inclusion on an "America's best" or "world's best" list. This pattern of imaging and commentary makes the program immediately recognizable as part of the documentary genre. For example:

Commentator: "No facility of this significance would overlook the demands of its glamorous guests . . ."

Image: A female guest is being served at a table by a male host.

Commentator: ". . . but just to make sure . . ."

Image: A male host, wearing a white shirt with a black coat and tie, rolls a white table-clothed cart full of strawberries and champagne into a guest room.

Commentator: ". . . the Breakers has an army of 17,000 staff . . ."

Image: A female host makes up a queen-sized bed.

Commentator: ". . . to ensure that everyone gets first-class service."

Image: In a guest room, a male host wearing a white shirt with a dark jacket and tie, opens a bottle of champagne for a female guest.

The World's Best Cruise Ships includes eight ships, the *World's Best American Beach Resorts* includes ten resorts, and the *World's Best Pleasure Palaces* includes ten palaces (see Table 3-1).

Travel Channel's *World's Best* was selected because (1) it airs on the only U.S. cable television station dedicated to travel and tourism; (2) each episode airs repeatedly throughout the programming week; (3) its title of *World's Best* signals that what this program shows is better than anything else that can be found in the world; and (4) it espouses to provide trustworthy information through its documentary-style format. Each of these characteristics provides an air of authority that serves to reinforce the authenticity of the images and representations in each episode. Each episode was viewed and analyzed, as described next.

Methodology

The authors and an assistant have reviewed each of the three Travel Channel *World's Best* episodes: *World's Best Cruise ships*, *America's Best Beach Resorts*, and *World's Best Pleasure Palaces*. Researchers viewed these episodes with the following questions in mind for each beach resort/cruise/pleasure palace:

1. What, according to this episode, is it about this cruise ship/beach resort/pleasure palace that sets it apart from others and thereby leads to its inclusion on the list of America's best or the world's best? That is, how is this cruise ship/beach resort/pleasure palace described as the top, or one of the top 10?

2. What images and physical symbols are used to represent this description(s) of quality? That is, what does this America's best or world's best cruise ship/beach resort/pleasure palace look like, and/or include, that lets the viewer know that it is high quality?

Following the viewing of each full episode, each researcher compared each of their individual cruise ship/beach resort/pleasure palace answers to identify common threads across the episode, as well as isolated characteristics or descriptors, in an overview of America's best or world's best cruise ship/beach resort/pleasure palaces. After viewing all three episodes, each researcher compared the overviews to identify common threads across the three episodes, as well as isolated characteristics or descriptors, in an overview of the best-quality tourism experiences (as provided by these specific types of tourism). Finally, the individual episode overviews and cross-episode overviews from each researcher were compared and contrasted to identify common threads across the three episodes, as well as isolated characteristics or descriptors. The findings are discussed here.

This research follows the cultural studies tradition of semiotic analysis of existing, commercially produced images as a way of revealing ideologies and cultural codes (Emmison and Smith, 2000; O'Brien and Kollock, 2001; Bowen, 2002) and the symbolic interactionist tradition of looking at the symbol, a representation of

Table 3.1 World's best episodes

World's Best Cruise Ships	America's Best Beach Resorts	World's Best Pleasure Palaces
Best Cruise Ship for Dining: *Norwegian Star*	#10: Casa Del Mar (California, USA)	#10: La Moumania Hotel (Marrakesh, Morocco)
Best Cruise Accommodations: *Radisson Mariner*	#9: Bahia Mar Resort (Texas, USA)	#9: Lanesborough Hotel (London, England)
Best Service Cruise: *Crystal Symphony*	#8: Ritz Carlton (Florida, USA)	#8: Cirigan Palace (Turkey) #7: Beverly Hills Hotel
Best Excursions Cruise: *Nantucket Clipper*	#7: The Cloister (Georgia, USA)	(California, USA) #6: Manele Bay Hotel
Best Family Cruise: *Disney Wonder*	#6: Manele Bay Hotel (Hawaii, USA)	(Hawaii, USA) #5: The Ritz (Paris, France)
Most Intimate Cruise: *Seabourn Spirit*	#5: Breakers Hotel (Florida, USA)	#4: Bellagio (Las Vegas, USA)
Fastest Cruise: *Olympic Voyager*	#4: Kahala Mandarin Oriental (Hawaii, USA)	#3: The Plaza (New York, USA)
Best Activities Cruise:	#3: Ritz Carlton Laguna	#2: Villa D'Este (Italy)
Carnival Pride	Niguel (California, USA) #2: Bacara Resort and Spa (California, USA)	#1: Burj Al Arab (Dubai, United Arab Emirates)
	#1: Four Seasons (Hawaii, USA)	

something that may or may not exist in tangible form, as the key to the puzzle about how individuals interact to construct meaning and structure in society (O'Brien and Kollock, 2001). Symbolic interactionism "focuses on subjective interpretations of events that occur in an *interactional* context. The assumption is that, whether we are dealing with someone face to face or having an internal dialogue with an imagined other, most human activity involves evaluating how to respond to others in specific contexts" (O'Brien and Kollock, 2001, p. 47).

In the analysis of the Travel Channel's *World's Best*, this type of interaction can be viewed as taking place on multiple levels. First, there is the observable interaction between participants in the tourism system depicted in the program episodes. Tourists and hosts are negotiating the tourism situation through the manner in which they play their respective roles, as they have been socially constructed to do. Because of the context and framing, this comes to represent for viewers how one is expected to act in a quality tourism setting (Santos, 2004). Second, there is an expected interaction between the actor or speaker (for example, the episode commentator or a site manager) and a potential tourist/viewer. Given the programming context and assumptions that can be made about a highly capitalistic society such as the United States, it is reasonable to assume that these travel documentaries were put together and aired with the expectation that the viewer would have some reaction, immediate or delayed, to seeing these images and hearing the descriptions or testimony of the commentators about what a superlative quality tourism experience entails.

In watching *World's Best*, we sought to capture the phenomenal features—the tourism related images and descriptions—in each of the three selected episodes and make these the objects of our analysis. In doing so, manifest content was taken to symbolize latent content within the context of a superlative program created by the only Travel Channel for a U.S. pay-television viewing audience. *Manifest content* is that which was visually apparent. *Latent content* is the underlying meaning as interpreted by the viewer, the referent to which the manifest content refers. The analysis of latent content takes into consideration the context in which the images are (intended to be) seen. This allows for culturally specific assumptions about symbolism and audience, as well as attention to potential effects of the message sender.

Characteristics that led to the inclusion of each of these cruise ships/beach resort/pleasure palaces on the Travel Channel's *America's Best* or *World's Best* list was used as a proxy for quality from the researchers' understanding of how *quality* is commonly defined, as well as the tourism-relevant dictionary.com definitions of *quality:*

n. An inherent or distinguishing characteristic; a property. Superiority of kind: an intellect of unquestioned quality. Degree or grade of excellence: yard goods of low quality. *Adj.* Having a high degree of excellence: the importance of quality health care.

Constructed Notions of Quality Tourism: Travel Channel

From our analysis we found Travel Channel's *World's Best* to define quality tourism experiences based on personal service, seclusion and solitude, pristine beauty, uniqueness, fine dining, luxurious accommodations, and the high expense required for purchase.

High Level of Service

Overall, the best beach resorts in the United States and the best cruises and pleasure palaces in the world are defined first and foremost by the high level of service they provide. The staff at these facilities looks after tourists on an individual basis, providing them with anything they could desire or imagine. This is accomplished by employing a high ratio of staff to guests, as well as personally getting to know guests by name and preferences, providing guests with every amenity they might ever conceivably need, and catering to their every whim.

For instance, to provide the highest level of service, the Breakers Hotel employs 17,000 staff and the *Crystal Symphony* has 550 crew members for up to 940 guests. Burj Al Arab greets guests at the airport in a chauffer-driven Rolls Royce, and wine glasses are never less than half full on the *Seabourn Spirit*. On the *Crystal Symphony*, which claims no request is outrageous, private butlers clean and press clothes, shine shoes, and pack for guests, as well as "just about anything else you can imagine" (Cruises, 2002). And at the Lanesborough Hotel, "the butler service is a special department that is not connected with other departments so here it's a separate part that is simply there waiting for guests to call and ask them to do things" (Pleasure Palaces, 2000). At the Ritz, Paris, a name that has become synonymous with quality, "no request is too ridiculous or too difficult. Their purpose is to make you happy" (Pleasure Palaces, 2000), and at the Four Seasons, "Anything that you could desire, they will make sure they can take care of or set up for you" (Beach Resorts, 2000).

The descriptions and images paint a picture of high-quality service as unlimited and guiltlessly excessive. Guests are free to do little or nothing for themselves because hosts are present to provide detailed personal service whenever, and however, it is desired. Images of how service is rendered and by whom are continually presented. For example, typical images include:

- Lounging tourists are served drinks on the beach.
- A male host, wearing a white shirt with a black coat and tie, rolls a room service cart covered in a white table cloth into a guest room.
- A female host makes a guest's large bed.
- A male host, wearing a white shirt with a dark jacket and tie, serves an alcoholic drink to a female guest.
- On an empty verandah, a female guest gets a massage from a male host. (Beach Resorts, 2000)

Seclusion and Solitude

Seclusion from the rest of society and opportunity for solitude characterize these best beach resorts, cruises, and pleasure palaces. Beaches are shown completely empty or with very few people on them. When people are present, there tends to be only a single female tourist or a lone heterosexual tourist couple. To preserve this notion, if need be, the image is shot in such a way that the one or two tourists in the foreground are in a space in which there are no other people. In these instances, in a first or quick glance at the image moving quickly onto and off the screen, the tourists appear to be alone. It does not seem to matter how big or small

45

a beach is, so long as it is private. Similar claims of privacy and seclusion are made about the Breakers' quarter-mile beach, Kahala Mandarin Oriental's 6.5 acres, and Manele Bay's entire island. The privacy and seclusion of each is touted as characteristic of a quality tourism experience.

Empty landscape in which one can find seclusion and solitude is not limited to the beach resorts. Descriptions of cruises and pleasure palaces include aerial shots of pristine landscape, empty and nearly empty beaches, hotel and cruise ship pools in which one or none swim, and restaurants in which only one couple dines, all showing the tourist as spatially removed from other people. Adult tourists are depicted as interacting only with one or two other tourists, most often their own heterosexual partner and occasionally their children, or with one or two serving hosts. In this way, they are spatially removed from the people and places of the world beyond their tourist bubble, as well as from other tourists and hosts who occupy this bubble with them. The constructed image is of each heterosexual couple having a quality tourism experience within their own personal bubble. A guest at the Four Seasons stated, "This is the second time we've been here and this time we have made up our minds that we are not going to leave the resort. It has everything that you need. It is very much self-contained. It's about as close to paradise as you are going to get" (Beach Resorts, 2000).

Given the stated number of rooms and guest space available, it cannot be realistically expected that the beaches, pools, and restaurants in these tourist places remain empty for one or two tourists at a time. However, this depiction gives the indication that tourists can behave as if they are the only one person or couple at a tourist location and are expected to interact with no one other than the staff designated to serve them. A guest at Manele Bay expresses this contradiction: "This place is what we had always imagined was paradise. We have all the amenities that you would really want or need and yet you have the feeling of privacy, the feeling of seclusion" (Beach Resorts, 2000).

Beautiful and Pristine, Yet Ordered and Controlled

Along with seclusion comes pristine beauty. Such adjectives are most often used to describe settings that have been specifically ordered and controlled to maintain this level of quality for guests. Lawns are manicured, bushes are trimmed, and all beaches are shown without litter from humans or nature. The management at the Kahala Mandarin Oriental Hotel shares that the hotel's 880 feet of white sand is "maintained and manicured every single morning" (Beach Resorts, 2000). And a guest at the Breakers notes, "The beach is clean, kept magnificently pristine" (Beach Resorts, 2000). Sweeping landscapes are shown with little or no human development. A staff member at Manele Bay explains that Lanai Island is owned by David Murdock, "and because it's privately owned, it's protected from any overdevelopment that you might find on the other islands. It's only been in tourism for about 10 years so it's really the way Hawaii was many, many years ago" (Pleasure Palaces, 2000). The *Norwegian Star* cruise is shown along with lush wooded landscapes and pristine white beaches. And, the *Nantucket Clipper* cruise is also shown on open empty blue water, next to lush wooded hills and manicured lawns with palm trees.

46

Unique or Superlative Feature or Activity

Often, that which defines these tourist destinations as the world's best is superlatively better than any other destination. The importance given to this superior aspect indicates that this characteristic is in some way expected in a quality tourism experience. Competing destinations expend great amounts of resources to be considered better than any other. The superlative characteristic may be uniqueness. Beach resorts, cruises, and pleasure palaces that strive to be the first to have something or do something that no other place has or does, are rated as high quality. Striving to be unique is important to attract tourists who are willing to pay for this difference. It appears that many beach resorts, cruises, and pleasure palaces have found their strategic competitive advantage through quality, as defined by an outstanding or unique characteristic.

For example, Manele Bay offers clay shooting in a golf-course–type setting in the woods. The *Seabourn Spirit* offers a helicopter cruise over the glaciers. The *Olympic Voyager* is the fastest cruise in the world and therefore "can reach more ports in less time than any other ship" (Cruises, 2002). The Four Seasons has a 2.5 million-gallon aquarium in which guests can actually swim. Burj Al Arab is a custom architectural structure, constructed in a very unique way. The sailboat shape of the hotel was designed to reflect the heritage of the seafaring nation of the United Arab Emirates. It has a double skin of Teflon-coated woven glass fiber and at 321 meters high is the world's tallest hotel, and it represents the largest use of these materials in any building, anywhere.

Other examples of strategic competitive advantage through quality include the Lanesborough Hotel, which offers its guests the latest in technology. Guests have access to mobile phones to take with them to the library bar at the hotel or to a business meeting in Paris. When someone calls for guests at the hotel, the hotel operators can ring guests' mobile phones wherever they are in Europe. And the *Disney Wonder*, which has the largest entertainment department anywhere in the world at sea, is the only cruise line in the world that can dock right next to its own private island.

Commentator: "When Disney decided to venture into the cruise ship business, they broke the mold, literally. They built state rooms 25 percent larger than industry standard . . ."

Image: A shot of the outside of the ship, which turns into a tour of a guest room.

Commentator: ". . . and did something that no other cruise line had ever done before. They actually bought one of the islands in the Bahamas."

Image: A shot of the ship from the island, highlighting guests walking on a roped walkway that leads to an empty, sandy white shore with cool green water.

Commentator: "It is absolutely immaculate and there is no better way to describe it than sheer paradise."

Image: Empty beach shot, to shot of ship in the distance with two kayakers paddling toward it in the foreground, to a shot of a group of about 20 tourists walking toward an empty beach with very well groomed flora, to a shot of 20 kids running toward the beach yelling.

Commentator: "Today the 1,000-acre island is known as Castaway Cay."

Image: Close-up shot of a child wearing a life jacket, snorkel, and mask.

Fine Dining

Superlative quality is also defined with food. As one guest on the *Norwegian Star* states, "Everything tastes better when you are cruising in Hawaii" (Cruises, 2002). These best resorts, cruises, and pleasure palaces highlight their fine dining. The *Crystal Symphony* claims, "We always say *Crystal Symphony* is the best restaurant in the town where it's parked" (Cruises, 2002). Often this characteristic of quality ties directly back to the high level of service discussed earlier. Similar images are repeatedly used to exemplify this high level of service, including white table cloths, stemmed glassware, formally dressed wait staff, tuxedos on waiters (and even decorated strawberries), and toasts with champagne. At the Four Seasons, personnel actually wait until a fish dish is ordered before they catch it from their on-site ponds. And this exemplary image is unique to the *Seabourn Spirit:*

Commentator: "*Seabourn* is internationally known for its over-the-top luxury, from champagne on demand to caviar in the surf."

Image: A female guest in a red bathing suit stands in thigh-deep water next to a floating table, where she is obviously being served by four male crew members, who, while also standing in the water, are fully dressed in crew white uniforms. Their cruise ship is in the background across blue water, beyond which are green wooded hills.

Well-Appointed Rooms

It is their accommodations that allow some of these facilities to differentiate themselves and develop a unique characteristic or competitive advantage. At the Ritz in Paris, César Ritz "introduced for the first time, one bathroom per room . . . a telephone in every room . . . [and] electricity in all the rooms" (Pleasure Palaces, 2000). The Cirigan Palace has Europe's biggest hotel room, the Sultan Suite, with a private entrance, its own personal staff, and a sunken bathtub big enough in which one may swim. The *Radisson Mariner* was the first ship to provide guests with a private balcony in every room. The *Disney Wonder* built staterooms 25% larger than industry standard and was the first to feature staterooms with a bath and a half. Quality rooms in these best beach resorts, cruise ships, and pleasure palaces are depicted as spacious and well-appointed with expensive furniture, tasteful décor, fresh flowers, and a balcony with ocean views. The large bathrooms come with deep tubs, and everyone has room service.

Expensive and Therefore Exclusive

All of these characteristics of quality cost money. For some of these beach resorts, cruise ships, and pleasure palaces explicit prices are used to indicate quality. The presidential suite in the Kahala Mandarin Oriental Hotel costs $3,700 per night. A cruise on the *Seabourn Spirit* can cost up to $10,000, the *Radisson Mariner* can cost up to $17,000, and the *Crystal Symphony* costs $38,000 to $175,000. A shot of vintage cognac at the Lanesborough Hotel can cost as much as $1,200. For others, the high price of quality is eluded to through the use of such descriptors as the "opulence" of the Cirigan Palace, the "luxury" of Burj Al Arab, references to "the rich and famous" guests at the Beverly Hills Hotel, and the royal treatment at the Lanesborough Hotel.

European Superiority

There is a noteworthy difference in the definition of quality for America's best beach resorts or an American pleasure palace, versus the world's best cruises and pleasure palaces outside the United States. American locations are qualified by association with Europe. For a tourist, the "colonial Mediterranean feel" to the Bacara Resort and Spa in California contributes to its status as "the ultimate get-away" (Beach Resorts, 2000). Management at the Breakers points out that " 'the Breakers experience' begins as you are coming up the main drive and you are see-ing this Italian influenced architecture" (Beach Resorts, 2000). The Bellagio, built to show that Las Vegas could compete with London or Paris, was designed to cap-ture "the exquisite look and feel of an Italian lake village" (Pleasure Palaces, 2000).

Constructed Notions of Quality Tourism: *The Australian*

Seeking to investigate whether televised representations are unique in their approach to what constitutes quality tourism experiences, the authors undertook an exploratory analysis of *The Australian's* travel section editorial commentaries. This exploratory analysis is intended to provide another example of the ways in which mass media characterize and construct notions of quality tourism experi-ences. It allows for consideration of another medium, and one constructed for an (Australian) audience with a different cultural perspective from a U.S. American audience.

Twelve editorial commentaries published in *The Australian* in 1982, 1992, and 2002 were selected as part of an exploratory longitudinal study and examined. Editorial commentaries from the first week of each Australian season—spring (September), summer (December), fall/autumn (March), and winter (June)—were selected, coded, and analyzed. Searching for a central topic, all editorial commen-taries were coded and analyzed individually by two graduate assistants and the authors. These four individual analyses were then brought together to identify and define common themes. This methodological approach used editorial commen-taries not as a window into an individual's experiences, but rather as a window into the social construction of tourism experiences. It particularly allowed the authors to enter the debate regarding quality tourism experiences by examining the mass-mediated commentaries of travel editors whose travel activities are shaped by socially constructed notions of tourism—hence, allowing for an exploration of notions of quality and its positioning within their commentaries.

Therefore, this section of the chapter is intended as a "check-point," an inquiry into the previous findings in order to assess the variety of approaches to what con-stitutes quality tourism experiences. It was particularly interesting to note that many of the same notions of quality tourism experiences were shared among media. For example, when describing their experiences, travel editors undoubtedly connected quality tourism experiences with notions of *high level of service.*

"While we may hardly be a mass organization, Hong Kong turned on hospitality that would have impressed somebody like the World Bank" (*The Weekend Australian*, March 6-7, 1982). "Prompt to supply top level accommodation . . . flew members to and from Hong Kong . . . arranged tours and supplied enough information to keep most inquiring travel writers happy for the rest of 1982" (*The Weekend Australian*, March 6-7, 1982). "I tell anyone who will listen that resort gardeners in Bali swish-swish their brooms and prune by hand" (*The Weekend Australian*, August 31-September 1, 2002). And, "Air India has always boasted their passengers get treated like maharajahs, but from the end of this year, visitors to India will get that sort of treatment on the ground too" (*The Weekend Australian*, June 5-6, 1982).

Notions of quality tourism experiences were also associated with notions of *seclusion and solitude*. In this case, quality tourism is meant to be without the loud sounds of work or other tourists. "The sound I do not want to hear on holiday is a lawnmower. And that means any mowing apparatus, except possibly those old fashioned pushers . . . but definitely including ride-on monsters" (*The Weekend Australian*, August 31-September 1, 2002). "The big winners will be the integrated spas . . . where accommodation is pavilion style and therapists can perform a range of treatments without guests leaving their rooms . . . so the guest room becomes a spa, a private cocoon" (*The Weekend Australian*, December 7-8, 2002).

As found in the Travel Channel analysis, notions of *beautiful and pristine, yet ordered and controlled* tourism experiences are also evoked: "An ideal setting—right on the headland near the famous aquarium with a view across the island" (*The Weekend Australian*, December 4-5, 1982), "two garden suites with French windows opening on to courtyards" (*The Weekend Australian*, September 12-13, 1992), "the only thing tourists . . . have to worry about is a possible change in the weather" (*The Weekend Australian*, September 4-5, 1982), and "every one of the 136 balcony rooms has the same outlook" (*The Weekend Australian*, December 4-5, 1982). In addition, *unique or superlative features or activities,* such as a four-week dining experience with the best chefs in Europe, "pate de foie gras which, when spread on a loaf of crusty bread, makes the ultimate cross-cultural Singapore picnic" (*The Weekend Australian*, September 12-13, 1992), a "restaurant specializing in cheese. . . . Every dish on the menu featured some sort of cheese . . . . between 100 and 120 different types of cheese" (*The Weekend Australian*, December 4-5, 1982), and "in an increasingly insecure world, the spa has become the sanctuary" (*The Weekend Australian*, December 7-8, 2002), are introduced as synonymous with quality tourism experiences. Discussions of *well-appointed rooms* are also introduced as essential for quality tourism experiences: "Stay in five star hotels like the Yak and Yeti or Everest Sheraton, or settle for not-much-less luxurious four-star places" (*The Weekend Australian*, September 4-5, 1982). "Appointments include two-toned marble bathrooms, embroidered sheets, stained glass panels, decorative wall friezes and shuttered windows" (*The Weekend Australian*, September 12-13, 1992).

Moreover, notions of quality tourism experiences are often evoked by discussions of how *expensive and therefore exclusive* an experience is. For instance, "India's rail system is bringing back genuine maharajah treatment with the state of Rajasthan contributing 18 refurbished carriages, once deemed suitable for the use of their princely rulers, to what will be known as The Maharajah's Express" (*The Weekend Australian*, June 5-6, 1982), "Its fine dining room, L'aigle d'Or, is affiliated with a restaurant of the same name in Paris, and chef Thierry Duflos has carved an enviable reputation" (*The Weekend Australian*, September 12-13, 1992), and "The original spas were not luxury retreats, but tiled torture chambers where one went for 'the cure'. . . and, by the look of the day, one was not administered to by petite temple maidens in white sarongs" (*The Weekend Australian*, December 7-8, 2002). Finally, just as it was found in the Travel Channel analysis, *The Australians'* travel editors made numerous reference to *Europe* in their description of quality tourism experiences. "The décor style of this hotel, which opened in October 1991, reminds you of a boutique Paris hotel" (*The Weekend Australian*, September 12-13, 1992), "it's hard to imagine the French Tourist Bureau deciding it could attract more visitors to Paris if the Gare de Lyon was reinvented as Flinders Street Station" (*The Weekend Australian*, March 2-3, 2002), and "L'aigle d'Or is affiliated with a restaurant of the same name in Paris" (*The Weekend Australian*, September 12-13, 1992).

Overall, this exploratory analysis revealed an emphasis on high level of service, seclusion and solitude in beautiful and pristine destinations, yet ordered and controlled tourism experiences that offer unique or superlative features and/or activities, as well as well-appointed rooms, expensive and therefore exclusive destinations, and European—particularly French—style. In their descriptions, travel editors evoke a certain entitlement to excess by relying on narratives that stress Frenchness, luxury, famous and royal individuals, tradition, aesthetically pleasing destinations, clean and orderly accommodations, fine food, high level of choreographed service, promptness, top-level accommodation, and special treatment for special people. It must be considered that these expectations are developed and constructed through their Australian editors and, as such, questions of aesthetics, for instance, are couched in what is aesthetically pleasing to an Australian audience. Moreover, these findings closely mirror the findings from our Travel Channel analysis, indicating that notions of the quality tourism experience are not only constructed through media representations but also presented as natural. Indeed, as discussed previously, travel media rely on established representations (Bowen, 2002; Santos, 2004), and, in so doing, we argue, notions of quality tourism experiences are recycled and reconstructed on a continuing basis.

Discussion

The overall image of quality tourism experiences presented in the analyzed Travel Channel episodes as the best in America or the best in the world, as well as the analysis of *The Australian's* travel section commentaries, is highly controlled, predictable, and expensive. Beautiful people enjoy service and privilege without distraction from the world they left or the place to which they have escaped. Safely inside their personal tourist bubble, they are free to consume resources at will, while avoiding both other tourists and hosts who are not actively engaged in serving them. This exclusive and elitist image is important to consider because pictorial images that have been widely distributed in the public sphere, such as those published in newspapers and magazines or broadcast on network and cable television, "are not only an indicator of shared beliefs and ideology, but are also presumed to have considerable influence in shaping them" (Emmison and Smith, 2000, p. 63). As introduced and discussed in Chapter Two,

"A person's reactions to the world depend on how he or she defines the situation" (O'Brien and Kollock, 2001, p. 5). How that person comes to define the situation is, at its root, based on cultural and contextual common sense. This common sense, a shared set of cultural rules for making sense of the world and interpreting one's reality, is learned through the process of socialization. And for this reason, reality is malleable.

In the case of these representations, quality tourism experiences are constructed by, and compliant with, socially shared notions of reality. In the process, the construction of reality in these destinations is therefore determined by official and unofficial tourism producers with tourists' best interests at heart. An individual's interpretation of reality, and how to interface with it, is culturally specific; what is seen to be true, good, and self-evident is learned through interactions and communications with individuals, groups, communities, and institutions. These interactions can occur in person, such as through participation in family life or a national tradition, or they can occur in a mediated form, such as by reading books or watching television. Continued participation in this learned social structure then helps to perpetuate the associated particular social construction of culture, and, in this case, continue to perpetuate notions of quality tourism experiences that are particular to a mass mediated culture. At the same time, not every individual or group has the same power to influence the construction of society or to shape the perpetuation of a cultural structure. For a wide variety of reasons, there are some who have the power to define reality in a certain way and have others act within their definition of reality. This issue of imbalanced power, if for no other reason, lends support to the project of analyzing how this takes place and what results (see the related discussions on power in Section Five: Political-Economic Construction of Quality Tourism Experiences.)

An implication is that every place that strives to provide quality service, or to be the best, will do so by imitating those characteristics common to all of the best places presented in these episodes. Given that these images represent the "world's best," quality tourism experiences become defined by what can be purchased and thereby limited to those who can pay. This institutionalization of quality tourism leads to limited choices and repetition of that which is good, as well as that which is bad. La Moumania Hotel in Marrakesh, Morocco, for example, is shown in juxtaposition with an impoverished street and market setting of that capital city. These images are framed for the viewer by the context in which they are being shown, as well as by the words that accompany them. Rather than celebrate the ways in which quality tourism may be experienced through the sights and sounds of Morocco's capital city, the message that comes across is that La Moumania provides a quality tourism experience and that such a quality tourism experience is not available outside the hotel's grounds. The rich culture and vibrant people of Marrakesh are discounted for the luxury and opulence that await tourists inside the hotel.

Many of the commonly presented images of seclusion and solitude are unrealistic. A solo swimmer in a pool or a lone couple on a beach at a facility with accommodations for over 1,000 begs the question, "Where are all the other guests?" Given the stated number of rooms and guest space available, it cannot be realistically expected that the beaches, pools, and restaurants in these beach resorts, cruise ships, and pleasure palaces remain empty for use by one or two tourists at a time. This depiction gives the indication that a guest can behave as if he or she is the only one present and is expected to interact with no one other than the staff designated to serve him or her.

As well as that which the tourism industry strives to provide, the characteristics common to all of the best places presented in these episodes become that which tourists seek. Personal service, seclusion and solitude, pristine beauty, uniqueness, fine dining, luxurious accommodations, and price become indicators of quality—of the "world's best"—against which tourists can measure their own tourism experiences. Although it is clear that the specific resort, cruise ship, and pleasure palace experiences presented by the Travel Channel may remain beyond the mass tourist budget, their common characteristics can be applied to that which is accessible in one's own income reality. See Chapter Five for a discussion of how mass tourists define the quality of their own tourism experiences. The frequency with which images and descriptions of these elite characteristics were repeated by the *World's Best* television episodes and in *The Australian* newspaper editorial columns from across the globe attests to the degree to which they have become established as equal to top-of-the-line tourism. And that they describe the "world's best" attests to their recognized importance in the conscious and subconscious minds of the tourists.

Framed as fact through the context of presentation by the only U.S.-dedicated Travel Channel, or by such travel commentaries as those written by travel editors, this mode of tourism comes to be seen as "natural" and clearly reinforces western individualism. Left out is any consideration of situations where quality tourism experiences defined as luxury and excess may be unrealistic, unethical, or unsustainable. Traveling in a world of "privilege," where their jobs allow for many perks (*i.e.*, all-paid expenses), travel writers, producers, and editors live and travel in a world that is not only outside of what most can afford, but at times outright impossible to find.

References

Bowen, H.E. (2002). Images of women in tourism magazine advertising: A content analysis of advertising in *Travel & Leisure* magazine from 1969 to 1999. *Dissertation Abstracts International* (UMI No. 3060773).

Emmison, M., and P. Smith. (2000). *Researching the Visual*. London: Sage.

Gnoth, J. (1999). Tourism expectation formation: The case of camper-van tourists in New Zealand. In A. Pizam and Y. Mansfeld (Eds.), *Consumer behavior in travel and tourism* (pp. 245-266). New York: Haworth Hospitality.

KAOS Entertainment (Producer). (2000, January 27). America's best beach resorts. [Cable television series episode]. *Travel Channel's World's Best*. Bethesda, MD: Discovery Communications Inc.

Kurosawa, S. (1992). Travel: Shades of old Singapore [and] The Duxton stands small. *The Weekend Australian*, September 12-13, p. 9.

Kurosawa, S. (2002). Departure lounge: Croc and a hard place. *The Weekend Australian*, March 2-3, p. 23.

Kurosawa, S. (2002). Departure lounge: Lawnmowers in paradise. *The Weekend Australian*, August 31–September 1, p. 15.

Kurosawa, S. (2002). Departure lounge: The eternal lure of the cure. *The Weekend Australian*, December 7-8, p. 3.

Lash, S. (1988). Discourse or figure? Postmodernism as regime of signification. *Theory, Culture and Society*, 5 (June): 311-336.

McQuail, D. (1994). *Mass Communication Theory: An Introduction* (3rd ed.). London: Sage. Michael Hoff Productions, Inc. (Producer). (2002, November 11). World's best cruise chips. [Cable television series episode]. *Travel Channel's World's Best*. Bethesda, MD: Discovery Communications Inc.

O'Brien, J., and P. Kollock. (2001). *The Production of Reality: Essays and Readings on Social Interaction* (3rd ed.). Thousand Oaks, CA: Pine Forge.

Potter, W.J. (2001). *Media Literacy* (2nd ed.). Thousand Oaks, CA: Sage.

Santos, C. (2004). Framing Portugal: Representational dynamics. *Annals of Tourism Research*, **31** (1), 122-138.

Shimp, T.A. (1997). *Advertising, Promotion, and Supplemental Aspects of Integrated Marketing Communications* (4th ed.). Orlando, FL: Dryden.

Sriber, C. (1982). Talking travel: Entente cordiale. *The Weekend Australian*, March 6-7, p. 17.

Sriber, C. (1982). Talking travel: Jazz on the high seas. *The Weekend Australian*, June 5-6, p. 17.

Sriber, C. (1982). Talking travel: Parlez-vous package. *The Weekend Australian*, September 4-5, p. 13.

Sriber, C. (1982). Talking travel: Sinful noshers' guide to Europe. *The Weekend Australian*, December 4-5, p. 16.

Stabler, M.J. (1990). The image of destination regions: Theoretical and empirical aspects. In B. Goodall and G. Ashworth (Eds.), *Marketing in the Tourism Industry: The Promotion of Destination Regions*. London: Routledge.

Surette, R. (1992). *Media, Crime and Criminal Justice, Images and Realities*. Pacific Grove, CA: Brooks/Cole.

Sussmann, S., and A. Unel. (1999). Destination image and its modification after travel: An empirical study on Turkey. In A. Pizam and Y. Mansfeld (Eds.), *Consumer Behavior in Travel and Tourism* (pp. 205-226). New York: Haworth Hospitality Press.

Termite Art Productions (Producer). (2000, December 12). World's best pleasure palaces. [Cable television series episode]. *Travel Channel's World's Best*. Bethesda, MD: Discovery Communications Inc.

Williamson, J. (1978/1995). *Decoding Advertisements: Ideology and Meaning in Advertising*. London: Marion Boyars Publishers.

Mediating Meaning

Section Two, while only constituted of one chapter, provides a bridge between Sections One and Three. In Section One, *Social Construction of Quality Tourism Experiences* we saw that meaning and interpretations in the world are socially constructed entities which are constantly changing and being mediated by influencing agents. Additionally, in Section One, the mass media was reported as playing a significant role in such constructions. In this Section, *Mediating Meaning,* the focus continues on social interactions and mediations of experiences. These mediations and interactions bridge across formal and informal participants in the tourism industry and related sectors as well as participants drawn from hosting communities. Further development is given to the latter, particularly, linkages between hosting communities, tourism development and quality tourism experiences in Section Three, *Interpretation of Meaning and Place*, as well as in Section Four, *Quality of life and Interpretation of Quality Tourism Experiences*, and variously in Section Five, *Political-Economic Construction of Quality Tourism Experiences*.

In Chapter Four, Gayle Jennings and Betty Weiler draw on social constructivism and postmodern perspectives to inform their discourse in regard to the social construction of meaning as well as meaning making or sensemaking of tourist experiences as a result of formal and informal mediation or brokering of tourism experiences. In addition, traveler typologies, politics of representation and communication theory as well as the concept of cultural brokering provide additional filters in regard to the interpretations presented by the authors in this chapter. Further, two heuristic models are used to highlight the nature and types of mediations required by tourists. The authors contend that in mediating tourism experiences—peoples, places, spaces, cultures and environments are subsequently mediated both informally and formally. Findings from research drawn across a number of studies are used to exemplify their commentary. Reflections are provided in relation to "When and how does mediation contribute to or enhance the quality of the tourist experience?". The authors conclude by offering insights into future research agendas that might be pursued by the different stakeholders situated in tourism industries and systems from the local through to the international level.

4

Mediating Meaning: Perspectives on Brokering Quality Tourist Experiences

Gayle Jennings
Betty Weiler

Purpose, Focus, and Definitions

". . . [h]uman beings do not find or discover knowledge so much as we construct or make it. We invent concepts, models, and schemes to make sense of experience, and we continually test and modify these constructions in the light of new experience. Furthermore, there is an inevitable historical and sociocultural dimension to this construction. We do not construct our interpretations in isolation but against a backdrop of shared understandings, practices, language, and so forth." (Schwandt, 2000, p. 197)

In the course of making these constructions, people often engage with others (and non-human elements) who and which serve to mediate their experiences. Specifically, within tourism contexts, these people, who may also be considered as "stakeholders," include other tourists, tourist providers, governments, communities, and indigenous groups as well as other interested and related organizations, agencies, and service providers. There are also, of course, *non-personal* mediators, including, for example, signage, design, aesthetics, overall settingscapes, activityscapes, peoplescapes, and experiencescapes. Although these media contribute to the mediation of experiences, they are not the focus of this chapter. The particular focus of this chapter is the role of the human mediator or broker in facilitating, or in some cases inhibiting, quality tourist experiences. We begin the chapter by defining the way in which we use these terms, and then we introduce the reader to a dichotomy of broker types based on whether the brokering role is a formal or informal one. After examining the experiential elements that are mediated by both types of brokers, we then introduce two heuristic models that provide theoretical lenses with which to explore how different types of tourists and different types of tourist settings may drive divergent needs and expectations for mediation from various types of brokers. In acknowledging that the dimensions and mechanisms of mediation are complex and poorly understood, the chapter concludes by highlighting a number of avenues for research to help demystify brokering and its important contribution to quality tourist experiences.

A common use of the term *brokering* in the tourism literature is in reference to "cultural brokering" (Cohen, 1985). In the mid-1980s, Cohen argued that the contemporary tour guide's role had moved away from its original role of pathfinder toward a mediatory role of which there are two components: social mediation and cultural brokerage. According to Cohen, social mediating involves being a go-between, linking visitors to the local population and to tourist sites and facilities and making the host environment non-threatening for the tourist. Cultural brokerage, or the bridging of cultural differences between hosts and visitors, and translating "the strangeness of a foreign culture into a cultural idiom familiar to the visitors" (p. 15) is the second component of the guide's mediatory role, also considered by Cohen as a primary role of the professional tour guide.

In this chapter we use the terms *brokering* and *mediating* interchangeably to encompass both of these roles. We define *brokering* as any active attempt by an individual to mediate the tourist experience of another individual. A broker or mediator is someone who assists in sense-making and in the tourist's (re)constructions of his or her experience as well as the (re)presentation of that experience.[1] Thus, we see it as much more than as Cohen proposed, "harmonizing the expectations and desires of the parties involved, and managing their interaction" (Cohen, 1992, p. 225). Nor do we see the role of brokering as limited to tour guides; indeed, a contribution of this chapter is to explore the roles played by those other than tour guides. Moreover, in contrast to what Cohen implies, brokering does not always facilitate a "quality" experience. The efforts of mediators can contribute positively, negatively, or neutrally to the sense-making processes of those with whom they are engaging. This is partly a consequence of sense-making being ultimately in control of the individual rather than the mediators. As intimated in the introductory quote, it is the individual herself or himself who makes the decisions regarding the (re)construction of the tourist experience, along with the subsequent evaluation of whether it was a quality experience or not.

Having discussed the terms *brokering/mediating* and *broker/mediator*, we turn our attention to a more detailed consideration of the term *quality tourist experience*. We have already seen in Chapter One that within the tourism literature

---

[1] The use of parentheses in this sentence in regard to "the tourist's (re)constructions of his or her experience as well as the (re)presentation of that experience" may appear unusual to some readers. However, the parentheses are specifically utilized to emphasize that the construction, interpretation, or making of knowledge, as per the introduction, is a continuous process between construction and reconstruction— that is, knowledge or meaning or sense making is constantly being mediated by us and others. Similarly, (re)presentation is used to indicate that presentations are not always authentic to the original version, since they too are socially constructed and reconstructed. They change during the course of presentation as well as representation, as was the case of construction and reconstruction, since these are processes and end states of social interactions. To prevent the somewhat clumsy format and use of "construction and reconstruction" as well as "presentation and representation" along with their plural forms, this chapter will use the parenthetical devices throughout to remind readers of this constant state of flux.

there are a plethora of meanings associated with the concept of a "quality tourism experience," as well as a "quality tourist experience." As previously stated, the term *quality tourist experience,* rather than *quality tourism,* is the focus of this chapter, since we are taking the perspective of the tourist when considering what quality is. Moreover, when the phrase *quality tourist experience* is broken down into its integral components of "quality" and "tourist experience," a range of individual interpretations and discursive representations results. This multiplicity of interpretations and constructions is due in turn to the multiple social (and political) constructions of reality (termed "lived experience" by Schutz, 1967).

For the purposes of this chapter, we define *quality* as a classificatory term used by, in this case, tourists to describe their (re)construction of a tourist experience. This term may mean excellence, a matching of expectations to lived experience, a perception of getting value for one's money, or however the individual tourist chooses to define it. Put more simply, "If [women and] men define situations as real [in this case, quality], they are real [quality] in their consequences" (Thomas and Thomas, 1928/1970, p. 572) regardless of other people's (re)constructions or attempts at (re)presentation(s) and evaluations. This latter social constructionist perspective is supported by postmodern writings in regard to the use of the terms *authentic* and *authenticity.* There are a number of parallels between the problematic nature of the term *authentic/ity* and the term *quality.* Primarily, each is dependent on who is doing the deconstruction and subsequent (re)construction or interpretation. Urry (1990, p.100) iterates this same point: "Tourism is a game, or rather a whole series of games with multiple texts and no single, authentic [quality] tourists' experience." Given the social constructionist/constructivist theoretical leanings of this chapter and postmodern skepticism to definitive conclusions, we maintain in this chapter a stance that "quality" is a self-defined term and that, in order to understand its meanings, researchers need to interact with the person using the term in order to gain an insider's (emic) perspective.

Just as quality remains a contested term, "experience" is also an elusive concept that can refer to both a process and an outcome/endstate or product. For example, experience may be described as an individual's inner state, brought about by something that is personally encountered, undergone, or lived through (Cohen, 2000, p. 251). It can also be a package that can be purchased—such as, "What an unforgettable experience! CANADA: FLY/DRIVE/FLY QANTAS TO VANCOUVER FROM $1399" or "Alaska: 7 NIGHTS NOW FROM $995. A special experience at a special price" (*The Courier Mail,* 23 February 2002). Another perspective that is generally supported in the literature is that the tourist experience is a process involving progression through a series of stages (beginning with anticipation and leading to planning, travel to, on-site [and multiple iterations of travel to and on-site activities], return travel, and recollection) (Jennings, 1997; Killion, 1992; Clawson, 1963). Although these multiple perspectives pose a special challenge for those wishing to research "the tourist experience," the point we wish to make here is that mediation can have an impact on many elements of the experiential product and therefore one's endstate and can occur at any and all stages of the experience. Consequently, the number and complexity of interactions as well as the historical/temporal and sociocultural nature of tourist experiences are manifold, involving numerous participants and contexts.

State of Knowledge

Types of Brokers

Participants who potentially contribute to the tourist experience include tourists, tourism providers, government bodies, hospitality employees, host community members, and others. Moreover, each of these may identify with numerous stakeholder groups and may thus interact directly and indirectly in multiple ways and at different stages of the travel experience. One way of making sense of these multiplicities is to distinguish between those who play a *formal* mediating or brokering role, and those who do so *informally*. For example, tour guides formally undertake brokering as one of a number of other job roles, such as group management, navigation, health care, and safety (Bras, 2000; Gurung et al., 1996). Guides are formally engaged in brokering, in the sense that it is a role associated with being a tour guide, and they are intentionally recruited, trained, and remunerated at least in part for playing the role of broker (Ap and Wong, 2001; Yu et al., 2001). This includes guides in the commercial and public sectors, those who work for protected areas/parks (year-round, seasonal, and volunteer), those who are tour managers and conduct extended tours, city-guides who lead mainly day tours, attraction and museum guides, and those who are employed as specialists, such as indigenous guides and study tour leaders. It is not only employers but also governments, protected area managers, host communities, and of course tourists who expect tour guides to broker experiences.

Photographer: Gayle Jennings.

Boat Captain and Hong Kong Aberdeen Harbour Tour Guide, 2004

Photographer: Gayle Jennings.

Formal Broker: Tour Guide at Olympic Park Ski Jump Salt Lake City, 2002

Others who are expected to mediate the tourist experience are shown in the upper half of Table 4-1, for example, travel agents and consultants, hotel concierges, information center staff (paid and volunteer), and many forms of non-personal mediation are also used to mediate the tourist's experience. These non-personal media can be considered as indirect mediation, in that someone determines what they will include or exclude, and, although critical to the tourist experience, they are not, as mentioned earlier, our focus here.

Having noted that tour guides and other formal brokers are "expected" to mediate the tourist's experience, it is important to comment here that the nature of this mediation is seldom monitored or assessed by tourism industry employers, let alone by other stakeholders. Nor are the outcomes of mediation evaluated, except where they are directly related to the goals of the business or organization. So, for example, an adventure tour operator might monitor the extent to which clients "had an adventure," typically gauged by tourist satisfaction, repeat travel, and profit margins. A historic site or zoo might also assess how well its staff mediated the experience by visitor numbers and profits, but also, say in the case of school groups, by how much the children learned (*e.g.*, factual recall), a rather crude measure of mediation effectiveness. So, generally speaking, being an effective mediator, although *expected,* is not necessarily a criterion of performance evaluation or reward, since we generally have no reliable ways of assessing it. The fact that we have a poor understanding of tourists' expectations and needs with regard to mediation makes it all the more challenging to implement appropriate mediation training and evaluation. We acknowledge that there is a wide body of literature that focuses on service quality and hospitality sector service experiences. However,

Table 4.1 Examples of mediators and brokers associated with the tourist experience

Nature of role	Planning and recollection (pre- and post visit)	En route (travel to and from site)	On-site
Formal mediating role:	Travel agents, travel consultants Government marketing bodies Marketing of tourism operations via promotional materials and events	Tour guides	Concierges in accommodation sector Staff and products in tourist information centers Local government tourism staff and products Tourism operations staff and products Tour guides (local—paid and volunteer)
Informal mediating role:	Friends and relatives Returning tourists Non-tourism destination/ site information employees Mass media Souvenirs, photos	Other hospitality and tourism staff, transport operators, and drivers Non-tourism employees	Other tourists Other hospitality and tourism staff Host/local community members Non-tourism employees Host family members Streetscapes

methods such as SERVQUAL do not attend directly to issues related to the quality of the service in mediating the tourist experience. For example, questions such as "Overall I thought the service from the staff was: Excellent Average Good Poor" are presented without explicit consideration of mediation. Of course, the original SERVQUAL instrument and its variations use multiple scale items, but generally they all seek to derive a single overall measure of "attitude toward service." And, to our knowledge, none of the scale items attempts to determine how different tourists experience and take away meaning from their experience-broker (Williams and Buswell, 2003). We believe the same is true of other quantitative and qualitative methods, such as transactional/exit surveys, total market surveys, and customer/ user surveys. These are not without their benefits, but to date the focus of these has not included an assessment of the effectiveness of the service encounter in mediating meaning for visitors and/or in helping tourists make sense of their experience in a way that is relevant to their own lives. This is, we argue, in part because these methods adopt an objective rather than an emic (social constructivist) perspective when trying to gauge the impact of service on the tourist experience.

With the exception of a few isolated studies in the tour guiding area (Bras, 2000; Yu et al., 2001), then, there has been limited investigation of mediation and the tourist experience. We really have a very poor understanding of the expectations of tourists regarding mediation, what factors influence the performance of mediators, and the impact of their brokering on the quality of the tourist experience.

Table 4-1 makes use of the formal/informal dimension to contrast those who are expected to mediate with those who are not required to do so as part of their job or role. Examples of the latter include waiters, back-of-house accommodation staff, local residents, taxi drivers, and employees at the local pub, gas station, and grocery store. Tourists themselves sometimes act as brokers (*e.g.*, a business traveler or student who returns home or who takes the family to a place where they once worked or studied), as does anyone hosting a visiting family member or friend.

> Tourism is a mediated activity. This mediation intervenes between and helps shape the relationships of the parties we usually think of as tourism's "hosts" and "guests" (cf., Smith, 1989). Recognition of tourism as a mediated activity, subject to a wide variety of interventions and an equally diverse array of interpretations as to the meaning of those interventions, encourages us to pay more systematic attention to those actors and institutions that stand outside the host/guest relationship but that so greatly influence the consequences of tourism. (Chambers, 1997, pp. 3-4)

These informal brokers/mediators differ from formal brokers in that they do not have a title, badge, or uniform that identifies them as a broker; their position does not require them to undertake the role of broker; and they are not recruited, trained, or remunerated for doing so.[2] Indeed, most mediators, and informal brokers in particular, share a tendency toward invisibility (Chambers, 1997, p. 6), and thus their mediation largely goes unnoticed and unrewarded. However, such mediation, whether formal or informal, plays a very important role and influences the tourist experience (see Chapters Seven and Eight).

This is not to say that the tourism industry is naïve with respect to the importance of customer service and communication with visitors. Superhost was developed in Canada in 1985 in preparation for the 1986 World Exposition in Vancouver, as a way of facilitating training and recognition for good customer service and community relations with visitors. Similar programs have since been developed in Great Britain, Australia, New Zealand, and several countries in Asia, and the program is widely acknowledged as important to the tourism industry. However, for the most part, these programs are aimed at delivering skills that will enhance sales and revenue and reduce customer dissatisfaction and complaints, rather than necessarily improving the ability of the resident or employee to mediate or broker the experience. And, of course, these programs are not focused in any way on researching mediation and its impact on the tourist experience. Thus, it is fair to say that we have only a vague understanding of visitors' needs and expectations regarding mediation. The ways in which tourists vary with respect to their mediation needs and expectations, and the reasons why particular tourists might make differing uses of formal versus informal brokers, are explored in a later section of this chapter.

To summarize, there are a myriad of individuals brokering the experience of the tourist both within and outside the tourism industry, beginning long before the

---

[2] It should be noted that the distinction may not always be clear cut—there are those in the tourism industry who may cross over between formal and informal, depending on the group or season. It is possible for an individual to move between being a broker and a nonbroker, and to move between being a formal broker (*e.g.*, an on-duty tour guide) and a nonformal broker (*e.g.*, an off-duty guide who lives, shops, and shares the community's leisure/recreation/tourism facilities with tourists).

Photographer: Gayle Jennings.

Informal Broker: Street Vendor, Dili, East Timor, 2002

tourist leaves home and continuing after his or her return. Many are stakeholders in the tourist experience, but most do not have a formal role to play in mediating the tourist's experience, and yet mediate they do. Moreover, the multiple interactions that occur between various stakeholders have ongoing and cumulative impacts on participants in all groups, so that the tourist experience is in a constant state of flux. The complexity is further iterated when all of the permutations of interactions with the overall tourism system (Mill and Morrison, 1992; Hall, 1994) are considered. This makes it difficult to identify and describe the nature of any one "mediation," let alone quantify and evaluate its contribution to the experience and to sense making.[3] And while it seems logical to suggest that people who are likely to come into contact with tourists should be trained in mediation skills, the enormity and complexity of this task, not to mention assessing and rewarding them for effective mediation, has meant that mediation has been largely ignored by the tourism industry, tourism educators, and researchers.

We have concluded that the role of a mediator is to contribute specifically to a tourist's meaning-making processes, essentially by mediating our constructions of experiences and interpretation of (re)presentations. Consequently, mediation is a process of interaction between the tourist and other individuals and/or groups, among whom some individuals will perform the role of mediator. From the perspective of the tourist, the mediator's primary purpose is to contribute to their sense-making processes in order to assist in interpreting settings, situations, people, and their (re)presentations.

Brokering of What?

But what exactly is being brokered, and what mechanisms can a broker use to mediate the tourist's experience? In a general sense, brokering is about providing or limiting access to a number of identifiable elements, such as particular places, spaces, people, information, cultures, and environments. Brokers can, for example, mediate a wildlife tourist experience by withholding or limiting directional information and other clues that help to locate hard-to-spot wildlife, which in turn can limit the tourist's level of access to this experience. Furthermore, while official or government personnel may broker access to specific sites and communities for specific time periods, local residents may find ways to discourage access through misleading and even false information. Mediators may also provide access by negotiating cheaper entry fees and deals on restaurant meals and other services, sometimes in return for benefits from service providers.

For example, during 1992-1999 fieldwork by Jennings, long-term yachtspersons sailing around the world reported having been officially granted cruising permits (site access and duration of access) but occasionally were "scared or warned off" by the locals. Similarly, local indigenous host community members talked about making some yachtspersons unwelcome and forcing them to move on,

---

[3] Sense making is used interchangeably with the construction of knowledge, meaning making, and interpretation of meaning in this chapter. Given the theoretical lens applied in this chapter, readers are reminded that all of these terms refer to social processes. For a further discussion of sense making, readers are referred to Weick (1995).

despite having permits for access. The reason for this action was based on the hosts at the local level perceiving a lack of quality (as in reciprocity) associated with the interactions between hosts and guests (refer to Chapters Seven and Eleven). Further, in some nations, although there may have been no cost to anchoring in some waters (only official or sociocultural mores), government officials would unofficially "charge" for initial entry, access, and/or duration of access. Rural farm families also act to mediate the public and private spaces of their farming operations and family life in order to manage the impacts of the introduction and integration of farm tourism into their lives, as well as the number and nature of interactions between family, farm employees, and tourists (Jennings and Stehlik, 2001).

Mediating is also associated with information giving and enrichment. Moreover, the way in which a broker provides (or withholds) information adds an effective dimension to the message, which can reinforce or indeed overpower the words. A broker can even be a role model and/or personally engage in the experience, providing access to a type (or quantity or duration) of experience not otherwise accessible to the tourist. Both informal and formal examples of this are simultaneously found in the work of Jennings (1999)—informal in that it was not managed by the tourism industry, but formal because it was brokered by the local authority figure. In the sections of her study dealing with tourist experiences of long-term yachtspersons, Jennings comments that the yachtspersons variously reported attending and being included in local cultural events that were off limits to other tourists. The brokering or mediation of this was managed by the local chief on behalf of the host community and the long-term yachtspersons (Jennings, 1992-1999 fieldnotes). The inclusions and information sharing were based on the yachtspersons respecting and following local sociocultural mores, engaging in acts of reciprocity, and having time to build relationships with the host community and authority figures. Consequently, based on positive host-guest interactions in day-to-day living, the brokering of "quality" tourist experiences was achieved by the yachtspersons. Chapter Eight pursues the theme of host-guest relations and quality tourism experiences in more detail.

Such examples are not limited to developing countries. So-called new Australians (first-generation immigrants) as well as international students often play an informal brokering role when hosting relatives and friends visiting Australia for the first time. It seems likely that they would select and interpret local sites, customs, and events through quite different lenses than a paid tourist guide might use, and quite possibly in a way that is more relevant, personal, and meaningful to the visitor. Research in the interpretation and guiding literature has demonstrated that facilitating meaning for visitors is very much affected by the guide's ability to connect with what the tourist knows and cares about (Weiler and Ham, 2001; Ham and Weiler, 2002). Informal brokers may in some cases be in a much better position to do this, particularly when, as in the case of visiting friends and relatives, they are likely to have more in common with the visitor than does the formal broker.

Of course, both formal and informal brokers are influenced by others, such as employers, communities, other tourists, and other stakeholders in regard to the access they provide. Tour operators and other employers may prescribe itineraries and even scripts that limit where tour guides can take visitors and what they can say. Protected area legislation may require the inclusion of particular messages and the exclusion of others or may restrict visitors to particular modes of transport, thereby restricting the ways the experience can be mediated. This in part occurs in the Great Barrier Reef Marine Park, where tourist access to sites is brokered by commercial operators. The operators' access is mediated in turn by a permit system that prescribes the number of passengers, number of sites, days of access, and times of access to those sites. Along with the permit system instituted by the Great Barrier Reef Marine Park Authority (GBRMPA), there is an expectation that during the "travel to" phase of the tourist experience the operators and guides will provide an educative component on how to behave in marine environments (*i.e.,* an explanation of codes of conduct). Payment of an environmental management charge is also added to each passenger's fare in order to assist with the further management and monitoring of tourist impacts on the reef. This charge generates funds for further research, which in turn results in decision making regarding brokering and mediating access to sites. The charge is also associated with the notion of "user pays" access, which in turn has ramifications for a tourist's interpretation of the quality of the experience in regard to "value for money." Whereas these last three comments are tied to management issues, they also serve to demonstrate the complexity and multiplicity of interactions that are associated with "front stage" and "back stage" management of mediation and brokerage of tourist experiences.

Apart from the types of management intervention in mediation and brokerage of tourist experiences discussed here, which attempt to positively influence quality, management can also directly influence the quality (and safety) of tourist experiences in a negative manner. In doing so, management may usurp the role of tour guides who also act as intermediaries between management and tourist as well as tourist and experience. Rafting guides, for example, size up skill and ability levels prior to the commencement of rafting experiences (Arnould et al., 1998; Holyfield, 1999). The turning away of unsuitable customers by rafting guides may, however, be in direct conflict with management's hands-off approach to mediation, in an effort to increase customer numbers and maximize profits (Holyfield, 1999). These differences in brokering by stakeholders with different agendas have implications not only for the tourist's experience but also for the environment and host communities.

Both formal and informal brokers often have the freedom to use their own judgment, colored by factors such as what they personally perceive to be the economic, social, and environmental benefits and costs of giving a tourist access to a particular experience. This is particularly the case for informal guides who, as mentioned earlier, are largely invisible and free to facilitate or inhibit access to experiences quite indiscriminately for different individuals and groups, and at different times of the day, week, or year. Even for formal brokers, the lack of monitoring and enforcement of legislation, standards, and ethics provides considerable latitude in how tourist experiences are mediated. As Bras (2000) concludes in her in-depth study of tour guides on the island of Lombok in Indonesia, "Mediation is an essential element in what they do, but the majority do not act as mediator out of a sense of the responsibility to satisfy all parties involved. . . . Their goal is not necessarily becoming a bridge actor defined as someone who flattens cultural differences and gets rid of other obstacles" (p. 207).

Thus, depending on the tourist, the guide sometimes tells accepted, controlled narratives and at other times combines familiar sites with unfamiliar ones within an integrated narrative. In some cases they provide behind-the-scenes access.

Because guiding is a risky business (from an employment perspective), guides propagate whatever approach brings them the expected benefits—for example, income and tips (Bras, 2000, p. 118).

Bras (2000) also observes that one cannot analyze Lombok tour guides as one homogeneous group—a point that has been reinforced elsewhere, including Yu's (2003a) research on guides of inbound Chinese tour groups to Australia. Some Chinese inbound tour guides have been known to mediate tourists' experiences in profound and positive ways, but at other times guides act in self-serving ways, such as restricting who tourists may interact with, where they may shop, and even when they can and cannot go outside their hotel. In some cases this is done by using dishonest and illegal means, such as holding the passports of tourists to control their experiences (Yu, 2003b). In these instances the broker is in a position to influence in a very significant way the quality of the tourist's experience.

To further address this issue of quality, given that quality is entirely self-defined, it is important to examine tourists' perspectives and to identify the factors that might contribute to the differing needs or expectations of tourists with respect to the experience and specifically mediating or brokering roles.

Theoretical Lenses

This section considers background information regarding factors that influence the tourist's need or desire for mediators or brokers. We draw on selected literature to present two heuristic models to assist in the study of the mediation of meaning in tourist experiences from a social constructivist perspective. The two heuristic models are Cohen's (1972) seminal work on traveler types and roles and Cohen's (1979) representation of tourist settings.

Factors That Influence the Tourist's Need or Desire for Mediators or Brokers

The tourism literature has engaged in considerable debate over the past few decades in trying to better understand the tourist, by developing categories, or *typologies,* of tourists. Some of these models are useful in informing a discussion of the relationship between mediation and a quality tourist experience. In reviewing these models, the reader will note that a common theme being explored here is the nature of the experience that the tourist desires or expects. These desires and expectations in turn influence the nature and type of mediation sought, including tourist self-mediation, as found in the work of Jennings (1999) regarding long-term cruising yachtspersons, and as discussed by Markwell (2001) regarding tourists mediating the tourist-nature experience.

A plethora of traveler types has emerged in the tourism literature, ranging from Cohen's (1972) fourfold typology to Pearce's (1982) 15 travel-related roles. Traveler roles and interactions have been explained by using either or both of two types of typologies: the interactive typology and the cognitive-normative typology (Craig-Smith and French, 1994). *Interactive typologies* focus on the interactions between tourists and host communities and destinations, whereas *cognitive-normative typologies* focus on tourists and their motivations. Although both are relevant to the role of the mediator, our focus here is on the interactive typologies since these are consistent with the theoretical paradigm informing the discussion in this chapter— social constructionist/constructivism or the interpretive social sciences. Interactive typologies provide a lens to view possible (re)constructions of reality. Again, these views are not definitive, as the "reality" of tourist experiences are always historically and socioculturally framed and constructed from the tourist's own (re)construction of such experiences. More specifically, the interactive typologies enable us to (re)present the lived experiences (*Erlebnis*) or achieve *verstehen* (empathetic understanding), as per Weber and Dilthey's application of the terms, in regard to mediated experiences.

There are various interactive typologies, but most are developments of either Smith's (1977) host-guest model or Cohen's (1972) familiarity-novelty model. Cohen's (1972) seminal paper on traveler types and roles emphasizes the relationship between tourists, on the one hand, and the tourism industry and host communities on the other. Based on the work of Schutz (1932/1972), who is credited with the founding of social phenomenology, Cohen's model is strongly linked to social constructionist perspectives and is useful as a heuristic device to learn more about the role of mediators and brokers regarding quality tourist experiences.[4]

In Cohen's typology, the world is ordered in categories of "strangeness and familiarity" (Dann and Cohen, 1991, p. 164), specifically using Schutz's (1967) terms *Wirbeziehung* (We-relationship) and *Ihrbeziehung* (They-relationship). Using Schutz's two categories/concepts, Cohen identifies four basic relationships depending on the degree of "familiarity" (We-ness) or "novelty" (They-ness) sought by travelers from the tourist industry and host communities as part of the overall travel experience. These four categories are *drifters* (who seek exotic experiences and immersion in a host culture), *explorers* (who arrange their own travel and seek experiences off the beaten track), *individual mass tourists* (who make use of travel agencies to preplan their travels and look for limited opportunities to encounter strangeness), and *organized mass tourists* (who travel in predetermined groups and largely avoid strangeness in their experiences) (Cohen, 1972). In his discussions, Cohen uses the term *novelty* interchangeably with *strangeness*. Dann (1993, p. 104) proposed that Cohen's typology is closely linked to Simmel's work on "the stranger" because "the tourist roles [in Cohen's typology] transcend spatial and temporal boundaries to the same degree that Simmeliam forms which they portray, and on which they are based, are also universal and perennial" (Simmel, 1950). The reader is also referred to the work of Gudykunst (1983) "Toward a Typology of Stranger-Host Relationships," for another discussion of the "stranger" and the sociology of tourism and to Yiannakis and Gibson (1992) for an overview of this literature.

---

[4] Cohen's typology is not assumed by us to be the "average" or definitive typology, as that is counterproductive to the underlying premise that there are multiple definitions, interpretations, and (re)constructions of quality tourist experiences.

Table 4.2 Model of tourist settings based on Cohen (1979)

		Nature of the Scene	
		Real	*Staged*
Tourist's Impression of Scene	Real	Authentic and recognized as such	Failure to recognize contrived tourist space
	Staged	Suspicion of staging authenticity questioned	Recognized contrived tourist space

Paralleling the development of tourist typologies has been an exploration of classificatory systems for the *setting* of the tourist experience. For example, MacCannell (1973), Cohen (1979), and Pearce (1982) have focused on the nature of front and back stage interactions, drawing on Goffman's dramaturgical references (1959) to discursively explain tourist experiences and (re)presentations of tourist experiences. Implicit in these classifications, especially MacCannell's work, was the pejorative notion that anything not back stage resulted in "duped tourists" and subsequently, by association, tourists who were not receiving quality experiences. Such a stance, however, does not take into account the expectations of the tourists themselves, and whether they believed that they had a quality experience or not. Perhaps the writers were assuming an etic (outsider's) perspective founded on an objective epistemological stance instead of attempting to achieve *verstehen* (empathetic understanding) (Weber, 1978). (See also the work of Schutz and Dilthey.) MacCannell's model was later modified by Cohen (1979). Cohen's modification considered touristic settings from two points of view—that of the setting and that of the tourist. From the *setting's* point of view, the experience can be either "real" or "staged," and from the *tourist's* point of view, the setting may be perceived as either "real" or "staged." This modification presents a two-by-two classification of touristic settings (see Table 4-2). This second work by Cohen (1979) is adopted as a second ideal type (heuristic device) from which to view the on-site phase of the tourist experience, particularly in regard to front-stage/back-stage settings.[5] Cohen's model is useful for highlighting how, even though hosts can control the level of authenticity provided by the setting, the perceptions of the same setting may be different for different tourists, as noted in the next section.

Discussion

Mediation, Tourist Typologies, and the Tourist Experience

We now revisit our formal/informal role distinction to explore the relative contribution that each plays for different types of tourists and in different tourist settings.

---

[5] Again, the same caveat that was mentioned above is relevant here and is repeated. This front- and back-stage typology is not deemed the definitive continuum; it is instead a heuristic tool.

All tourists have a need for both novelty and familiarity in their travel experiences, but some may desire more novelty and/or may be in a position (*e.g.*, have the confidence, skill, or resources) to explore further beyond the familiar than others. It is evident, for example, that some tourists for whom the destination is new and who have little familiarity with the host community and environment will find it helpful to seek out both formal and informal mediators to broker their experience via language translation, cultural interpretation, information, and so on.

How, then, do the tourist types differ in their need or desire for mediation? We suggest that the mass tourist will expect and be comfortable with formal mediation delivered in a group setting, while the explorer and drifter may shun all forms of formal mediation and seek out informal mediators instead. This, then, implies that those who are seen to be mediators by virtue of their employment (*e.g.*, tour guides, tourist information officers, and concierge staff) may be sought out for information by a narrower range of tourists than those who are informal mediators. On the other hand, formal brokers are easier to identify and may therefore be utilized by mass tourists more than informal brokers, particularly those with considerable mediation needs due to their limited travel experience, the nature of their travel party (*e.g.*, children, persons with disabilities), limited time, inflexible itineraries, and limited resources (*e.g.*, language skills) to seek out informal brokers.

Some experiences may simply demand mediation; for example, in some places it is not possible to swim with a seal or dolphin in the wild unless traveling with a group and accompanied by a licensed operator. Access to backcountry areas of some national parks requires visitors to book in advance and travel by public transport (*e.g.*, Denali National Park in the United States)—there is simply no other way of accessing the experience. This issue is explored in the context of guiding on cruise ships, where tourists are highly dependent on their guide, and this affects the nature of the guiding and the experience (Ham and Weiler, 2002). However, in most cases tourists have considerable latitude in their choice of mediation, whether it be formal or informal, pre-visit, on-site, or at all stages, and most visitors self-select the media they wish to use (Ham, 1999).

Returning to Cohen's front- and back-stage model, it seems likely that mediation by a formal broker would be perceived as appropriate in a staged setting. Such a view is supported in the writings of Feifer (1985). Feifer, assuming a postmodern perspective, noted that "institutionalized tourists" (Cohen, 1972) recognize that they are engaging in a game or hyper-reality (Ecco, 1986). This was a view also espoused by respondents in Jennings' (1999, p. 415) study of long-term ocean yachtspersons. "An advantage of a package recognized by cruisers was that when tourists buy a travel experience package—a commodity, they know up front what they are paying and what they are getting for that money. Consequently, the package standardizes the experience and ensures a familiarity about the experience."

As one participant commented, "You might be in Tahiti and they will have the girls doing the lei-lei dance. You know they will have their plastic girdles on and it won't be the real lei-lei that they normally do in the dances [for themselves]" (Jennings, 1999, p. 417).

In such contexts, the broker's role in facilitating a quality experience would seem to be to ensure that visitors knowingly expect a staged setting, including at the pre-visit phase. As Jennings and Stehlik (2001) comment in regard to the representation of different types of farm tourism experiences, the formal broker has a mediating role; however, so too have the tourists:

> Tourists will select from the array of farm experiences offered . . . based on the experience they desire to engage. Consequently, tourists also mediate the nature of the authenticity of the farm tourism product they purchase. The challenge for operators, however, is to ensure that they present the farm experience authentically and ethically rather than as something it is not, in order that the tourists can make the right choices. (Jennings and Stehlik, 2001)

This contrasts with the broker's role in a real (back-stage) setting. The role of the broker here might be considerably more complex in facilitating appropriate access without compromising the experience, while preserving the integrity of the host community and environment. For example, beach boys, particularly in the Caribbean and South East Asia, operate as small-scale entrepreneurs in the informal sector to offer romance tourism (as opposed to sex tourism) experiences to women tourists (Dahles, 2002). However, in assuming these brokering roles, the beach boys are adopting positions that are counter to their mainstream societal values. Similarly, some of the tourist women would also be acting counter to their own societal values. Subsequently, beach boys may or may not provide quality tourist experiences depending on how long women tourists are able to support the beach boys before their interest wanes when the women's money runs out (Dahles, 2002) and also as a result of the host community's reaction to the relationship between beach boys and women tourists. The roles of beach boys are not considered to be ones that maintain the integrity of the host community on a variety of levels—earning an income, following traditional pathways to relationships and lifestyle living. Similarly, the women tourists may be viewed derisively by the host community. The nature of interactions with others in the host community may be impacted.

The roles that the formal and informal brokers play and their impacts on the quality of the tourists' experiences in these scenarios are largely unknown. However, two key factors appear to be relevant from a number of the foregoing examples: relationship building and clear and unambiguous communication. Relationship building and communication are elements of mediation that are fruitful avenues for further research, a point to which we return in the final section of this chapter.

In summary, it seems likely that formal and informal brokers would play different roles not only with respect to the tourist types for whom they are mediating and the types of settings they provide access to but also the nature and timing of the access and mediation they provide. This is another area in need of further research, also addressed at the end of this chapter.

Implications

Recognizing that mediation is central to any tourist experience (Chambers, 1997), it is important to develop an understanding of how mediation contributes to enhancing the tourist experience. Using the formal/informal dichotomy of broker types together with Cohen's two heuristic models, we begin to see some of the reasons why visitors might seek out mediation and the mechanisms by which the experience might be enhanced and negated by mediation.

When and How Does Mediation Contribute to or Enhance the Quality of the Tourist Experience?

In mediating tourist experiences, we have discussed the notion of mediating people, places, spaces, cultures, and environments. The extent to which a broker provides information or otherwise facilitates spatial and temporal access to a desired experience, whether it is front stage or back stage, will enhance or inhibit quality in the experience. Precisely how to match mediators and mediated spaces to traveler types and desired travel experiences, however, is unclear. Moreover, given the self-defined nature of quality and in turn the sense-making processes of tourists, there may well be no way of determining the extent to which mediation contributes to a quality tourist experience. Thus, until such time that research tackles some of these issues and relationships, it is difficult to provide formulas for industry as to how to better manage mediation, how to market the broker's expertise and potential roles, and how to improve the recruitment, training, and rewarding of good mediators.

Furthermore, while we are suggesting further research, we need to remember that the travel experience is in a constant state of change and flux. It is ever dynamic and yesterday's answers may not necessarily fit tomorrow's context. The tourist experience is also temporally, historically, socially, and culturally bounded. It is constituted of a multiplicity of interactions, some of which may be managed but others which may well not be. To say otherwise would be to deny the theoretical lenses that have been applied to consider the mediation of travel experiences and the consequences for quality—that is, the theoretical lenses of a social constructionist/constructivist approach with a hint of postmodern skepticism in regard to definitively capturing reality. That being said and so as not to adopt nihilistic tendencies, we offer the following suggestions. First, when broadly considering the research agenda in regard to mediating meaning and its contribution to quality tourist experiences, researchers need to adopt more integrated and collaborative enterprises. This will enable a more holistic view to be obtained. Second, when determining the impact of mediators/brokers on the quality of tourist experiences, researchers and the tourism and travel industry/system need to engage in emic as well as etic research. Emic research achieves an "insider's" perspective. Such a perspective asserts that "cultural behavior should always be studied and categorized in terms of the inside view—the actor's definition—of human events" (Pelto and Pelto, 1978, p. 54). In adopting such an approach, understanding of the sense-making and (re)construction and (re)interpretation of tourist experiences by tourists themselves will be grounded in the everyday experiences of those tourists.

Having commented on the nature of an overall research agenda to be pursued in regard to mediating tourist experiences and perspectives of quality, we turn our attention to what makes a good mediator. Through our explorations of literature, the application of heuristic models, and our own research, there appear to be two resonating themes—relationships built on mutual respect and trust at the relevant time and place, and effective communication. Education and training in regard to mediating and brokering quality tourist experiences hinge on these two elements: "good relationship building" and "honest and open two-way communication between visitor and mediator." Both are terms we would again suggest as also self-defined by users. Insights into the multiplicity of usage should also be part of any research agenda pursued.

If brokers are to facilitate an experience that is matched to a tourist's needs, desires, and setting expectations, there must be two-way communication so that the tourist's perspective is being heard. Communication theory has long recognized that, to be effective, communicators need to make their messages and communication style relevant to their listeners, and, to do this, they need a sound knowledge of what the listener (the visitor) already knows and what the listener cares about. These make it possible for the communicator, in this case the mediator, to provide access to information, places, spaces, people, cultures, and environments that will connect with the visitor. Connecting with the tourist's current schema or dataset of knowledge and feelings is essential if the tourist is going to be able to make sense of what she or he experiences. Further discussion of the theoretical underpinnings of communication and meaning making are provided in Ham (2002).

These points regarding communication theory also overlap into relationship building. Taking the time to know others beyond surface-level interactions is important when we recall the point that meaning, knowledge, and sense making are social processes. Relationship building, at the formal and informal levels, has critical implications for the mediation of meaning as well as the quality of tourist experiences. We realize that the chaotic nature of interactions associated with tourist experiences will not necessarily be amenable to positive relationship experiences; however, for those in the tourism industry and related stakeholder sectors, such knowledge is paramount for "business."[6]

For tourism industry stakeholders interested in engaging in relationship building, there exists a body of knowledge that addresses this very aspect in marketing (specifically, relationship marketing). Other theoretical perspectives useful for informing or counterpointing a research agenda into mediation of quality tourist experiences include dependency theory, imperialism and neocolonialism, power theories, politics of decision making, communication theory (cross-cultural communication and understanding), stranger theory (familiarity, novel, strangeness), uncertainty avoidance theory, politics of representation, space, and place, stakeholder theory, and community perspectives such as decision making and autonomy, to identify just a few.

Toward a Specific Research Agenda

Generally, we believe that both formal and informal brokers have the potential to influence the quality of the experience in a profound way, both individually and cumulatively, but the roles of both, and in particular informal brokers, have been overlooked in research on the tourist experience. Based in part on our use of

---

[6] Unless, of course, tourists directly seek to experience negative relationships as part of the overall tourist experience, such as in the BBC production, *Fawlty Towers*, which was allegedly based on experiences at the Gleneagles Hotel located in Torquay, Britain, when managed by a Mr. Sinclair (BBC America, 2004) or in experiencing thanna tourism, which can be confronting or trying for tourists and during which positive relationship building may not be able to be achieved due to the overall nature and gravity of experience.

Cohen's two heuristic models, we offer the following research questions as starting points for exploring how mediation relates or contributes to a quality tourist experience:

- What are the key attributes and characteristics of an effective mediator/broker?
- How and when do different types of brokers contribute to a quality tourist experience?
- What are the relative roles of informal and formal brokers in the experience?
- What processes can be used to better match tourist requirements in regard to brokering (*e.g.,* differing tourist types) in respect to quantity and quality of "access" and therefore subsequent influence on the quality of tourist experiences?
- Can interactions with formal and informal mediators and brokers be planned and managed to effect a higher-quality tourist experiences?
- How is the role of the mediator/broker changing in relation to changing visitor profiles, including growth in independent travel by relatively inexperienced travelers?
- How can the industry better respond (*e.g.,* recruitment, training, accreditation, reward systems) to improve the effectiveness of mediators/brokers?
- How can mediators/brokers respond to increasing demand for more travel options, specialization, and flexibility in travel, destinations, tours, and products?

We are not providing answers to these questions, but rather we suggest that they are questions to which tourism industries and tourism system(s) would benefit from answers at the local, regional, national, and international levels. Bringing any one of the theoretical perspectives mentioned in the previous section to bear on any of these research questions would certainly make a valuable contribution to the literature.

As stated in the introductory quote, "[N]o process of meaning making exists in isolation" (Dunn, 1998, p. 136); many parties are involved that serve to mediate the tourist experience and have an impact on the quality of the experience. And yet, it is not unusual to hear a tourist refer to a particular individual—a guide or a local resident or even a taxi driver—as "making the experience" for them. How brokering mediates meaning and thereby facilitates quality tourist experiences at both an individual and a collective level is certainly a phenomenon in need of much further study.

References

Ap, J., and K. Wong. (2001). Case study on tour guiding: Professionalism, issues and problems. *Tourism Management, 22,* 551-563.

Arnould, E., Price, L., and P. Tierney. (1998). Communicative staging of the wilderness staging of the wilderness servicescape. *The Service Industries Journal,* **18** (3), 90-115.

BBC America. (2004). Fawlty Towers. *http://www.bbcamerica.com/genre/comedy_games/fawlty_towers/ft_facts.jsp.* Downloaded 3 February 2004.

Bras, K. (2000). *Image-Building and Guiding on Lombok: The Social Construction of a Tourist Destination.* Amsterdam: Tilburg University.

Chambers, E. (Ed.). (1997). *Tourism and Culture: An Applied Perspective.* Albany: State University of New York Press.

Clawson, M. (1963). *Land and water for recreation: Opportunities, problems and policies.* Chicago: Rand Mc Nally.

Cohen, E. (1972). Toward a sociology of international tourism. *Social Research*, **39**, 164-182.

Cohen, E. (1979). A phenomenology of tourist experiences. *Sociology*, **13**, 179-201.

Cohen, E. (1985). The tourist guide: The origins, structure and dynamics of a role. *Annals of Tourism Research*, **12**(1), 5-29.

Cohen, E. (1992). Pilgrimage centers: Concentric and excentric. *Annals of Tourism Research*, **19**, 33-50.

Cohen, E. (2000). Experience. In J. Jafari (Ed.), *Encyclopedia of Tourism* (pp. 215-216). London: Routledge.

Courier Mail, The. (2002). Travel section, February 23. Canada advertisement (p. 5) and Alaska advertisement (p. 9).

Craig-Smith, S., and C. French. (1994). *Learning to Live with Tourism*. Melbourne: Pitman.

Dahles, H. (2002), Gigolos and rastamen: Tourism, sex, and changing gender identities. In M. B. Swaine and J. H. Momsen (Eds.), *Gender/Tourism/Fun(?)* (pp. 180-194). New York: Cognizant Communication.

Dann, G.M. (1993). Limitations in the use of 'nationality' and 'country of residence' variables. In Pearce, D.G., and R.W. Butler (Eds.). *Tourism Research*. London: Routledge.

Dann, G.M., and E. Cohen. (1991). Sociology and tourism. *Annals of Tourism Research*, **18**, 155-169.

Dunn, D.R. (1998). Home truths from abroad: Television representations of the tourist destination. Unpublished thesis, University of Birmingham, England.

Ecco, U. (1986). *Travels in Hyper-Reality*. London: Picador.

Feifer, M. (1985). *Going Places*. London: Macmillan.

Goffman, E. (1959). *Presentation of Self in Everyday Life*. Garden City, NY: Doubleday Anchor.

Gudykunst, W.B. (1983). Toward a typology of stranger-host relationships. *International Journal of Intercultural Relations*, **7**, 401-413.

Gurung, G., Simmons, D., and P. Devlin. (1996). The evolving role of tourist guides: The Nepali experience. In R. Butler and T. Hinch (Eds.), *Tourism and Indigenous People* (pp. 107-128). United Kingdom: International Thomson Business.

Hall, C.M. (1994). *Tourism in the Pacific Rim: Development, Impacts and Markets*. South Melbourne: Longman Cheshire.

Ham, S.H. (1999). One Perspective on the Evolution of Interpretive Research. Keynote presentation to the International Symposium on Society and Resource Management (ISSRM), Brisbane, Australia, July 6-10. *http://www.cnr.uidaho.edu/rrt/sam_list.htm*

Ham, S.H. (2002). Meaning Making—The Premise and Promise of Interpretation. Keynote address to Scotland's First National Conference on Interpretation, Royal Botanic Gardens, Edinburgh, April 4. *http://www.cnr.uidaho.edu/rrt/sam_list.htm*

Ham, S.H., and B. Weiler. (2002). Toward a theory of cruise-based interpretive guiding. *Journal of Interpretation Research*, **7** (1), 29-49.

Holyfield, L. (1999). Manufacturing adventure: The buying and selling of emotions. *Journal of Contemporary Ethnography*, **28** (1), 3-32.

Jennings, G.R. (1997). The travel experience of cruisers. In M. Oppermann (Ed.), *Pacific Rim 2000: Issues, Interrelations, Inhibitors* (pp. 94-105).London: CAB International.

Jennings, G.R. (1999). Voyages from the Centre to the Margins: An Ethnography of Long Term Ocean Cruisers. Unpublished Ph.D. thesis. Murdoch University, Perth, Australia.

Jennings, G.R., and D. Stehlik. (2001). Mediated authenticity: The perspectives of farm tourism providers. *2001: A Tourism Odyssey*. TTRA 32nd Annual Conference Proceedings, June 10-13.

Killion, K.L. (1992). *Understanding Tourism, Study Guide*. Rockhampton: Central Queensland University.

MacCannell, D. (1973). Staged authenticity: Arrangements of social space in tourist settings. *American Journal of Sociology*, **79** (3), 589–603.

Markwell, K. (2001). An intimate rendezvous with nature? Mediating the tourist-nature experience at three tourist sites in Borneo. *Tourist Studies*, **1** (1) 39-57.

Mill, R.C., and A. Morrison. (1992). *The Tourism System: An Introductory Text* (2nd ed). Englewood Cliffs, NJ: Prentice-Hall.

Pearce, P.L. (1982), *The Social Psychology of Tourist Behavior*. Oxford: Pergamon.

Pelto, P.J., and G.H. Pelto. (1978). *Anthropological Research: The Structure of Inquiry* (2nd ed.). Cambridge: Cambridge University Press.

Schultz, A. (1932/1972). *The Phenomenology of the Social World*. London: Heinemann.

Schutz, A. (1967). *The Phenomenology of the Social World*. (G. Walsh and F. Lehnert, Trans.) Chicago: Northwestern University Press.

Schwandt, T.A. (2000). Three epistemological stances for qualitative inquiry: Interpretivism, hermeneutics, and social constructionism. In N.K. Denzin and Y.S. Lincoln (Eds.), *Handbook of Qualitative Research* (2nd ed., pp. 189-213). Thousand Oaks, CA: Sage.

Simmel, G. (1950). *The Sociology of George Simmel*. (K.H. Wolff, Trans.) Glencoe, IL: Free Press.

Smith, V. (Ed.). (1977). *Hosts and Guests: The Anthropology of Tourism*. Philadelphia: University of Pennsylvania Press.

Smith, V. (Ed.). (1989). *Hosts and Guests: The Anthropology of Tourism* (2nd ed.). Philadelphia: University of Pennsylvania Press.

Thomas, W.I., and D. Swaine Thomas. (1928/1970). *The Child in America: Behavior Problems and Programs*. New York: Knopf.

Urry, J. (1990). *The Tourist Gaze, Leisure and Travel in Contemporary Societies*. London: Sage.

Weber, M. (1978). *Economy and Society: An Outline of Interpretive Sociology*, Vol. 1, edited by G. Roth and C. Wittich. Berkeley: University of California Press.

Weick, K.E. (1995). *Sensemaking in Organizations*. Thousand Oaks, CA: Sage.

Weiler, B., and S. Ham. (2001). Tour guides and interpretation. In D. Weaver (Ed.), *Encyclopedia of Ecotourism* (pp. 549-564).Wallingford, UK: CAB International.

Williams, C., and J. Buswell. (2003). *Service Quality in Leisure and Tourism*. Wallingford, Oxon, UK: CAB International.

Yiannakis, A., and H. Gibson. (1992). Roles tourists play. *Annals of Tourism Research*, **19**, 287-303.

Yu, X. (2003a). Conceptualizing and Assessing Intercultural Competence of Tour Guides: An Analysis of Australian Guides of Chinese Tour Groups. Unpublished Ph.D. thesis, Monash University, Melbourne, Australia.

Yu, X. (2003b). Chinese tour guiding in Australia: Current status, issues and recommendations. In R. Black and B. Weiler (Eds.), *Interpreting the Land Down Under: Australian Heritage Interpretation and Tour Guiding* (pp. 186-203). Golden, CO: Fulcrum Publishing.

Yu, X., Weiler, B., and S. Ham. (2001). Intercultural communication and mediation: A framework for analyzing intercultural competence of Chinese tour guides. *Journal of Vacation Marketing,* **8** (1), 75-87.

Interpretation of Meaning and Place

The phenomenon of tourism occurs in various places and spaces and each of these places and spaces have associated meanings which are socially constructed by peoples within and without those places and spaces. In this section, the interpretation of meaning and place is the key focus along with meaning making processes and the related linkages to quality tourism experiences. The section is composed of two chapters. Chapter Five considers connecting experiences to quality by understanding the meanings behind visitors' experiences. Chapter Six explores the notion of sense of place and its relationship to sustainable quality tourism experiences.

In Chapter Five, Kathleen Andereck, Kelly S. Bricker, Deborah Kerstetter, and Norma Polovitz Nickerson review the related literature to determine the meanings of "experience" in both a recreational and travel sense as well as to highlight the different theoretical and methodological focuses used. Some of the related literature investigated includes, for example, motivation theories and personal construct theories, as well as satisfaction approaches, benefits-based approaches, experience-based approaches, and meanings-based approaches. Following the review of the literature, the authors draw on research related to three different tourism experiences to examine the nature of the meaning and emotions associated with visitor experiences from the visitor, tourist, or recreationalist's experience. These three experience studies constitute three case studies. The first involves automobile travelers who completed a diary relating to their travel experience in Arizona. The second involves personal interviews with visitors to the state of Montana, and the third involved white water recreationalists and utilized a mail questionnaire using open-ended questions. As a result of interpreting these three case studies based on mixed methods approaches as well as reference to the literature, the authors intimate that settings and tourist expectations can influence the meaning and evaluation of tourist experiences and the nature of the quality of such experiences. Moreover, that the meaning of visitors' experiences are varied and that knowledge and understanding of this along with knowledge and understanding that visitors will have varied expectations will assist tourism providers in presentations of quality tourism experiences.

In Chapter Six, Kelly S. Bricker and Deborah Kerstetter reverse the focus from the consideration of visitors, tourists, and recreationalists to host communities. In particular, the authors use sense of place theories, development theory, dependency theory, the notion "tourism as a panacea," resident impact, and power constructs to explore the role of sense of place in relation to tourism development. Their writings reflect a leaning to critical theory orientation as well as some elements of postpositivism. Through the use of a case study that centers on a specific tourism development in Serua and Namosi Provinces, Fiji, the authors demonstrate how meanings that local people ascribe to places and spaces can have impacts on the development of sustainable quality tourism experiences. In regard to sense of place, it is important for local people to maintain social ties, traditions, feelings of connectivity or rootedness, and respect for the environment. The authors caution that, in order to achieve sustainable quality tourism experiences, both the hosts and the guests need to be considered.

The emphasis in Chapter Six on hosts leads readers into the next section, *Quality of Life and Interpretation of Quality Tourism Experiences*. As the title suggests, the following section further examines the issue of residents' quality of life related to tourism developments and the subsequent nature of the "quality" of tourism experiences. A number of other issues presented in Chapter Six are further developed in Chapter Ten, particularly in regard to community participation in sustainable tourism developments and support for conservation.

5

Connecting Experiences to Quality: Understanding the Meanings Behind Visitors' Experiences

Kathleen Andereck
Kelly S. Bricker
Deborah Kerstetter
Norma Polovitz Nickerson

I like the grandeur of the mountains. To me it's, I guess you'd say it's my church, going to the high peaks, as far as experiencing any closeness to God or spirituality. I feel it in our wilderness areas, most definitely. I'm going to take home images of those glacially carved mountains and what I experience when I am up high like that. It's where I just feel in tune with myself and with nature I suppose. I'll take that back and be able to visualize that for a long time. (Nickerson et al., 2003, p. 41)

The "meaning" of experiences, such as the one described above, is of interest to researchers who find that people seek an optimal experience (*i.e.*, flow) through which they may feel deep involvement, intense concentration, lack of self-consciousness, and transcendence of a sense of self, all of which lead to an intrinsically rewarding experience (Csikzentmihalyi and Csikzentmihalyi, 1988). Is this true for tourists? And why is it important that we understand the way in which tourists consider and reminisce about their experiences?

According to Pine and Gilmore (1999), to be successful in any business, including tourism, we must recognize that we have entered into a new economic era—the experience economy—an era in which consumers' demands for inherently personal experiences is growing (LaSalle and Britton, 2003) and an expectation for customized relationships is commonplace (Baker, 2003). As Sir Colin Marshall, former chairman of British Airways, suggests, we have moved from thinking "that a business is merely performing a function . . . [to going] beyond the function and compet[ing] on the basis of providing an experience" (in Prokesch, 1995, p. 103).

So, what does this mean for the travel and tourism industry? In this chapter we explore the very nature of "experience" as defined by three different groups of tourists. We introduce tourists' reflections on their experiences and the meanings found through different methodologies for understanding tourist experiences. By understanding the experience, we hope to show what aspects within an experience provide a "quality" tourism experience. These visitor reflections on their experiences provide tangible clues to a hard-to-define phenomenon—the experience—and allow us to provide insight to how tourism businesses can create unforgettable, intrinsically rewarding quality-based experiences.

Experience

No two people can have the same experience (Lounsbury and Polik, 1992), because it is derived from an interaction or series of interactions between the consumer, the environment, and the provider (O'Sullivan and Spangler, 1998). This interaction leads to a reaction which, when positive, "results in the recognition of value" (LaSalle and Britton, 2003, p. 30)—value that remains in one's memory long afterward (Pine and Gilmore, 1999).

An experience is not a snapshot, but rather a complex process, that involves multiple parties, evolves over time, and retains value long into the future. An experience also is primarily visual, whereby tourists purposefully "gaze" on something different from everyday life (Urry, 1995); it can be positive or negative (Lee et al., 1994), dynamic (Hull et al., 1992), transitory (Mannell, 1980; Tinsley and Tinsley, 1986), exceptional in its function (MacCannell, 1976), and dependent in part on context (Bell, 1993; Borrie and Roggenbuck, 2001). Moreover, the true value of an experience is derived from the process consumers go through when attempting to obtain an experience (Omodei and Wearing, 1990; Otto and Ritchie, 1996). This process involves personal reactions and feelings, as discussed in Chapter Eight.

Experience in a Recreational or Travel Context

Researchers study various qualities (*e.g.*, attributes, dimensions) of recreational or travel experiences. For example, according to Arnould and Price (1993), Hull and Michael (1995), and Hull and colleagues (1992), experiences are dynamic and fluctuate over the course of engagement. McIntyre and Roggenbuck (1998), on the other hand, note that "there is a transaction among environmental context, mood states, focus of attention and perceptions of risk and competence which shapes the character and quality of the experience" (p. 417). While the researchers' results are provocative, they have been built on the notion that experience can be studied through looking at a series of stages or events (see Clawson and Knetsch, 1966), an approach Kelly (1955) suggests is not reflective of an "experience." Hence, various authors have chosen to apply and elaborate on Personal Construct Theory (PCT) in their study of recreation or travel experiences. Personal Construct Theory "posits that the *sine qua non* of human existence is our tendency to attribute unique meanings to the data of our experience. These meanings, termed 'personal constructs,' serve not only as interpretation of past events but as hypotheses about events yet to be encountered" (Epting and Neimeyer, 1984, p. 2). While PCT is built around the individual perspective, it is not to say the social construction concept discussed in Chapter Two is lacking. Instead, PCT evolves based on how the individual sees reality and constructs his or her social world. The two concepts are intertwined.

Botterill and Crompton (1996), whose conceptual framework was driven by PCT, conducted a series of structured interviews in an effort to understand "experience" from the perspective of individual tourists. Their findings indicate that emotional states are integral to understanding optimal leisure experiences. Although quite different from a conceptual standpoint, Montag (2000), Kearns (2001), and Ashton-Shaeffer and colleagues (2001) also conducted studies to address the notion of experience from an individual perspective. Kearns (2001), for example, in her study of wildlife enthusiasts, notes that an important factor in how individuals interpret their experience is the character, or context, of the interaction they're seeking. Lee and associates (1994), building on Denzin's (1984) modes of lived emotions (*i.e.*, sensible feelings, lived body feelings, intentional value feelings, and self and moral feelings), argue that individuals are more likely to address sensible (*e.g.*, physical sensations in the body) and intentional value (*i.g.*, forms of emotionality such as being attractive) feelings when discussing their leisure experiences. Cohen (1979) and Vallee (1987), on the other hand, suggest that the travel experience is, for many consumers, akin to a religious experience or pilgrimage, offering more than the reward of just being there.

According to Jackson and colleagues (1996), tourists are most likely to refer to an experience as positive when they can reflect on the culture and heritage of an area, appreciate social factors, have control of their experience, experience positive exchanges between members of the host community and themselves, and respond to external factors such as beautiful scenery and appealing attractions. Negative experiences, on the other hand, are most likely to be attributed to "bad luck" or other external factors, such as bad service in the tourism industry or the host population.

In many studies, the visitor experience is typed and molded into concrete descriptors. However, as Stewart (1998, p. 392) indicates, "There is a growing uneasiness regarding dominant research perspectives that still rely on concepts and methods depicting leisure experiences as something that individuals can easily frame, that endures through time, and whose essential qualities are captured in a single image."

Experience as Understood through Different Methodological Lenses

How visitor experiences are measured is undergoing an evolution. According to Borrie and Birzell (2001), the four most common approaches to studying visitor experiences include satisfaction approaches, benefits-based approaches, experience-based approaches, and meanings-based approaches. Both satisfaction and benefits-based approaches have historically been built on quantitative methods, such as mail-back surveys and on-site questionnaires. In the satisfaction approach, visitors, using a Likert scale, indicate their degree of satisfaction toward such things as a destination or hotel services. High satisfaction means the visitor had a good experience. The benefits-based approach, on the other hand, requires individuals to indicate their level of agreement on various benefits associated with their experience, such as "to escape," "to reduce stress," and so forth (Manfredo et al., 1983). This benefits-based approach, according to Glaspell (2002, p.12), "has limited utility for developing a deeper understanding of the nature of experiences or specific influences on those experiences." This is because the visitor is simply checking a box and not explaining what that box means to them.

In an effort to develop a deeper understanding of "experiences," researchers began to use experienced-based approaches in the 1990s; visitors were required to report their thoughts and feelings in a diary or record answers to specific questions about their feelings at certain times during their trip (Borrie and Roggenbuck, 2001). Results indicated that experiences are dynamic rather than static in nature, but researchers continued to have little understanding of what experiences actually meant to individuals. Hence, the fourth approach, meanings-based, has been introduced in an attempt to further delineate what the actual experience "means" to individuals. More specifically, experiences are treated as windows into participants' ongoing constructions of the world and their places in it, rather than as discrete, on-site engagements (Arnould and Price, 1993; Patterson et al., 1998). Only after deeper discussion (*i.e.*, in-depth interview) or total emergence (*i.e.*, participant observation) is the researcher able to elicit life-enriching stories told by participants.

Clearly, experience can be documented at a multitude of levels and through different methodological approaches. However, understanding what those experiences mean is difficult, if not impossible, using quantitative methods (i.e., satisfaction approaches, benefits-based approaches). Thus, recognizing that "tourism holds the potential to elicit strong and emotional and experiential reactions by customers" (Otto and Ritchie, 1996, p. 168), in this chapter we address the meaning and emotions attached to very different tourism experiences—travel through two states, Arizona and Montana, and river rafting in California—via a case study approach. The three case studies are presented separately. They are followed by a discussion of visitors' interpretations of their experiences as well as how such information can be used to create and maintain quality experiences in a tourism environment.

The Arizona Experience

Whether it's golfing at a luxurious resort, rafting through the Grand Canyon, or taking a leisurely hike through the northern pines or desert cacti, Arizona invokes images of sun, blue skies, spectacular scenery, and fun. To elicit information on visitors' experiences in Arizona, a random sample of 1,059 automobile travelers who stopped at the state welcome center were asked to complete a diary. (See MacKay et al., [2002] for more information regarding the questionnaire and sampling methods.)

The diaries, which included space to comment on each day's highlights, unexpected occurrences, and disappointments, allowed for qualitative analysis. A subsample of 107 of the most highly descriptive and insightful diaries was selected in order to provide the level of detail needed for the qualitative analysis.

When asked about their experience in Arizona, individuals are most likely to mention "pull" factors, including attractions and activities, driving, landscape viewing and scenery, and weather. Pull factors are the external forces drawing tourists to a destination (Dann, 1981). They also mention social interaction with other people and support and customer service components, including accommodations and food services, public facilities or areas, highway/road conditions/traffic, tourism information, and service delivery. Table 5-1 provides a summary of categories, the percentage of respondents who commented on each category, and a corresponding definition.

Pull Factors

A majority of tourists described their experiences largely in terms of the quality of attractions and activities experienced. For example, one individual referred to the highlight of his day as visiting Homolovi Ruins State Park. He "loved being able to walk among the ruins and see where they are excavating." Another respondent

Table 5.1 Arizona travel experience categories

Experience Categories	Highlights	Disappoint-ments	Unexpected Events	Description
Pull Factors				
Attractions and activities	55.6%	21.5%	15.9%	Visiting a place or doing a recreational activity
Driving	8.6	0.9	0.5	Using a car to see scenery, driving as an activity
Landscape viewing/ scenery	17.5	4.4	28.5	Scenery, wildlife, animals
Weather	2.2	10.9	16.4	Temperatures, precipitation
Social Interaction				
Social	7.8	0.6	1.2	Spending, enjoying time spent with family and friends
Support and Customer Service				
Accommodations and food services	4.2	9.1	4.8	Purchase of or experiences with buying services to satisfy need for shelter and food
Public facilities or areas	0.2	5.3	4.1	Places open to the public (i.e., rest stops, campgrounds)
Highway/road conditions/traffic	0.1	8.3	6.5	Physical areas where motorists drive, conditions of the roads, signage along roads
Tourism information	0.6	6.2	1.9	Assistance in the form of brochures, billboards, maps to assist the vacationer
Service delivery	2.8	3.8	8.2	Service provided by a host or employee to a tourist

noted her daily highlight as "experiencing so many magnificent works—both by Native Americans and nature itself (Meteor Crater, Wupatki National Monument)." A third tourist indicated that the "Grand Canyon was *beyond* expectations! Incredible—awe inspiring."

Tourists also referenced meaningful, quality experiences in terms of the unexpected. With respect to attractions and activities, one individual mentioned the "Town of Jerome—what a setting! What a drive to get there!" while another found "the beauty of San Xavier del Bac Mission" unexpected. Because attractions and activities are important to tourists, disappointing experiences also provide meaning to the experience. One tourist, for example, commented that her visit to Sunset Crater was disappointing "just for the fact that you couldn't walk up and see into it for yourself." Others noted unmet expectations with respect to attractions: "Thought there were more trees in Petrified Forest" and "Agua Caliente no longer actually has hot springs. Old ruins are not interesting enough to justify the drive." When landscapes and scenery are viewed as disappointments, it is most often due to personal preferences of the individual. For example, one person commented on the scenery in northeastern Arizona by writing: "Rocks are rocks. I got bored, tired and hot." A more common type of comment, however, refers to human-caused impacts on the landscape, essentially the quality of the physical environment: "Too many junkyards between Holbrook and Flagstaff within sight of I-40."

Weather, an additional example of a pull factor, is most often noted as affecting the experience in a disappointing or unexpected manner, such as weather inhibiting planned activities. For example, one tourist was disappointed that "the rain

Photographer: Kathleen Andereck.

On the Rim of the Grand Canyon

prevented us from seeing all the sights we wanted to see at the Grand Canyon and were unable to go to Oak Creek Canyon and Sedona."

The Social Component

Interaction with friends and family is a significant aspect of the tourism experience (Dunn Ross and Iso-Ahola, 1991; Prentice et al., 1998) and influences perceptions of quality. Most of the time, social aspects of the experience are viewed as highlights, contributing to perceived experience quality. According to one family, "We took our foreign exchange student (from Germany) from Phoenix, through the saguaros—Sedona Red Rocks—Slide Rock Park to Flagstaff." Occasionally, tourists have social experiences they consider unexpected: "We met people at breakfast in Tucson that we met at the Grand Canyon. It was like meeting old friends and we don't even know their names." It is rare that social interaction is viewed as a disappointing experience. In cases where this happens, it is often related to leaving friends and family during the course of the trip: "Leaving our friends in Arizona. We went to Nevada without them!!!"

Support and Customer Service Components

In Arizona, support services and customer services, important aspects of quality experiences, are most often viewed as disappointing facets of the tourism experience. When viewed as positive experiences, they are most often considered unexpected occurrences rather than highlights: "Swiss Village Lodge in Payson—the price is right, the dinner was two for the price of one and the place is spacious and quiet." Services also can cause disappointments: "Anasazi Inn and Restaurant—Grossly overpriced for accommodations."

Public facilities are most frequently reported when they are not clean and well-kept: "Rest area near Flagstaff dirty." As with other supporting services, travel information is most often mentioned when it is deficient: "Flagstaff road signs that didn't give me enough notice of how to get onto I-40." Tourists also cite information perceived as inadequate. For example, one man commented, "In general, information at the Grand Canyon was repetitive and a very low intellectual level. I was very disappointed that there was no way to get more detailed information. Canyon de Chelly seemed much better."

Finally, customer service is most frequently mentioned as a positive, but unexpected, aspect of the tourism experience. For example, an unexpected positive experience included: "Tour was excellent—Weather perfect—Driver/guide was polite, informative, helpful and made our day special." An unexpected negative experience, on the other hand, included: "Person who sold me 5-day fishing license did not know trout stamp was necessary and did not have AZ fishing regulations available."

In summary, the revelation of deeper meanings behind individuals' experiences is limited due to individuals' focus on more superficial aspects of the experience within the diary instrument rather than in-depth personal feelings regarding the consumption of the experience. Hence, the experience, as reflected by individuals through their comments in the diary, was meaningful but varied with respect to specific attractions, activities, and scenery.

The Montana Experience

Montana, the fourth largest state in the United States, includes prairies and bad-lands in the east to the Rocky Mountain range in the west. Movies such as *A River Runs Through It*, and the 1998 movie, *The Horse Whisperer*, have resulted in organic images (Pritchard and Morgan, 1996) that portray Montana as a majestic yet serene place to "find oneself."

Despite the images portrayed by the media and the state destination marketing organization, visitors are primarily attracted to Montana's national parks (*i.e.*, Glacier and Yellowstone) (Nickerson and Dillon, 2002). However, after arriving in Montana, their vacation experience becomes more than a visit to the national parks or a pre-determined set of expectations. In a study of vacationers in Montana (see Nickerson et al., 2003), 53 visitors were intercepted and interviewed in-depth about what a Montana vacation means to them. The interviews were tape-recorded and analyzed with the use of the N-Vivo qualitative software program. A Montana vacation, as defined by these tourists, is comprised of four dimensions: (1) environment, (2) activities, (3) western frontier, and (4) spirituality (see Table 5-2). These dimensions are interrelated, yet the "environment" appears to drive the experience and the meanings associated with it.

Environment

Visitors to Montana have images of wide valleys and big mountains with little or no development and, in most cases, find that their images are correct. In their minds, California, Colorado, and the east coast have lost that authentic connection to nature; Montana has not. Visitors notice the environment in Montana and com-pare it to other places not as "well endowed." They point out the diversity that Montana has from plains to peaks. As one visitor said, "The mountains are green, velvet, suede—green, green, green!" The badlands and plains capture the rawness of the west and elicit questions such as, "What was it like for the pioneers?" Interestingly, the environment also brings out disappointments, especially for return visitors. As one visitor noted, "There's a lot more sprawl than I expected. I haven't been here since '61, so it's been a long time, but I was surprised at how many people and how much spread of suburban Montana there was."

Activities

Many visitors allude to an activity such as fishing, hiking, rafting, camping, horse-back riding, birding, or photography as a way of getting out into nature. Certainly, some individuals visit particular areas in Montana for the physical exertion or the ability to say, "I did it." Many, however, want, and are able to get, a reprieve from their daily routine. Montana provides the escape they so desire. As the catalyst, activ-ities rejuvenate them, provide accomplishment, and even food (*e.g.*, fish). But, over-whelmingly, these same visitors are not visiting Montana for the activity alone. Montana provides visitors with a chance to relax, to be at one with nature, and to escape. As one visitor mentioned, "It's exercise and being outdoors and seeing the

Table 5.2   A Montana vacation – the meaning behind the experience

Environment: The natural beauty provided for the full experience.

"You should have seen the people on the mountain yesterday when they saw that mother mountain goat and the baby. They were all beside themselves. It's something most people never get to see and don't expect to see except at a zoo or at Disney World or something. There are a lot of people that think it's a real blessing to be able to actually see something in the wild."

"I just think that's just a very magical place to be [rivers], and I'm right. Rivers bring peace. I just think they're God's gift. They're just so peaceful and they're lovely and clean and glorious surroundings. There's a magical quality about these Montana rivers."

"The Missouri River is very scenic with the cliffs and the rock formations. It's very wild. We camped alone almost every night. When we got past the bad weather and we started to adjust to the rhythm of life on the river, we loved it. So after a few days, that becomes the rhythm of life and you've forgotten all that other stuff—going to work and buying groceries. (ha ha!)"

"[My mountain experience is] oh God, I don't know. I just want to absorb it. They're just beautiful because I never see them when I go back home. I get a sense of peace and I get a sense that just kind of clears my mind. I just got a sense of inner peace."

Activities: The activities were engaged in so one could be in the natural environment.

"Mountains, fly-fishing. Is there anything else to life? Fly-fishing is a passion. It's serenity. It's the beauty of the surroundings, nature, sounds. Coming to a bend and having a deer standing in the stream. It all comes together and it's peaceful, it's relaxing, it's my way of getting rid of stress."

"[The adventure of hiking is] to possibly see some kind of an animal, a wild animal. If I were riding my motorcycle I wouldn't see it. When you hike there's so much more. Slower pace. It's just the basics of getting back to nature. You leave the hectic world behind and you just kind of relax."

Western Frontier: Visitors felt a connection to the past, as if they were emerged in it themselves.

"Wide open, beautiful, untamed. It's pretty much what I've been told. It's the open land. Everything's really clean. It's expansive. It means that this land is so untouched, like it was hundreds of years ago. Like it must have looked exactly the same with the pioneers."

"You just can't realize what Lewis and Clark went through. There were no machines; there were no horses until they got to the top of the Rocky Mountains. Then when they came back, I can just feel what they were feeling."

Spirituality: The Montana experience brought visitors' appreciation of God and creation.

"I think it's restorative, body, soul, and spirit. I believe we are part of nature, part of God's creation . . . particularly in an undisturbed way, as one still finds quite a bit out here."

"Montana is the most beautiful place in the world. Wide open space, few people, and just glorious, pristine beauty. There's no place like it. I think I can come into our humanity here. I think people are living in a more nature way and closer to the earth, closer to God. So I can breathe, I can truly breathe here. Just unparalleled beauty. It never fails to amaze me."

animals and living a little more simply for a brief while. It kind of reinvigorates me in a lot of ways."

Western Frontier

Montana provides a link to the past and an authentic immersion into what people say were "the good ol' days." Some visitors comment that Montana is a living past open to visitors. Thus, history is a big part of many Montana vacations. Visitors try to understand the plight of the Native Americans who traveled along the Nez Perce Trail or the interaction between the Indians and the Lewis and Clark expedition: "In other states tourists can 'see' where Lewis and Clark went, but in Montana, we can 'feel' it."

Spirituality

Seeing and feeling the open space induces a feeling of the past, but it also engenders a spiritual element for many visitors. For some individuals, the "sound of silence" brings about a sense of spirituality. Silence, in their minds, is golden. In fact, many individuals describe a connection to God—that the beauty of Montana is part of God's creation. Such beauty is the epitome of unplugging and removing oneself from the struggles and problems of everyday life. This aesthetic and spiritual aspect of the land and environment is considered to be one of the most powerful parts of "experiencing" Montana.

Visitors describe their Montana vacation in terms of the renewal and escape they experience through their exposure to the environment. They also recognize the importance of their involvement in activities, including exposure to the state's history, many of which are integrally tied to the environment.

California and the River Running Experience

Promoted as California's most popular whitewater recreation river, and the second most popular commercial rafting river in the United States, the South Fork of the American River (SFAR) is located in El Dorado County, northern California—the heart of Gold Rush Country (Bricker and Kerstetter, 2002). To explore the meaning of visitors' experiences on the SFAR, a random sample of nearly 1,200 boaters was selected to participate in a mail questionnaire. (See Bricker [1998] for more information regarding the questionnaire and sampling methods.)

Individuals responded to a series of open-ended questions regarding places along the SFAR (Bricker and Kerstetter, 2002; Schroeder, 1996). Their responses were then analyzed through qualitative methods of analysis. The meanings whitewater recreationists attached to special places along the SFAR were condensed into three dimensions: (1) recreation-environmental, (2) human-recreation, and (3) heritage-environmental' (see Table 5-3).

Note: Total responses represent the number of comments made within each category. This number does not depict the number of individuals who responded; some individuals may have cited one or more places that fit the category. This table has been slightly modified from the results presented by Bricker (1998) and Bricker and Kerstetter (2002). For a complete review of quotes and results, see Bricker (1998).

Recreation-Environmental

The majority of visitors to the SFAR described meanings affiliated with a recreation-environmental dimension (REC) (Table 5-3). Visitors to the river wrote of aesthetics and an appreciation for the environment, the need to protect and preserve the

Table 5.3 The California river experience

Dimension Categories	Examples of Visitor Descriptions
Recreation—Environmental (n = 264) *Aesthetic—Recreation:* Meanings combining the natural beauty of an area with descriptions or ideas about the recreational activity taking place	"A place of wilderness (or at least it was 15 years ago) few people see or experience because of lack of access. A section that includes quiet float sections and exciting rapids. The famous gorge with far more to offer than whitewater."
Protect / Preserve: Meanings associated with protecting environment and recreational pursuits	"The whole area around the river was wonderful. I would love for the whole area to be left untouched. I don't think the nature should be disrupted. Everything should be left alone. There was not just one special place; all the land around the river was important."
Access: Access to the recreational experience and/or environment in which the activity takes place (positive and negative associations)	"There is no place that really stood out more than any other spot, but what attracts me to this area is a quiet secluded place that is pretty easily accessible."
Human—Recreation (n = 179) *The Gathering Place:* Place meanings that recognized the social nature of a place or experience in addition to the recreation component	"Some people gathered around enjoying the river, watching others run the rapid. Had fun running the rapid and hanging out on shore for a while afterward, [socializing] with the other river runners and spectators."
Challenge—Growth: Place meanings associated with personal growth or witnessing the growth of others within the context of a recreational pursuit	"This is the first big rapid on Chili Bar. I have some good memories of being nervous before it. It was definitely one good confidence boost after running it."
Shared Experience: Place meanings associated with recreational experiences with special emphasis on sharing the experience with family and friends	"Exciting, wet, exhilarating, swirling water, refreshing. Sharing the thrills with friends and relaxation."
Enjoyment: The enjoyment of watching others engaged in a recreational pursuit	"I like the excitement of the rapids and I also enjoy seeing all the other people just having a good time on the river, fishing, swimming, panning for gold—people of all ages were enjoying themselves."
Heritage—Environmental (n = 48) *Natural Appreciation:* An event in a place that is shared and refers to the natural attributes of that environment	"I cherish the sighting of a golden eagle flying overhead with a snake dangling from its talons, and a hard rain beating the river's surface into a froth. I love its sameness. In an ever-changing world, sameness is comforting."

Continued

Table 5.3   The California river experience—cont'd

Dimension Categories	Examples of Visitor Descriptions
Native Environments: Meanings associated with places that evoked a sense of kinship with humans that lived in the area prior to present day (cultural heritage)	"The sense of being part of a long history of different people associated with a river of beauty. The merger of human endeavor and natural habitat."
Protect and Preserve: Environmental messages shared with others or emphasized within the context of special places	"As the sun was sinking low on the horizon the deer made their way to the river to drink, the turkey vultures bathed and hung their wings to dry, and a river otter hauled out on one of those cottonwoods that dared to fall to the floods. My spirit was lifted to see that the river corridor continues to provide habitat to El Dorado's wildlife even with 100,000 boaters each season and the free hand of capitalism at work this spring after the floods. Please preserve this educational resource!"

river corridor (including concerns about the preservation of the natural areas and overcrowding), seasonality and the various "moods" of the river, as well as access to the river. As one boater reports, the quality of his experience hinges on nature and perhaps solitude: "Upper Stretch. This is more a time than a place. Last fall, [when] hardly anyone was out on the river . . . the air was crisp, fall colors were out, and the birds were generally undisturbed. The low water made for some significant changes in some of the rapids, creating rock gardens and narrow chutes."

Human-Recreation

The human or social aspect of the river experience, combined with the recreational component, is the second dimension associated with the meaning individuals assign to the SFAR (Table 5-3). Visitors referred to the SFAR as a "gathering place," a place for personal challenge and growth, a place to share experiences with others, and a source of enjoyment. More specifically, visitors highlight the importance of sharing family experiences, as well as the development of a sense of teamwork or camaraderie. They described the enjoyment they had in sharing the place and the associated recreation activities with others. Individuals also emphasized the social component of creating quality experiences: "Bridging many years into the future on cold winter days, no one there but friends with kayaks. Many layers of polypro and dry suits. Always glad to be there. I've met a lot of friends there, almost a second home. Each day on the river is like a little homecoming."

Heritage-Environmental

Whitewater recreationists highlight the importance of sharing the experience with others through an environmental or cultural heritage lens. In comparison to the other dimensions, the primary difference reflected in this dimension is that visitors do not emphasize the recreational activity. Instead, visitors report the importance of environmental attributes, an environmental message, or natural appreciation of the river corridor or a cultural heritage component coupled with shared experiences with others, the impacts of humans on the environment, and signs of human influences (both past and present). In essence, environmental attributes are tied to the local heritage of the area (community, environmental, and cultural) (Table 5-3). For example, one boater reflected on the temporal coexistence of humans and nature: "The sense of being part of a long history of different people associated with a river of beauty. The merger of human endeavor and natural habitat."

The meanings individuals associate with places along the SFAR are multidimensional. Visitors refer to environmental, social, and recreational contexts when imbuing meaning into descriptions of their experiences along the SFAR. And, quality tourism experiences are demonstrated through a variety of socially constructed meanings, placing emphasis on elements of the micro and macro landscapes, heritage, and people of the river corridor.

Discussion

According to various researchers (e.g., Borrie and Roggenbuck, 2001; Hull et al., 1992; Lounsbury and Polik, 1992), the tourism experience is dynamic and interpreted differently by every visitor. Our review of tourists' experiences supports these notions and provides evidence that tourists articulate three dimensions of meaning: the social aspects of the experience, the environmental aspects of the experience, and the aspect of activities within those environments as the experience. For example, interaction with others provides meaning to the experience (Prentice et al., 1998). In Arizona, tourists ran into the same individuals at multiple destinations and unexpectedly found a social group with whom they could relate. In addition, setting is a primary conduit of the experience and meanings associated with it (McIntyre and Roggenbuck, 1998). Being on a river or sitting next to a mountain brings up intense feelings about the need to protect and preserve fragile resources. Such feelings result in awe and profound respect for the environment and all it represents. Hence, the meaning that tourists ascribe to their experiences support the notion that the environment is relevant to quality tourism experiences.

In terms of activities, witnessing living history (i.e., remnants via grinding stones or the "real west") in Montana and California evokes intense feelings, lending support to Botterill and Crompton's (1996) contention that individuals' emotions and feelings are part and parcel with the meaning they attach to an experience. How these tourism experiences are interpreted and the meanings they evoke, however, depend on the research method used.

The three case studies highlighted in this chapter demonstrate that different methods (i.e., diary, in-depth interviews, and open-ended questions in a mail-back questionnaire) have somewhat parallel results. For example, the diary method reveals what is important to visitors based on what they perceive as experience highlights, unexpected occurrences, and disappointments. Tourists visiting Arizona recognized specific attractions, activities, and settings as important to their overall experience—enough so that they wrote them down in their diaries. It can be interpreted that highlights correlate to quality tourism experiences and that disappointments correlate to those aspects that deter from quality experiences. However, while it is clear that certain aspects were part of the experience and important to visitors, the diary responses did not provide as much depth with respect to the "meaning" behind the experience. This is partly due to the question to which the visitor was responding in the diary. The question did not focus on *why* that highlight was important or *what* it meant to them.

With respect to the California river-running experience, visitors expressed their feelings, emotions, and thoughts about the river by responding to open-ended questions in mail-back questionnaires. As a result, visitors dug deeper into their soul to relive the experience (positive and negative) and the meaning of the experience was expressed through their recollection. They also spoke to the importance that geographic location (from a macro to micro perspective) had on the meaning(s) they attributed to their experience. Quality experiences on the river were interpreted as those responses where the individual used emotive connecting words, exclamation points, and told us how wonderful the experience was to them. Again, the disappointments or concerns expressed in their diaries suggest aspects that take away from their quality experience.

Finally, the richest experience-related information was derived through the use of on-site in-depth interviews with tourists visiting Montana. In this situation, interviewers asked tourists to discuss their experience as they were embracing it. Hence, tourists were given the opportunity to describe the environment, but also the feelings they were experiencing while in that environment. Through tourists' body language, the excitement they exhibited when describing their experiences and the tenor of their conversation, interviewers were able to interpret what factors contributed as well as took away from their quality tourism experiences.

Regardless of method used, there is support for Lounsbury and Polik's (1992) assertion that no two people can have the same experience and, as a result, will describe its meaning differently. For example, in the Montana vacation experience one visitor described Montana as "the most beautiful place in the world with wide open spaces, few people, and glorious pristine beauty," while another visitor was disappointed in the urban sprawl and the number of people.

There is also evidence that an experience evolves through a complex process that has positive and negative components to it and is dependent in part on context. One Arizona visitor was disappointed that he or she couldn't see into a crater, and river runners in California described their distaste for over-development. Such disappointments are often due to personal expectations or preferences, yet these do impact individuals' interpretations of their experiences.

Further, it is clear from the findings that when the interaction between the consumer, the environment, and a provider is positive, individuals assign value to that experience (LaSalle and Britton, 2003) and remember it for a long period of time (Pine and Gilmore, 1999). A California visitor, for example, remembered being nervous before going through the rapids as well as the confidence gained after experiencing the rapid. An Arizona visitor, on the other hand, wrote that the Grand Canyon was "beyond expectations, incredible—awe inspiring." And one Montana visitor, after commenting about the beauty and spirituality of the mountains, said, "I'll take that back and be able to visualize that for a long time." In Chapter Four, the authors point out the impact of mediators on individuals' interpretations of their experiences. For example, a mediator for Arizona visitors could have been an article about the Grand Canyon in *National Geographic Traveler*. If visitors' experiences did not meet or exceed the experiences described in the article, they would not be satisfied and might reference the quality of their experience as sub-par.

Finally, in any tourism destination, the setting establishes the context for the experience. According to LaSalle and Britton (2003), an experience of value is "a product or service that when combined with its surrounding experience events goes beyond itself to enhance or bring value to a customer's life. This is the ideal—to deliver such overall value that a product transcends the ordinary to become extraordinary or even priceless" (p. 38)

Creating Quality Experiences

Tangible clues provided by visitors through the meanings they attach to their experiences can help improve or create a quality tourism experience. The clues vary from the simple to the complex, from the obvious to the little known. On the simple side, experiences are affected by bad service providers—front-line people who do not respond politely to a visitor. Poor service brings out negative comments and taints the quality of an experience. Certainly this is nothing new to the tourism industry, but it emphasizes that providing training in good customer service techniques on a continual basis is necessary.

Weather is frequently mentioned as a primary travel motivator among visitors to Arizona when addressed through quantitative studies (Andereck, Knopf, and Vogt, 2003; Andereck, Vogt, and LeClerc, 2003) as well as the diary approach presented here. Weather, however, is almost always a negative when it is mentioned. From a destination marketing point of view, it is imperative to supply potential visitors with the truth about weather possibilities to establish realistic expectations. Destination marketers can also suggest that the visitor choose between good weather surrounded by many other tourists enjoying the destination, or potentially bad weather with fewer people around. In sum, tourism providers must be prepared to guide visitors toward different destinations or activities when the weather is not optimal.

Another simple clue with not-so-simple solutions is tied to signage and road conditions. Some visitors in Arizona were frustrated with either the lack of signs or the interpretive signs that did not adequately address the setting. Roads and traffic were also a negative for many Arizona visitors. Solutions to these problems are generally tied up with funding issues as well as state and national regulations. However, destination marketers can provide up-to-date information via their websites that indicate changes in road conditions or where construction occurs. Given the advances being made in hand-held and auto-based geographic positioning systems, providers should also consider how they can tap into such technology.

Appreciation for the cleanliness of an area or the surprise echoed by tourists as they confront a good price or friendly people suggest that they, too, have a lasting impact on visitors. Businesses should continually add a "twist" to their service so the visitor has that pleasant surprise. Once that twist is copied by others, however, it becomes expected by the consumer. Thus, as Pine and Gilmore (1999) and LaSalle and Britton (2003) suggest, a new surprise or customized experience should be waiting in the wings.

In regard to the natural environment, visitors want to be able to access public lands now but preserve them for future generations. This issue is complex because, in essence, change is not desired. However, change takes place every time visitors access public lands. In addition, changes near access sites such as commercial development may create unease in the minds of the visitors. Thus, when changes do occur, it is important that information regarding such changes be available to potential visitors; otherwise, their expectations will not be met and dissatisfaction will set in.

In summary, tourism experiences can and will be affected by the setting as well as visitors' expectations. Hence, travel and tourism providers need to be conscious (as much as possible) of the expectations tourists bring to their site. As Davenport and colleagues (2000) and the authors in Section One of the book mention, if managers understand the types of experiences expected and valued by their customers, they will be able to develop more effective strategic initiatives, including communication (*e.g.*, advertising, publicity, or public relations), a cornerstone of an effective marketing campaign.

References

Andereck, K.L., Knopf, R.C., and C.A. Vogt. (2003). *Arizona Office of Tourism Marketing Conversion Study, Final Report FYs 2002/2003*. Phoenix: Arizona State University West, Department of Recreation and Tourism Management.

Andereck, K.L., Vogt, C.A., and D. LeClerc. (2003). *Arizona Welcome Center Study Report*. Phoenix: Arizona State University West, Department of Recreation and Tourism Management.

Arnould, E., and L. Price. (1993). River magic: Extraordinary experiences and the extended service encounter. *Journal of Consumer Research*, **20**, 28-45.

Ashton-Shaeffer, C., Gibson, H., Autry, C., and C. Hanson. (2001). Meaning of sport to adults with physical disabilities: A disability sport camp experience. *Sociology of Sport Journal*, **18**, 95-114.

Baker, S. (2003). *New Consumer Marketing: Managing a Living Demand System*. West Sussex, England: John Wiley & Sons.

Bell, M. (1993). What constitutes experience? Rethinking theoretical assumptions. *The Journal of Experiential Education*, **16** (1), 19-24.

Borrie, B., and J. Roggenbuck. (2001). The dynamic, emergent, and multi-phasic nature of on-site wilderness experiences. *Journal of Leisure Research*, 33 (2), 202-228.

Borrie W.T., and R. Birzell. (2001). Approaches to measuring quality of the wilderness experience. In W.A. Freimund and D.N. Cole (Eds.), *Visitor Use Density and Wilderness Experience: Proceedings* (pp. 29-38). Ogden, UT: U.S. Department of Agriculture, Forest Service, Rocky Mountain Research Station.

Botterill, D., and J. Crompton. (1996). Two case studies: Exploring the nature of the tourist's experience. *Journal of Leisure Research*, **28** (1), 57-82.

Bricker, K.S. (1998). Place and Preference: A Study of Whitewater Recreationists on the South Fork of the American River. Unpublished doctoral dissertation, The Pennsylvania State University, University Park, State College, PA.

Bricker, K.S., and D. Kerstetter. (2002). An interpretation of special place meanings whitewater recreationists attach to the South Fork of the American River. *Tourism Geographies*, **4** (4), 396-425.

Clawson, M., and J. Knetsch. (1966). *Economics of Outdoor Recreation*. Baltimore: Johns Hopkins Press.

Cohen, E. (1979). A phenomenology of tourist experiences. *Sociology*, **13**, 179-201.

Csikzentmihalyi, M., and I. Csikzentmihalyi. (1988). *Optimal Experience: Psychological Studies of Flow in Consciousness*. Cambridge: Cambridge University Press.

Dann, G.M.S. (1981). Tourist motivation: An appraisal. *Annals of Tourism Research*, **8**, 187-219.

Davenport, M., Freimund, W., Borrie, W., Manning, R., Valliere, W., and B. Wang. (2000). *Examining Winter Use in Yellowstone National Park* (p. 15). Ogden, UT: USDA Forest Service, Rocky Mountain Research Station.

Denzin, N. (1984). *On Understanding Emotion*. San Francisco: Jossey-Bass.

Dunn Ross, E.L., and S.E. Iso-Ahola. (1991). Sightseeing tourists' motivation and satisfaction. *Annals of Tourism Research*, **18**, 226-237.

Epting, F., and R. Neimeyer. (1984). *Personal Meanings of Death: Applications of Personal Construct Theory to Clinical Practice*. New York: Hemisphere.

Glaspell, B.S. (2002). Minding the Meaning of Wilderness: Investigating the Tensions and Complexities Inherent in Wilderness Visitors' Experience Narratives. Unpublished Dissertation, The University of Montana-Missoula.

Hull, R., and S. Michael. (1995). Nature-based recreation, mood change, and stress reduction. *Leisure Sciences*, **17**, 1-14.

Hull, R., Stewart, W., and Y. Yi. (1992). Experience patterns: Capturing the dynamic nature of a recreation experience. *Journal of Leisure Research*, **24** (3), 240-252.

Jackson, M., White, G., and C. Schmierer. (1996). Tourism experiences within an attributional framework. *Journal of Leisure Research*, **17** (1), 1-13.

Kearns, S. (2001). Viewing Grizzly Bears in Captivity: An Exploration of Visitor Dialogue and Meanings Associated with the Experience. Unpublished masters thesis, The University of Montana-Missoula.

Kelly, G. (1955). *The Psychology of Personal Constructs*. New York: Norton.

LaSalle, D., and T. Britton. (2003). *Priceless: Turning Ordinary Products into Extraordinary Experiences*. Boston: Harvard Business School Press.

Lee, Y., Dattilo, J., and D. Howard. (1994). The complex and dynamic nature of leisure experience. *Journal of Leisure Research*, **26** (3), 195-211.

Lounsbury, J., and J. Polik. (1992). Leisure needs and vacation satisfaction. *Leisure Sciences*, **14** (1), 105-119.

MacCannell, D. (1976). *The Tourist*. New York: Schocken.

MacKay, K.J., Andereck, K.L. and Vogt, C.A. (2002). Understanding vacationing motorist niche markets. *Journal of Travel Research*, 40, 356-363.

Manfredo, M.L., Driver, B.L., and P.J. Brown. (1983). A test of concepts inherent in experience based setting management for outdoor recreation areas. *Journal of Leisure Research*, **3**, 263-282.

Mannell, R. (1980). Social psychological techniques and strategies for studying leisure experiences. In S. Iso-Ahola (Ed.), *Social Psychological Perspectives on Leisure and Recreation* (pp. 62-88). Springfield, IL: Charles C Thomas.

McIntyre, N., and J. Roggenbuck. (1998). Nature/person transactions during an outdoor adventure experience: A multi-phasic analysis. *Journal of Leisure Research*, **30** (4), 401-422.

Montag, J. (2000). Experiencing Wolves in Yellowstone National Park: The Wolf-Watching Story. Unpublished masters thesis, The University of Montana-Missoula.

Nickerson, N., and T. Dillon. (2002). *Nonresident Summer Visitor Profile*. Missoula, MT: Institute for Tourism and Recreation Research, College of Forestry and Conservation, The University of Montana.

Nickerson, N., Ellard, J.A., and R. Dvorak. (2003). *The Montana Vacation Experience, Part 1.* Missoula, MT: Institute for Tourism and Recreation Research, School of Forestry, The University of Montana.

Omodei, M., and A. Wearing. (1990). Need satisfaction and involvement in personal projects: Toward an integrative model of subjective well-being. *Journal of Personality and Social Psychology*, **30** (4), 762-769.

O'Sullivan, E., and K. Spangler. (1998). *Experience Marketing: Strategies for a New Millennium.* State College, PA: Venture Publishing.

Otto, J., and J.B. Ritchie. (1996). The service experience in tourism. *Tourism Management*, **17** (3), 165-174.

Patterson, M.E., Williams, D.R., Watson, A.E., and J.W. Roggenbuck. (1998). An hermeneutic approach to studying the nature of wilderness experiences. *Journal of Leisure Research*, **30**, 423-452.

Pine II, J., and J. Gilmore. (1999). *The Experience Economy: Work is Theatre & Every Business is a Stage.* Boston: Harvard Business School Press.

Prentice, R.C., Witt, S.F., and H. Claire (1998). Tourism as experience: The case of heritage park. *Annals of Tourism Research*, **25**, 1-24.

Pritchard, A., and N.J. Morgan. (1996, September). Selling the Celtic Arc to the USA: A comparative analysis of the destination brochure images used in the marketing of Ireland, Scotland and Wales. *Journal of Vacation Marketing*, **2**, 346-365.

Prokesch, S. (1995). Competing on customer service: An interview with British Airways' Sir Colin Marshall. *Harvard Business Review*, **73** (6), 103.

Schroeder, H. (1996). *Voices from Michigan's Black River: Obtaining Information on "Special Places" for Natural Resource Planning.* St. Paul, MN: U.S. Department of Agriculture, Forest Service, North Central Forest Experiment Station.

Stewart, W. (1998). Leisure as multiphase experiences: Challenging traditions. *Journal of Leisure Research*, **30** (4), 391-400.

Tinsley, H., and D. Tinsley. (1986). A theory of the attributes, benefits and causes of leisure experience. *Leisure Sciences*, **8** (1), 1-45.

Urry, J. (1995). *Consuming Places.* London: Routledge.

Vallee, P. (1987). Authenticity as a Factor in Segmenting the Canadian Travel Market. Unpublished masters thesis, University of Waterloo, Canada.

6

Saravanua ni vanua: Exploring Sense of Place in the Rural Highlands of Fiji

Kelly S. Bricker
Deborah Kerstetter

People acquire a sense of belonging and purpose that gives meaning to their lives through personal attachment to places (Buttimer, 1980; Relph, 1976; Tuan, 1980). This "meaning" manifests in emotional attachment to one's family and residence, respect and caring for the Earth, and a special complex set of relations between individuals and nature, for example (Moore and Graefe, 1994; Tuan, 1980). Thus, attempting to delineate the meaning individuals attach to places (*i.e.*, sense of place) helps researchers to "understand a good deal about culture, values and concerns of the people who built and use [them]" (Raitz, 1987, p. 49).

This chapter focuses on "sense of place" for residents of Nakavika Village of Namosi Province and Nabukelevu Village of Serua Province, two villages recently introduced to tourism development in the remote mountainous highlands of Viti Levu in the Republic of Fiji. (Saravanua ni vanua directly translated to English means "tourism and land"; see Bricker [2001] for more information.) Fiji lies nearly 1,900 miles north of Sydney, Australia, and just over 3,000 miles southwest of Honolulu, Hawaii. The largest of its 330 islands is Viti Levu, which accounts for 59% of the land and 70% of the population. Unlike the coastal areas of Fiji, tourism was not introduced to the highlands until 1998. Hence, the purpose of this chapter is to examine the meanings residents attach to their village (*i.e.*, sense of place) and how they can potentially affect the development of sustainable quality experiences for tourists and residents alike.

Sense of Place

Sense of place is holistic, including social, cultural, environmental, psychological, geographic, and demographic dimensions of peoples' lives (Bricker, 1998; Jackson, 1994;

Tuan, 1977). According to Jackson (1994), sense of place is "a lively awareness of the familiar environment, a ritual repetition, [and] a sense of fellowship based on a shared experience, . . . which in the long run creates our sense of place, and of community" (pp. 159-160). Further, Shamai (1991) states that sense of place is "part of the social and political reproduction process of each society" (p. 355). However, Burr (1995) contends that the actual definition of sense of place comes inherently from the individual.

Historically, sense of place within the context of travel and tourism has been addressed through research on the host community. "Community in its very nature is a social artifact which represents a body of individuals sharing common cultural values and tools" (Potts et al., 1992, p. 9). Understanding the relationship between local community members and the place in which they live assists tourism planners, operators, and marketers in their development of sustainable quality tourism experiences. This understanding contributes in several ways. First, it assists tourism developers in determining the appropriateness of the tourism product. Second, it contributes to understanding the aspirations and desires of the local community, which enhances development of and communication about tourism impact strategies. And, third, responding to the value people assign to the place in which they live minimizes potential negative impacts on local cultures.

Certification and tourism guideline programs such as Green Globe 21 International Ecotourism Standard (IES) (2003), the National Ecotourism Accreditation Program (NEAP) (2003), and Rights and Responsibilities: A Compilation of Codes of Conduct for Tourism and Indigenous & Local Communities (2003) exemplify the importance of understanding cultural sensitivities within the context of tourism. For example, within the Green Globe 21 IES, there are sections of the

Photographer: N.K. Bricker.

A young Fijian on a billi-billi, rafting Fijian style in Namosi Province.

certification criteria that specifically address community benefits, cultural respect, and sensitivity. Further, in developing the tourism product, most certification programs include guidelines for community consultation processes and education and training for local staff support (Green Globe 21, 2003; NEAP, 2003; Rights and Responsibilities, 2003).

Vanua: Place and Its Meaning in Fiji

Within Fijian society, *vanua* is a term utilized to describe place meaning that combines land, culture, history, and beliefs, and it has been suggested as an expression of Fijian values (Batibasaga, 2000). "[Vanua] does not mean only land and the area one is identified with, and the vegetation, animal life, and other objects on it, but also includes the social and cultural system—the people, their traditions and customs, beliefs and values, and the various other institutions established for the sake of achieving harmony, solidarity, and prosperity within a particular social context" (Ravuvu, 1983, p. 70). Thus, understanding the people and their relationship to their vanua is important for tourism developers interested in creating tourism experiences that harmonize with the "place" for which they are proposing development.

Tourism Development

Historically, tourism development has been promoted as a panacea to the economic woes of small, rural communities (Bookbinder et al., 1998; Christie and Simmons, 1999; Curzon, 1993; Spenceley, 2001), where there is generally an absence of market protectionism, technological and human resource demands are low, and there tend to be fewer environmental and structural constraints than would be experienced with other types of economic development (Kinnaird et al., 1994). Tourism provides a source of employment that, in some cases, helps to preserve ties to the community and prevent migration from rural communities (Ashley and Roe, 2002; Ceasar, 2000; Christie and Simmons, 1999; Colvin, 1996; Spenceley, 2001). Additionally, there is some indication that tourism can be a catalyst for improved health care (Ceasar, 2000; Christie and Simmons, 1999; Curzon, 1993; Honey, 1998; Spenceley, 2001). Tourism may also provide support for other related economic opportunities that support the tourist experience, such as increased options for income generation in local communities through creation of other businesses, including tours, taxi services, and handicrafts (Bookbinder et al., 1998; Ceasar, 1998, 2000; Curzon, 1993; Fullerton, 2002; Hviding and Bayliss-Smith, 2000; Koeppel, 2000; Yu et al., 1997).

This argument for the economic benefits of tourism development faces challenges, however. Cohen (1984), Dogan (1989), and Stevens (1991) note that changes in the local value system as a result of economic gains through tourism lead to power struggles and conflicts of interest. And Laxson (1991) suggests that there is a dehumanizing effect on members of the local community (*e.g.*, Native Americans) when they are "the tourist attraction." (See Chapter Ten for a case analysis of Native Americans and casino development concerning meaningful spaces and subsequent use of these places within their community.)

From a positive sociocultural perspective, tourism development contributes to enhanced cultural pride and provides opportunities for residents to develop a sense of identity, place, and self-worth as well as a chance to educate others about the unique characteristics of their particular culture (Butler, 1991; Sweet, 1990; Ziffer, 1989). Tourism development may also maintain or revive the performing arts, resulting in income for local residents, enhanced tourism experiences, and a means to maintain cultural authenticity (Colvin, 1996; Spenceley, 2001).

Yet, challenges abound with respect to the sociocultural benefits of tourism development. Inskeep (1987), for example, argues that ill conceived and poorly managed tourism development "can erode the very qualities of natural and human environments that attract visitors in the first place" (p. 460). Tourism development can also negatively impact the art, customs/rituals, and architecture of indigenous people (Fridgen, 1991). As a result, it is imperative that we study the impact of tourism on small-scale or rural communities to " ensure survival of local culture and its artifacts" (Potts et al., 1992, p. 10).

One of the problems in developing countries has traditionally been that "local communities are rarely consulted about infrastructure and development decisions" (Hill, 1990, p. 18). To ensure that the local culture and its artifacts survive, we must respond to the people, ideas, and meanings that are attached to the places we study as they represent the unique cultures that attract tourists in the first place (Burr, 1995; List and Brown, 1996; Potts et al., 1992).

Tourism Development in Fiji

In response to indigenous Fijians' concerns about tourism development in rural areas (e.g., environmental degradation, rights of indigenous landowners, poverty alleviation, and rural migration), Fiji's Ministry of Tourism and Transport developed the National Ecotourism and Village-based Policy (NEVP). 'The primary objective of the NEVP document [is] to ensure that socio-cultural and environmental impacts [are] minimized and the quality of tourism products [is] enhanced or sustained, thereby achieving maximum benefits for rural residents of Fiji" (Bricker, 2002, p. 271). Because nearly 60% of Fijians live outside urban areas, this policy has significance for rural tourism development. The NEVP prompted the re-formation of the Fiji Ecotourism Association, which gives small and medium nature-based and village-based tourism operators a voice in the Ministry of Tourism (Bricker, 2003).

Tourism Development in Serua and Namosi Provinces

In 1998, tourism was introduced to Serua and Namosi, provinces in the highlands of Fiji, through a whitewater rafting company called Rivers Fiji (RF). This did not occur overnight, however. Managers of RF researched the potential of introducing ecotourism to the highlands of Fiji from 1992 to 1997. Then, due to the nature of land tenure in Fiji (i.e., ownership is held by tribal groups called *matagali*), several meetings were held with provincial leaders and matagali to secure hundreds of signatures supporting tourism development. Additionally, RF secured permission from the Fiji Trade and Investment Bureau (FTIB). (For further information on the details of RF, see Bricker [2001].)

Village Residents and Their *Vanua*

The remainder of this chapter focuses on the results of a multiphased study of sense of place for residents of two villages within the highlands of Fiji. The intent is to document how information can and has been used by suppliers, including RF, and other stakeholders to guide the development of sustainable quality tourism experiences.

Constructing the Data

In an effort to understand villagers' "sense of place," the study was conducted in two phases.

Phase I—Sense of Place as Described by Village Residents

Phase I of the study began in 1998 with a Sevu Sevu in each village. A *Sevu Sevu* is a ceremony whereby guests present a gift of kava (*i.e.*, the local plant used for ceremonies and social purposes) to the chief and the elders of the village and describe their particular issue or need. In this context, permission to conduct a study was requested. Permission was granted and interviews began with key informants or village leaders selected by the village elders. A Fijian member of the research team conducted each interview in the vernacular. He then transcribed the interviews into English with the help of Fijian transcribers.

In the Village of Nakavika, within the province of Namosi, 10 individuals were interviewed: the Chief of the Yavusa (male); the Catechist for the Catholic Church (male); the head of Matagali (*i.e.,* the male village leader); a rugby coach/youth leader (male); the treasurer of the women's association (female); the chairperson of the women's organization and women's representative to the District Council (female); the chairman for the development and upkeep of the church (male); the village headman/speaker (male); a youth leader for the village and the District of Wainikoroiluva (male); and a spokesperson for traditional education (female). In the village of Nabukelevu, within the province of Serua, the six individuals interviewed included the Church Deacon for the District of Burenitu (male); the Matagali Chief (male); the village Headman (mediator) (male); a member of the women's prayer group (female); the manager of the village school (male); and the Chief of the Clan Burenitu (male).

The key informants and village leaders were asked a series of questions extracted from sense of place literature, including but not limited to:

- What can you tell me about the place in which you live?
- What is the meaning of this place to you?
- What is happening in this place that is important?
- What is really important to your quality of life in this place?
- How sorry would you be to have to leave this place?
- What are your main concerns for the future of this place?

Given that the questions were open-ended, a classification system (*i.e.*, typologies) was developed (see Patton, 1990) to make sense out of respondents' expressions.

Using an iterative process, individuals' comments were condensed into five coherent themes: Commodity, Social, Heritage/Legacy, Rootedness, and Environment. *Commodity,* the first theme, includes items that relate to safety, food, and overall health and well-being. *Social* addresses the unity within a village, including love, cooperation, and respect. Tradition, and the importance of it being carried on, comprises the *Heritage/Legacy* dimension. The willingness of villagers to leave the place in which they live is the focus of the fourth dimension—*Rootedness.* The final dimension, *Environment,* represents the profound respect villagers have for the environment, including the need to conserve and protect it.

The five themes are represented in the sense of place (*i.e.,* thematic) statements listed in Table 6-1, all of which formed the basis of Phase II of this study.

Phase II—Residents' Level of Agreement with Sense of Place Statements

In order to understand the cultural salience of the results identified in Phase I, researchers returned to Nakavika and Nabukelevu in May and June 2003. During Phase II, data were collected by way of a survey administered to adults 18 years of age and older. A Fijian member of the research team represented the study and conducted survey interviews. The surveys were translated into the Fijian vernacular for ease of completion. In addition, the Fijian investigator was present to explain each statement, if necessary. Seventy-eight individuals from Nakavika and seventy-nine individuals from Nabukelevu completed the survey.

The results indicated that residents were most likely to agree with the statements, "It is important to continue the traditions of our village" and "We must conserve the environment for future generations" (see Table 6-2). Respondents were more neutral in their level of agreement with the statements, "The place in which we live is safe from natural disasters" and "I would leave this village only if I was asked to leave." Are these results representative, however, of how individuals in

Table 6.1   Place meaning statements

Theme	Statement
Commodity	• The place in which we live sustains us with as much food as we need. • The place in which we live is safe from natural disasters.
Social	• There is love and respect among the people of my village. • There is unity and cooperation among the people of my village.
Heritage/Legacy	• It is important for our youth to carry on our traditions. • It is important to continue the traditions of our village. • Our village maintains a genuine Fijian way of life.
Rootedness	• I will live in this village until I die. • I would leave this village only if I was asked to leave. • I would leave this village for an opportunity to make more money. • I would leave this village if necessary due to family obligations.
Environment	• We must conserve the environment for future generations. • We must protect our natural resources for the future of tourism.

Table 6.2 Level of agreement with statements that describe the village (*i.e.*, place)

Statement	Strongly Disagree	Disagree	Neither Agree nor Disagree	Agree	Strongly Agree	Mean[a]	SD[b]
It is important to continue the traditions of our village. (n = 155)	0.0%	0.6%	0.0%	65.2%	34.2%	4.33	.51
We must conserve the environment for future generations. (n = 155)	0.0%	0.6%	0.0%	65.2%	34.2%	4.33	.51
It is important for our youth to carry on our traditions. (n = 157)	0.0%	0.6%	0.0%	66.9%	32.5%	4.31	.50
We must protect our natural resources for the future of tourism. (n = 157)	0.0%	0.6%	0.0%	73.9%	25.5%	4.24	.47
The place in which we live sustains us with as much food as we need. (n = 157)	0.0%	0.0%	0.6%	81.5%	17.8%	4.17	.40
There is love and respect among the people of my village. (n = 156)	0.6%	4.5%	0.0%	80.1%	14.7%	4.04	.62
There is unity and cooperation among the people of my village. (n=156)	0.6%	5.1%	0.6%	81.4%	12.2%	3.99	.63
I will live in this village until I die. (n = 153)	2.0%	3.3%	4.6%	75.8%	14.4%	3.97	.71
I would leave this village for an opportunity to make more money. (n = 152)	1.3%	4.6%	4.6%	77.6%	11.8%	3.94	.68
Our village maintains a genuine Fijian way of life. (n = 156)	0.6%	10.3%	1.3%	70.5%	17.3%	3.94	.81
I would leave this village, if necessary, due to family obligations. (n = 147)	2.7%	20.4%	5.4%	67.3%	4.1%	3.50	.95
I would leave this village only if I was asked to leave. (n = 143)	4.9%	23.8%	7.7%	59.4%	4.2%	3.34	1.04
The place in which we live is safe from natural disasters. (n = 151)	4.0%	28.5%	10.6%	55.0%	2.0%	3.23	1.01

[a]Mean value was derived from individuals' response to a five-point Likert scale ranging from 1 (strongly disagree) to 5 (strongly agree).
[b]SD = Standard deviation.

105

each village feel about their place of residence? To find out, the researchers further explored differences in response to the place statements between Nakavika and Nabukelevu villagers.

To determine whether residents from Nakavika and Nabukelevu differed in their response to the sense of place statements, a series of t-tests were performed. The results demonstrated that the residents of Nakavika and Nabukelevu differed significantly in their response to five statements. In all cases, residents of Nakavika were less likely than residents of Nabukelevu to agree that village traditions should be maintained, that they would leave the village for an opportunity to make money, and that the environment/natural resources should be protected/conserved (see Table 6-3).

Table 6.3 Differences in place meaning between residents of Nakavika and Nabukelevu

Statement	*Residents*	*N*	*Mean*	*SD*	*t*
The place in which we live sustains us with as much food as we need.	Nakavika Village	78	4.17	.38	−.167
	Nabukelevu Village	79	4.18	.42	
The place in which we live is safe from natural disasters.	Nakavika Village	72	3.36	.91	1.58
	Nabukelevu Village	79	3.10	1.09	
There is love and respect among the people of my village.	Nakavika Village	78	4.10	.41	1.29
	Nabukelevu Village	78	3.97	.77	
There is unity and cooperation among the people of my village.	Nakavika Village	78	4.01	.59	.38
	Nabukelevu Village	78	3.97	.66	
It is important for our youth to carry on our traditions.	Nakavika Village	78	4.18	.48	−3.38*
	Nabukelevu Village	79	4.44	.50	
I will live in this village until I die.	Nakavika Village	76	3.87	.79	−1.85
	Nabukelevu Village	77	4.08	.60	
I would leave this village only if I was asked to leave.	Nakavika Village	68	3.47	.94	1.40
	Nabukelevu Village	75	3.23	1.12	
I would live this village for an opportunity to make more money.	Nakavika Village	76	3.82	.63	−2.89*
	Nabukelevu Village	76	4.07	.72	
I would leave this village, if necessary, due to family obligations.	Nakavika Village	72	3.47	.98	−.30
	Nabukelevu Village	75	3.52	.94	
It is important to continue the traditions of our village.	Nakavika Village	78	4.22	.50	−2.78*
	Nabukelevu Village	77	4.44	.50	
We must conserve the environment for future generations.	Nakavika Village	78	4.21	.41	−3.12*
	Nabukelevu Village	77	4.45	.57	
We must protect our natural resources for the future of tourism.	Nakavika Village	78	4.13	.44	−3.08*
	Nabukelevu Village	79	4.35	.48	
Our village maintains a genuine Fijian way of life.	Nakavika Village	77	3.95	.76	.19
	Nabukelevu Village	79	3.92	.86	

[1]Means ranged from 1 to 5, with 1 representing "strongly disagree" and 5 representing "strongly agree."
*Significant beyond the .05 level of significance.

Discussion

The unique culture, natural environment, social atmosphere, and political environment within which rural Fijian highlanders live influences their sense of place. In Phase I of the study, key informants and community leaders introduced comments that were condensed into five themed sense of place categories (*i.e.*, Commodity, Social, Heritage/Legacy, Rootedness, and the Environment), none of which was more important than the others. For example, respondents commented on the cooperation that is inherent in, as well as the tradition that exemplifies, village life. They also recognized that their daily existence depends on the respect they receive from other residents, many of whom work with them to protect and conserve the natural environment upon which the entire village depends. This finding supports Burr's (1995) contention that people perceive multiple senses of place as important reasons for living where they do. Further, the dimensions culled from the open-ended responses reinforce findings previously presented by Eyles (1985) and Burr (1995), both of whom introduced social ties/relationships, a sense of rootedness, and respect for the natural environment in individuals' descriptions of sense of place.

The results also suggest that individuals who live in the highlands of Fiji are of one society, but separate and distinct cultures. Culture is generally considered to be a complex system of messages and signals (D'Andrade, 1995; Kuper, 2001) or, more simply, comprised of "the knowledge people use to live their lives and the way in which they do so" (Handwerker, 2001, p. 107). Residents of Nakavika and Nabukelevu initially introduced a variety of themes regarding sense of place and, during Phase II of the study, attached significantly different levels of importance to the sense of place statements reflecting those themes. These findings suggest that each village has its own unique culture. Why is this important? It is imperative that developers focusing on tourism products for the highlands understand the context in which the tourism product is being introduced and the sense of place held by residents. For example, since the early 1980s, residents of Nabukelevu have been exposed to outsiders bringing logging development to their village, which has affected their thinking about tourism. As noted by one resident,

Tourism is very different from other industries such as the logging industry or the fishing industry. The logging and the fishing industry will take away from our land our resources, in a way depriving us of our resources. Whereas for tourism, tourists would not take away any of our resources. They will just come, watch and experience our resources that also include our culture, and us the people. When the logging company departed from here, they departed with our forests. The land is stripped bare. When the fishing company departed from our waters, they departed with our marine life and our waters are scarce or even extinct with marine life. Our resources must be safeguarded so that our future generations can also utilize them. (Bricker, 2001, p. 242)

Developing quality tourism experiences while keeping in mind the culture, including sense of place, of a travel destination is challenging, but feasible. For example, in the context of Fiji, RF proposed a lease for conservation on the Upper Navua river corridor and was met with overwhelming support by villagers, the logging company, and eight different matagali. This has long-term implications for quality tourism experiences along the river, as no commercial development will take place within the 25 km corridor for at least 25 years. This area is called the

Upper Navua Conservation Area and remains home to unique and once thought extinct species such as parrots, iguana, and fish on the island of Viti Levu.

Respondents from each village differed in the importance they attach to maintaining tradition. Residents of Nabukelevu are more concerned about youth carrying on the traditions of the village than are residents of Nakavika. Given this sentiment, it appears that tourism developers who introduce tourism to the area will need to place much greater emphasis on maintaining and celebrating the traditions of Nabukelevu. For example, when RF hires guides for the Upper Navua River, it does so through traditional channels, including going through a process with elders to select individuals with the necessary qualifications. Additionally, RF encourages guides to tell "their" story on the river, and is exploring the possibility of introducing ancient village sites as part of the tourist experience while continuing traditional uses within the Upper Navua Conservation Area.

An interesting result lies in the fact that residents of Nabukelevu are inclined to agree that they will leave the village for the "opportunity to make more money," which makes it difficult for them to maintain the traditions of the village, including those that are tied to the environment. Hence, developers interested in promoting tourism in Nabukelevu must consider how they can involve residents in tourism in a way that not only preserves what makes the area special, but also allows them to make money while doing so. A successful example lies in the Upper Navua Conservation Area, where RF delivers a percentage of the income generated from each tourist to the village and various matagali. Additionally, due to a rotational hiring process for guides, RF provides each matagali with the opportunity to have a family member earn income from the company.

In order to maintain peace and harmony within rural tourism destinations such as Nakavika and Nabukelevu, tourism developers must be sensitive to village traditions and consult with residents before introducing a tourism product that could be offensive to everyday life or traditions. This practice has been crucial for the sustainability of RF and in gaining support for conservation efforts within the river corridor. For example, early in the development of the business, RF made a commitment (despite outside pressure from tour companies, tourists, etc., to include Sunday trips) to (1) operate trips Monday through Saturday only, as Sunday is an important religious and family day for village residents; (2) implement a dress code for all tourists entering the village; and, (3) visit only with permission and the traditional sevu sevu. RF has also worked on a process for addressing grievances based on the traditional ways of dealing with issues that may arise. The implementation of this process has minimized conflict and increased guides' satisfaction with RF.

In Chapter Four, Jennings and Weiler address the importance of engaging in tourism research from the emic, or "insiders," perspective. This chapter highlights one technique for doing so and the importance of engaging stakeholders when commencing the development of a quality tourism experience. Jennings, in Chapter One, also points out the consequences of not representing the identities of a community accurately. The results of this chapter demonstrate that adopting the emic perspective allows tourism operators to adjust elements of the operation—such as guide selection, visitation, and rules for visiting the village—in response to villagers' concerns for conservation.

Further, in Chapter Ten, Bricker, Daniels, and Carmichael recognize that decision making at the local level is critical to the development of sustainable products and garnering support for conservation of the natural environments in which tourism operates. The results of this study provide support for their argument. Communication with villagers at the onset of tourism development by RF guided the development of the tourism product and eventually led to the protection of a river corridor.

In closing, quality tourism experiences depend on maintaining the sense of place held by residents of a tourism destination. If the development of tourism negatively affects residents' sense of place, the quality of experiences sought by tourists and the unique characteristics of the place that attracted them initially might ultimately disappear. Thus, tourism developers must assess how residents feel about their place and what impacts they are willing to accept throughout the tourism development process.

References

Ashley, C., and D. Roe. (2002). Making tourism work for the poor: Strategies and challenges in southern Africa. *Development Southern Africa*, **19** (1), 61-82.

Batibasaga, K.K. (2000). Personal correspondence, October 11.

Bookbinder, M.P., Dinerstein, E., Rijal, A., Cauley, H., and A. Rajouria. (1998). Ecotourism's support of biodiversity conservation. *Conservation Biology*, **12** (6), 1399-1404.

Bricker, K.S. (1998). Place and Preference: A Study of Whitewater Recreationists on the South Fork of the American River. Unpublished doctoral dissertation, The Pennsylvania State University, University Park, PA.

Bricker, K.S. (2001). Ecotourism development in the rural highlands of Fiji. In D. Harrison (Ed.), *Tourism and the Less Developed World: Issues and Case Studies* (pp. 235-250). Wallingford, UK: CABI Publications.

Bricker, K.S. (2002). Fiji: Small island ecotourism planning amidst political unrest and rising tides. In M. Honey (Ed.), *Ecotourism and Certification: Setting Standards in Practice* (pp. 265-297). Washington, DC: Island Press.

Bricker, K. S. (2003). Ecotourism development in Fiji: Policy, practice, and political instability. In D.A. Fennell and R.K. Dowling (Eds.), *Ecotourism Policy and Planning* (pp. 187-203). Wallingford, UK: CABI Publications.

Burr, S.W. (1995, October). The problem with sense of place within a context of sustainable tourism development: A qualitative study [abstract]. *Abstracts from the 1995 Symposium on Leisure Research* (p. 77). Arlington, VA: National Recreation and Park Association.

Butler, R. (1991). Tourism, environment, and sustainable development. *Environmental Conservation*, **18** (3), 201-209.

Buttimer, A. (1980). Home, reach, and the sense of place. In A. Buttimer & D. Seamon (Eds.), *The Human Experience of Space and Place* (pp. 167-187). London: Croom Helm.

Ceaser, M. (1998). Wildlife News: Phinda wins tourism award. *African Wildlife*, **52**, 37.

Ceaser, M. (2000). Bolivia's lodge for nature [Electronic Version]. *Americas*, **52** (3), 4-5.

Center on Ecotourism and Sustainable Development and The International Ecotourism Society. (2003). *Rights and responsibilities: A compilation of codes of conduct for tourism and indigenous and local communities*. Washington DC: Center on Ecotourism and Sustainable Development and The International Ecotourism Society.

Christie, L., and N. Simmons. (1999). Wild places: Kapawi Lodge in Ecuador's Amazon. *Wildlife Conservation*, **102** (6), 56-59.

Cohen, E. (1984). The sociology of tourism: Approaches, issues and findings. *Annual Review of Sociology*, **10**, 373-392.

Colvin, J. (1996). Indigenous ecotourism: The Capirona programme in Napo Province, Ecuador. *Unasylva* **187** (47), 32-37.

Curzon, C. (1993). Ecotourism—Conservation ethics—Profit: Getting it right in the eastern Transvaal. *Africa -Environment and Wildlife*, **1** (2), 36-42.

D'Andrade, R. (1995). *The Development of Cognitive Anthropology.* Cambridge: Cambridge University Press.

Dogan, H. (1989). Forms of adjustment: Sociocultural impacts of tourism. *Annals of Tourism Research*, **16** (2), 216-233.

Eyles, J. (1985). *Sense of Place.* Cheshire, England: Silverbrook.

Fridgen, J.D. (1991). *Dimensions of Tourism.* Michigan: Educational Institute of the American Hotel and Motel Association.

Fullerton, E. (2002). Mexico's fledging ecotourism struggles to survive. *Planet Ark.* Retrieved October 8, 2003, *http://www.planetark.org/dailynewsstory.cfm?newsid= 15676&newsdate=26-Apr-2002.*

Garro, K. (2000). Remembering what one knows and the construction of the past: A comparison of cultural consensus theory and cultural schema theory. *Ethos*, **28**, 275-319.

Green Globe 21 International Ecotourism Standard for Ecotourism Products. (2003). Ecotourism Australia and CRC for Sustainable Tourism. Green Globe 21, Asia Pacific Region. Accessed December 31, 2003, *http://www.greenglobe.com/ documents/general/ecotourismstandard.pdf.*

Handwerker, W. (2001). The construct validity of cultures: Cultural diversity, culture theory, and a method for ethnography. American Anthropologist, **104** (1), 106-122.

Hill, C. (1990). The paradox of tourism in Costa Rica. *Cultural Survival Quarterly*, **4** (1), 14-19.

Honey, M. (1998). Where's the "eco" in "ecotourism"? Americas.org. Retrieved September 19, 2003, *http://www.americas.org/events/travel/tourism_turns_green.htm.*

Hviding, E., and T. Bayliss-Smith. (2000). Rumors of Utopia: Conservation and ecotourism. In E. Hviding and T. Bayliss-Smith (Eds.), *Islands of Rainforest: Agroforestry, Logging and Eco-tourism in Solomon Islands* (pp. 291-320). Burlington, VT: Ashgate Publishing.

Inskeep, E. (1987). Environmental planning for tourism. *Annals of Tourism Research,* **14**, 118-135.

Jackson, J.B. (1994). *A Sense of Place, a Sense of Time.* New Haven, CT: Yale University Press.

Kinnaird, V., Kothari, U., and D. Hall. (1994). Tourism: Gender perspectives. In V. Kinnaird and D. Hall (Eds.), *Tourism: A Gender Analysis* (pp. 1-28). New York: John Wiley & Sons.

Koeppel, D. (2000). Costa Rica: Me rainforest, you Jane. *Travel Holiday*, **183**, 94-101.

Kuper, A. (2001). *Culture: The Anthropologists' Account.* Cambridge: Harvard University Press.

Laxson, J. (1991). How "we" see "them": Tourism and Native Americans. *Annals of Tourism Research*, **18**, 365-391.

List, P., and P. Brown. (1996). Moving toward an expanded land management ethic. In B. L. Driver, D. Dustin, T. Baltic, G. Elsner, and G. Peterson (Eds.), *Nature and the Human Spirit* (pp. 457-465). State College, PA: Venture Publishing.

Moore, R.L., and A.R. Graefe. (1994). Attachments to recreation settings: The case of rail-trail users. *Leisure Sciences*, **16**, 17-31.

National Ecotourism and Accreditation Program (NEAP). (2003). Retrieved November 25, 2003, *http://www.ecotourism.org.au/neap.asp*.

Patton, M.Q. (1990). *Qualitative Evaluation and Research Methods* (2nd ed.). Newbury Park, CA: Sage.

Potts, T., Backman, K., Uysal, M., and S. Backman. (1992). Issues in rural community tourism development. *Visions in Leisure and Business*, **11** (1), 5-13.

Raitz, K. (1987). Commentary: Place, space, and environment in America's leisure landscapes. *Journal of Cultural Geography*, **8** (1), 49-61.

Ravuvu, A. (1983). *Vaka I Taukei: The Fijian Way of Life*. Suva, Fiji: Institute of Pacific Studies, University of the South Pacific.

Relph, F. (1976). *Place and Placedness*. London: Pion Ltd.

Romney, A., Batchelder, W., and S. Weller. (1987). Recent applications of cultural consensus theory. *American Behavioral Scientist*, **31** (2), 163-177.

Shamai, S. (1991). Sense of place: An empirical measurement. *Geoforum*, **22** (3), 347-358.

Spenceley, A. (2001). Ecotourism - Local community benefit systems at two nature-based tourism operations in South Africa. *UNEP Industry and Environment*, **24** (3), 50-53.

Stevens, S. F. (1991). Sherpas, tourism, and cultural change in Nepal's Mount Everest region. *Journal of Cultural Geography*, **12** (1), 39-58.

Sweet, J. (1990). The portals of tradition: Tourism in the American Southwest. *Cultural Survival Quarterly*, **14** (2), 6-8.

Tuan, Y. (1977). Space and Place: The Perspective of Experience. Minneapolis, Minnesota: University of Minnesota Press.

Tuan, Y. (1980). *Space and Place: The Perspective of Experience*. Minneapolis: University of Minnesota Press.

Yu, D., Hendrickson, T., and A. Castillo. (1997). Ecotourism and conservation in Amazonian Peru: Short-term and long-term challenges. *Environmental Conservation*, **24** (2), 130-138.

Ziffer, K. (1989). Ecotourism: The Uneasy Alliance. A working paper prepared for Conservation International by Ernst & Young.

Quality of Life and Interpretation of Quality Tourism Experiences

As already noted in Section Two, *Mediating Meaning*, and Section Three, *Interpretation of Meaning and Place*, the interchange of residents and tourists can impact on overall evaluations on the nature of the quality of tourism experiences. Associated with such interchanges are related perceptions, attitudes, and experiences of residents and tourists alike, as well as various social, cultural, economic and environmental impacts and related consequences for resident quality of life and tourist quality of experience. In this Section, particular emphasis is placed on the both the perceived and realized interaction of residents (hosts) and tourists (guests). The dominant theoretical lens used to inform this chapter is post-postivism. Additionally, elements of the interpretation of meaning and place resonate in Chapters Seven and Eight, and an overlying theme is consideration of the social constructions of quality of life and their relationships to quality tourism experiences.

In Chapter Seven, Barbara A. Carmichael presents a detailed overview of literature related to resident perceptions and attitudes to tourism and tourists as well as to tourism impacts on resident quality of life. The chapter includes consideration of the development over time of theoretical and methodological frameworks used in resident studies. In particular, social exchange theory, social representation theory, life cycle, and carrying capacity and quality of life constructs resonate in the literature, albeit that the latter is more implied than explicitly stated. The nature of such interaction between residents and tourism, however, has ramifications for the overall nature of the "quality" of tourism experiences.

In Chapter Eight, Kathleen Andereck and Claudia Jurowski further develop the quality of life construct and proffer a tourism quality of life (TQOL) measurement tool. In particular, this chapter highlights from the relevant literature the positive and negative experiences associated with economic aspects of resident quality of life, sociocultural aspects of resident quality of life, and environmental aspects of resident quality of life. Attention is also given to predictors of tourism attitudes. The chapter concludes with a case study drawn from Arizona to demonstrate the use of the TQOL index to measure residents' perceptions of tourism impacts, the perceived strength of feeling associated with such impacts, and levels of satisfaction with specific impacts.

7

Linking Quality Tourism Experiences, Residents' Quality of Life, and Quality Experiences for Tourists

Barbara A. Carmichael

"The tourist may have his [or her] vacation spoiled or enhanced by the resident. The resident may have his [or her] daily life enriched or degraded by the unending flow of tourists" (Knox, 1982, p. 77, cited in Ap, 1992, p. 669).

The purpose of this chapter is to identify the role and importance of research on resident attitudes to tourism as part of our understanding of quality tourism experiences. The chapter presents a literature review of the current state of knowledge on residents' perceived impacts of tourism. It looks at how these impacts affect residents' attitudes and reactions toward tourism and residents' quality of life. This is based on the premise that such reactions influence the quality of tourists' experiences. The literature review focuses on the theoretical and methodological advances made in these studies in recent years. Specifically, the driving questions are: What theories are used to frame resident attitude studies? And, how are perceived impacts and resident attitudes measured, classified, scaled, and modeled? Discussion of how quality of life variables for residents and tourists are integrated into these studies is also a theme of this review. As far as possible, research gaps are identified. It is suggested that some of the theories that have been applied to the study of resident attitudes toward tourists may also be applied to understanding tourist perceptions and attitudes toward residents. These linkages are conceptualized in Figure 7-1 and discussed in more detail throughout the chapter.

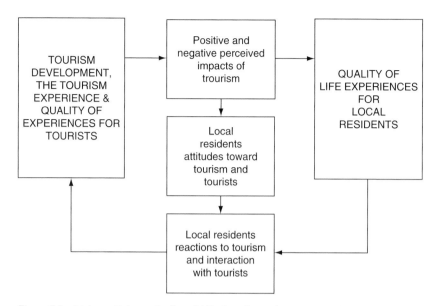

Figure 7.1   Linkages Between Quality of Life Experiences for Local Residents and Tourists.

Role of Local Residents in Quality Tourism Experiences

Vacations play a multiple role in influencing a tourist's quality of life, for example, they can provide physical and mental rest and relaxation, they can provide space for personal development and the pursuit of personal and social interests, and they can also be used as a form of symbolic consumption enhancing status (Richards, 1999). However, these experiences do not occur in a vacuum but are influenced by conditions in the host community, in the regions where tourism occurs. Local residents in host communities are an integral part of the tourism experience, influence its quality, and, as a consequence, impact on a tourist's "quality of life." Other tourists and local residents, both directly and indirectly, are inseparable from the environmental settings of the experiences. However, the exact nature of how resident attitudes toward tourism actually affect quality tourism experiences is under-researched, partly because of measurement difficulties but also because of the prevailing research directions in marketing and tourism research.

Perdue and colleagues (1999) note that much of the current services marketing literature focuses on the "services marketing triangle" (Kotler, 1994, p. 470; Zeithaml and Bitner, 1996, p. 23). The three corners of this triangle are the company, its employees, and its customers, linked by internal marketing, external marketing, and interactive marketing (Kotler et al., 2003, p. 47). Similarly, the service quality literature focuses on "point-of-service" evaluations and tends to ignore the wider community in terms of external marketing and interactive marketing. For example, a new text on service quality in leisure and tourism (Williams and

Buswell, 2003) fails to mention the host community effects. A fuller description of a product's marketing environment is provided by Kotler and associates (2003). They propose that six environmental factors shape the destination "macro-environment": demographic, economic, natural, technological, political, and cultural forces. It is implied that these forces develop an environmental effect that directly influences tourist perceptions and experiences. However, much of the marketing literature has had little to say about social factors, such as the friendliness of local people, the languages spoken, family structures, occupations, urban layout, population density, poverty levels, and living conditions—all of which are part of the tourism environment and influence experiences.

Tourism scholars have suggested that a fourth corner, representing community residents, needs to be added to the "services marketing triangle" (Fick and Ritchie, 1991; Le Blanc, 1992, cited in Perdue et al., 1999). Residents who are supportive of tourism tend to be receptive and friendly to tourists, which, in turn, provides a positive experience for tourists. This influences their intention to return, as well as their word-of-mouth recommendations. Murphy (1985) was one of the first to identify the need for a community approach to tourism destination planning and marketing. He suggests that "the product and image that intermediaries package and sell is a destination experience, and as such creates an industry that is highly dependent on the goodwill and co-operation of the host communities. . . . It is the citizen who must live with the cumulative outcome of such developments and needs to have a greater input into how his [sic]community is packaged and sold as a tourism product on the world market" (p. 16).

More recent research by tourism scholars in marketing has identified the importance of the community factor as part of the tourism experience. Mo and colleagues (1993) show that the destination environment factor described as a "Destination Orientation Dimension" (of social and cultural attributes) is the primary factor in an international tourist's experiential desires of the destination product. Murphy and associates (2000) use a Partial Least Squares analysis to test a hypothesis that positive experience with the elements of the destination's macro environment will positively affect trip quality. The destination environment in terms of climate, scenery, ambiance, friendliness, and, to a lesser extent, cleanliness was found to be a predictor of quality (beta = 0.36) for visitors to Victoria, BC, British Columbia. This reveals implications for the importance of the tourism industry working with local government, particularly in its strategic planning goals and general quality-of-life objectives. It also suggests that "managers will be well advised to focus on the more general environmental conditions of a destination, as well as the infrastructure and businesses over which they have more direct control" (Murphy et al., 2000). Management in this context refers to tourism management at a number of scales (governments, destinations, firms). Nevertheless, as yet, tourism researchers have had little to say about the effects of resident attitudes and behaviors on quality tourism experiences.

Perceived Impacts of Tourism

What is a quality experience for the tourist may not be so for the local (Bramwell, 2003). There is a range of tourism factors that influence resident attitudes toward tourism and affect quality of life. Most studies suggest that, although residents perceive many of the economic impacts as positive, they are less agreed on the nature and direction of the perceived environmental and social impacts (Caneday and Zeiger, 1991; Carmichael et al., 1996; Carmichael, 2000). In fact, developing a local tourism industry offers no guarantee of improved quality of life for residents (Long, 1996, p. 341). A detailed discussion of resident perceptions of the impact of tourism is provided in Chapter Eight and in the case study in Chapter Eleven and so will not be repeated here. Furthermore, there are a number of thorough reviews in the tourism literature of resident attitudes toward tourism (Ap and Crompton, 1998; Pearce et al., 1996; Haralambopoulos and Pizam, 1996), which indicate in depth some of the perceived consequences of tourism development.

Unfortunately, some of these studies have methodological flaws. For instance, many did not create their own item pool of perceived impacts but relied on previous studies from which to derive the variables used in the empirical analysis. One difficulty with this type of analysis is that it may be difficult for residents to distinguish between the effects of tourism itself and other forces for modernization that are experienced by communities (Wall, 1996). Another methodological issue lies in assessing which of the many impacts has salience to the individual residents or to subgroups of the population and whether the importance of these impacts varies over space and time. Even in very early stages before tourism infrastructure is introduced, residents show differing degrees of ambivalence toward tourism development (Hernandez et al., 1996). These researchers recommend that "various components of attitudes toward tourism should be weighted by respondents in terms of their importance, to better understand how overall attitudes are shaped" (Hernandez et al., 1996, p. 775). To address the latter problem, a case study is presented in Chapter Eight in which the diversity of the perceptions that have an impact on tourism is measured using a tourism and quality-of-life index. This index is comprised of three measures: residents' assessments of the importance of quality-of-life indicators; residents' assessments of their satisfaction with these indicators; and residents' assessments of tourism's influence on the indicators.

Resident Attitudes Toward Tourism

Attitudes have been defined as an enduring predisposition toward a particular aspect of one's environment. This predisposition can be reflected in the way one thinks, feels, and behaves with respect to that aspect (McDoughall and Munro, 1987, p. 87). Thus, attitudes are structured along three dimensions: (1) cognitive (beliefs, knowledge, perceptions); (2) affective (likes and dislikes); and (3) behavioral (action taken or expressed, instinct to act with respect to a particular object or place). For example, in the case of overall attitude toward tourism, residents hold beliefs about the effects of tourism; they know if they like or dislike these effects and may react accordingly. The level of their reaction is likely to depend on the importance that they place on the perceived impact and the likelihood of it affecting their quality of life.

Resident attitudes toward tourism are influenced by both external factors (*i.e.*, the perceived impacts of tourism and community development) and internal factors (*i.e.*, related to the residents' personal characteristics and those of the tourists). A number of tourism researchers have provided lists of such factors that potentially contribute to theory development in understanding the relationships between perceived impacts and resident attitudes. Butler (1975) identifies five characteristics of the destination area that influence perceived impacts of tourism by residents: economic state of the area, degree of local involvement in tourism, spatial characteristics of tourism development, viability of the host culture, and other characteristics (political attitudes). He describes five factors related to the nature of the tourists that were important to influencing interaction with residents: number of visitors, length of stay of visitors, ethnic characteristics of visitors, economic characteristics of visitors, and activities of visitors. Drawing from the previous literature, Lankford and Howard (1994) identify several variables that related to the personal characteristics of the residents themselves. They include length of residence, economic dependence on tourism, distance of tourism center from respondent's home, resident involvement in tourism decision making, birthplace, level of knowledge, level of contact with tourists, and demographic characteristics. These relationships all have implications for theory development. With such a variety of factors influencing perceived impacts of tourism on individuals and communities, it is not surprising that there are a variety of attitudes expressed by residents. Recent studies have explored this diversity among resident opinions and have focused on the analysis of the attitudes of sub-groups of the population (Ryan and Montgomery, 1994; Ryan et al., 1998; Madrigal, 1995; Davis et al., 1988; Williams and Lawson, 2001; Weaver and Lawton, 2001).

Theory Development

More than a decade ago, Ap (1990, 1992) bemoaned the lack of theory in the growing number of studies of resident attitudes toward tourism. He stated that "unless researchers launch out of the elementary descriptive stage of the current state of research and into an explanatory stage where research develops some sort of theoretical framework, they may find themselves none the wiser in the next ten years time" (1990, p. 615). Theoretical frameworks examining tourism's impacts have received increasing attention following Ap's (1992) critique.

Moreover, some earlier studies could be reframed within these new frameworks (Pearce et al., 1996; Perdue et al., 1999). In this section, a number of recent directions in theory development are reviewed within the context of life cycle and carrying capacity models, social disruption, social exchange, and social representations theory. Conceptual frameworks developed first for tourism as a whole, but more recently they have evolved to focus on specific types of tourism development, such as special events (Fredline and Faulkner, 2000) and casino tourism (Roehl, 1999). Early frameworks for understanding resident attitudes involved the destination *life cycle model* (Butler, 1980) and the concept of critical carrying capacity constraints and limits to growth (Long et al., 1990; Madrigal, 1993). Allen and colleagues (1993, p. 28) suggest that there is a threshold beyond which tourism development may in fact be detrimental to quality of life. Doxey's "Irridex" descriptive scale (1975) outlines unidirectional changes in resident attitudes as destinations move through the tourism destination growth cycle. In the early stages, residents are in the state of euphoria, which changes to apathy, annoyance, and perhaps even antagonism as the number of tourists increases with destination growth and consolidation. Doxey's model is simplistic but it is useful in explaining how attitudes toward tourism may become more negative over time (Smith and Krannich, 1998).

Longitudinal models for a single destination are preferable methodologies for testing out these concepts (Carmichael et al., 1996; Getz, 1994; McCool and Moisey, 1996; Johnson et al., 1994; Lee and Back, 2003), although a cross-sectional design using destinations at different stages in the product life cycle has been mostly used (*e.g.*, Ryan et al., 1998; Long et al., 1990; Akis et al., 1996, in rural areas; Gilbert and Clark, 1997, in urban areas).

Perdue and associates (1999) contrast the carrying capacity concept implied in the resort cycle model and in Doxey's "Irridex" with a social disruption hypothesis that also can be used to explain changes in residents' quality-of-life perceptions and their attitudes toward tourism (England and Albrecht, 1984). This hypothesis was developed for so-called boomtown communities that are in the process of responding to a period of rapid economic change. Through this process, resident quality of life is expected to initially decline (as a result of the stress on infrastructure) and then improve as the community and its residents adapt to the new situation. Evidence for the framework of social carrying capacity is provided in a study by Long and associates (1990). However, in another study by Carmichael and colleagues (1996), there was a decline in the quality of life for some variables (crime and traffic worsened, perceived historic value decreased, and the town was a less desirable place to live). In contrast, a different variable based on responses to the statement "It would be better if the tourism infrastructure had never been built" showed evidence for the social disruption hypothesis (Carmichael et al., 1996).

Most studies of resident attitudes are made after tourism develops, although there are exceptions (Keogh, 1990; Mason and Cheyne, 2000; Hernandez et al., 1996). These latter studies show that in the pre-tourism and early tourism stage, when residents mainly hold positive attitudes toward tourism, not everyone is uncritical and in a state of euphoria. Hernandez and associates (1996) report that respondents were generally in favor of the future development of an "instant" resort enclave but had mixed feelings. They were especially concerned about the end of tranquility as part of their way of life. Indeed, it is likely that, at all stages of tourism development, residents will hold a variety of attitudes toward tourism and tourists.

One model developed in the geographical literature to describe cultural contact (Abler et al., 1975) was suggested by Butler (1975) to have application in understanding the diversity in resident attitudes and behaviors toward tourism. This model is discussed later in this chapter, as it is useful in understanding the link between resident attitudes and behaviors.

The variety of attitudes among residents may also be explained by perceptions of the social exchange relationship between residents and tourists. Ap (1990, 1992) suggests that *social exchange theory* provides a basis for the identification and definitions involved in the measurement of resident perceptions of the impact of tourism. The social exchange of resources related to tourism may provide opportunities for satisfying exchanges. The basic premise of social exchange theory is that people will favor tourism if the benefits exceed the costs of tourism and if they value these benefits. Residents are asked to hypothesize an evaluation of tourism in terms of social exchanges and the expected benefits and costs that are realized in exchange for resources and services. Ap (1992) formulates a number of propositions that can be used as hypotheses. He suggests that positive attitudes toward tourism occur when perceived benefits, compared to costs, are satisfactory and balanced. Principles of rationality, satisficing, reciprocity, and justice must be met. In an unbalanced relationship, if the resident hosts are advantaged, then their perceptions of tourism will be positive; if they are disadvantaged, their perceptions will be negative. This hypothesis is often implicitly recognized even though it may not be related to social exchange theory; for example, consider Eadington (1986) comments in referring to casino tourism: "One's attitude toward the casino project will depend largely on whether those changes are going to improve or deteriorate one's present quality of life in that community" (p. 280).

Perdue, Long, and Allen (1990) first mention social exchange theory as a conceptual framework for understanding resident attitudes in their study of Colorado communities, and tested out the theory in some of their later work (Perdue et al., 1999). A number of more recent studies use social exchange theory as a basis for hypothesis testing and modeling (Gursoy et al., 2002; Jurowski et. al., 1997; Lee and Back, 2003). In Chapter Eleven of this book, this theory is used to understand how residents weigh the costs and benefits of tourism and form attitudes toward tourism development. Many of the costs and benefits are not evenly spread, which helps explain diversity of opinion among residents and their behavioral responses. Furthermore, the encounter between tourist and host may be symmetrical and balanced in the sense of power and control over resources or it may be asymmetrical or unbalanced (de Kadt, 1979). In a study by Waitt (2003), the social exchange framework and the life-cycle concept are both used to explain the changing enthusiasm and support for the Sydney Olympics between 1998 and 2000 and the different responses in Sydney neighborhoods.

Another theory has recently been introduced into the tourism literature by Pearce and associates (1996). They suggest that *social representations theory* offers potential for understanding commonalities in resident perceptions and attitudes rather than focusing on their differences. Social representations theory is concerned with describing and understanding how and what people think in their ongoing everyday experiences and how a wider social reality influences these thoughts (Billig, 1993; Moscovici, 1984). Social representations are meta-systems that include values, beliefs, and common-sense explanations of how the world operates. Moscovici (1973) defines social representations as "cognitive systems with a logic and language of their own and a pattern of implication, relevant to both values and concepts, and with a characteristic kind of discourse. They do not represent simple 'opinions about,' 'images of,' or 'attitudes towards' but 'theories' or 'branches of knowledge' in their own right for the discovery and organization of reality" (p. xiii, cited in Pearce et al., 1996, p. 38). These systems he describes as having two main functions: "First to establish an order which will enable individuals to orientate themselves in their material and social world and to master it; and secondly to enable communication to take place among members of a community by providing them with a way of social exchange and a code for naming and classifying unambiguously the various aspects of the world and their individual and group history" (Moscovici, 1973, p. xiii, cited in Pearce et al., 1996, p. 38).

A core function of social representations is to make the unfamiliar familiar (Moscovici 1981, 1984, 1988). Two processes, anchoring and objectification, are important in the naming, classifying, and defining functions of social representations. Anchoring, according to Moscovici (1981), allows us to name, classify, and categorize a new and unfamiliar object by comparing it to what we know already. Objectification enables one to take abstract concepts and ideas and make them ordinary and concrete. It is concerned with building up images of the concept or idea.

Social representations are particularly useful for explaining social conflict or reactions to salient issues such as the creation of a new tourism attraction within the community that may alter the balance of existing power relations. Conflict brings social representations out in the open and individuals in arguments are more likely to use social representations to support their judgments (Billig, 1993). Differences in representations held by the parties in conflict help to explain why they are unable to agree on simple facts, since evidence is interpreted differently by using different "branches of knowledge." These ordinary world-views or social representations have a very powerful influence on people's perceptions, decisions, and actions. Although social representations can and do influence individual thinking, they are not deterministic. Individuals have a role in the construction and development of social representations and can choose between alternative social representations (Pearce et al., 1996).

As already noted, individual resident perceptions and attitudes toward tourism were recently linked to the study of social representations by Pearce and colleagues (1996). Through secondary analysis of existing studies from Hawaii and New Zealand, they found strong evidence for the utility of recasting or developing a new conceptual framework under the lens of social representations. Their results show that different social representations are likely to be held by different groups—for example, "tourism developers and beneficiaries, tourism workers, the broad community and specific community groups with strongly identified moral and ethnic traditions" (p. 138). This finding is consistent with "social representation theory," as the benefits and costs of tourism are neither actually or perceived to be distributed equally. They conclude with a series of Australian examples that demonstrate social representations in action. Some research in recent studies has been based on this theoretical framework (Fredline and Faulkner, 2000; Lee et al., 2003), and they are now including reference to the theory in their identification of cluster sub-groups.

Pearce and colleagues (1996, p. 95) suggest that initially the social representations may be emancipated, and a large proportion of the population holds a variety of such representations (for example, tourism as an economic force, a local environmental concern, or as a positive mix of people). A few tightly knit groups may hold more detailed hegemonic social representations (for example, tourism as a savior, tourism as an environment wrecker, or tourism as an agent of over-development). At times of crisis, perhaps when tourism develops too fast and is perceived as being out of control, individuals holding emancipated views may be drawn to the polemic positions. Polarized views may be further deepened if the community is divided on an ethnic basis (Wyllie, 1998; D'Hauteserre, 2001). After the crisis, such polemic positions may fade. This theorizing has parallels in the concept of social disruption as communities adapt to change and also as part of an issue attention cycle whereby the issue becomes less salient and community concerns shift elsewhere.

Some researchers have developed scales to indicate overall attitude toward tourism by combining perceptions of the impacts of tourism (Lankford and Howard, 1994; Ap and Crompton, 1998; Smith and Krannich, 1998; Carmichael, 2000). Pearce and associates (1996) suggest that this logic could be reversed and that perhaps it is the overall image of tourism and tourists and associated beliefs that structure the way impacts are perceived and felt.

Traditionally, attitude research has focused on individual and group differences instead of searching for commonalities and consensus, as suggested in a social representations framework. If social representations are present, it is likely that within a group or sub-group there may be uniformity in the way people perceive and react to tourism impacts. A few studies have used cluster analysis to define groups on the basis of their attitudes toward tourism (Davis et al., 1988; Madrigal, 1995; Ryan and Montgomery, 1994). However, these studies do not link the consensus found within the community sub-groups to social representations or to the processes of anchoring and objectification.

There is some common ground between life-cycle concepts and social representations theory. Ryan and colleagues (1998) compare resident attitudes toward tourism in rural areas in a town in the United Kingdom with a town in New Zealand, both at different stages in the development of tourism. They identify the importance of studying residents' value systems in understanding resident attitudes. "It is not tourism itself that is a determinant of attitude but rather tourism development is simply a catalyst for the expression of a view which is in accordance with a person's value system" (Ryan et al., 1998, p. 117). They suggest that in more mature destinations, where tourism is more noticeable, such core values may be triggered so that residents tend to become more strongly opposed or supportive of tourism. In addition, work by Lindberg and Johnson (1997) emphasizes the importance of value systems in resident attitude research, and Williams and Lawson (2001) identify the importance of understanding the "community issues" profile of their cluster groupings of residents and suggest the potential of a values-based approach.

In summary, three theories—life cycle theory, social exchange theory, and the theory of social representations—provide a sound basis for understanding resident attitudes toward tourism. Before outlining the links between these theories and quality tourism experiences, this section concludes with a few suggestions for future directions in theory development.

It seems that resident attitudes are influenced by (1) the types of tourism and tourism development and (2) the types of residents. First, there is the potential for theory development in examining *different types of tourism* and their effect on perceived impact, resident attitudes, and resident quality of life. Large-scale quality resort developments consume local resources and local access to space. They may create more resentment than smaller-scale developments. For example, in the case of Malta, Boissevain and Theuma (1988) argue that "quality tourism's infrastructure include luxury hotels, golf courses and marinas. These consume more natural resources than mass sun, sand and sea tourism for which the infrastructure was already in place. Recent public protests about threats to Malta have all concerned new projects aimed at attracting up-market tourists" (pp. 98-99). Bramwell (2003) suggests the need to examine resident attitudes and reactions to various forms of tourism that develop in different ways and at changing rates, often producing complex and ambiguous impacts and responses. Although current thinking attests that independent travelers may have greater impact on resident attitudes because of the greater direct level of contact, it may be the effects of tourism infrastructure and the scale of development that lead to more negative attitudes.

Second, focus on the *types of residents* and sub-groups within the resident population offers potential for theory development. A grounded theory and emic approach could be taken toward theory development and qualitative research methodologies used, as in the study by Brunt and Courtney (1999). A number of questions may be raised here about the types of tourists and the types of residents that could become the basis of new conceptual frameworks. How similar are hosts to visitor populations? Are residents newcomers to the area? What is the mix of foreign residents (developers, condo owners) and indigenous native residents? What is their sense of place and community attachment? What are their values? What are their views on acceptable levels of change? What is important to their quality of life? What is their level of contact with tourists? It should be possible to link some of these questions about residents and tourists with all, or at least some, of the existing theories (described earlier) to produce a dynamic conceptual model. Such a model would include change over time, social interactions, and different perspectives and viewpoints of different types of residents and visitors. Some progress toward the application of different theoretical frameworks applied to different resident groups was made in a recent study by Banks (2004).

The traditional life-cycle model suggests a worsening in resident attitudes over time, but this is not always the case (Getz, 1994). The different trajectories of resort cycle development, as hypothesized by Weaver (2000), means that there could be a series of resident attitude change models reflecting different levels of sustainability in resort development.

One strong theme that has emerged in this literature review that relates to resident attitudes is the need for community input into tourism decision making (see also Chapter Six). Embedded in this concept is access to power (Madrigal [1995] based on Molotch's [1976] growth machine ideas). The case study in Chapter Ten of this book explores further power relationships in communities in the analysis of contested spaces, access to resources, and power changes within the context of Native American casino developments in southeast Connecticut.

It is clear that tourism communities are not static but constantly evolving places in terms of tourism development, resident attitudes toward tourism, resident power relationships, and resident control over resources. Such changes have implications for residents' attitudes toward tourists, residents' interaction with tourists and tourists' perception of the quality of their tourism experience. Just as theory has begun to develop to conceptualize and explain changing and diverse resident attitudes within a tourism context, there are now emerging methodological advances in the measurement of resident attitudes toward tourism.

Advances in Methods: Measurement, Scales, and Modeling

In Ap's review of the research literature on resident attitudes, as well as critiquing the lack of theoretical orientation, he suggests that "operational definitions of central concepts are underdeveloped and reliability and validity measures typically have not been reported" (1990, p. 666). Despite criticisms of its lack of theoretical foundation (Pearce et al., 1996) and reservations about the use of a standard scale (Preglau, 1994), an excellent methodological advance was made by Lankford and Howard (1994) in their innovative attempt to create a Tourism Impact Attitude Scale (TIAS) for resident attitudes in a rural area in Oregon. They were first to provide a standardized tool for measuring resident attitudes toward tourism in different contexts. They generated a large item pool (92 items) from a literature review and panel of experts. Scale purification and Cronbach's alpha was used to reduce the item pool to 50. The item pool was further reduced to 27 after consistency analysis. These scale items were measured on a five-point Likert scale. Principal components analysis with an oblique rotation was used on the scale variable, and two factors were revealed: Factor 1: concern for local tourism development and Factor 2: personal and community benefits. Follow-up studies have used the TIAS for tourism in general (Rollins, 1997) and for a specific type of tourism, where the scale was modified to use the word *casino* instead of *tourism* (Jones, 2003). The Rollins (1997) study in Nanaimo, British Columbia, uncovered four factors: Factor 1: general opinions about tourism; Factor 2: perceived benefits to the community; Factor 3: perceived negative impacts; Factor 4: perceived personal benefits. Although these factors were different from those identified by Lankford and Howard, Rollins suggests that the four-factor solution is very similar and offers a more descriptive explanation. Rollins also raised the question, "Is it appropriate to lump all tourism together and measure host perceptions or is it more useful to measure host responses to a particular activity?"

Jones (2003) developed a 24-item TIAS to apply to the measurement of resident perceptions of the Mohegan Sun casino in Montville, Connecticut. She used principal axis factor analysis with oblique rotation to identify three factors: Factor 1: development issues; Factor 2: standard of living; Factor 3: change and promotion. Closer inspection of the items that loaded on these factors shows that factor 3 includes many environmental quality-of-life variables that are impacted negatively by the change, whereas Factor 2 has more of the positive economic variables. Bachleitner and Zins (1999) used a modified version of the TIAS that added a distinct dimension of environmental influences in a study of cultural tourism impacts on residents in Styria, Austria.

Ap and Crompton (1998) followed rigorous scale development and scale purification procedures to develop a tourism impact scale comprising of seven domains: social and cultural, economic, crowding and congestion, environmental, services, taxes, and community attitudes. There were acceptable levels of internal consistency and relatively high convergent validity. It was tested in three diverse Texas communities and the consistency in the results showed that it could easily be adapted and applied in other communities. This scale differs in that an index was developed for each variable that was derived from the beliefs about the variable multiplied by the respondent's level of like or dislike of the change. The use of the multiplicative function is based on Fishbein's (1963) theory of reasoned action multiattribute model. Respondents reply on a Likert-type scale about their beliefs that tourism brings the changes and then also evaluate the degree to which they like or dislike the changes. Quality of life is inferred rather than directly measured in the variables included in the scale.

However, one scale does not fit all conditions. Tourism scholars have recently developed resident attitude scales for different types of tourism—for example, river-based casinos (Chen and Hsu, 2001), limited stakes casino gambling (Kang et al., 1996), and special events social impacts (Fredline et al., 2003). In these scales, it is usually implied that the "composite score of each factor could be treated as an indicator monitoring the change in quality of life" and "that such indicators can assist tourism planners, community leaders and business owners to render strategies for sustaining quality of life" (Chen and Hsu, 2001, p. 463).

The scale development process used in these studies is sophisticated in analytical techniques, typically involving exploratory factor analysis, item-total inter-correlation, reliability testing using Cronbach's alpha, and various validity assessment procedures as well as confirmatory factor analysis. Nevertheless, the variety of factors revealed in these studies suggests little consistency of results that can be well integrated into theory development. Part of the problem might be the limited degree to which the studies use the concept of *quality of life* explicitly in the analysis. Often, quality of life is merely inferred from the array of impacts measured. Sometimes regression analysis is used to predict the relationship between perceived impacts and a quality-of-life overall assessment variable, as in the study by Roehl (1999). However, rarely are theoretical frameworks used that focus explicitly on quality-of-life issues in this way. A notable exception to this is the study by Perdue and associates (1999) that used a specific quality-of-life scale based on four items (alpha 0.88): I would like to move away from_____; I am satisfied with_____ as a place to live; The future of _____ looks bright; and Taking everything into account (family, work, leisure, safety, etc.) how satisfied are you with the quality of life in_____?

In addition, there is recent progress in modeling resident attitudes with the use of structural equation modeling (Gursoy et al., 2002; Lee and Back, 2003; Ko and Stewart, 2002) with trade-off analysis (Lindberg et al., 1999; Lindberg et al., 2001) and multidimensional scaling (McNicol, in press; Lawson et al., 1998). This research provides evidence of the importance of different perceived benefits and costs in influencing attitudes toward tourism and makes incremental progress in theory development.

Resident Attitudes and Their Link with Resident Behaviors and Coping Strategies

Do local residents demonstrate their attitudes toward tourism through follow-up behavior and reactions and interactions with tourists? It is more likely that the three components of attitudes (cognitive/affective/behavioral) described earlier will be related in a consistent manner, if measurement is directed toward a specific attraction rather than toward tourism in general. However, the cognitive/affective/behavior relationship is not deterministic and the strength of the relationship seems to be influenced by a number of factors, including situation factors, the manner in which attitudes are formed, and the relevance or importance of an attitude (Ajzen and Fishbein, 1980). It is recognized that previous studies have not always found this link. Indeed, many residents do nothing about their negative feelings about tourism and tourists, possibly due to perceived lack of behavioral control (Ajzen, 1991), which has been found to be an important variable in predicting behavior.

Abler and colleagues' (1975) model takes into account variation in resident attitudes and behaviors within the same geographic area. A four-cell matrix is used to classify persons by their attitudes and behaviors. On any given issue, one's attitude may be negative or positive and one's behavior may be active or passive. Therefore, four combinations are possible: active-positive: aggressively promoting a position in favor of something; active-negative: aggressively opposing something; passive-positive: passively agreeing with and accepting something; and passive-negative:

resigned acceptance of something one disagrees with. The model does not indicate the relative importance of the four categories, and, although it suggests there will be change over time, it does not outline the anticipated direction of change over time. Nor does it allow for neutral categories on either dimension. Carmichael (2000) operationalized this model, and residents were successfully segmented by their attitudes and behaviors. In addition, this model can help to explain the political reaction to tourism by small groups (Getz, 1994).

Limited support for this model comes from Ap and Crompton (1993), who reported on resident reactions to tourism in four Texas communities. They suggested that resident reactions to tourism could be placed on a continuum comprising four strategies: embracement, tolerance, adjustment, and withdrawal. *Embracement* mirrored *aggressive promotion; tolerance* (or take it or leave it ambivalence) was consistent with *passive acceptance; adjustment* and *withdrawal* did not fit the scheme suggested by the matrix model; and they found no evidence for resistance through aggressive opposition. However, their objectives and research design did not enable them to test the attitude/behavioral relationship empirically.

Another scheme developed by Dogan (1989) focused on behavioral coping strategies of indigenous peoples as a reaction to the effects of international tourism. The suggested strategies of adoption, boundary maintenance, retreatism, and resistance exhibit similar characteristics to the model put forth by Abler and colleagues (1975), while not specifically testing its findings. Dogan's (1989) and Ap and Crompton's (1993) models are similar in that they are both behavioral models but they may both be critiqued in that they do not sufficiently link or explore the attitude/behavior relationship.

There are some subtle coping strategies that residents use when living in areas that receive large numbers of tourists, which could relate to the adjustment and withdrawal strategies discussed by Ap and Crompton (1993). Joseph and Kavoori (2001) describe the coping strategies of a Hindu religious community when reconciling the threats of western tourists to their religious traditions while enjoying the economic benefits from tourists. This ambivalence is resolved through "mediated resistance" that allows the host community to condemn tourism collectively while participating in it on an individual basis. Adjustment occurs through rhetoric and psychological rationalization of behavior. A different kind of withdrawal is observed in Malta, where residents retreat into speaking the Maltese language, even though they can speak English, when tourists are around, so that they can maintain control over their personal space (Bramwell, 2003).

In summary, different types of residents cope in different ways to their perceived impacts of tourism development and tourists in their midst. Such reactions may be passive or active, masked or open, and will, subtly or markedly, affect the quality of tourism experiences for tourists.

Resident Coping Strategies and the Link with Tourism Experiences and Tourist Behaviors

This section returns briefly to the three key frameworks that have informed and progressed theoretical understanding of residents' perceptions and attitudes toward tourism and their relevance to quality tourism experiences. Social exchange theory has implications for tourists' perceptions of residents and communities as well as residents' perceptions of tourists and tourism. It can partly answer the question: How do tourists feel about residents and how do residents influence quality tourism experiences? Where the exchange relationship is balanced or unequal but to the advantage of tourists, then they will perceive positive benefits from social interaction with host community residents. In marketing terms, they will get "value for money" (what you get for what you pay). It is debatable whether tourists prefer an equal situation or one that is weighted in the tourist's favor. It is tempting to think they would prefer the latter in an economic transaction. However, for cultural learning and mutual understanding the equal situation is likely to be preferable not just for the tourism experience but for the long-term balance to locals for sustainability.

Life-cycle models also offer potential for understanding quality tourism experiences. As resort development occurs, the quaintness and uniqueness leaves the place (Christaller, 1964; Young, 1982) and the tourist as well as the resident is faced with the negative impacts related to physical, environmental, and social constraints. Doxey's "Irridex" model (1975), although developed to apply to residents, might apply also to tourist experiences, either as the tourists visit the same destination at different time periods or as they change attitudes during the duration of a single trip. The author is unaware of any research that applies such a model within the tourism context. Suitable destinations for such research might be in Caribbean countries in which high levels of visitor harassment occurs (De Albuquerque and McElroy, 2001). The framework might also apply in understanding visitors' annoyance with each other—for example, other members of the participants on a bus group tour or cruise. Suggested stages might be anticipation and excitement; annoyance; and adjustment and coping strategies. The culture shock literature, although developed to apply to long-term sojourners, gives some insight into how the quality of a tourist's experience may change over the course of a trip. Reisinger and Turner (2003) explain that many tourists experience different types of culture shock (role shock, language shock, culture fatigue, transition shock, re-entry shock) during their travel to and from a foreign destination. *Culture shock* is defined as "reaction of sojourners to problems encountered in dealing with host members" (Bochner, 1982, p. 172, cited in Reisinger and Turner, 2003, p. 57). Culture shock influences the quality of the tourism experience in stages that may be likened to the framework suggested by Doxey (1975) for the resident "Irridex." For example, Oberg (1960) identifies four stages of culture shock: (1) a honeymoon stage (fascination and optimism); (2) a hostility stage (negative attitudes toward host society and other sojourners); (3) a recovery stage (increased ability to cope in the new environment), and (4) an adjustment stage (acceptance and enjoyment of the new environment). Reisinger and Turner (2003, p. 62) summarize the patterns of culture shock and adjustment as suggested in a number of culture shock stage models (Oberg,1960; Gullahorn and Gullahorn, 1963; Brein and David, 1971; Hofstede, 1997; Jandt, 1998). All involve similar transitions from early honeymoon, optimism, and euphoria toward later stages of hostility and irritation followed by recovery, adaptation, and adjustment. Gullahorn and Gullahorn (1963) add stages of reverse culture shock and readjustment after returning home.

While these culture shock models imply simple unidirectional changes similar to Doxey's model, they do not offer attempts to theorize the quality of the tourism experience, either for different types of tourists (see Chapter Five) or in contact situations with different types of local residents. The intensity and the duration of culture shock are likely to depend on length of stay, type of tourist, type of travel arrangements, and cultural differences between the foreigner and the local resident. Depending on the length of stay, some tourists may never leave the honeymoon stage—a fact that some tourism marketers, tour companies, and tour guides may find appealing.

Social representations theory has been suggested to explain how residents make sense of their knowledge about tourism. This theory may also be used in explaining how tourists interpret the quality of their tourism experience. As Schwandt (2000, p. 197) suggests, "We do not construct our interpretations in isolation but against a backdrop of shared understandings." Some residents are able to play a role in assisting with the social construction of the tourism experience for the tourists. Tour guides may act as mediators in making the unfamiliar familiar, at least to the extent that tourists are seeking familiarity. This may partly explain the varying degrees of quality tourism experiences among tourists within the same setting. Chapter Four further explores issues of brokering, familiarity, and their relationship to quality tourism experiences.

Chapter Implications

The theme of this chapter is the linkage between quality of life for local residents in a tourism region and quality of life for tourists, as shown in Figure 7-1. Although there is some development of theory that has taken place over the last 10 years, we still have a variety of different hypotheses that make up a theoretical mismatch. Social exchange theory, social representations, and life cycle and carrying capacity concepts help to explain variety in resident attitudes toward tourism and tourists over time, space, and place, as well as at a personal level. However, there are a number of gaps in theory development that need to be addressed, such as the type of tourist and the type of resident in the context of different levels of social interaction. It may be worth exploring the desired levels of social interaction of both residents and visitors, whether those desired levels of interaction are achieved, and how that relates to quality. Does quality mean being comfortable and relaxed with the level and type of social interaction accepted and nonthreatened but at the same time stimulated?

It is further suggested in this review that there is the potential to use the theory developed for understanding resident attitudes and apply this theory to tourists. The quality tourism experience could be framed in life-cycle concepts and an "Irridex" scale for tourists, conceptualized in a similar manner to models posed in the culture shock literature. Social exchange theory offers a framework for understanding tourists' attitudes toward residents and the resulting impact on quality tourism experiences. Such a framework would be based on perceived benefits and costs for the tourist. Similarly, social representations and tourist values research may help explain how different types of tourists perceive the quality of their tourism experiences and form images of residents. Perhaps an application of such theory could be used to explore tourist and guide interaction and its effect on perceptions of quality. Perceptions of tourists and their attitudes toward host communities remains an area about which we know relatively little and which offers the potential for theory development. Furthermore, practitioners and destination marketing organizations would benefit from knowing how locals are perceived and how they may, or may not, contribute to quality tourism experiences.

To reiterate, this review has shown that there are a number of common factors that influence both the quality of life for residents and quality tourism experiences. These factors are (1) the number and type of residents, (2) the number and type of tourists, (3) social exchange relationships between residents and tourists, (4) social representations of each other, and (5) the type of tourism development. It is suggested that this describes a dynamic situation and that the life-cycle trajectory of the resort cycle will mean that these relationships need to be investigated over time. Figure 7-2 describes how experiences for both visitor and local residents are linked by such situational factors.

In addition to theory development, the resident perceptions/attitudes/impacts literature has developed methods and measurement scales. However, the explicit use of the quality-of-life concept in such studies is not usually addressed, although it is implicitly applied. In response to this research gap, a case study is presented in the next chapter that gives a new way of measuring quality of life and resident attitudes toward tourism. A tourism quality-of-life scale is created that includes the beliefs about a specific quality-of-life variable, the importance of that variable to residents' quality of life, and the degree to which tourism has had an impact on that specific variable.

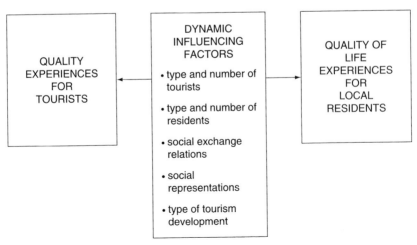

Figure 7.2 Factors Influencing Quality of Life for Residents and Quality Experiences of Tourists within a Tourism Context.

References

Abler, R., Janelle, D., Philbrick, A., and J. Sommer. (1975). *Human Geography in a Shrinking World*. North Scituate, MA: Duxbury Press.

Ajzen, I. (1991). The Theory of Planned Behavior. *Organizational Behavior and Human Decision Processes*, 50, 179-211.

Ajzen, I., and M. Fishbein. (1980). *Understanding Attitudes and Predicting Social Behavior*. Englewood Cliffs, NJ: Prentice-Hall.

Akis, S., Peristianis, N., and J. Warner. (1996). Resident attitudes to tourism development: The case of Cyprus. *Tourism Management*, **17** (7), 481-494.

Allen, L.R., Hafer, H.R., Long, P.T., and R.R. Perdue. (1993). Rural residents' attitudes toward recreation and tourism development. *Journal of Travel Research*, **1** (4), 27-37.

Ap, J. (1990). Residents' perception research of the social impacts of tourism. *Annals of Tourism Research*, **17** (4), 610-616.

Ap, J. (1992). Residents' perceptions of tourism impacts. *Annals of Tourism Research*, **19**, 665-690.

Ap, J., and J.L Crompton. (1993). Resident strategies for responding to tourism impacts. *Journal of Travel Research*, **32** (1), 47-50.

Ap, J., and J.L.Crompton. (1998). Developing and testing a tourism impact scale. *Journal of Travel Research*, **37** (2), 120-130.

Bachleitner, R., and A.H. Zins. (1999). Cultural tourism in rural areas: The residents' perspective. *Journal of Business Research*, **44**, 199-209.

Banks, S. (2004). Tourism Impacts as Perceived by Three Resident Typology Groups. Paper presented at the International TTRA Conference, Montreal, Canada.

Billig, M. (1993). Studying the thinking society: Social representations, rhetoric and attitudes. In G.M. Breakwell and D.V. Canter (Eds.), *Empirical Approaches to Social Representations* (pp. 39-62). Oxford: Clarendon Press.

Bochner, S. (1982). *Cultures in Contact: Studies in Cross-Cultural Interaction*. Oxford [Oxfordshire]; New York: Pergamon.

Boissevain, J., and N. Theuma. (1998). Contested space, planners, tourists, developers and environmentalists. In S. Abram and J. Walden (Eds.), *Anthropological Perspectives on Local Development* (pp. 96-119). London: Routledge.

Bramwell, B. (2003). Maltese responses to tourism. *Annals of Tourism Research*, **30** (3), 581-605.

Brein, M., and K.H. David. (1971). Intercultural communication and the adjustment of the sojourner. *Psychology Bulletin*, **76** (3), 215-230.

Brunt, P., and P. Courtney. (1999). Host perceptions of socio-cultural impacts. *Annals of Tourism Research*, **26** (3), 493-515.

Butler, R. (1974). Social implications of tourism development. *Annals of Tourism Research*, **2** (2), 100-111.

Butler, R. (1975). Tourism as an agent of social change. *Tourism as a Factor in Regional and National Development* (Occasional Paper 4., pp. 85-90). Peterborough, Ontario: Department of Geography, Trent University,

Butler, R. (1980). The concept of a tourist area cycle of evolution: Implication for management of resources. *Canadian Geographer*, **24**, 5-12.

Caneday, L., and J. Zeiger. (1991). The social, economic and environmental costs of tourism to a gaming community as perceived by its residents. *Journal of Travel Research*, **27** (2), 2-8.

Carmichael, B.A. (2000). A matrix model of resident attitudes and behaviors in a rapidly changing tourism area. *Tourism Management,* **21,** 601-611.

Carmichael, B.A., Peppard, D.M. Jr., and F. Boudreau. (1996). Mega-resort on my doorstep: Local resident attitudes toward Foxwoods Casino, and casino gambling on nearby Indian reservation land. *Journal of Travel Research,* **34** (3), 9-16.

Chen, J.S., and Hsu, C.H.C. (2001). Developing and validating a riverboat gaming impact scale. *Annals of Tourism Research,* **28** (2), 459-476.

Christaller, W. (1964). Some considerations of tourism locations in Europe. *Papers and Proceedings of the Regional Science Association,* **12,** 95-105.

Davis, D., Allen, J., and R.M. Cozenza. (1988). Segmenting local residents by their attitudes, interests and opinions towards tourism. *Journal of Travel Research,* **27** (2), 2-8.

De Albuquerque, K., and J.L. McElroy. (2001). Tourism harassment: Barbados survey results. *Annals of Tourism Research.* **28** (2), 477-492.

de Kadt, E. (1979). *Tourism: Passport to Development?* New York: Oxford University Press.

D'Hauteserre, A.M. (2001). Representations of rurality: Is Foxwoods Casino Resort threatening the quality of life in southeast Connecticut? *Tourism Geographies,* **3** (4), 405-429.

Dogan, H.F. (1989). Forms of adjustment: Socio-cultural impacts of tourism. *Annals of Tourism Research,* **16,** 216-236.

Doxey, G.V. (1975). A Causation Theory of Visitor-Resident Irritants, Methodology and Research Inferences. *The Impact of Tourism. Sixth Annual Conference Proceedings of the Travel and Tourism Research Association* (pp. 195-198). San Diego.

Eadington, W.R. (1986). Impact of casino gambling on the community: Comment on Pizam and Pokela. *Annals of Tourism Research,* **13,** 279-285.

England, J.L., and S.L. Albrecht. (1984). Boomtowns and social disruption. *Rural Sociology,* **49,** 230-246.

Fick, G.R., and J.R.B. Ritchie. (1991). Measuring service quality in the travel and tourism industry. *Journal of Travel Research,* **30,** 2-9.

Fishbein, M. (1963). An investigation of the relationship between beliefs about an object and attitude toward that object. *Human Relations,* **16,** 233-240.

Fredline, E., and B. Faulkner. (2000). Host community reactions. A cluster analysis. *Annals of Tourism Research,* **27** (3), 763-784.

Fredline, E., Jago, L., and M. Deery. (2003). The development of a generic scale to measure the social impacts of events. *Event Management,* **8** (1), 23-37.

Getz, D. (1994). Resident attitudes towards tourism. A longitudinal study in the Spey Valley, Scotland. *Tourism Management,* **15** (4), 247-258.

Gilbert, D., and M. Clark. (1997). An exploratory examination of urban tourism impact, with reference to residents attitudes in the cities of Canterbury and Guildford. *Cities,* **14** (6), 343-352.

Gullahorn, J.E., and J.T. Gullahorn. (1963). An extension of the U-curve hypothesis. *Journal of Social Issues,* **19** (3), 33-47.

Gursoy, D., C. Jurowski, and M. Uysal. (2002). Resident attitudes: A structural modelling approach. *Annals of Tourism Research* **29** (1), 79-105.

Haralambopoulos, N., and A. Pizam. (1996). Perceived impacts of tourism: The case of Samos. *Annals of Tourism Research,* **22** (3), 503-526.

Hernandez, S.A., Cohen, J., and H.L. Garcia. (1996). Resident attitudes towards an instant resort enclave. *Annals of Tourism Research,* **23** (4), 755-779.

Hofstede, G. (1997). *Culture and organizations: Software of the mind: New intercultural cooperation and its importance for survival.* New York: McGraw Hill.

Jandt, F.E (1998). *Intercultural Communication* (2nd ed.). Thousand Oaks, CA: Sage.

Johnson, J.D., Snepenger, D.J., and S.Akis. (1994). Residents' perceptions of tourism development. *Annals of Tourism Research,* **21** (3), 629-642.

Jones, J. L. (2003). Modifying the Tourism Impact Scale (TIAS) to Explore Casino Impacts and Resident Attitudes. Unpublished doctoral dissertation, Storrs: University of Connecticut.

Joseph, C.A., and Kavoori, A.P. (2001). Mediated resistance tourism and the host community. *Annals of Tourism Research,* **28** (4), 998-1009.

Jurowski, C., M. Usal, and R.D. Williams. (1997). A theoretical analysis off host community resident reactions to tourism. *Journal of Travel Research* **36** (2), 3-11.

Kang, Y-S., Long, P.T., and Perdue, R.R. (1996). Resident attitudes toward legal gambling. *Annals of Tourism Research,* **23** (1), 71-85.

Keogh, B. (1990). Public participation in community tourism planning. *Annals of Tourism Research,* **17,** 449-465.

Knox, J.M. (1982). Resident-visitor interaction: A review of the literature and general policy alternatives. In F. Rajotte (Ed.), *The Impact of Tourism Development in the Pacific* (pp. 76-107). Peterborough, Ontario: Environmental Resources Study Programme, Trent University.

Ko, D-W., and W.P. Stewart. (2002). A structural equation mode of residents' attitudes for tourism development. *Tourism Management,* **23,** 521-530.

Kotler, P. (1994). *Marketing Management: Analysis, Planning and Implementation* (8th ed.). Engelwood Cliffs, NJ: Prentice-Hall.

Kotler, P., Bowen, J., and J. Makens. (2003). *Marketing for Hospitality and Tourism* (3rd ed.). Englewood Cliffs, NJ: Prentice-Hall.

Lankford, S.V., and D.R. Howard. (1994). Developing a tourism impact attitude scale. *Annals of Tourism Research,* **21,** 121-139.

Lawson, R.W., Williams, J., Young, T., and J. Cossens. (1998). A comparison of residents' attitudes towards tourism in 10 New Zealand destinations. *Tourism Management,* **19** (3), 247-256.

LeBlanc, G. (1992). Factors affecting customer evaluations of service quality in travel agencies: An investigation of customer perspectives. *Journal of Travel Research,* **30,** 10-16.

Lee, C-K., and K.J. Back. (2003). Pre- and post-casino impact of residents' perceptions. *Annals of Tourism Research,* **30** (4), 868-885.

Lee, C-K., Kim, S-S., and S. Kang. (2003). Perceptions of casino impacts—A longitudinal study. *Tourism Management,* **24** (1), 45-55.

Lindberg, K., Andersson, T.D., and B.G.C. Dellaert. (2001). Tourism development: Assessing social gains and losses. *Annals of Tourism Research,* **28** (4), 1010-1030.

Lindberg, K., Dellaert, B.G., and C.R. Rassing. (1999). Resident tradeoffs: A choice modeling approach. *Annals of Tourism Research,* **26** (3), 555-569.

Lindberg, K., and R.L. Johnson. (1997). Modeling resident attitudes toward tourism. *Annals of Tourism Research,* **24** (20), 402-424.

Long, P.T. (1996). Early impacts of limited stakes gambling on rural community life. *Tourism Management,* **117** (5), 341-353.

Long, P.T., Perdue, R.R., and L. Allen. (1990). Rural resident tourism perceptions and attitudes by community level of tourism. *Journal of Travel Research,* **28** (3), 3-9.

McCool, S., and N. Moisey. (1996). Monitoring resident attitudes toward tourism. *Tourism Analysis*, **1**, 29-37.

McDoughall, G., and H. Munro. (1987). Scaling and attitude measurement in tourism and travel research. In J.R.B. Ritchie and C. Goeldner (Eds.), *Travel Tourism and Hospitality Research*. New York: Wiley.

McNicol, B. (2004, in press). Group destination images of proposed tourism resort developments: Identifying resident and developer contrasts. *Tourism Analysis*.

Madrigal, R. (1993). A tale of tourism in two cities. *Annals of Tourism Research*, **20**, 336-353.

Madrigal, R. (1995). Residents' perceptions and the role of government. *Annals of Tourism Research*, **22** (1), 86-102.

Mason, P., and J. Cheyne. (2000). Residents' attitudes to proposed tourism development. *Annals of Tourism Research*, **27** (2), 391-411.

Mathieson, A., and G. Wall. (1982). *Tourism: Economic, Physical and Social Impacts*. New York: John Wiley and Sons.

Mo, C., Howard, D.R., and M.E. Havitz. (1993). Testing an international tourist role typology. *Annals of Tourism Research*, **14** (2), 319-335.

Molotch, H. (1976). The city as a growth machine: Towards a political economy of place. *American Journal of Sociology*, **82**, 309-322.

Moscovici, S. (1973). Foreword. (D. Graham, Trans.). In C. Herzlich (Ed.), *Health and Illness* (pp. ix-xiv). London: Academic Press.

Moscovici, S. (1981). On social representations. In J.P. Forgas (Ed.), *Social Cognition: Perspectives on Everyday Understanding* (pp. 181-209). London: Academic Press.

Moscovici, S. (1984). The phenomenon of social representations. In R.M. Farr and S. Moscovici (Eds.), *Social Representations* (pp. 3-69). Cambridge: Cambridge University Press.

Moscovici, S. (1988). Notes towards a description of social representations. *European Journal of Social Psychology*, **18**, 211-250.

Murphy, P., Pritchard, M.P., and B. Smith. (2000). The destination product and its impact on traveler perceptions. *Tourism Management*, **21**, 43-52.

Murphy, P.E. (1985). *Tourism: A Community Approach*. New York: Methuen.

Oberg, K. (1960). Culture shock: Adjustment to new cultural environments. *Practical Anthropology*, **7**, 177-182.

Pearce, P., Moscardo, G., and G.F. Ross (1996). *Tourism Community Relationships*. Oxford, UK: Elsevier Science Ltd.

Perdue, R.R., Long, T.L., and L. Allen. (1990). Resident support for tourism development. *Annals of Tourism Research*, **17** (4), 586-599.

Perdue, R.R., Long, P.T., and Y.S. Kang. (1999). Boomtown tourism and resident quality of life: The marketing of gaming to host community residents. *Journal of Business Research*, **44**, 165-177.

Preglau, M. (1994). Is TIAS a valid tourism impact management tool? *Annals of Tourism Research*, 828-829.

Reisinger, Y., and L.W. Turner. (2003). *Cross-Cultural Behaviour in Tourism: Concepts and Analysis*. Jordan Hill, Oxford: Butterworth-Heinemann.

Richards, G. (1999). Vacations and the quality of life: Patterns and structures. *Journal of Business Research*, **44**, 189-198.

Roehl, W. (1999). Quality of life issues in a casino destination. *Journal of Business Research*, **44**, 223-229.

Rollins, R. (1997). Validation of the TIAS as a tourism tool. *Annals of Tourism Research,* **24** (3), 740-756.

Ryan, C., and D. Montgomery. (1994). The attitudes of Bakewell residents to tourism and issues in community responsive tourism. *Tourism Management*, **15** (5), 258-369.

Ryan, C., Scotland, A., and D. Montgomery. (1998). Resident attitudes to tourism development—A comparative study between Rangitikei, New Zealand and Bakewell, United Kingdom. *Progress in Tourism and Hospitality Research*, **4**, 115-130.

Schwandt, T.A. (2000). Three epistemological stances for qualitative inquiry: Interpretivism, hermeneutics, and social constructionism. In N.K. Denzin and Y.S. Lincoln (Eds.), *Handbook of Qualitative Research* (2nd ed., pp.189-213). Thousand Oaks, CA: Sage.

Smith, M.D., and R.S. Krannich. (1998). Tourism dependence and resident attitudes. *Annals of Tourism Research*, **25** (4) 783-802.

Waitt, G. (2003). Social impacts of the Sydney Olympics. *Annals of Tourism Research*, **30** (1), 194-215.

Wall, G. (1996). Perspectives on tourism in selected Balinese villages. *Annals of Tourism Research,* **23** (1), 123-127.

Weaver, D. (2000). A broad context model of destination development scenarios. *Tourism Management*, **21**, 217-224.

Weaver, D.B., and L.J. Lawton. (2001). Resident perceptions in the urban-rural fringe. *Annals of Tourism Research*, **28** (2), 439-458.

Williams, C., and J. Buswell. (2003). *Service Quality in Leisure and Tourism.* Wallingford, Oxon: CABI Publishing.

Williams, J., and R. Lawson. (2001). Community issues and resident opinions of tourism. *Annals of Tourism Research*, **28** (2), 269-290.

Wyllie, R.W. (1998). Not in our backyard: Opposition to tourism development in a Hawaiian community. *Tourism Recreation Research*, **23** (1), 55-64.

Young, B. (1982). Touristization of traditional Maltese fishing-farming villages. *Tourism Management*, **4** (1), 35-41.

Zeithaml, V.A., and M.J. Bitner. (1996). *Services Marketing.* New York: McGraw-Hill.

8

Tourism and Quality of Life

Kathleen Andereck
Claudia Jurowski

Social and natural conditions of the community in which tourism experiences take place play a pivotal role in the ability of a destination to offer quality tourism experiences. Commonly, a community adapts tourism for its economic benefits based on the theory that an increase in income from tourists will improve the quality of life in the community. Yet, development programs that fail to address goals beyond those related solely to economics may actually degrade the quality of life within a community by worsening social conditions and failing to preserve the natural environment. It is particularly important for tourism development programs to address quality-of-life issues because quality tourism experiences depend on a receptive host population and an attractive natural environment. This chapter adds to current knowledge about how tourism affects the quality of life within the tourist destination and presents a tool that can be used to assess tourism's effect on community quality of life.

Quality-of-Life Measures

Community quality of life is commonly assessed using an aggregate of several economic measures. However, when measures of economic wealth are used alone in evaluating the well-being of a community, many other factors that affect quality of life are discounted (Dowrick et al., 2003; Lawn, 2003; Massam, 2002; Max-Neef, 1995). For example, economic measures often evaluate the efficiency of a project but fail to address equity issues. Increasing income from tourism may have little effect on community welfare when the benefits from the income are not spread throughout the community. (The reader is referred to Chapter Eleven for a detailed discussion of the efficiency and equity issues of community development.) The gross domestic product (GDP) is a clear example of the weakness of an economic measure; it does not consider how income is distributed nor how production affects the environment. Therefore, growth in GDP does not necessarily have a positive impact on community well-being. The value of continued economic growth is questionable when one considers that there is a threshold at which continued growth will result in a lower quality of life because the benefits will be exceeded by the ensuing costs (Lawn, 2003; Max-Neef, 1995). Assessments that combine economic measures with measures of social and environmental conditions relating to the desirability of living and working conditions and perceptions of these life conditions afford a more comprehensive representation of well-being and community quality of life (Pembina, 2001). Ecological economists claim that measuring only the benefits of economic growth without subtracting the costs of attaining the gain gives an inaccurate assessment of success of a development program. The cost of economic development to community quality of life (QOL) include factors such as the weakening of family structure, disruption of social networks, loss of cultural integrity, loss of historical infrastructure, and environmental degradation (crowding, noise, litter, traffic congestion, driving hazards, and air or water pollution).

One such measure, the Human Development Index (HDI), is a composite index that evaluates achievement in three dimensions: a long and healthy life, knowledge, and a decent standard of living (Massam, 2002; United Nations Development Program, 2003). The World Bank's Wealth Accounting system measures four types of assets on a per-capita basis where human-made assets (equivalent to the GDP) are given only 20% of the weight. Other assets used to measure the prosperity of the state are families, communities and institutions, environmental assets, human resources, and social capital (Massam, 2002). Using a similar index, the Genuine Progress Indicator (GPI), the Pembina study concluded that although the production of goods and services increased in Alberta, Canada, over 40 years, the aggregate quality of life declined. The Sustainable Net Benefit Index (SNBI) responds to the environmental economics demand for a cost-benefit analysis. This index separates factors into costs and benefits and present results on a balance sheet, allowing for a clear comparison of the benefits and costs of economic growth (Lawn, 2003). The cost-benefit analysis indices provide a better measure of quality of life because they include aspects that detract from quality of life, as well as those that improve it. For example, in this type of measure the benefits of increased income, tax revenues, and jobs within a community are weighed against the costs that might include the loss of green space, polluted air, or cultural degradation. Community planners can use such indices to determine when the costs of growth outweigh the benefits.

Quality-of-Life Dimensions

The objective measures, even those that broaden the concept to include measures of environmental and social conditions, are incomplete without subjective measures of how individuals evaluate their quality of life. Hence, quality of life has two dimensions—an objective dimension that is external to the individual and a subjective dimension that reflects individual feelings and perceptions. Consequently, quality of life in a community is comprised of the sum of the objective conditions and individual community members' feelings about and perceptions of the objective conditions within the community (*i.e.*, economic activity, climate, social/cultural institutions, and environmental conditions) (Cutter, 1985). The subjective dimension of quality of life is emotive and value-laden, encompassing factors such as life satisfaction, happiness, feelings of well-being, and beliefs about one's standard of living (Davidson and Cotter, 1991; Diener and Suh, 1997; Dissart and Deller, 2000; Grayson and Young, 1994). The inclusion of subjective measures such as personal feelings and perceptions about the external factors is critical to accurately evaluating community quality of life (Dissart and Deller, 2000).

Consequently, policymakers need information about how an area is doing not only from a broad-based quantitative perspective but also from a subjective perspective that incorporates how citizens perceive the factors that contribute to their own quality of life and how they collectively think their region or area is doing (Morrison Institute, 1997). To that end, decision makers need to understand the perspective of community residents in relation to how they experience tourism—in other words, the extent to which residents feel tourism improves or worsens their quality of life. To create quality tourism experiences for both residents and tourists, it is important to identify specific aspects of tourism that reduce the quality of experiences so measures can be taken to mitigate problems. Knowledge of the way residents assess costs and benefits of tourism as well as the extent to which they feel tourism is responsible for those costs and benefits is vital to decision makers. In addition, knowledge of how important various impacts are to residents' quality of life in relation to life satisfaction is critical. This chapter's study addresses these issues and demonstrates a method for determining how tourism experiences are perceived to affect the quality of life of residents of a tourism destination. It extends the findings from traditional resident attitudes studies through the development of a quality-of-life index related to experiences with tourism. The Tourism and Quality of Life index (TQOL) is comprised of three measures: (1) residents' assessments of the importance of quality-of-life indicators; (2) residents' assessments of their satisfaction with indicators; and (3) residents' assessments of tourism's influence on the indicators. The three measures are combined to create the TQOL index and broad domains are identified from 38 tourism-related quality-of-life items. To better understand why residents perceive tourism experiences differently, several variables are investigated as predictor variables for the TQOL domains. The study provides a method useful for describing the subjective dimension of a community's quality of life and for identifying aspects of tourism that need improvement to provide quality tourism experiences.

Tourism and Resident Quality-of-Life Studies

To fully evaluate tourism's role in the quality of life of residents of a tourist destination, residents' perceptions of how tourism impacts their lives must be evaluated. (Chapter Seven discusses a number of theories and resident attitude studies all of which demonstrate the range of residents' experiences with tourism, some of which are positive, and others negative.) Tourism products and facilities such as festivals, restaurants, natural and cultural attractions, and outdoor recreation opportunities facilitate enjoyable tourism experiences for residents in addition to the economic benefits of a higher personal standard of living, increased tax revenues and increased employment that some members of the community enjoy. These positive experiences, however, can be overridden by negative effects such as crowding, traffic and parking problems, increased crime, increased cost of living, friction between tourists and residents, and changes in residents' way of life (Ap

Photographer: Claudia Jurowski

Social and Economic Interaction between Residents and Tourists.

and Crompton, 1993; Bastias-Perex and Var, 1995; McCool and Martin, 1994; Ross, 1992).

The theories presented in the preceding chapter explain factors that affect residents' evaluation of tourism, noting that the factors fall into three basic categories: (1) economic, such as tax burdens, inflation, and job availability; (2) sociocultural, such as community image, the availability of festivals and museums, and awareness of cultural heritage; and (3) environmental, such as crowding, air, water and noise pollution, wildlife destruction, and litter (Andereck, 1995; Marcouiller, 1997; Ryan, 1991). Whereas Chapter Seven includes an in-depth discussion of issues related to resident assessment of tourism impacts, this chapter reviews specific studies in each category related to the positive and negative aspects of resident experiences with tourism. Further, it addresses predictors of residents' evaluation of tourism experiences.

Economic Aspects of Resident Quality of Life

With respect to economic factors, there is evidence that residents perceive the positive benefits of tourism in the form of increased employment, investments, and profitable local businesses, as well as negative economic effects, including an increase in the cost of living. It appears as if residents perceive a positive rise in the standard of living more than the negative impact of a rise in the cost of living

(Liu and Var, 1986). The economic impacts of tourism experiences on residents vary considerably within a community. For example, vacation home development can create a tax burden on local residential property owners (Fritz, 1982) and tourism development has been found to increase government debt and the cost of living for residents (Crotts and Holland, 1993).

Sociocultural Aspects of Resident Quality of Life

Although the economic benefits of tourism are usually considered to improve quality of life, the sociocultural factors may not always be as positive (Liu et al, 1987). The local community and culture can experience changes due to tourism and these can have an effect on resident quality of life. Areas with high levels of tourism activity often experience an increase in population, especially as a result of new residents relocating from out of state, which results in significant changes in the social character of the community (Christensen, 1994; Perdue et al., 1991). Loss of residential identity and local culture often occurs when a high growth rate with poor planning and growth management are combined (Rosenow and Pulsipher, 1979). Tourism development directly affects residents' habits, daily routines, social lives, beliefs, and values, which may lead to psychological tension. Other negative sociocultural consequences of tourism include a decline in traditions, materialism, increase in crime rates, and social conflicts (Dogan, 1989).

The residents of some destinations agree that tourism does not affect the crime rate and they do not attribute social costs to tourism (Liu and Var, 1986). However, other residents perceive an increase in negative sociocultural consequences such as brawls, drug addiction, vandalism, and individual crimes. The same residents identified improvements in attitudes toward work and hospitality toward strangers as positive social effects of tourism (Haralambopoulos and Pizam, 1996). Other positive effects are cultural benefits, including improved entertainment, historical and cultural exhibits, a means for cultural exchange, cultural events, and a strengthening of cultural identity (Liu and Var, 1986).

Environmental Aspects of Resident Quality of Life

Although the tourism industry is often considered a clean industry that does not harm the natural environment, in reality, it can cause significant environmental damage because it is often developed in areas that have attractive but fragile environments. The principal negative environmental consequences of tourism are air pollution, such as emissions from vehicles and airplanes; water pollution, such as waste water discharge, fertilizer leakage, and road oil; wildlife destruction as a result of hunting, trapping, and fishing and disruption of natural habitats; plant destruction, deforestation, overcollection of specimens, forest fires, and trampling of vegetation; and destruction of wetlands, soil, and beaches. In addition, there are other environmental consequences of tourism that concern residents. These include large buildings that destroy views; clashing architectural styles that do not fit the style of the area; noise pollution from planes, cars, and tourists; damage to geological formations due to erosion and vandalism; fishing line and tackle left by anglers; and graffiti (Andereck, 1995).

The impacts of tourism on the environment are evident to scientists, but not all residents attribute environmental damage to tourism. Residents commonly have positive views on the economic and some sociocultural influences of tourism on quality of life, but their reactions to environmental impacts are mixed. Some residents feel tourism provides more parks and recreation areas, improves the quality of the roads and public facilities, and does not contribute to ecological decline. Many do not blame tourism for traffic problems, overcrowded outdoor recreation, or the disruption of peace and tranquility of parks (Liu and Var, 1986). Alternatively, some residents express concern that tourists overcrowd the local fishing, hunting, and other recreation areas or may cause traffic and pedestrian congestion (Martin and McCool, 1992; Reid and Boyd, 1991). Some studies suggest that variations in residents' feelings about tourism's relationship to environmental damage are related to the type of tourism, the extent to which residents feel the natural environment needs to be protected, and the distance residents live from the tourist attractions (Jurowski et al., 1997; Jurowski and Gursoy, 2004).

Predictors of Residents' Perceptions of Tourism

Most importantly, studies have found that residents who perceive greater levels of personal benefit from tourism express more positive attitudes toward tourism and are more supportive of tourism development than those who do not feel they receive tourism's benefits (Jurowski et al., 1997; Lankford and Howard, 1994; Liu and Var, 1986; McGehee and Andereck, 2004; Perdue et al., 1990). When residents are categorized into those who are directly economically dependent on tourism and those who are not dependent, it becomes evident that the former perceive the tourism industry in a more positive light (Haralambopoulos and Pizam, 1996; Liu et al., 1987). Residents who themselves or who have family employed in the tourism industry tend to have more positive perceptions of tourism's impact than other residents (Brunt and Courtney, 1999; Deccio and Baloglu, 2002; Haralambopoulos and Pizam, 1996; Jurowski et al., 1997; Lankford and Howard, 1994; Sirakaya et al., 2002). The social exchange theory offers an explanation for this phenomenon. The theory proposes that those who value the benefits of tourism and evaluate the benefits as greater than the costs will be supportive of tourism development efforts. On the other hand, those who see greater costs or who have little value for the rewards will not be supportive of tourism. (Readers are referred to Chapter Eleven for a complete discussion on social exchange theory.)

Similarly, resident attitudes toward tourism are often found to be related to involvement with the tourism industry. Residents who feel they are knowledgeable about tourism, as well as those who are more involved in tourism decision making (Lankford and Howard, 1994), are often more positively inclined toward the industry. In like manner, those who are more engaged with the industry through high levels of contact with tourists are more positively inclined toward tourism and express more positive attitudes than the uninvolved (Brougham and Butler, 1981; Lankford and Howard, 1994).

Sentiments about one's community appear to be a reasonable predictor of attitudes about tourism. However, research findings have not demonstrated a clear relationship between community attachment and support for or opposition to tourism (Davis et al., 1988; Deccio and Baloglu, 2002; Gursoy et al., 2002; Jurowski et al.,

1997; Lankford and Howard, 1994; McCool and Martin, 1994; Um and Crompton, 1987). This has also been true of the relationship between demographic characteristics and attitudes; generally, no consistent relationships, except for employment in the industry, have emerged in the analysis of the connection between traditional demographic variables and tourism attitudes (King et al., 1993; Lankford, 1994; Liu and Var, 1986; Mok et al., 1991; Perdue et al., 1990; Ross, 1992; Sirakaya et al., 2002; Tosun, 2002).

A number of studies based on social exchange theory have verified a relationship between support for tourism development and attitudes toward tourism. For example, structural equation models have verified a relationship between support for tourism development and economic involvement, ecocentric attitudes, residents' perceptions about impacts, the state of the economy, how far residents live from the tourist activities, residents' evaluation of costs and benefits, and, in some instances, community attachment (Gursoy et al., 2002; Jurowski, 1994; Jurowski and Gursoy, 2004). Other models, most often using regression analysis, have found that various attitude domains predict resident support for tourism (Andereck and Vogt, 2000; McGehee and Andereck, 2004; Perdue et al., 1990). These models verify the direct relationship between residents' assessments of the impacts of tourism and their support for tourism. However, they do not address the question of how important the factors are in the evaluation of quality of life and the extent to which these factors are related to tourism. The following study of Arizona residents' attitudes examines the relationship between tourism experiences and quality of life by investigating which factors have the greatest impact on quality of life and the role that tourism plays in the factors.

Arizona Residents

This study examines the effect of tourism experiences on the quality of life (QOL) of the residents of tourism destinations in a manner that considers not only residents' assessments of the impacts of tourism but also how important these impacts are to QOL and the satisfaction of residents with the current situation related to impacts. The method includes an examination of the role tourism experiences play in affecting QOL. A telephone survey and a self-administered mail survey were used to collect data for the study. To ensure a representative sample, the state population was stratified based on census data. Sample quotas for each county in Arizona and for Hispanic respondents were determined. A telephone survey company that used a computer-generated random sample from a statewide voter registration list conducted the telephone survey portion of the study. The person who answered the telephone was selected as the interviewee, providing he or she met the age requirement. Names and addresses were confirmed for the follow-up mail survey.

For the second portion of this study, a questionnaire was administered to the respondents identified from the telephone portion of the study. The questionnaire was used to determine the perceived effects of 38 tourism-related economic, sociocultural, and environmental factors on the quality of life of Arizona residents.

After agreeing to participate in the survey, each subject was mailed a questionnaire, a cover letter, a stamped and pre-addressed return envelope, and an Arizona Council for Enhancing Recreation and Tourism (ACERT) map of recreational and tourism sites in Arizona as incentive to return the survey. In the cover letter, each person was asked to complete the questionnaire and mail it back. In return for their time and assistance, the potential respondents were also notified that their names would be entered in a drawing for a gift set from a popular clothing line. A postcard reminder followed the initial mailing one week later. As a final effort to increase the response rate, a second survey packet was mailed to those prospective respondents who had not yet returned their completed questionnaire three weeks after the initial mailing.

Measurement

The questionnaire included several sections. The QOL items of concern for this chapter include (1) importance scales with respect to tourism and quality-of-life indicators where 1 = not all important and 5 = extremely important; (2) satisfaction scales with respect to quality-of-life indicators where 1 = not at all satisfied and 5 = extremely satisfied; and (3) effects of tourism on quality-of-life scales where 1 = tourism greatly decreases and 5 = tourism greatly increases. The first section asked respondents to rate how important each of the 38 tourism-related quality-of-life items were to them *personally*, then to rate how satisfied they were with each quality-of-life factor *in their community*. In the second section, the same or very similar tourism-related quality-of-life factors were used to measure respondents' opinions about how much tourism decreases or increases each characteristic *in their community*. The items are listed in Table 8-1. Note that wording differences for the set of tourism effects scales are parenthetically included in the table.

The measurement items used for the three Likert-type scale sets of the mail survey instrument are attributed to, and modified from, a combination of tourism and quality-of-life–related studies, including Allen and associates (1993); Andereck and associates (1999); Inglehart and Rabier (1986); McCool and Martin (1994); Morrison Institute (1998); Perdue and associates (1990); Ross (1992); and Schalock (1990).

Data Analysis

Data analysis uses a combination of methods. To begin, a QOL score has been computed for each respondent using a method developed by Brown and colleagues (1998) and further used by Massam (2002). This method uses importance and satisfaction ratings of items to determine a QOL score ranging from −10 to +10. For example, an item rated as extremely important with which a respondent is extremely satisfied receives a score of +10. If the item is extremely important and the respondent is not at all satisfied, an item is given a score of −10. If both importance and satisfaction are rated as 3, the QOL score is a 0. (See Table 11 in Massam [2002, p. 192] for the QOL score calculation method.) A tourism and quality-of-life (TQOL) index is then computed by using the respondents' perceptions of tourism's effect on the QOL items. The QOL score is computed by multiplying the QOL score by the tourism effects score recoded as follows:

Table 8.1 Means for QOL indicators

Items	Impor-tance[a]	Satis-faction[b]	Tourism Effects[c]	QOL Score[d]	TQOL Score[e]
Awareness of natural and cultural heritage	3.7	3.4	3.8	1.5	3.9
Plenty of festivals, fairs, and museums	3.5	3.3	4.0	1.1	4.9
Opportunities to participate in local culture	3.4	3.3	3.4	1.2	2.5
An understanding of different cultures	3.8	3.2	3.5	1.0	2.6
The image of my community to others	4.0	3.4	1.8	3.9	5.0
Having live sports to watch in my community	3.2	3.3	3.8	1.3	4.4
Quality recreation opportunities	4.1	3.3	3.8	1.3	4.7
Controlled traffic (Traffic)	4.4	2.7	3.8	−1.5	4.6
Controlled urban sprawl and population growth (Urban sprawl and population growth)	4.3	2.6	3.4	−2.2	2.4
The prevention of crowding and congestion (Crowding and congestion)	4.4	2.7	3.7	−1.4	4.1
Proper zoning/land use (Conflicts over zoning/land use)	4.3	2.9	3.3	−0.7	1.5
Litter control (Litter)	4.5	2.9	3.4	−0.3	2.1
Preservation of natural areas	4.4	3.1	3.6	0.5	2.9
Preservation of wildlife habitats	4.2	3.1	3.5	0.4	2.1
Preservation of cultural/historical sites	4.2	3.2	3.7	1.0	3.7
Clean air and water	4.8	3.0	3.2	0.1	1.5
Feeling safe	4.7	3.4	3.4	2.0	3.0
Preserving peace and quiet (Peace and quiet)	4.5	3.2	3.1	1.0	1.1
City services like police and fire protection	4.6	3.8	3.6	3.7	6.3
The beauty of my community	4.4	3.4	3.6	1.9	4.2
A stable political environment	4.0	3.0	3.3	0.0	1.2
The preservation of my way of life	4.3	3.4	3.0	2.0	1.7
Having tourists who respect my way of life	3.9	3.2	3.2	0.9	1.2
My personal life quality	4.7	3.8	3.2	4.0	4.1
Good public transportation	3.6	2.4	3.6	2.4	2.3
Strong and diverse economy	4.1	3.2	3.8	0.7	4.4
Enough good jobs for residents	4.3	2.9	3.6	−0.4	3.9
The value of my house and/or land	4.4	3.7	3.4	3.1	5.2
Plenty of retail shops and restaurants	3.6	3.5	4.1	1.9	6.5
Stores and restaurants owned by local residents	3.6	3.1	1.5	3.4	1.7
The prevention of crime and vandalism (Crime and vandalism)	4.7	3.1	3.3	0.6	2.7
The prevention of drug and alcohol abuse (Drug and alcohol abuse)	4.5	2.9	3.2	−0.4	1.0
Fair prices for goods and services	4.3	3.2	0.9	3.5	2.5
A feeling of belonging in my community	4.0	3.4	3.2	1.8	2.8
Resident participation in local government	3.8	3.1	3.2	0.3	0.7
Community pride	4.1	3.4	3.6	1.6	4.1
Quality roads, bridges, and utility services	4.4	3.1	3.6	0.4	3.8
Tax revenue, such as sales tax/bed tax	3.9	3.0	3.8	−0.1	3.5

[a]Scale: 1 = not at all important to 5 = extremely important
[b]Scale: 1 = not at all satisfied to 5 = extremely satisfied
[c]Scale: 1 = tourism greatly decreases to 5 = tourism greatly increases
[d]Range: −10 to 10 (see Massam, 2002, p. 192)
[e]Range: −30 to 30

1. Positive impact items effects scale scores recoded where tourism greatly decreases = −3, tourism decreases = −2, tourism has no effect = 1, tourism increases = 2, tourism increases = 3.
2. Negative impact items effects scale recoded where tourism greatly decreases = 3, tourism decreases = 2, tourism has no effect = 1, tourism increases = −2, and tourism greatly increases = −3.

For example, a positive impacts item with a QOL score of 10 and a tourism effects rating of 4 ("tourism increases," which has been recoded as 2), then becomes a tourism and quality of life (TQOL) score of 20; and an item with a QOL score of 8 and an effects rating of 3 ("tourism has no effect," recoded as 1) remains an 8. On the negative side, if the QOL score is a 10 and the perceptions rating is a 2 ("tourism decreases," which as been recoded as −2), the TQOL score is a −20. However if the QOL score is a −3 but the tourism perceptions rating is a 5 ("tourism greatly increases," which has been recoded as a −3), the TQOL index becomes a 15. If residents feel tourism improves positive aspects of community QOL, the TQOL index is a positive number; if residents feel tourism exacerbates negative QOL indicators such as traffic, the TQOL number is negative. Next, the TQOL indices are factor analyzed to develop TQOL domains.

Results

Table 8-1 presents the mean responses for each of the series of scales, the QOL index, and the TQOL index. The higher the TQOL index, the more residents feel that tourism contributes to this indicator, even if the indicator is negative, such as crowding and congestion, which has a TQOL mean score of 4.1.

The principal component factor analysis with varimax rotation of TQOL items ultimately results in eight factors with items that load reasonably well, have reasonably strong reliability, and make conceptual sense (Table 8-2). Although some of the alpha coefficients are somewhat lower than the ideal, the domains are conceptually cohesive. To improve reliability and conceptual coherence, an item has

Table 8.2 Factor analysis of TQOL domains

Domains	Factor Loadings	Eigenvalue	Variance Explained
Cultural awareness and amenities			
Awareness of natural and cultural heritage	.673		
Plenty of festivals, fairs, and museums	.651		
Opportunities to participate in local culture	.583		
An understanding of different cultures	.565		
The image of my community to others	.507		
Having live sports to watch in my community	.401		
Quality recreation opportunities	.395		
Scale statistics: mean=4.0; std. dev.=3.8; α=.71		6.54	17.9

Continued

145

Table 8.2   Factor analysis of TQOL domains—cont'd

Domains	Factor Loadings	Eigenvalue	Variance Explained
Urban Issues			
Controlled traffic	.772		
Controlled urban sprawl and population growth	.749		
The prevention of crowding and congestion	.671		
Proper zoning/land use	.610		
Litter control	.595		
Scale statistics: mean=2.9; std. dev.=7.4; α=.75		3.44	9.56
Natural/Cultural Preservation			
Preservation of natural areas	.865		
Preservation of wildlife habitats	.833		
Preservation of cultural/historical sites	.658		
Scale statistics: mean=2.8; std. dev.=7.3; α=.82		2.15	6.0
Community Well-Being			
Clean air and water	.682		
Feeling safe	.623		
Preserving peace and quiet	.616		
City services like police and fire protection	.508		
The beauty of my community	.389		
Scale statistics: mean=3.2; std. dev.=6.1; α=.66		1.5	4.1
Personal Way of Life			
A stable political environment	.594		
The preservation of my way of life	.552		
Having tourists who respect my way of life	.543		
My personal life quality	.498		
(Good public transportation)	.445		
Scale statistics: mean=2.1; std. dev.=4.6; α=.61 (.58)		1.3	3.6
Economic Strength			
Strong and diverse economy	.684		
Enough good jobs for residents	.590		
The value of my house and/or land	.523		
Plenty of retail shops and restaurants	.488		
Stores and restaurants owned by local residents	.370		
Scale statistics: mean=4.4; std. dev.=4.6; α=.59		1.3	3.5
Crime and Substance Abuse			
The prevention of crime and vandalism	.633		
The prevention of drug and alcohol abuse	.626		
Scale statistics: mean=1.9; std. dev.=7.24; α=.56		1.2	3.4
Community Connection			
(Fair prices for goods and services)	−.637		
A feeling of belonging in my community	.486		
Resident participation in local government	.441		
Community pride	.415		
Scale statistics: mean=2.5; std. dev.=4.5; α=.68 (.55)		1.2	3.4
Excluded Variables			
Quality roads, bridges, and utility services			
Tax revenue (sales tax/bed tax)			

been removed from each of two of the factors to improve reliability (included in parenthesis in Table 8-2). Good public transportation was removed from the *life quality* factor, and fair prices for goods and services was removed from the *community connection* factor. As well, two items were removed (quality roads, bridges, and utility services and tax revenue) during iterations of the analysis because they did not load well on any factor. The eight domains are (1) *cultural awareness and amenities,* which includes items related to cultural aspects of the community; (2) *urban issues,* which includes items typically considered negative impacts of tourism and often associated with urban areas; (3) *natural/cultural preservation,* which includes the three preservation-oriented items; (4) *community well-being,* which includes items related to safety and cleanliness; (5) *personal way of life,* which includes items related to political, environmental, and social circumstances; (6) *economic strength,* which includes the items related to economic impacts; (7) *crime and substance abuse,* which is made up of the two crime-oriented items; and (8) *community connection,* which consists of items related to community belongingness.

Next, regression analysis is conducted to examine variables that help explain residents' perceptions of the effects of tourism on QOL by investigating predictor variables for the TQOL domains. The following items have been used as independent variables:

1. Employment in the tourism industry where 1 = not employed, 2 = indirectly employed, and 3 = directly employed
2. Perceived personal benefit from tourism where 1 = not at all to 5 = a lot
3. Amount of contact with tourists in the community where 1 = no contact to 4 = a large amount of contact
4. Perceived knowledge about the tourism industry where 1 = not at all knowledgeable to 4 = very knowledgeable
5. Involvement in tourism-related community decision making where 1 = not at all to 4 = a lot
6. Demographic variables including education, age, income, ethnicity, and year living in the community

Table 8-3 presents the series of final regression models.

The two negative domains, *urban issues* and *crime,* are both predicted only by *ethnicity* with white respondents and non-Latino respondents indicating they are more likely to feel tourism contributes to these sorts of problems, respectively. This is particularly interesting, given that ethnicity is rarely a predictor of tourism attitudes alone. *Cultural awareness and amenities* is predicted by two variables, *level of contact with tourists* and *personal benefit from tourism,* with those who have more contact with tourists and those who feel they benefit more from tourism reporting that tourism contributes to the cultural QOL amenities in the community. *Natural/cultural preservation* is predicted by *education, age,* and *personal benefit,* with respondents who are less educated, are older, and perceive greater personal benefits from tourism indicating they feel tourism contributes to the preservation of natural and cultural resources. The TQOL domain *community well-being* is predicted by three variables, including *age,* with older people being more likely to feel tourism contributes to this domain; *ethnicity,* with non-Anglos feeling tourism contributes to this domain; and *personal benefit,* with those who perceive more benefits from tourism reporting they feel tourism is a contributor

Table 8.3 Final regression models

	Dependent Variable	
Independent Variables	*Beta*	*t*
Model 1	*Urban Issues*	
Ethnicity (Anglo)	0.12	2.96
Model Statistics	*(Adjusted R-Square=.01, F=8.77, p=.00)*	
Model 2	*Crime and Substance Abuse*	
Ethnicity (Hispanic)	−0.08	−2.06
Model Statistics	*(Adjusted R-Square=.01, F=4.25, p=.04)*	
Model 3	*Cultural Awareness and Amenities*	
Contact	0.08	Contact
Benefit	0.20	Benefit
Model Statistics	*(Adjusted R-Square=.06, F=20.94, p=.00)*	
Model 4	*Natural/Cultural Preservation*	
Benefit	0.15	3.67
Age	0.09	2.12
Education	−0.08	−2.09
Model Statistics	*(Adjusted R-Square=.03, F=7.06, p=.00)*	
Model 5	*Community Well-Being*	
Benefit	0.19	5.00
Age	0.17	4.24
Education	−0.13	−3.27
Ethnicity (Anglo)	−0.16	−4.01
Model Statistics	*(Adjusted R-Square=.09, F=16.49, p=.00)*	
Model 6	*Personal Way of Life*	
Benefit	0.28	7.28
Age	0.16	4.16
Ethnicity (Anglo)	−0.14	−3.57
Model Statistics	*(Adjusted R-Square=.10, F=23.56, p=.00)*	
Model 7	*Economic Strength*	
Benefit	0.23	5.93
Model Statistics	*(Adjusted R-Square=.05, F=35.20, p=.00)*	
Model 8	*Community Connection*	
Benefit	0.27	7.01
Age	0.17	4.28
Ethnicity (Anglo)	−0.12	−3.19
Model Statistics	*(Adjusted R-Square=.09, F=22.13, p=.00)*	

to community well-being. *Personal way of life* and *community connection* are both related to the same three variables, including *ethnicity, age,* and *personal benefit from tourism*. Non-Anglos, younger respondents, and those who perceive great tourism benefits feel tourism is a greater contributor to these domains than Anglos, older respondents, and those who do not perceive tourism's benefits accrue to them. Finally, *economic strength* has only one predictor variable, *personal benefit from tourism*, with those who benefit more feeling tourism is a contributor to the economy.

Discussion

The TQOL index offers new insight into the way residents of destinations evaluate the role tourism plays in their quality of life by adding two dimensions not previously studied. Not only are residents' perceptions regarding the effects of tourism experiences within their communities measured and explained, but also measured are the importance of those indicators and the level of satisfaction with the indicators. Existing research can tell us, for example, if residents in a community perceive that tourism results in increased cultural awareness in the community; however, it cannot tell us if residents feel that increased cultural awareness is important, nor does it offer an understanding of the level of resident satisfaction with this attribute. The TQOL measure takes all of these factors into account in an effort to better understand the way in which residents experience tourism.

Most resident attitude studies have identified negative aspects of residents' tourism experiences. The two negative domains found in this study are consistent with those studies. Residents of Arizona communities feel tourism can detract from their quality of life in some ways in that they experience the negative results of tourism in the form of urban-related issues, especially traffic and crowding, as well as more crime. These aspects of community life are very important to residents; they are not satisfied with existing conditions and they feel tourism exacerbates the problems. What is not consistent with existing research is the relationship between ethnicity and negative tourism effects within the community. Ethnicity and marginality theories explain that ethnic and racial minority groups have differing perceptions than majority groups due to economic, cultural, and social differences, as well as discrimination (Valentine, 1999). They are differentially impacted by forces within the community, place different levels of importance on community attributes, and experience different levels of satisfaction with community attributes. As a result, minorities perceive quality of life differently than majority groups. Thus, it is perhaps not surprising that ethnic and racial minorities sense the resident tourism experience in a different way than do majority groups, especially with respect to negative consequences of tourism. Interestingly, in this case, Hispanics tend to feel that tourism is less of a problem than do Anglos. The latter tend to blame tourism more for urban-related negative consequences than Hispanic residents who are less inclined to perceive tourism as a significant contributing factor to crime and substance abuse problems.

Even though they recognize the negative impacts of tourism, the majority of the Arizona residents in this study feel tourism improves their quality of life and generally experience tourism within their communities in positive ways. The positive TQOL domain with the highest mean is *economic strength*. The individual items within this domain—with the exception of *stores and restaurants owned by local residents*—have relatively high TQOL scores, especially the items *plenty of retail shops and restaurants* and *the value of my house and/or land*. Residents feel these aspects of community life are important; they have varying levels of satisfaction with the attributes, but feel tourism is a contributor to these attributes in a constructive way. This domain is predicted only by *personal benefit from tourism,* which is quite consistent with the many studies that have found personal benefit to be one of the strongest predictors of tourism attitudes. Although residents seem to realize that tourism is a contributor to a good economy within the community, those who realize the greatest personal benefit from tourism are the most cognizant of the positive quality of life influences of tourism.

The TQOL domain that explains the most variance is *cultural awareness and amenities*—a domain that also has a fairly high mean score. Although some of the individual items emerge as only moderately important and residents tend to be moderately satisfied with such amenities, they feel tourism substantially enhances their quality of life with respect to having cultural awareness and activities within the community. In this way, residents experience tourism within their communities in a positive way. The item *image of my community to others* stands out as an item with a fairly high TQOL score, as does *plenty of festivals, fairs and museums*. This domain is explained by two variables, *level of contact with tourists* and *personal benefit from tourism*. Again, perceived personal benefit emerges as an important variable in explaining resident perceptions of how tourism affects their quality of life. Similarly, residents who have more contact with tourists are more cognizant of the way in which tourism can enhance a community's cultural resources. Perhaps these variables are related because residents who take advantage of cultural opportunities in a community are the people who feel such opportunities are the most important, and via participation come into contact with more tourists than do other residents.

Community well-being is the TQOL domain with the next highest mean. The items within this domain are rated as some of the most important to residents, and although satisfaction is moderate, residents feel tourism increases these community attributes to a moderate extent. *City services like police and fire protection* is an item within this domain that is viewed as extremely important by residents, and they feel tourism contributes to the quality of this community attribute to some extent. Individuals who receive more personal benefits from tourism are more inclined to feel tourism contributes positively to community QOL. Three demographic segments perceive tourism as a factor in improving their quality of life; these include older respondents, less educated respondents, and ethnic minorities.

The residents also indicated that *natural and cultural preservation* is important. They appear to be only moderately satisfied with the community attributes in this domain and perceive that tourism is a means for improving the preservation of their natural and cultural heritage. Personal benefit from tourism is again a predictor variable, as are age and education. Just as for domains already discussed, residents who feel they gain more tourism benefits also feel tourism contributes to quality of life to a greater extent. Individuals who are older and those who have lower education levels view tourism as a greater contributor to community quality of life than do younger or more highly educated residents.

The final two domains, *life quality* and *community connection*, have some similarities in that they are viewed as fairly important with moderate satisfaction levels (except public transportation, with which residents are not particularly satisfied). Residents seem to feel that good public transportation, community pride, and quality roads, bridges, and utility services are positively influence by tourism. As in the other domains, the *life quality* and *community connection* domains are positively related to personal benefit from tourism, age, and ethnicity.

Implications

This study clearly demonstrates that residents' quality of life is both positively and negatively affected by tourism experiences. Although the prevailing belief is that educating residents about the economic benefits of tourism will increase support within the community for tourism development, it is clear that there are other community quality-of-life attributes that may be even more important to local residents. Arizona residents valued not only the economic benefits of tourism but also community well-being and preservation of their natural and cultural heritage. Economic development plans based on tourism that focus solely on the economic benefits risk losing the support of the local population. Plans that fail to incorporate programs to protect and improve valued social and environmental elements are likely to meet with resistance. Pursuance of such plans can result in outright animosity toward tourists and the tourism industry. Those who benefit financially from the tourism industry should understand that residents recognize both the positive and negative influences tourism can have on their lives. Communicating benefits of tourism that are valued by the community is likely to result in positive attitudes toward tourism and amenable community relationships with tourists and the tourism industry. The TQOL can be a valuable tool for achieving such relationships because of its ability to identify elements the tourism industry affects that are valued by the residents.

An aspect of this study that is different from traditional resident attitude studies is particularly worth noting, and that is the predictive nature of demographic variables with respect to the TQOL domains. It is uncommon to find a relationship between demographic characteristics and tourism attitudes; however, the Arizona study shows that demographic characteristics influence residents' perceptions of how tourism impacts their quality of life. The older, less educated, and ethnic minorities appear to view tourism as having a greater effect on positive quality-of-life domains and a lesser effect on the negative ones than do other groups. Additional research is needed to discover the reason for the differences. Does tourism improve the quality of life of these groups more than others? Is the perception based on a greater need for economic growth? Is the difference the result of experiences with tourism? Or are some groups less likely to attribute negative consequences within their communities to tourism?

Most important, the newly developed TQOL index is an effective and valuable instrument for monitoring residents' tourism experiences. As demonstrated in the Arizona study, it identifies what is important to the residents and how the residents interpret the effect of tourism experiences on their own lives. Consequently, the TQOL index is useful for measuring the subjective nature of quality of life. When the TQOL index is used in conjunction with objective and external indicators, a clear description of the impact of tourism on the quality of life of residents can be achieved. The index allows for the analysis of population segments to identify potential inequities in the distribution of the benefits and costs of tourism. An added benefit of the index is its ability to identify inequalities in the distribution of the costs and benefits of tourism to various segments within the community. Thus, the index responds to the recommendations of economists that advocate noneconomic measures to justify the benefits and the costs of growth. The TQOL index can be as effective in determining when increased income from tourism is reducing rather than improving the community quality of life.

The quality of tourism experiences for residents of tourist destinations is measured by residents' perceptions of how tourism affects their QOL. Quality experiences are those that improve rather than detract from the quality of life of residents. The TQOL index assesses the true effect of tourism experiences on residents' QOL and identifies those experiences that enhance and detract from community QOL.

References

Allen, L.R., Hafer, H.R., Long, P.T., and R.R. Perdue. (1993). Rural residents' attitudes toward recreation and tourism development. *Journal of Travel Research*, **31** (4), 27-33.

Andereck, K.L. (1995). Environmental consequences of tourism: A review of recent research. In S.F. McCool and A.E. Watson (Eds.), *Linking Tourism, the Environment, and Sustainability* (pp. 77-81). General Technical Report No. INT-GTR-323. Ogden, UT: Intermountain Research Station.

Andereck, K.L. Knopf, R., Valentine, K., and C. Vogt. (1999). *Tourism and Quality Of Life*. Phoenix: Arizona State University West, Department of Recreation and Tourism Management.

Andereck, K.L. and C. A. Vogt. (2000). The relationship between residents' attitudes toward tourism and tourism development options. *Journal of Travel Research* **39** (1), 27-36.

Ap, J., and J.L. Crompton. (1993). Residents' strategies for responding to tourism impacts. *Journal of Travel Research*, **32** (1), 47-50.

Bastias-Perex, P., and T. Var. (1995). Perceived impacts of tourism by residents. *Annals of Tourism Research*, **22**, 208-209.

Brougham, J.E., and R.W. Butler. (1981). A segmentation analysis of resident attitudes to the social impact of tourism. *Annals of Tourism Research*, **8**, 569-589.

Brown, I., Raphael, D., and R. Renwick. (1998). *Quality of Life Profile* (Item #2). Toronto: Quality of Life Research Unit, Center for Health Promotion, University of Toronto.

Brunt, P., and P. Courtney. (1999). Host perceptions of sociocultural impacts. *Annals of Tourism Research*, **26,** 493-515.

Christensen, N. A. (1994). A study of the relationships of tourism and potential impacts on Montana counties. Misc. Rep. Missoula, MT: The University of Montana, School of Forestry, Institute for Tourism and Recreation Research.

Crotts, J.C., and S.M. Holland. (1993). Objective indicators of the impact of rural tourism development in the state of Florida. *Journal of Sustainable Tourism*, **1**, 112-119.

Cutter, S.L. (1985). *Rating places: A geographer's view on quality of life*. Resource Publications in Geography, the Association of American Geographers.

Davidson, W.B., and P.R. Cotter. (1991). The relationship between sense of community and subjective well-being: A first look. *Journal of Community Psychology*, **19**, 246–253.

Davis, D., Allen, J., and R.M. Cosenza. (1988). Segmenting local residents by their attitudes, interests, and opinions. *Journal of Travel Research*, **27** (2), 2-8.

Deccio, C., and S. Baloglu. (2002). Nonhost community resident reactions to the 2002 Winter Olympics: The spillover impacts. *Journal of Travel Research*, **41**, 46-56.

Diener, E., and E. Suh. (1997). Measuring quality of life: Economic, social, and subjective indicators. *Social Indicators Research*, **40**, 189-216.

Dissart, J.C., and S.C. Deller. (2000). Quality of life in the planning literature. *Journal of Planning Literature*, 15 (1), 135-161.

Dogan, H. (1989). Forms of adjustment: Socio-cultural impacts of tourism. *Annals of Tourism Research*, **16**, 216-236.

Dowrick, S., Dunlop, Y., and J. Quiggin. (2003). Social indicators and comparisons of living standards. *Journal of Development Economics*, **70** (2), 501-529.

Fritz, R.G. (1982). Tourism, vacation home development and residential tax burden: A case study of the local finances of 240 Vermont towns. *American Journal of Economics and Sociology*, **41**, 375-385.

Grayson, L., and K. Young. (1994). *Quality of Life in Cities: An Overview and Guide to the Literature*. London: The British Library.

Gursoy, D., Jurowski, C., and M. Uysal. (2002). Resident attitudes: A structural modeling approach. *Annals of Tourism Research*, **29**, 79-105.

Haralambopoulos, N., and A. Pizam. (1996). Perceived impacts of tourism: The case of Samos. *Annals of Tourism Research*, **23** (3), 503-526.

Inglehart, R., and J. Rabier. (1986). Aspirations adapt to situation–But why are the Belgians so much happier than the French? A cross-cultural analysis of the subjective quality of life. In F.M. Andrews (Ed.), *Research on the Quality of Life* (pp. 1-56). Ann Arbor: University of Michigan Press.

Jurowski, C. (1994). The Interplay of Elements Affecting Host Community Resident Attitudes toward Tourism: A Path Analytic Approach. Unpublished Ph.D. dissertation. Virginia Polytechnic Institute and State University, Blacksburg, VA.

Jurowski, C., and D. Gursoy. (2004). Distance effects on residents attitudes toward tourism. *Annals of Tourism Research*, **31** (2), 296-312.

Jurowski, C., Uysal, M., and D.R. Williams. (1997). A theoretical analysis of host community resident reactions to tourism. *Journal of Travel Research*, **34** (2), 3-11.

King, B., Pizam A., and A. Milman. (1993). Social impacts of tourism: Host perceptions. *Annals of Tourism Research*, **20** (4), 650-665.

Lankford, S.V. (1994). Attitudes and perceptions toward tourism and rural regional development. *Journal of Travel Research*, **32** (3), 35-43.

Lankford, S.V., and D.R. Howard. (1994). Developing a tourism impact attitude scale. *Annals of Tourism Research*, **21** (1), 121-139.

Lawn, P.A. (2003). A theoretical foundation to support the Index of Sustainable Economic Welfare (ISEW), Genuine Progress Indicator(GPI), and other related indexes. *Ecological Economics*, **44** (1), 105-118.

Liu, J.C., Sheldon, P.J., and T. Var. (1987). Resident perception of the environmental impacts of tourism. *Annals of Tourism Research*, **14**, 17-37.

Liu, J.C., and T. Var. (1986). Resident attitudes towards tourism impacts in Hawaii. *Annals of Tourism Research*, **13,** 193-214.

Marcouiller, D.W. (1997). Towards integrative tourism planning in rural America. *Journal of Planning Literature*, **11** (3), 337-357.

Martin, S.R., and S.F. McCool. (1992). Attitudes of Montana residents toward tourism development. Res. Rep. 23. Missoula: The University of Montana, School of Forestry, Institute for Tourism and Recreation Research.

Massam, B.H. (2002). Quality of life: Public planning and private living. *Progress in Planning,* **58** (1), 141-227.

Max-Neef, M. (1995). Economic growth and quality of life. *Ecological Economics*, **15,** 115-118.

McCool, S.F., and S.R. Martin. (1994). Community attachment and attitudes towards tourism development. *Journal of Travel Research*, **32** (3), 29-34.

McGehee, N.G., and K.L. Andereck. (2004). Factors predicting rural residents' support of tourism. *Journal of Travel Research*, **43**.

Mok, C., Slater, B., and V. Cheung. (1991). Residents' attitudes towards tourism in Hong Kong. *Journal of Hospitality Management*, **10,** 289-293.

Morrison Institute for Public Policy. (1997). *What Matters in Greater Phoenix: 1997 Indicators of Our Quality of Life*. Tempe: Arizona State University.

Pembina Institute. (2001). *Alberta Sustainability Trends 2000: The Genuine Progress Indicators Report 1961 to 1999*. Dayton Valley, Alberta: Pembina Institute.

Perdue, R.R., Long, T.L., and L. Allen. (1990). Resident support for tourism development. *Annals of Tourism Research*, **17** (4), 586-599.

Perdue, R.R., Long, P.T., and L.D. Gustke. (1991). The effects of tourism development on objective indicators of local quality of life. In *Travel and Tourism Association 22nd Annual Proceedings* (pp. 191-201). Salt Lake City: Travel and Tourism Research Association.

Reid, L., and A. Boyd. (1991). The social impacts of tourism and their effects on attitudes toward a major cultural attraction. In *Travel and Tourism Association 22nd Annual Proceedings* (pp. 123-133). Salt Lake City, UT: Travel and Tourism Research Association.

Rosenow, J.E., and G.L. Pulsipher. (1979). *Tourism: The Good, the Bad and the Ugly.* Kansas City, MO: Media Publishing.

Ross, G.F. (1992). Resident perceptions of the impact of tourism on an Australian city. *Journal of Travel Research*, **30** (3), 13-17.

Ryan, C. (1991). *Recreational Tourism: A Social Science Perspective.* London: Routledge.

Schalock, R.L. (Ed.). (1990). *Quality of Life: Conceptualization and Measurement,* Vol. 1. Washington DC: American Association on Mental Retardation.

Sirakaya, E., Teye, V., and S. Sönmez. (2002). Understanding residents' support for tourism development in the central region of Ghana. *Journal of Travel Research*, **41,** 57-67.

Tosun, C. (2002). Host perceptions of impacts: A comparative tourism study. *Annals of Tourism Research*, **29,** 231-253.

Um, S., and J.L. Crompton. (1987). Measuring resident's attachment levels in a host community. *Journal of Travel Research*, **26** (1), 27-29.

United Nations Development Program. (2003). *Human Development Reports.* Retrieved December 27, 2003, from *http://www.undp.org/hdr2003/indicator/indic_8_1_1.html.*

Valentine, K. (1999). Tourism and Quality of Life in Arizona: A Cross-Cultural Study of Hispanics and Anglos. Unpublished M.S. thesis. Arizona State University, Tempe.

Political-Economic Construction of Quality Tourism Experiences

This section of *Quality Tourism Experiences* draws readers' focuses onto the interplay between economics, politics, planning, and tourism. Although *Quality Tourism Experiences* has emphasized that tourism is a complex and multi-faceted phenomenon, such a viewpoint is re-emphasized in this section wherein tourism as an industry is examined essentially from a supply side perspective. The section opens by acknowledging the resultant challenges inherent in the complexity of the tourism industry even when adopting a systems approach. It recognizes the challenges associated with defining and measuring its impact as well as in modeling the supply-demand interactions. The organizing construct in this section is political-economic theory, especially in regard to tourism as an economic development tool. Various theoretical paradigms inform the research reported in the chapters. For example, critical theory influences Chapters Nine, Ten, Eleven, and Twelve. Additionally, social constructivism variously informs Chapters Ten and Twelve and postpositivism shapes the research in the case study in Chapter Ten.

In total, Section Five is constituted of four chapters. The first chapter overviews the section and political-economic theory. The following three chapters respectively consider the related elements of quality tourism development and planning and the distribution of tourism benefits, as well as the political nature of tourism decision making. To elaborate further, in the first chapter of this section, Chapter Nine, Margaret J. Daniels and Lori Pennington-Gray introduce the political-economic theory and make connections between tourism and economic development, particularly the impact of economic development on the quality of tourism experiences as well as residents' "quality of life." A case study of Alachua County, Florida, is provided, which demonstrates how governments and community residents can jointly develop a tourism plan that uses a participative process in line with resident views and that also ensures quality tourism outcomes.

In the next chapter, Chapter Ten, Kelly S. Bricker, Margaret J. Daniels, and Barbara A. Carmichael discuss how powerful and well-resourced elites can impact tourism development decision making processes for self-serving rather than community interests with resultant consequences for quality tourism experiences for all stakeholder groups. Theoretical concepts of power, planning, decision making, sustainability, and politics of representation pervade this chapter. The interpretation of meaning and place in regard to resident communities and quality of life, already considered in Section Three, is apparent again in this chapter. Two case studies are integrated into the discussion. The first presents a meta-analysis of global biodiversity hotspots, an examination of constituency building, conservation funding, and the distribution of economic benefits in relation to the environment. The second case study examines the development of a large scale casino on Native American land in southeast Connecticut. The case study highlights the subsequent contested spaces and power interactions between a traditional "center" and a "periphery" as well as associated "quality of life" and sustainability issues for both "center" and "periphery" residents.

In the third chapter in this section, Chapter Eleven, Claudia Jurowski, Margaret J. Daniels, and Lori Pennington-Gray consider economic growth and development and associated consequences for the distribution of tourism benefits and costs as a result of tourism development. The chapter notes that tourism as a development tool does not always necessarily generate a better quality of life for residents. In particular, the chapter draws on the theoretical constructs related to efficiency and equity and social exchange theory. A case study of Daytona Beach, Florida is presented as an application of social exchange theory in practice as a mechanism to assess and monitor tourism development equity issues. The chapter makes linkages back to Section Four, *Quality of Life and Interpretation of Quality Tourism Experiences*, and Chapter Eight, especially the Tourism Quality of Life (TQOL) index. Chapter Eleven shows that, depending on the nature of exchanges related to tourism development and the subsequent cost or benefit of those exchanges from the perspectives of residents, there will be resultant flow-on effects for both the nature and quality of any related tourism experiences.

In Chapter Twelve, Lori Pennington-Gray and Barbara A. Carmichael conclude Section Five with an emphasis on tourism and politics, and, as the preceding chapters have done, show in a consideration of decision making practices and processes, particularly in this chapter, that tourism decision making tends to be undemocratic in nature and infused with top-down decision making rather than bottom-up decision making. The chapter focuses on the theoretical constructs of social equity, sustainability and economic vitality, and ecological integrity. A model of planning and development is offered and two cases studies are used to demonstrate the degree that democratic decision making infuses the construction of quality tourism experiences. The first case study is drawn from Ontario, Canada, and the second from Alachua County, Florida.

9

Introduction to Political-Economic Construction of Quality Tourism Experiences

Margaret J. Daniels
Lori Pennington-Gray

The purpose of this chapter is to introduce the political-economic construction of tourism. This chapter is divided into six parts. First, an overview of tourism as an "industry" is offered. Second, tourism is described as an economic development strategy. Third, economic base theory is used to describe tourism as export driven. Fourth, the distributional consequences of economic development are summarized, with specific emphasis on political economic theory as a means of understanding these consequences. Fifth, a case study of no-growth policy is used to illustrate the ties between tourism, politics, and economics. Finally, the intent, justification, and goals of the remaining chapters comprising this section of the text are offered. The guiding principle of this section as a whole is that development is politically and economically charged in a way that often undermines quality tourism outcomes, especially for host destination residents.

Tourism as an "Industry"

Tourism suffers from an industrial identity crisis. As Smith notes (1988), "The lack of an adequate industrial definition has regrettable consequences for tourism. One of the most serious consequences is that tourism perennially suffers from a poor reputation in the eyes of policy analysts, government officials, economic analysts, and industry leaders not involved with tourism. Many of these individuals even express doubts as to whether tourism is truly an industry" (pp. 181-182).

Smith explains that the difficulty in defining tourism as an industry arises in part due to the fact that there is not a single industrial code for tourism. Instead, tourism is made up of an abundance of disparate industries, such as transportation, food services, and retail services. Thus, identifying expenditures that are tourism based is inherently complicated. Smith argues that a supply-side definition of tourism should be applied when addressing tourism in terms of the goods and services produced. The supply-side definition focuses on commodities produced such that "tourism is the aggregate of all businesses that directly provide goods or services to facilitate business, pleasure, and leisure activities away from the home environment" (Smith, 1988, p. 183).

An additional, related problem with defining the tourism industry is noted by Chadwick (1992), who explains that economists are concerned that "any attempt to account for travel and tourism is liable to lead to double counting because activities of all establishments are already allocated to existing industries" (p. 72). Chadwick states that different groups have identified industrial areas that relate, in varying degrees, to tourism. For example, she notes that the United Nations identified accommodation, travel agents and tour operators, restaurants, passenger-transport enterprises, retail manufacturers, recreation facilities, and government agencies as seven areas engaged in tourism activities. She concludes with a systems approach to travel and tourism by stating that tourism links together "*people* who require *services* outside their community of residence in order to achieve certain *objectives*" (p. 75).

Leiper (1990) also uses a systems approach when considering the multi-industry nature of tourism: "Travel and tourism industries can be regarded as sub-systems of whole tourism systems" (p. 28). He breaks the travel and tourism industry into seven sectors, while noting that some overlap may occur, including: marketing, public transportation, accommodations, attractions, tour operators, government coordination, and miscellaneous (*e.g.*, retail, restaurants, banking). Crompton (1999), in an adaptation of Gunn's (1988, 1997) supply-demand view of tourism, offers a pictorial representation of this systems approach, which has been further adapted in Figure 9-1. This figure illustrates the interdependencies between supply and demand, emphasizing the need for a systems view to clearly understand the economic forces driving tourism.

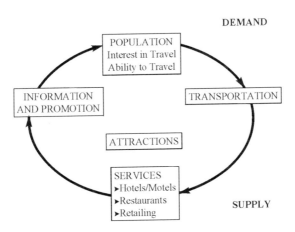

Figure 9.1 Systems Representation of Travel and Tourism (Adapted from Crompton, 1999).

Despite the potential complexity in defining tourism as an industry, it has become an increasingly popular target of community and regional economic development. An understanding of the international growth of services can help explain why tourism is touted as a viable means of development.

Tourism and Economic Development

Development is a multivalued social goal, a specific component of which is economic development. As Galston and Baehler state, "While development cannot be equated with steadily increasing incomes, it is hardly imaginable without income growth" (1995, p. 25). Blakely (1994) asserts that in planning local economic development, regional and community planners must implement strategies that best utilize the local resource base. For example, since 1950, the base of the U.S. economy has shifted to services (Freshwater, 2000). The growth in the service industries is an international phenomenon, with one result being an increasing demand for services associated with recreational activities. Further, in some countries, competitive industries are also needed to replace manufacturing plants that are filtering down to international locations or industries with little growth potential. Freshwater (2000) notes that tourism and recreation are two areas frequently touted as replacement industries. Whitson and Macintosh (1996) agree, and explain:

So important, indeed, are leisure and consumption in the new service economy that cities of widely varied sizes and geographical locations are seeking to rebuild the postindustrial economics around shopping and entertainment . . . to 're-image' themselves as places with things to see and do. This strategy is not employed by provincial centers as well as major national cities and, although at one level it is a strategy to keep local leisure spending at home, it is also very much a competition to attract outside money in the form of tourism. (p. 280)

As will be discussed in detail in Chapter Ten, the economic promise of tourism is pushing growth of this industry in developed and developing countries throughout the globe. For example, in Australia and New Zealand, tourism is seen as a "sunrise industry" that can boost export income and act as a source of employment (Hall et al., 1997, p. 16). In small, resource-limited countries, such as Mauritius, tourism has compensated for the output growth stagnation of once dominant industries, in this case, sugar (Durbarry, 2002). As tourism is a significant export industry for many countries, it is not surprising that community planners would consider it as a development strategy. One way to understand tourism as an export is through the articulation of economic base theory.

Tourism as an Export: Economic Base Theory

Blakely (1994) argues that no single theory completely explains regional or local economic development. He goes on to explain that the sum of economic development theories can be expressed as: "Local/Regional Development = f (natural resources, labor, capital investment, entrepreneurship, transport, communication, industrial composition, technology size, export market, international economic situation, local government capacity, national and state government spending, and development supports)" (p. 53).

The economic practitioner must determine which factor or factors should be given the greatest weight when making program and policy decisions and should lean toward programs that maximize the community's competitive advantage. Policymakers who are considering tourism as an economic development strategy must determine its export potential. Accordingly, while economic base theory cannot explain all aspects of regional development, it is an appropriate theory to address tourism as a development strategy.

Nelson (1993) offers an introduction to economic base theory by explaining:

Economic base theory presumes that regional development is driven by economic rules applied to space. Regional development is sustained through vertical and complementary linkages among industries. Three kinds of external relationships are critical for regional development: trade characterized by imports and exports of goods and services; migration of people in their capacities as both consumers and workers; and migration of other factors, principally capital for investment. (p. 29)

Nelson (1993) describes how development is an integration of imports, exports, people and capital, but the export component is primary to economic base theory. Thus, economic base theory is also known as export base theory. The premise of the theory is that "the external demand for a region's products is the primary determinant of regional prosperity" (Malizia and Feser, 1999, p. 51). To better understand the basis of economic base theory requires the following definition of income:

$$Yi = C + I + G + X - M$$

where:

Yi = income of region i
C = consumption through consumer (household) spending
I = investment
G = government spending
X = export sales
M = import purchases

Although each of the five components making up income is a possible source of regional economic development, "the economic base model explicitly recognizes only export expansion. In short, export expansion is considered to be the sole or primary engine of regional economic growth" (Davis, 1993, p. 9).

The economic activities in a given area can be broken down into two categories: basic and nonbasic (Healey and Ibery, 1990). Basic activities are those that have an export market, thus bringing outside dollars into the region. Blakely (1994) explains, "Adherents of economic base theory postulate that the determinants for economic growth are directly related to the demand for goods, services, and products from areas outside the local economic boundaries of the community. In essence, the growth of industries that use local resources, including labor and materials for final export elsewhere, will generate both local wealth and jobs" (p. 54).

The goods, services, and products that are in demand are the basic activities (Rainey and McNamara, 1997). Nonbasic activities, on the other hand, are those goods, services, and products produced for local consumption. Economic base theory emphasizes the need to increase basic activity, which will in turn increase nonbasic activity as "a growth in basic activities will increase the flow of labor into the region, increasing the demand for goods and services within it and bring about a corresponding increase in the amount of nonbasic activities" (Healey and Ibery, 1990, p. 302). Malizia and Feser (1999) offer a thorough explanation of the connections between basic and nonbasic sectors:

The two sectors are linked in two ways. First, the basic sector directly purchases goods and services from the nonbasic sector. Second, workers employed in the basic sector purchase food, clothing, shelter, public services, and other commodities for the nonbasic sector. Greater demand for the region's exports generates export sales and income for the basic sector, while basic-sector purchases provide income to the nonbasic sector. Consumption spending by basic-sector workers also generated income for the nonbasic sector; nonbasic firms and workers then engage in additional rounds of spending. These rounds of spending generate what is called the "multiplier effect." Through the multiplier effect, an initial increase in basic-industry income generates even greater total income for the area. In parallel fashion, a decrease in basic industry income leads to a greater decrease in total area income. (pp. 51-52)

Economic base theory is a readily understandable explanation of regional development, and as tourism services continue to expand internationally, it is no wonder that community planners consider tourism as a potential means of increasing an export base. Freshwater (2000) warns, however, that some communities are better suited to tourism opportunities than others. Walo and associates (1996) name the resources that contribute to tourism development: "Conducive regional factors would include a clean environment, adequate facilities and infrastructure, a genuine range of events and attractions, friendly host population, and local government receptive to the wishes of the host population and more" (p. 96). Walo and colleagues assert that communities without the above resources may realize significant opportunity costs in attempting to become tourist-friendly. Thus, the costs associated with attracting tourists may make tourism an unrealistic export strategy in many regions. Bull (1991) explains that the most successful tourism products combine natural and created features, the latter of which require capital investment. Malizia and Feser (1999) note that the most important task for an economic base developer is to make sure that the region possesses industries whose products are in heavy demand from outside the region. Further, while a region may possess any number of export industries, economic base theory allows a researcher to focus on critical industries, which are "industries that, if lost, would constitute the greatest loss to the community" (Malizia and Feser, 1999, p. 61). An important next step, then, is to consider the distribution of development benefits and costs.

The Distributional Effects of Economic Development

Historically, patterns of land development were assumed to make the best use of an area's environment (Holupka and Shlay, 1993). More recently, experts have determined that this is not always the case, and the assumption that development always results in positive outcomes has led to problematic consequences. Political economic theory offers a means of understanding the potential distributional effects of tourism.

Political economic theory operates on three premises. The first premise is the recognition that "specific local actors and institutions play key roles in determining how local development occurs" (Holupka and Shlay, 1993, p. 177). In other words, powerful individuals and organizations with significant economic resources at their disposal often make development decisions that are in the best interest of their businesses rather than the community as a whole.

The second premise of political economic theory is that "the distribution of benefits from development are highly skewed; those at the top reap the benefits of development while the public largely pays the cost of development" (Holupka and Shlay, 1993, pp. 177-178). Those most likely to lose are the lower class and minorities who suffer from a system of "exclusion, segregation, and labor segmentation" (Betancur and Gills, 1993, p. 192).

The third premise of political economic theory is that "metropolitan development decision making processes tend to be undemocratic; critical decisions are typically hidden from the public view and the public serves to legitimize decisions rather than to play a material role in making them" (Holupka and Shlay, 1993, p. 178). Holupka and Shlay argue that growth machines present a façade of democracy to local communities by selling the public on the benefits of development while deemphasizing or neglecting to report the associated risks and costs of development.

Political economic theory stresses that development is not inherently natural; instead, it is often the result of actions taken by self-interest groups. By considering the political economic perspective, resistance groups can identify the primary institutions and actors implementing development and determine ways to "best intervene to change some of the most damaging consequences of the current development process" (Holupka and Shlay, 1993, p. 187).

In sum, development decisions are not always made in the best interest of all individuals impacted by the development. Bartik (1991) summarizes specific groups of households that are gainers and losers in the short run (3 to 10 years) due to development. Table 9-1 summarizes the social impacts of local economic development policies. The assumption of this model is that, in the short run, households are relatively immobile. Bartik goes on to explain that in the long run (more than 10 years), with the assumption of limited mobility removed, the employed will break even on average, and the unemployed (*e.g.*, retirees) will lose on average, due to higher prices of goods and services and, in the case of unemployed property owners who do not sell, higher property taxes.

Table 9.1   Short-run household distributional effects of state and local economic development policies

Group	Effect
Employed homeowners	Gain due to wage and property value increase
Employed renters in labor sub-markets whose workers are relatively mobile	Gain because real wage increases
Employed renters in labor markets with inflexible wages	Loss because real wage drops
Unemployed who get jobs	Gain in employment benefits
Unemployed homeowners who don't get jobs	Gain in property values, but loss due to increase in local prices
Unemployed renters who don't get jobs	Loss due to increase in local prices

Adapted from Bartik (1991).

164

In short, increasing a community's export base via tourism does not necessarily translate into increased income or quality of life for the host residents. The long-term negative impacts of tourism growth, such as higher taxes, increased rents, cultural degradation, and depletion of natural resources, can outweigh any short-term economic benefits (e.g., Faulkenberry et al., 2000; Mitchell and Reid, 2001). Even short-term tourism events lead to undesirable social impacts such as increases in congestion, noise, and crime (Mules and Faulkner, 1996). However, these potential problems may be understated or misunderstood by community residents when tourism development is introduced as a potential economic stimulus (Swindell and Rosentaub, 1998). The political environment of an area may dictate development impacts. For example, when comparing the cultural impact of tourism development on the countries of Denmark and Singapore, Ooi (2002) concludes that Singapore's political structure has created a situation where "commercial interests can be forcefully and deliberately integrated into local cultures by the authorities" (p. 702).

One way to ensure that tourism benefits outweigh the drawbacks is through directed, sustainable planning efforts that emphasize quality through community involvement. Lankford (1994) suggests that the key to successful destination planning is the inclusion of local residents through participation in the decision making process. For the resident, as evidenced in Chapter Eight, quality-of-life experiences are directly influenced by positively and negatively perceived impacts of tourism and indirectly influenced by attitudes toward tourism and tourists in general as well as the outcomes of interactions with tourists. For the tourist, quality tourism experiences are likely to result in repeat behavior, positive word of mouth, and overall positive experiences. The following case study examines how multiple parties in a Florida county have come together to plan for tourism using a Smart Growth approach to development.

Case Study: No Growth Policy in Alachua County

Alachua County is located in the heart of north central Florida about 120 miles north of Orlando. It is considered a medium-sized county in Florida, with just under 200,000 residents (Figure 9-2). In 1996, a nonprofit, public-interest organization called Sustainable Alachua County, Inc. (SAC) was formed. This organization

Figure 9.2   Map of North-Central Florida and Alachua County.
Source: *http://www.co.alachua.fl.us/content/maps/index.asp* (accessed 6/6/04).

consists of residents of Alachua County who are expressly interested in creating a sustainable future for the county. One of the main missions of the organization is to change public and private policy in order to protect the environment and ensure an equitable society and healthy local economy, including the development of tourism.

There are two major areas in the Smart Growth plan that involve tourism: (1) the planning process in the county and (2) ongoing planning of the county. First, in June 1997, a one-day community summit involving focus groups was convened with involved citizens of Alachua County. Out of that summit, community goals for a sustainable future were developed (Table 9-2). These goals were adopted by the Board of County Commission and are currently used to guide responsible growth decisions that the commission makes on behalf of the county. There were seven areas of emphasis tied to the goals: agriculture and food, education and culture, land use, natural systems, resource efficiency/pollution prevention, transportation, and the economy.

Table 9.2   Goals for sustainable Alachua county

Goal 1 - Health and the Environment
Ensure that every person enjoys the benefits of clean air, clean water, and a healthy environment at home, at work, and at play, and further ensure that every person has access to an effective health-care delivery system.

Goal 2 - Economic Prosperity
Achieve a healthy local economy that develops an adequate number of meaningful, living wage jobs, eliminates poverty, and provides the opportunities for a high quality of life in an increasingly competitive global economy.

Goal 3 - Equity
Ensure that all are afforded justice and have the opportunity to achieve economic, environmental, and social well-being.

Goal 4 - Conservation of Nature
Use, conserve, protect, and restore natural systems and resources—land, air, water, energy, and biodiversity—in ways that help ensure long-term social, economic, and environmental benefits for ourselves and future generations.

Goal 5 - Stewardship
Create a widely held ethic of stewardship that values diversity and strongly encourages individuals, institutions, and corporations to take full responsibility for the economic, environmental, and social consequences of their actions.

Goal 6 - Civic Engagement
Create full opportunity for citizens, businesses, and communities to participate in and influence the natural resource, environmental, and economic decisions that affect them, while ensuring that each geographic and socioeconomic sector bears costs and impacts equitably.

Goal 7 - Capital
Create facilities, and produce and purchase products, based on long-term environmental and operating costs, and find ways to include environmental and social costs in short-term prices. Establish economic measures of the value of biodiversity and ecosystems.

Goal 8 - Education
Ensure that all citizens have equal access to education, culture, and life-long learning opportunities that will prepare them for meaningful work, a high quality of life, and an understanding of the concepts involved in sustainable development.

Goal 9 - Communication and Culture
Foster a cultural climate that provides opportunities for a full range of entertainment, creative expression, artistic experience, and modes of communication.

Table 9.2   Goals for sustainable Alachua county—cont'd

Goal 10 - Agriculture
Define, develop, and promote local systems to foster a diverse and sustainable agriculture, protect farmland and the rural environment, and establish food security and a high standard of nutrition for the entire community.

Goal 11 - Land Use
Create land use patterns that promote a walkable community, minimize sprawl, preserve natural resources, preserve regional identity, and provide appropriate locations for community services and industry.

Goal 12 - Transportation
Provide transportation choices: car, bus, bicycle, and walking. Increase the efficiency of existing transportation resources. Create transportation that supports neighborhoods, protects the environment, and enhances the mobility of all ages and incomes.

Source: *http://www.afn.org/~links/sustainable/#SAC%20GOALS* (accessed 5/19/05).

One of the focus groups, which included members of the Alachua County Visitor and Convention Bureau (VCB), discussed several issues. One of the main areas of discussion was tourism. A general consensus of this focus group was that the community should promote eco-heritage tourism. Discussions surrounding eco-heritage tourism promotion centered on key values held by citizens of the community. These key values included low impact, managing carrying capacities of the natural resources; respecting local heritage, culture, and nature; respecting the local inventory (rather than building large attractions); not trading off the community for economic gain; and planning and promoting tourism that is consistent with the needs and wants of the community.

At the end of the summit, it was determined that there was widespread acceptance of eco-heritage tourism as an important element of future economic development plans. The focus group on economics decided that tracking the number of visitors to the natural and historic sites was a good indicator of sustainability (smart growth).

The second area of involvement for tourism in the Smart Growth plan is the execution of the goals from the summit. The first step in executing the plan in relation to tourism was to hold a tourism-visioning workshop. Therefore, in 2000, the commission, through the VCB and Tourism Development Council (TDC), hosted a visioning process for tourism in Alachua County. Representatives from local sports organizations, municipal governments, arts alliances, local tourism operators, faculty at the University of Florida, and members of the community were present for a two-day workshop. Consistent with the goals of Sustainable Alachua County, the tourism visioning process resulted in the development of a plan for sustainable tourism in the County, called the Vision for Tourism (Figure 9-3).

This plan is now used to make decisions regarding tourism in Alachua County. Decisions are guided by the nine-member TDC appointed by the Board of County Commission. Florida State Statute guides the composition of the board and dictates that the Tourism Development Council must consist of one county commissioner, one commissioner from the largest municipality, one commissioner from another municipality, three citizens-at-large, and three owner/operators in the lodging sector.

The TDC is responsible for ensuring that recommendations regarding tourism development are consistent with both the Vision for Tourism in the county as well

Located in north central Florida, Gainesville/Alachua County is a unique, family-friendly, university community, well known for its exciting blend of cultural, historic, and natural attractions as well as fine arts and sporting events. Home of the University of Florida Gators, the area draws business and convention travelers from throughout the world to the state-of-the-art research, medical, and conference facilitates. Careful preservation and use of the natural and man-made resources draw leisure visitors to enjoy the county's unique eco-systems. Tourism is an important contributor to the economic development in Gainesville/Alachua County and is woven into the fabric of the community in a way that enhances the residents' quality of life and the long-term viability of the community's cherished natural resources.

Figure 9.3   *Vision for Tourism in Alachua County.*
Source: Destination Consultancy Group (2000).

as the Smart Growth plan. The TDC evaluates projects that represent four categories of tourism in the county: (1) operations of the VCB; (2) a grant program to support meetings and conventions; (3) a destination enhancement fund that is used to support the arts and eco-heritage development; and (4) the Commission's Special Projects Fund. Evaluation tools have been created that aid the TDC in making recommendations to the commission on funding of specific projects. Tourism decisions in Alachua County are guided by the values that were expressed by citizens at both the Smart Growth summit as well as the Visioning Workshop. Quality of life for residents is at the cornerstone of tourism development. Ultimately, decisions that are not consistent with community values (*e.g.*, preservation of natural resources, historical resources, and culture) are not likely to be funded. Therefore, the Smart Growth plan and the results of the Visioning Workshop have minimized the negative impacts of tourism.

This case illustrates how government and residents can work together to develop a plan for tourism that is consistent with the vision of the county (the residents). The tourism visioning process lays the foundation that guides any future decisions regarding tourism planning and development. At the heart of these decisions is the residents' quality of life. This bottom-up, participative process is one method of developing tourism destinations that provide quality tourism experiences for both residents and tourists.

Justification and Goals

While tourism, economic, and political research abounds, there is a lack of literature that deliberately and clearly illustrates the linkages between the three areas within the context of quality tourism planning and development. Using the premises of political-economic theory, the next three chapters will seek to create these linkages. The goal of Chapter Ten is to demonstrate how powerful political actors influence tourism development and planning. Chapter Eleven illustrates how the distribution of benefits from tourism development is highly skewed. Chapter Twelve examines how tourism decision making tends to be undemocratic. Together, the chapters comprising this section are used to illustrate how tourism development is often guided by political and economic principles and practices that can either uphold or degrade quality tourism experiences.

References

Alachua County Board of Commissioners. (2001–2002). *Alachua County, Florida: Maps.* Downloaded 6 June 2004. [*www.co.alachua.fl.us/content/maps/index.asp*].

Bartik, T.J. (1991). *Who Benefits from State and Local Economic Development Policies?* Kalamazoo, MI: W.E. Upjohn Institute for Employment Research.

Betancur, J.J., and D.C. Gills. (1993). Race and class in local economic development. In R.D. Bingham and R. Mier (Eds.), *Theories of Local Economic Development: Perspectives from across the Disciplines* (pp. 191-209). Newbury Park, CA: Sage.

Blakely, E.J. (1994). *Planning Local Economic Development: Theory and Practice* (2nd ed.). Newbury Park, CA: Sage.

Bull, A. (1991). *The Economics of Travel and Tourism.* New York: John Wiley and Sons.

Chadwick, R.A. (1992). Concepts, definitions, and measures used in travel and tourism research. In J.R. Brent Ritchie and C.R. Goeldnew (Eds.), *Travel, Tourism and Hospitality Research: A Handbook for Managers and Researchers* (2nd ed., pp. 65-80). New York: John Wiley and Sons.

Crompton, J.L. (1999). *Measuring the Economic Impact of Visitors to Sports Tournaments and Special Events.* Ashburn, VA: Division of Professional Services, National Recreation and Park Association.

Davis, H.C. (1993). *Regional Economic Impact Analysis and Project Evaluation.* Vancouver: UBC Press.

Destination Consultancy Group (2000). The Alachua County Visioning Process Report. Unpublished Document. Lafayette, IN.

Durbarry, R. (2002). The economic contribution of tourism in Mauritius. *Annals of Tourism Research,* **29** (3), 862-865.

Faulkenberry, L.V., Coggeshall, J.M., Backman, K., and S. Backman. (2000). A culture of servitude: The impact of tourism and development on South Carolina's coast. *Human Organization,* 59 (1), 86-96.

Freshwater, D. (2000). Rural America at the turn of the century: One analyst's perspective. *Rural America,* 15 (3), 2-7.

Galston, W.A., and K.J. Baehler. (1995). *Rural Development in the United States: Connecting Theory, Practice, and Possibilities.* Washington, DC: Island Press.

Gunn, C.A. (1988). *Tourism Planning* (2nd ed.). New York: Taylor and Francis.

Gunn, C.A. (1997). *Vacationscape: Developing Tourist Areas.* New York: Taylor and Francis.

Hall, C.M., Jenkins, J., and G. Kearsley. (1997). Introduction: Issues in tourism planning and policy in Australia and New Zealand. In C. M. Hall, J. Jenkins, and G. Kearsley (Eds.), *Tourism Planning and Policy in Australia and New Zealand: Cases, Issues and Practice* (pp. 16-36). Sydney: Irwin Publishers.

Healey, M.J., and B.W. Ibery. (1990). *Location and Change: Perspectives on Economic Geography.* Oxford, England: Oxford University Press.

Holupka, C.S., and A.B. Shlay. (1993). Political economy and urban development. In R.D. Bingham and R. Mier (Eds.), *Theories of Local Economic Development: Perspectives from across the Disciplines* (pp. 175-190). Newbury Park, CA: Sage.

Lankford, S. (1994). Attitudes and perceptions toward tourism and rural regional development. *Journal of Travel Research,* **24** (3), 35-44.

Leiper, N. (1990). Tourism systems: An interdisciplinary perspective. *Occasional Papers,* **2,** 1-40.

Malizia, E., and E. Feser. (1999). *Understanding Local Economic Development.* New Brunswick, NJ: Center for Urban Policy Research (CUPR) Press.

Mitchell, R.E., and D.G. Reid. (2001). Community integration: Island tourism in Peru. *Annals of Tourism Research,* **28** (1), 113-139.

Mules, T., and B. Faulkner. (1996). An economic perspective on special events. *Tourism Economics,* **2** (2), 107-117.

Nelson, A.C. (1993). Theories of regional development. In R.D. Bingham and R. Mier (Eds.), *Theories of Local Economic Development: Perspectives from Across the Disciplines* (pp. 27-57). Newbury Park, CA: Sage.

Ooi, C. (2002). Contrasting strategies: Tourism in Denmark and Singapore. *Annals of Tourism Research,* **28** (3), 689-706.

Rainey, D.V., and K.T. McNamara. (1997). New and Existing Manufacturing Establishments: Differential Growth Impact. Paper presented at the annual meeting of the Regional Science Association International, Buffalo, New York.

Smith, S.L.J. (1988). Defining tourism: A supply side view. *Annals of Tourism Research,* **15,** 179-190.

Swindell, D., and M.S. Rosentaub. (1998). Who benefits from the presence of professional sports teams? The implications for public funding of stadiums and arenas. *Public Administration Review,* **58** (1), 11-20.

Sustainable Alachua County Inc. (1996, 1997). *Sustainable Development Seminar Series: "Sustainable Community," Goals of Sustainable Alachua County Inc.* Accessed 19 May 2005. [*http://www.afn.org/-links/sutainable/#SAC%20GOALS*].

Walo, M., Bull, A., and H. Breen. (1996). Achieving economic benefits at local events: A case study of a local sports event. *Festival Management and Event Tourism,* **4,** 95-106.

Whitson, D., and D. Macintosh. (1996). The global circus: International sport, tourism, and the marketing of cities. *Journal of Sport and Social Issues,* **20** (3), 278-295.

10

Quality Tourism Development and Planning

Kelly S. Bricker
Margaret J. Daniels
Barbara A. Carmichael

The continuing sacraband of struggle and compromise nearly obliterated the last of the ancient Forests in the Pacific Northwest, precipitated the alarming loss of wetlands everywhere in the country, reduced the nation's reserves of true wilderness, impaired the natural qualities of national parks, accelerated the extinction of species, destroyed the financial base and quality of life in human communities, and weakened the fabric of biodiversity. And so it has tended to go: while the principles get lost in the dust clouds of conflict over policies, proposals, and programs, the overall abundance and quality of natural habitat is steadily diminished. (Nelson, 1994, p. xiii)

Nelson's (1994) commentary on the diminishing state of public lands (*i.e.,* national parks, wildlife refuges, hotspot areas, etc.) pertains not only to land development in general but also specifically to tourism development, planning, and policy. The first purpose of Chapter Ten is to detail how powerful individuals and organizations with significant resources often make tourism development decisions that serve their own interests rather than considering the community as a whole. An extended analysis of 263 case studies will then be used to illustrate the benefits and limitations of sustainable tourism development practices in terms of constituency building, local economic benefits, and conservation funding. The chapter will conclude by tying together issues of quality tourism experiences, power, and land use and development by considering a case of contested spaces and casino development on Native American land.

Development and Tourism

Historically, land abuse has taken place due to unchecked private initiatives (Zaslowsky and Watkins, 1994). In considering development processes, "there is

strong evidence that various features of the factor endowments of these three categories of New World economies—including soil, climates, and the size or density
of the native population—predisposed them toward paths of development associated with different degrees of equality, wealth, human capital and political power"
(Sokoloff and Engerman, 2000, p. 223).

Public lands were established to mitigate development problems. As explained by
Zaslowsky and Watkins, "The public land systems compensate for the chief short-
coming of free enterprise – which is its inability to respond to any but its own press-
ing demands, all of them originating, understandably, in the need to maximize
profits as quickly as possible" (1994, p. 2). Unfortunately, according to Nash
(2001), this same preservation may lead to the degradation of public lands.
Although unprecedented tourist visitation may preclude protected areas from development, these visitors may lead these same areas to be "loved to death" (p. 316).

Unchecked tourism development also creates problematic effects in urban areas,
in particular those with a sensitive resource base (Russo, 2002). Using Venice as
an example, Russo (2002) discusses the "vicious circle" (p. 169) of tourism development in heritage cities, where "unguided expansion of the industry is followed
by decline, because high private and collective costs emerge and disrupt economic
and tourism performance of the city" (p. 166). Hence, long-range planning in both
natural and urban environments remains a critical factor in tourism development
and visitor impact management.

So, the stage is set for development and tourism. Far too often, tourism development decisions are made in ways that emphasize short-term economic gain over
long-term stability. For example, Gil (2003) explains the tourism development crisis
in the Canary Islands succinctly, "In a society where the language of economics and
its indicators distance the public from politicians, tourism and its economic weight
are creating a situation that, in many cases, is irreversible" (p. 745). Due to unmiti-
gated accommodation growth, coupled with poor maintenance, a changing tourist
profile and increased Mediterranean competition, the forecasted accommodation
supply of the Canary Islands is far surpassing the forecasted demand (Gil, 2003).

Tourism planning in developing countries, in particular, tends to be controlled
by the political elite. For example, Göymen (2000) discusses the state's dominant
role in tourism development in Turkey, where only over time did the central government consider tourism partnerships:

It was the collective efforts of private entrepreneurs investing in tourism, indigenous managers proving their competence, and the dynamism, resourcefulness exhibited by the new
players that helped convince the state to eventually redefine its role in the industry.
Admittedly, this cooperative partnership approach had its limitations and shortcomings. In
most cases, the public partners still dominated the scene. This was not only because they
wielded incomparable authority and resources but that the nongovernmental partners felt
subservient in most cases, exhibiting a timidity deeply embedded in the local political culture. (p. 1035)

Even though these partnerships hold promise for local involvement, a history of
deference to the state impacts the development governance of tourism in Turkey
and reinforces regional socioeconomic disparities (Göymen, 2000). Further,
tourism growth in Turkey has led to "environmental destruction (particularly along
coastal areas), cultural alienation, and the loss of social control and identity among
host communities" (Göymen, 2000, p. 1041).

Whereas highly centralized government control of tourism development can be problematic, external commercial involvement creates significant local distributional issues as well. Walpole and Goodwin (2000) use Komodo National Park (KNP) in Indonesia as an illustration of tourism development gone awry. The growth of tourism to KNP has led to increased external involvement and dependency, where "a large portion of businesses—be they hotels, restaurant, or charter boat operations—are not locally owned. . . . This will compromise the ability of local people to control and capitalize upon the development and commodification of their environment" (Walpole and Goodwin, 2000, p. 571). In the case of KNP and other tourism areas heavily dependent on external capital, "the existence of local economic elites serves to further constrain the distribution of benefits" (Walpole and Goodwin, 2000, p. 572). Walpole and Goodwin (2000) emphasize that the drawbacks of the current distribution of tourism benefits are being increasingly recognized and that initiatives to improve equity are underway. They stress, however, that the success of the equity programs requires the cooperation of local community and external business representatives.

Interestingly enough, placing tourism development in the hands of local community members creates its own set of difficulties. Cohen (2001) explains how indigenously based weavers have contributed greatly to tourism development in Oaxaca, Mexico. However, the relationships between contract weavers, independent producers, and merchants are rife with mistrust, competition, and inequality; "Thus, community-based tourism development, in this example, plays a central role in the growth of class divisions and increasing social tensions within the community" (Cohen, 2001, p. 390). The system comes full circle, as independent producers and contract weavers turn to state and federal representatives to create programs to control merchant dominance (Cohen, 2001).

Addressing Tourism Development

No easy answer to tourism development and power relationships exists, but researchers have set forth a number of explanations and recommendations that can assist stakeholders when considering the political and economic dimensions of development. For example, although shared development decisions are generally desirable, there are times when government intervention is necessary to contain development. Piga (2003) contends that in cases where sensitive natural environments are involved, if a private developer's plans are viewed to have unbeneficial consequences in the long run, the government should "exploit its first-mover advantage" (p. 904) and set a land use tax at a rate that deters development.

Gil (2003) goes a step further by explaining that, in some cases, an outright moratorium on tourism development is necessary. Although this can produce undesirable consequences (Gil, 2003), it may be necessary for the long-term protection of an area's factor endowments.

Up-marketing is another policy that can be initiated to control tourism development. Durbarry (2002) uses the country of Mauritius as an example of successful up-market tourism, which involves promoting to primarily high-spending tourists. Thus, Mauritius is successfully emphasizing quality over quantity by attracting a smaller market of high spenders. Simultaneously, the country has contained leakage by minimizing the amount of foreign hotel investment: "In cases where foreigners are involved, the hotels are owned in joint ventures with local share-holders" (p. 864).

Partnerships and shared decision making, while often complex and time con-suming, can also foster successful tourism development (Araujo and Bramwell, 2002). Araujo and Bramwell (2002) stress that particular attention must be paid to power differentials to ensure that mutual arrangements are indeed mutual. For example, in discussing a regional tourism partnership in northeast Brazil, the authors explain that the poverty in the majority of the region, in conjunction with "high unemployment, low pay, seasonal jobs, poor welfare and education provi-sion, low literacy levels, and high rates of disease" (p. 1147) create a planning dilemma because "poor social groups may be uninterested in being involved in planning as they are preoccupied with making ends meet or because of their his-tory of being excluded from decision making" (p. 1141). Thus, crisis intervention to increase local social welfare and decrease uncertainty must take place before meaningful local participation can occur (Araujo and Bramwell, 2002).

As is discussed more thoroughly in Chapters Eleven and Twelve, development teams should also carefully consider the views, needs, beliefs, and attitudes of community members. Using a case study of Nazareth, Uriely and colleagues (2002) found that individuals who felt that their heritage was well represented and positively portrayed were more supportive of tourism development than those whose heritage was not represented. When community members feel misrepre-sented or abused by the tourism system, their attitudes toward development are likely to be negative. For example, in Ghana, "wages in tourism are below subsis-tence level, even by Ghanian standards, while working conditions are deplorable" (Teye et al., 2002, p. 684). Understandably, those holding tourism-based jobs in Ghana have a degree of resentment, both toward tourism development and tourists themselves.

Having established a basis for understanding tourism, development, and power, the next goal of this chapter is to explore tourism's relationship to protection of natural areas using an extended analysis of case studies. The analysis considers tourism development, planning, and balancing power relationships from a biodi-versity conservation perspective, in terms of constituency building, local economic benefits, and conservation funding.

A Meta-Analysis of Current Research in Tourism and Environment Relationships Relative to Biodiversity Hotspots

The World Tourism Organization (WTO) is guided by the understanding of qual-ity in tourism as "the result of a process which implies the satisfaction of all the legitimate product and service needs, requirements and expectations of the con-sumer, at an acceptable price, in conformity with the underlying quality determi-nants such as safety and security, hygiene, accessibility, transparency, authenticity and harmony of the tourism activity concerned with its human and natural envi-ronment" (WTO, 2003).

The WTO (2003) argues there should be "common, irrevocable criteria of qual-ity, which are vital for the consumer independently of category or class of the prod-uct, establishment, facility or service sophistication." These include safety and security, hygiene, accessibility, transparency, authenticity, and harmony. The concept of *harmony* with the human and natural environment is directly relevant to sustainability. The World Tourism Organization clearly links quality tourism with sustainable tourism development.

We generally accept that sustainable tourism development must be inclusive of not only environmental considerations but also social and economic pillars as part of the equation. Moreover, while we understand that sustainable tourism must safeguard the natural environment in order to meet the needs of the host population and satisfy tourists, we have yet to determine whether this is actually taking place in practice (Cater, 1993). By exploring tourism's relationship to protection of natural areas, including protected areas such as national parks, we can begin to understand ways in which sustainability is incorporated into aspects of this complex industry. As Butler (2000) suggests, "The relationship between tourism and national parks will never be an easy one, but for the mutual well-being of both partners, the relationship must not only continue, but become more symbiotic if parks are to continue to perform their multiple functions into the third millennium" (p. 335).

In February 2002, Conservation International convened a comprehensive workshop on Tourism and Biodiversity, with international representatives from Conservation International, the United Nations Environment Program, World Conservation Monitoring Center (WCMC), International Institute for Environment and Development (IIED), African Conservation Corp-Kenya, and West Virginia University. The discussion focused on tourism development and biodiversity on two levels: macro and micro (Bricker et al., in press). One of the outcomes of this workshop was a need to collect and synthesize the results of research on the relationship between tourism development and biodiversity conservation via meta-analyses of case studies from around the globe (Bricker et al., in press). The overriding hypothesis guiding this analysis was: "Tourism development implemented according to the principles of environmental sustainability, nature conservation, and contributing to the well-being of local peoples will have a net positive or a neutral impact on biodiversity" (Conservation International, 2001, p. 1).

Returning to the focus of this chapter, a meta-analysis of case study research on tourism and environment relationships relevant to biodiversity hotspot areas was conducted. According to Conservation International (2003),

Hotspots are regions that harbor a great diversity of endemic species and, at the same time, have been significantly impacted and altered by human activities. Plant diversity is the biological basis for hotspot designation; to qualify as a hotspot, a region must support 1,500 endemic plant species, 0.5 percent of the global total. Existing primary vegetation is the basis for assessing human impact in a region; to qualify as a hotspot, a region must have lost more than 70 percent of its original habitat. Plants have been used as qualifiers because they are the basis for diversity in other taxonomic groups and are well known to researchers. Typically, the diversity of endemic vertebrates in hotspot regions is also extraordinarily high.

A meta-analysis is a form of qualitative research whereby research articles, rather than what people say, is content analyzed. Specifically, a systematic review was initiated to:

- Understand basic relationships, performance indicators, achievements, impacts of tourism, and biodiversity conservation relationships;
- Provide a comprehensive aggregation of results of case studies conducted between 1977 and 2003; and

■ Understand what has been studied and where more research is required for monitoring and evaluation of tourism growth in biodiversity hotspot areas.

Through key-word searches of several databases the following criteria were used to sift through the case studies from around the world. (Note: A complete database list will be published in Bricker, *et al.,* in press.)

■ Case studies must be published in peer reviewed journals;
■ Geographic area(s) described must be in a biodiversity hotspot;
■ The case-study must be written in English; and
■ Cases must address relationships between tourism and the environment.

Based on these criteria, 263 articles from 56 countries around the world were selected for the meta-analysis. The largest percentage (20%) was from the Indo-Burma hotspot area, followed closely by Mesoamerica (Bricker et al., in press). In general, key benefits to conservation and community were documented, as well as sociocultural and environmental impacts related to tourism development. The key benefits included the following principles:

Principle 1: Source of Financing. Tourism can be a source of financing for conservation through a variety of mechanisms, such as the Belizean tax on airfare that supports conservation at a national scale – or entry fees to parks that support their management.

Principle 2: Justification for Conservation. Tourism can provide a strong economic rationale to preserve areas rather than converting them to alternative uses such as crop or pasture land. Economic valuation has demonstrated the value of the wildlife and wild lands given what tourists are willing to pay to see them. These methods were increasingly used to reflect the costs and benefits of ecotourism over other land uses.

Principle 3: Providing Local People with Economic Alternatives. Protected areas and surrounding lands are often the most remote and agriculturally marginal lands in many countries. Tourism can generate benefits for local communities that support lives and livelihoods that reduce involvement in less sustainable endeavors (*e.g.,* poaching, unsustainable logging), which may avert environmental degradation by providing employment, income-generating opportunities, and financing for community projects.

Principle 4: Constituency Building. Tourism can build constituencies for conservation at local, national, and international levels. Locally, it provides a direct link between conservation objectives and livelihood needs. It can help build national-level constituencies both for specific site-based protection and for conservation policies more generally. Both national and international eco-tourists may be willing to donate their time, energy, and money to lobby for or against policies or activities that threaten the areas visited.

Principle 5: Impetus for Private Conservation Efforts. Worldwide, private nature reserves, operated by both for-profit and nonprofit organizations, were established to generate income and preserve habitats. Such reserves supplement *public* protected areas, broaden the range of habitats, and help serve as wildlife corridors. Private conservation areas are frequently multiple-use areas that combine areas for consumptive resource use (*e.g.,* grazing, forestry, and fishing) with areas for wilderness and recreation (such as wildlife viewing, birding, or sport-hunting or fishing) (Brandon, 1996, pp. 1-4).

Representation of Biodiversity Hotspots and Countries

Table 10-1 depicts the hotspot areas included in the study and number of countries represented by each hotspot area. Of the hotspot areas listed, all but two biodiversity areas are represented by case studies. The California Floristic Province, designated on the western coast of the United States, and the Mountains of South Central China were not represented by case studies. The Indo-Burma Hotpot area represented the majority of case studies covered in this study. Mesoamerica followed closely, with 50 case studies, or 19% of the total number of case studies represented. Surprisingly, very little attention has been given to the majority of hotspot areas around the globe. For example, within the Caribbean hotspot area, only 10 of 26 countries had been studied with respect to tourism and environment relationships. Additionally, within the Mediterranean Basin, only one-third of all countries represented within the hotspot had been researched and the results presented in case studies. West Africa, Caucasus, and Sundaland also had very low representation. The majority of cases represented case study research at the park or site level (55%), with national coverage following at 24% and regional coverage at 21%. (Note: The results presented in this study are a portion of a larger study conducted with Conservation International, 2002-2004. The comprehensive report will be published in Bricker *et al.,* in press.)

So what does this case study research related to tourism and the environment tell us? For the purposes of this chapter, we focused on three questions related to sustainable development, tourism benefits, and quality tourism experiences:

Table 10.1   Biodiversity hotspot areas represented by case studies

	N = Case Studies	Percent
Atlantic Forest	4	1.5
Brazilian Cerrado	1	0.4
Cape Floristic Region	10	3.8
Caribbean	17	6.5
Caucasus	1	0.4
Central Chile	3	1.1
Choco-Darien-Western Ecuador	7	2.7
Eastern Arc Mountains and Coastal Forests	19	7.2
Guinean Forests of West Africa	5	1.9
Indo-Burma	53	20.2
Madagascar and Indian Ocean Islands	10	3.8
Mediterranean Basin	18	6.8
Mesoamerica	50	19.0
New Caledonia	1	0.4
New Zealand	10	3.8
Philippines	1	0.4
Polynesia and Micronesia	9	3.4
Southwest Australia	5	1.9
Succulent Karoo	10	3.8
Sundaland	6	2.3
Tropical Andes	7	2.7
Wallacea	8	3.0
Western Ghats and Sri Lanka	8	3.0

- Does tourism encourage constituency building, which promotes conservation?
- Does tourism provide local people with economic alternatives to minimize encroachment into conservation areas?
- Why was funding from tourism not providing benefits to conservation?

Constituency Building

The findings in relationship to constituency building are summarized in Table 10-2. Some 17% of the cases reported that tourism encourages constituency building, which promotes biodiversity conservation. Only 8% reported that it did not, and an overwhelming majority of the case studies did not address the issue. Of those case studies reporting that constituency building occurred, they ranged from a local to a national scale.

On community and government levels, protected areas were either expanded or initiated, including marine and land areas. Locally, tourism encouraging constituency building surfaced through evidence of participation in conservation programs or associations, formation of new conservation associations, and increased volunteerism in local conservation efforts by landowners. There was also evidence that tourism employees (*e.g.,* tour guides) were volunteering their time in local conservation programs. Jointly, local communities and government demonstrated increased concern for the environment through the establishment of regulations for pollution and waste. Locals also became involved in establishing environmental education and awareness programs within their communities. Last, some case studies referred to increased participation by tourists in fund raising for conservation efforts (Bricker et al., in press). From a national scale, tourism was an impetus for government to increase funds to support enterprise-based approaches to biodiversity conservation. There was also evidence of increased cooperation and communication between government, nongovernment organizations (NGOs), and private enterprise in sustainable tourism development efforts.

Of those cases reviewed that did not demonstrate tourism's contribution to encouraging constituency building (*i.e.,* 8%), the evidence demonstrated the lack of the local community's involvement in tourism initiatives. For example, some cases suggested that indigenous landowners were in conflict with park managers concerning wildlife, doubting the sincerity of park officials to engage with local communities. Locals also have threatened to kill wildlife outside of reserves if not compensated appropriately. Other cases gave evidence of local community members feeling disenfranchised and left out of the planning processes for tourism development. The lack of opportunities for gainful employment or ability to generate income was also depicted in case studies. Additionally, local community members were denied access to traditional areas for activities such as fishing and farming, thwarting other possibilities for income generation. And, in some instances, case studies reflected the dominance of local elites who have monopolized tourism development (Bricker et al., in press).

Although the majority of cases (75%) did not address whether or not tourism encourages constituency building, it does appear to be an important link to protecting the environment long term. Hence, it is critical that we take a more holistic approach to examining the outcomes of tourism as a means of constituency building for conservation—locally, nationally, and with tourists. In a recent study

Table 10.2 Does tourism promote constituency building to promote conservation? (From Bricker et al., in press)

Does tourism promote constituency building to promote conservation?
- Some 17% (n = 45) of all cases reviewed identified and addressed this issue. Another 8% of the case studies reviewed determined that this principle was not evident, leaving 75% (n = 197) of all case studies not addressing this principle at all.

Mesoamerica (50 cases)
- Some 66% of cases did not address this principle (33 cases).
- Of the remaining 34% that did address this principle, 30% (15 cases) showed evidence of this occurring, with 4% (2 cases) suggesting this does not occur at all.

Caribbean (17 cases)
- Some 82% (14 cases) reviewed in the Caribbean hotspot region did not address this principle. The remaining 18% (3 cases) that did address this principle showed evidence of the principle occurring.

Madagascar and Indian Ocean Islands (10 cases)
- Some 70% of cases reviewed in this hotspot did not address this principle. The remaining 3 cases (30%) showed evidence of this occurring.

Eastern Arc Mountains and Coatal Forests (19 cases)
- Some 58% of cases did not address this principle (11 cases). Of the remaining 42% that did address this principle, 10% (2 cases) showed evidence of this occurring, and 32% (6 cases) suggested this does not occur at all.

Cape Floristic Region (10 cases)
- Some 80% of cases did not address this principle (8 cases). The remaining 20% showed evidence of this occurring.

Succulent Karoo (10 cases)
- Some 70% of cases reviewed in this hotspot region did not address this principle. Of the three cases addressing this principle, two cases (20%) showed evidence of this occurring.

Mediterranean Basic (18 cases)
- Some 89% of the cases reviewed in the Mediterranean Basin region did not address this principle.
- The remaining 11% (2 cases) showed evidence of this principle occurring.

Indo-Burma (53 cases)
- Some 70% of cases reviewed in this region did not address this principle (37 cases). Of the remaining 30% that did address this principle, 10 cases (19%) showed evidence of this occurring; with six cases (11%) suggesting that this does not occur at all.

New Zealand (10 cases)
- Some 90% of the cases reviewed in the New Zealand hotspot region did not address this principle (9 cases). The remaining 10% showed evidence of this principle occurring.

Summary
- The majority of the cases (74%) did not address this principle: "Does tourism promote constituency building to promote conservation?"
- The hotspot regions that did address this principle, with the exception of the Eastern Arc Mountains and Coastal Forests and Indo-Burma hotspot regions, showed a greater percentage of the principle occurring (17%) than the principle not occurring (8%).
- The Caribbean, Madagascar and Indian Ocean Islands, Cape Floristic Region, Mediterranean Basin, and New Zealand hotspot regions showed that, for all cases that addressed the issue of promoting consituency building to promote conservation, 100 percent showed evidence of this principle occurring.

179

jointly conducted by the Travel Industry Association of America (TIA) and National Geographic Traveler (2003), the majority of travelers found outstanding scenery (80%) and a clean and unpolluted environment (73%) as two of the most important attributes in taking leisure trips (p. 13). This natural capital attracts tourists to a destination and provides an important component of quality tourism experiences.

Economic Benefits

Another issue considered in the review of cases was whether tourism provides local people with economic alternatives to minimize encroachment into conservation areas. This issue is summarized in Table 10-3. Once again, the majority (*i.e.,* 60%) did not address this issue in discussing tourism and environment relationships. Another 15% of the case studies reviewed determined that this principle was not evident at all. However, of the 25% of cases that did address the issue, several interesting examples emerged.

Direct and indirect employment opportunities were a common thread throughout the case studies. This was evidenced through descriptions of the percentage of local people employed in tourism, types of positions held, development of human resource potential via education and training opportunities, and types of alternative employment opportunities produced (*i.e.,* development of handicraft trade, guiding/outfitting services, food services). Additionally, financial incentives included mention of income from leases, government incentives, community development funds, and creation of infrastructure benefits, including better transportation and increased community resources and social services. Also, when addressing economic alternatives to exploitation, some cases referenced regional benefit—tourism strengthened the economy, general trading, and real estate value (Bricker et al., in press).

Not surprisingly, negative impacts of tourism development were also evident. In these case studies, tourism did not provide economic alternatives to exploitation. Reasons for this included:

- Inadequate compensation for locals displaced by parks or protected areas;
- Unsuccessful revenue sharing schemes, creating tension among local communities and tourism enterprises; and
- Low-paying jobs and low status jobs (Bricker et al., in press).

A significant portion (71%) of the travel market (American travelers) believed that "people must live in harmony with nature in order to survive" (TIA and National Geographic Traveler, 2003, p. 16). Hence, mechanisms to build a relationship between economic benefits to local communities and protecting the natural environment are critical to the sustainability of quality environments. For example, Bookbinder and associates (1998) explain that "25 years of experience in the buffer zones of [Royal Chitwan National Park] convince us that local support for biodiversity conservation requires a combination of co-ownership, co-management, and policy change" (p. 1403). Additionally, to maintain quality tourism experiences in destinations while providing real economic benefits to host communities, more work needs to be done to:

Table 10.3   Does tourism provide local people with alternatives to exploiting conservation areas?

(From Bricker et al., in press)

- Of all cases reviewed, 25% (n = 67) identified this principle as addressed. Another 15% of the case studies reviewed determined that this principle was not evident, leaving 60% (n = 157) of all case studies not addressing this principle at all.

Mesoamerica (50 cases)
- Some 70% of cases did not address this principle (35 cases).
- Yet of the remaining 30% that did address this principle, 24% (12 cases) showed evidence of this occurring, with 6% (3 cases) suggesting this does not occur at all.

Caribbean (17 cases)
- Some 88% (15 cases) reviewed in the Caribbean hotspot region did not address this principle. The remaining 12% (2 cases) that did address this principle showed evidence of the principle occurring.

Madagascar and Indian Ocean islands (10 cases)
- Some 60% of cases reviewed in this hotspot did not address this principle.
- Of the 4 cases addressing this principle, 3 cases showed evidence of this occurring.

Eastern Arc Mountains and Coastal Forests (19 cases)
- Some 32% of cases did not address this principle (6 cases).
- Yet of the remaining 68% that did address this principle, 21% (4 cases) showed evidence of this occurring, with 47% (9 cases) suggesting this does not occur at all.

Cape Floristic Region (10 cases)
- Some 50% of cases did not address this principle (5 cases).
- The remaining 50% showed evidence of this principle occurring.

Succulent Karoo (10 cases)
- Some 30% of cases reviewed in this hotspot region did not address this principle.
- Yet, of the 7 cases addressing this principle, 6 cases (60%) showed evidence of this principle occurring.

Mediterranean Basin (18 cases)
- Some 56% of the cases reviewed in the Mediterranean Basin region did not address this principle.
- The remaining 44% (8 cases) showed evidence of this principle occurring.

Indo-Burma (53 cases)
- Some 45% of cases reviewed in this region did not address this principle (24 cases).
- Yet, of the remaining 55% that did address this principle, 15 cases (28%) showed evidence of this occurring; with 14 cases (26%), suggesting that this does not occur at all.

New Zealand (10 cases)
- A total of 100% of the cases reviewed in the New Zealand hotspot region did not address this principle.

Summary
- The majority of the cases (60%) did not address: "Does tourism provide local people with alternatives to exploiting conservation areas?"
- The hotspot regions that did address this principle, with the exception of the Eastern Arc Mountain and Coastal Forests hotspot region, showed a greater percentage of the principle occurring (25%) than the principle not occurring (15 percent).
- The Eastern Arc Mountains and Coastal Forests hotspot region showed a larger percentage (47%) of this *Principle 3* not occurring than the principle actually occurring (21%). This was also evident in *Principle 4*, with 32% of the cases from this hotspot region showing that, the principle did not occur, and only 10% showing that the principle did occur.
- The Caribbean, Cape Floristic Region, and Mediterranean Basin hotspot regions showed that, for all cases that addressed this principle, 100% showed evidence of this principle actually occurring.

- Develop training programs for staff, incorporating sensitivity and consideration for local cultures and customs (Pearl, 1993).
- Structure wage and tipping programs considering equity and local norms (Pearl, 1993).
- Construct programs where local people are involved in tourism, participate fully, and secure fair and equitable benefits from tourism development (Colvin, 1996).

Funding for Conservation?

Within the range of articles reviewed, 55 articles addressed why funding from tourism was not providing benefits to conservation. Results demonstrated that several factors inhibit tourism's ability to benefit biodiversity conservation, including process and planning, land tenure and ownership, mismanagement and distribution of funds, and access to visitors and visitor dollars (Bricker et al., in press).

Process and Planning

Process and planning issues encompassed a wide range of concerns. The case studies described the necessity to capture economic surplus from travel consumers and funnel funds into conservation efforts. Another issue was the lack of resources within protected areas, including staff and operations. Lack of integrated planning and enforcement and control capabilities were identified as issues that inhibit tourism funds from directly contributing to conservation. Some of the cases presented inferred that there was a lack of coherent policies and legislation, resulting in lack of enforcement in protected areas. Others referred to a general lack of expertise in science and conservation management as well as institutional capacity for sustainable development. Additionally, these case studies referenced an overall lack of communication and dialogue between park managers, local residents, and the tourism industry. Finally, there was some mention of an unwillingness of the tourism industry to invest in conservation (Bricker et al., in press).

Land Tenure and Ownership

Concerning ownership issues, several factors that inhibit tourism dollars from benefiting conservation efforts were described. First, several cases referenced high leakage rates due to foreign ownership—tourist dollars were not reinvested locally. Second, despite the establishment of protected areas, poaching continued to thwart conservation efforts. Last, the laws reflecting land tenure were incongruent with reality, often resulting in unclear ownership and responsibilities (Bricker et al., in press).

Mismanagement and Distribution of Funds

Corruption, lack of accountability, inadequate entrance fees, and lack of funds funneling directly back to the resource were issues tied to the mismanagement of funds. The primary issues surrounding the distribution of funds included limited benefits to communities. Simply, only a few benefited directly from tourism revenues, leaving a majority to find other mechanisms for income generation—which included illegal extraction of natural resources. Unfortunately, in some cases absolutely no benefit filtered directly to the local communities. Another issue relevant to the distribution of funds was the fact that in some areas tourists dollars went into general funds instead of being allocated directly back to the natural areas collecting the fees (Bricker et al., in press).

Access to Visitors and Visitor Dollars

The meta-analysis of case studies in biodiversity hotspot areas substantiated the fact that in order for a country or destination to attract and sustain tourism visitation levels, there must be political stability. Additionally, the high cost of travel to destinations, as well as poor infrastructure development, contribute to low arrivals, which ultimately affects the amount of revenue generated for conservation and other needs (Bricker et al., in press). Supporting these ideas relative to quality tourism experiences, TIA and National Geographic Traveler (2003) also found that, in their recent study of American travelers, only 8% of travelers preferred to travel internationally rather than in the United States (p. 11). In times of political uncertainty and risk of terrorism, this is not surprising. Results of this survey and the meta-analysis raise further questions for the viability of remote travel destinations located in crisis areas. Hence, sustaining biodiversity must also consider a range of sustainable activities to assist in a healthy economy in addition to tourism activities, enabling not only mechanisms for environmental protection but also mechanisms locally controlled and sustained by communities for poverty alleviation and increased quality of life.

Discussion

The meta-analysis of biodiversity and tourism studies reveals that there are many barriers to the realization of the sustainable development of tourism. Some of these barriers are related to political factors in terms of the control held by powerful elites and the lack of involvement of local communities in planning for the pace and scale of tourism development. Little wealth is spread in terms of the "equalization principle," and there may be mismanagement of funds. As described in Chapter Nine, one of the premises of political economic theory recognizes that specific local actors and institutions play key roles in determining how local development occurs (Holupka and Shlay, 1993). The key to this process is that power rests in the hands of individuals and groups, whether it is in the form of land, labor, or capital. The following section of this chapter will tie together issues of power, quality, land use, and tourist development within the context of Native Americans and their recent ventures in economic development through tourism and casino gaming. Changing power relations, contested space, and social representations of different ethnic groups form the themes of discussion. A case study of Native American gaming in southeast Connecticut reveals how economic, social, and environmental impacts of tourism are perceived as the development takes shape on reservation land. Loss of environmental integrity and quality-of-life issues are blamed on the Native American developers, and local residents resent this emerging power group who, in this area at least, are no longer an underprivileged sector of society.

Case Study: Native Americans in Southeast Connecticut— Contested Spaces and Tourism Developments

In 1992, the opening of the Foxwoods Resort Casino by the Mashentucket Pequot tribe brought many changes to the quiet rural area in southeastern (SE) Connecticut where the reservation is located. For the tribe it meant rapid economic growth, which contrasted sharply with their past poverty and lack of economic success at previous economic development efforts. Since opening, the casino has undergone a number of expansions and it is now the biggest casino resort development in the world. For the residents of the three rural towns of Ledyard, North Stonington, and Preston that are situated in close proximity to the casino, this tourist attraction represents an unwelcome intrusion and is perceived by many as negatively affecting their quality of life. In 1996, a second mega-resort casino, the Mohegan Sun, was opened by the Mohegan tribe in nearby Montville. With the recent application for federal recognition of the Eastern Pequots, there are contested plans for further developments on their reservation land (Hutt Scott, 2003). Since the developments occur on Native American lands, with the tribes in power as sovereign nations, this situation is unusual in that there are two host communities to understand—the tribes and their surrounding U.S. residents not residing on native lands. The tribes are in control of their land and the pace and nature of the development. The local towns control the zoning and development on their land but are unable to affect what happens on reservation land.

In geographical thought, there is a recent emergence of a "new economic geography" that attempts to contextualize the "economic" by locating it within the cultural, social, and political relations through which it takes meaning and direction (Lee and Wills, 1997). Cultural politics, therefore, has become important in understanding local economic development (McCann, 2002). *Cultural politics* is defined as "the process enacted when a set of social actors shaped by, and embodying, different cultural meanings and practices come into conflict with each other" (Alvarez et al., 1998, p. 7). This takes place within a spatial context. Social actors engage in politics and mobilize representations and understandings of their place as they articulate competing visions for the future of their locality (McCann, 2002). As the host communities for casino developments in SE Connecticut are further divided on an ethnic basis, it is not surprising that there are differing visions and representations for growth, prosperity, quality of life, and "identity" of the region. These conflicting views are shaped by the history of changing power relations in the region and historical arguments over land tenure, land use, and space.

Contested Landscapes—Historical Background

At the time of European arrival in New England in the early seventeenth century, the Pequots controlled hundreds of square miles of land between the Thames and

Pawcatuck rivers along Long Island Sound (Waldman, 1994). They were described by British and Dutch traders as "the most numerous, the most warlike, the fiercest, and the bravest of all the aboriginal clans of Connecticut" (Eisler, 2001). The translation of their name itself means "destroyers." The Pequots fished, hunted, farmed, and traded furs with Europeans. Before contact with the Europeans, the Pequots numbered an estimated 15,000, but infectious diseases and conflict with the European settlers decimated 80% of their population. During the Pequot War in 1637, at least 400 Pequots were killed in Mystic when their fort was attacked and burned (Carmichael and Peppard, 1998). In 1667 a 3,000-acre reservation was established for the Pequots at Mashentucket in a heavily wooded area of rocky knolls and swamps. The size of the reservation fell rapidly to 1,600 acres in 1721, 989 acres in 1761, and 204 acres in 1855. During the twentieth century, no new housing was constructed and housing deteriorated. By 1970, only two elderly women lived on the reservation. At this time the tribe was under great threat because, if the land was completely vacated, it could be seized by the state. The two women fought to hold on to the tribal land and encouraged Pequots to return to the reservation. By 1974, the Pequots adopted a constitution and filed a land claims suit. They gained federal recognition in 1983 and received a $900,000 settlement and access to federal loans. The reservation land base has grown to 3,600 acres and there are plans to annex nearby land (Stansfield, 1996).

This history reflects the uneasy tension between subjugated Native Americans and white Americans. The Native Americans lost their power base and land and were relegated to small reservations on poorer unproductive land. Giddens (1985) conceptualizes the integration of power in regionalization as the interaction of "front" and "back regions." Front regions are areas where interaction is open, on show, and often official (modern capitalist state, normal behavior, the accepted). Back regions are areas of underdevelopment, often hidden, ignored, marginalized, and represent the "other." A further aspect of regionalization occurs in the notions of center and periphery, which Giddens (1985) equates with those who establish themselves as having control over resources and those who are outside of that control. White American heritage, culture, and representations dominated in the SE Connecticut region. Other histories, cultures, and representations were marginalized at least until the 1990s.

The Mashentucket Pequot tribe, after various unsuccessful ventures in economic development (horticulture, pig farming), opened a successful Bingo hall in 1986 and, after the Indian Gaming Regulatory Act was passed in 1988, they applied to open a casino. After much opposition from the state and against the wishes of many local residents, the tribe gained permission from the Secretary of the Interior to open Foxwoods Resort casino in 1992. After a series of expansions, the casino development is now an immense entertainment complex. The tribe is no longer the neglected rural "other" that experiences exploitation and deprivation but a dominant economic force in the region.

Changing Power Relations

Skip Hayward, former tribal leader who shaped the initial casino development, described the casino as a way for the Pequots to have a voice in the region and "to tell their story." Part of the new development includes a museum of tribal heritage to encourage native pride. Despite an investment of $193 million, this museum is not profitable. It seems that casino visitors and museum visitors are different market segments (Bowles, 2003). More significantly, a statue of the English leader who slaughtered the Pequots in the massacre during the Pequot war, as described above, was removed from its long-standing position in the town of Windsor, Connecticut. Hence, removal of an icon such as this may reflect the change in power relations in the region.

The tribe is now a dominant economic presence, contributing economic benefits and employment. In 1993, the tribe negotiated with the state to operate slot machines and, in return, gave 25% of their gross revenue from slots to the state. Since that point, the tribe has contributed $1.6 billion to Connecticut. A recent statement from a tribal spokesman, Peter Johnson, reflected the Pequot attitude toward this contribution: "States should not balance their budgets on the backs of Indian tribal governments" (Abrahms, 2003). In fact, 3% of the state's revenue comes from slot machine proceeds from the Mashentucket Pequot and the Mohegan casinos (Abrahms, 2003). Each casino is a mega-attraction that draws 30,000 to 40,000 visitors per day. The tribes have been so successful that "they have turned centuries of social and political relations on their heads" (D'Hauteserre, 2001, p. 420). The Mashentucket Pequot tribe is contributing generously to the region's infrastructure and has provided opportunities for partnerships with local organizations (Carmichael and Peppard, 1998). These partnerships mostly create goodwill and enhance their corporate image. However, set against this force for positive relationships, there are perceived threats as the tribe begins to assert the new power that goes along with their economic prosperity. These threats are visible in discourses on contested boundaries, land annexation, infrastructure growth, quality of life, and sustainability and even the authenticity of the tribe themselves.

Boundaries, Land Annexation, and Infrastructure—Contested Spaces

According to D'Hauteserre (2001), the Mashentucket Pequot are represented as threatening to take over their ancient lands, leaving U.S. residents powerless to direct the future trajectories of the area. The local residents want to be assured of specific and fixed boundaries for the reservation to strictly control Pequot space. This is ironic, considering the history of Pequot space in the region. However, it is not surprising, since boundaries, like the spaces they delineate, are socially constructed as different actors seek to define the scope and extent of their sociospatial relations (D'Arcus, 2003). The Pequots are expanding their land base but only in a very limited way, as yet. There are local action groups (for example, the Connecticut Alliance Against Casino Expansion) that are centers of resistance to such development, not just in terms of reservation land but also to infrastructure expansion for regional growth. Specifically, opposition is strong to the superhighway expansion plan to replace Route 2A, which links Foxwoods to the Mohegan Sun. This expansion would be at taxpayers' expense, would require $76 million federal funding, and is directly linked to gambling expansion. Foxwoods is planning a $99 million expansion to compete with the recently completed $1 billion expansion to the Mohegan Sun that included a hotel, casino, arena, and convention center (Scarponi, 2003).

Quality of Life and Sustainability—Perceived Impacts and Social Representations

A second discourse described by D'Hauteserre (2001) is the representation by the nearby U.S. residents that the Mashentucket Pequots are pursuing destructive actions against the quaint picturesque environment of SE Connecticut. She explains this as an attempt to challenge and discredit the new spatial arrangements developed in the region. D'Hauteserre suggests that "residents of the towns closest to Foxwoods, who have always resisted Indian presence in their midst, have had to construct 'values' for their rural space as a strategy of social resistance to the transformed relationships that the commoditization of the reservation has established" (p. 414).

While residents of nearby towns are concerned about the environmental impacts of the casino developments (Carmichael et al., 1996), the tribe is a member of the National Tribal Council that has a proactive policy rather than a reactive response to environmental issues. There is a new sewage plant on the reservation that is more environmentally sound than the septic disposal tanks used in the surrounding townships. However, as the casino and related golf course developments expand, water supply is becoming a major issue (Lyman, 2003).

Resident attitude surveys conducted in 1992, 1993, and 1995, soon after the casino opened, reveal deterioration in the perceived quality of life for the residents in the three surrounding towns (Carmichael et al., 1996). There were four overall assessment variables in the surveys:

1. The casino is making my town a less desirable place to live. (LESS DESIRABLE)
2. In general, it would be better for this area if the casino had never been built. (NEVER BUILT)
3. In general, the benefits of the casino and related development outweigh the costs to my town. (TOWN BENEFIT)
4. In general, the benefits of the casino and related development outweigh the costs to the region. (REGION BENEFIT)

Table 10-4 shows the changes in resident responses to quality-of-life variables over time. Regression analysis and logit analysis reported elsewhere (Carmichael et al., 1996) showed that perceived casino impacts predicted quality-of-life variables and, notably, that perceived environmental impact was a significant independent variable in all models.

The same surveys revealed that attitudes toward the tribe have deteriorated more than they have improved (Carmichael et al., 1996). Table 10-5 summarizes the direction of change but does not reveal overall attitude.

Respondents were asked to explain these changes in attitudes. Those whose attitudes toward the tribe became more favorable commented about perceived positive benefits and support for the tribe with such statements as, "They are good people," "They have already had such misfortune, they deserve better," and "They are using the land wisely." In contrast, a second representation was revealed by some whose attitudes had deteriorated, in comments such as, "They are not real Indians." Intermarriage, particularly with African Americans means that many do not fit their physical stereotype. Furthermore, there is no poverty. Instead, the Mashentucket Pequot attracted many tribe members back to the reservation under the rule that they should be at least one-sixteenth Pequot; they enjoy the benefits

Table 10.4   Changes in resident responses to quality of life variables over time

Quality-of-Life Variable	Agree 1992	Agree 1993	Agree 1995	Disagree 1992	Disagree 1993	Disagree 1995
LESS DESIRABLE—The casino is making my town a less desirable place to live.	38.4%	49.8%	62.1%	53.7%	37.7%	30.0%
NEVER BUILT—In general, it would be better for this area if the casino had never been built.	33.2%	44.9%	34.5%	55.3%	41.7%	45.4%
TOWN BENEFIT—In general, the benefits of the casino and related development outweigh the costs to my town.	NA	36.4%	31.5%	NA	49.4%	51.7%
REGION BENEFIT—In general, the benefits of the casino and related development outweigh the costs to the region.	NA	47.0%	42.9%	NA	40.9%	40.4%

of economic success. Some local residents show their resentment in comments such as, "I think there are a number of people with little Indian blood getting all the money" and "They are not real Indians, they are wealthy" (Carmichael and Peppard, 1998).

This case study shows the cultural politics of a region in action and resistance, as tourism in the form of a mega-resort casino is used for economic growth. The geographical core of colonialism, particularly in its settler form, is about the displacement of people from their land and its repossession by others (Harris, 2003). The recognition of sovereign nations and the politics of difference rather than assimilation opened the path to economic prosperity for Native Americans through an often despised activity: casino gaming. The discussion has revealed the changing power relations that resulted from this process in southeastern Connecticut, as well as the struggle, resistance, and coping strategies of the traditional "center" as it gives way to the influence of the "periphery."

Table 10.5   Changes in resident attitudes toward the Mashentucket Pequot tribe over time

ATTITUDE- Have your attitudes toward the tribe become	Agree 1992	Agree 1993	Agree 1995
Generally more favorable	16.9%	18.8%	17.8%
Generally less favorable	20.6%	29.4%	30.7%
Stayed about the same	62.4%	51.4%	51.5%

Implications

Tourism development decisions are usually made by powerful elites. Such decisions may be motivated by short-term gain rather than long-term sustainability in terms of quality of life for local residents. Are overall benefits perceived to be outweighing overall costs? Perceived impacts are often more important than actual impacts of tourism development in influencing quality of life. Numerous barriers are present to the achievement of sustainable tourism development, as the meta-analysis of case studies in biodiversity hot spots shows. Political stability is vital for tourism sustainability. However, such stability often comes with control from powerful elites who superimpose their vision of quality in tourism development and tourism experience. In the concluding case study of a small region with changing power elites, a struggle for space, control, and prescription for quality tourism is illustrated. Local U.S. communities have no control over the tourism developments that are rapidly growing on nearby Indian Reservation Land. While this case study involves the development of casino gaming as an example of tourism, there are parallels between the cultural politics in this small region and the general issues raised by the meta-analysis of nature-based tourism initiatives. These issues involve themes of ownership and control, power through access to funding, and the changing dimensions of cooperation and control. Behind each case lies the political construction of tourism and, as a consequence, influences the development of tourism products, residents' perceptions of tourism growth and development, residents' quality of life, and the natural, social, and physical environments in which they reside and tourists visit.

References

Abrahms, D. (2003). States get too greedy, tribes say: The Mashentuckets are among those testifying. *www.norwichbulletin.com*, July 10, accessed 12/18/03.

Alvarez, S.E., Dagnino, E., and A. Escobar. (1988). Introduction: the cultural and political in Latin American social movements. In S.E. Alvarez, E. Dagnino, and A. Escobar (Eds.), *Cultures of Politics and Politics of Cultures: Revisioning Latin American Social Movements* (pp. 55-70). Albany: State University of New York Press.

Araujo, L.M., and B. Bramwell. (2002). Partnership and regional tourism in Brazil. *Annals of Tourism Research,* **29** (4), 1138-1164.

Bookbinder, M.P., Dinerstein, E., Rijal, A., Cauley, H., and A. Rajouria. (1998). Ecotourism's support of biodiversity conservation. *Conservation Biology,* **12** (6), 1399-1404.

Bowles, A. (2003). Tribe's focus slips from museum. *www.norwichbulletin.com*, August 10, accessed 12/18/03.

Brandon, K. (1996). *Ecotourism and Conservation: A Review of Key Issues, Environmental Department Papers* (No. 033). Washington DC: The World Bank.

Bricker, K., Brandon, K., Matus, S., and C. Christ. (in press). *Meta-Analysis of Tourism and Biodiversity Conservation Relationships*. Joint Report by Conservation International and West Virginia University. Washington DC.

Butler, R.W. (2000). Tourism and national parks in the twenty-first century. In R.W. Butler and S.W. Boyd (Eds.), *Tourism and National Parks: Issues and Implications* (pp. 323-335). Chichester: John Wiley and Sons.

Carmichael, B.A., and D.M. Peppard, Jr. (1998). The impact of Foxwoods Resort Casino on its dual host community: South East Connecticut and the Mashentuckeet Pequot tribe. In A.A. Lew and G.A. Van Otten (Eds.), *Tourism and Gaming on Indian Lands* (pp. 128-144). Elmsford, NY: Cognizant Communications.

Carmichael, B.A., Peppard, D.M., Jr., and F.M. Boudreau. (1996). Mega-resort on my doorstep: Local resident attitudes toward Foxwoods Casino and casino gambling on nearby Indian reservation land. *Journal of Travel Research*, **34** (3), 9-16.

Cater, E. (1993). Ecotourism in the Third World: Problems for sustainable tourism development. *Tourism Management,* **14** (2), 85-90.

Cohen, J.H. (2001). Textile, tourism and community development. *Annals of Tourism Research,* **28** (2), 378-398.

Colvin, J. (1996). Indigenous ecotourism: The Capirona programme in Napo Province, Ecuador. *Unasylva,* **187** (47), 32-37.

Conservation International. (2001, February). *The Tourism Sector and Biodiversity Conservation.* Workshop summary presented by Conservation International, Washington, DC.

Conservation International Biodiversity Hotspots of the World. (2003). *http://www.biodiversityhotspots.org/xp/Hotspots/hotspotsScience/*, accessed 3/31/04.

D'Arcus, B. (2003). Contested boundaries: Native sovereignty and state power at Wounded Knee, 1973. *Political Geography*, **22,** 415-437.

D'Hauteserre, A.M. (2001). Representations of rurality: Is Foxwoods Casino Resort threatening the quality of life in southeast Connecticut? *Tourism Geographies,* **3** (4), 405-429.

Durbarry, R. (2002). The economic contribution of tourism in Mauritius. *Annals of Tourism Research,* **29** (3), 862-865.

Eisler, K.I. (2001). *Revenge of the Pequots: How a Small Native American Tribe Created the World's Most Profitable Casino.* New York: Simon and Schuster.

Giddens, A. (1985). Time space and regionalization. In D.Gregory and J.Urry (Eds.), *Social Relations and Spatial Structures.* London: Macmillan, 1985.

Gil, S.M. (2003). Tourism development in the Canary Islands. *Annals of Tourism Research,* **30** (3), 744-747.

Göymen, K. (2000). Tourism and governance in Turkey. *Annals of Tourism Research*, **27** (4), 1025-1048.

Harris, C. (2003). *Making Native Space.* Vancouver, BC: University of British Columbia Press.

Holupka, C.S., and A.B. Shlay. (1993). Political economy and urban development. In R.D. Bingham and R. Mier (Eds.), *Theories of Local Economic Development: Perspectives from Across the Disciplines* (pp. 175-190). Newbury Park, CA: Sage.

Hutt Scott, K. (2003). $500,000 buys tribe a voice in capital. A top lobbyist works to get the Eastern Pequots federal recognition. *www.norwichbulletin.com*, September 22, accessed 12/18/03.

Lee, R., and J. Wills. (1997). *Geographies of Economies.* New York: Wiley.

Lyman, B. (2003). Anti-casino groups open new battle lines. *www.norwichbulletin.com*, September 4, accessed 12/18/03.

McCann, E.J. (2002, September). The cultural politics of local economic development: Meaning-making, place-making and urban policy process. *Geoforum,* **433,** 385-389.

Nash, R.F. (2001). *Wilderness and the American Mind*. New Haven, CT: Yale University Press.

Nelson, G. (1994). Foreword. In D. Zaslowsky and T.H. Watkins (Eds.), *These American Lands* (pp. xi-xv). Washington, DC: Island Press.

Pearl, M. (1993). *Subsistence Farming and Ecotourism: Crater Mountain Wildlife Management Area, Papua New Guinea*. Airlie, VA: United States Department of Agriculture.

Piga, C.A.G. (2003). Territorial planning and tourism development tax. *Annals of Tourism Research,* **30** (4), 886-905.

Russo, A.P. (2002). The "vicious circle" of tourism development in heritage cities. *Annals of Tourism Research,* **29** (1), 165-182.

Scarponi, D. (2003). Foxwoods plans expansion, route 2 bypass. *www.lasvegassun.com*, April 3, accessed 12/18/03.

Sokoloff, K.L., and S.L. Engerman. (2000). History lessons: Institutions, factor endowments, and paths of development in the New World. *Journal of Economic Perspectives,* **14** (3), 217-232.

Stansfield, C. (1996). Reservations and gambling: Native Americans and the diffusion of legalized gaming. In R. Butler and T. Hinch (Eds.), *Tourism and Indigeneous Peoples*. International Thompson Business Press.

Teye, V., Sönmez, S.F., and E. Sirakaya. (2002). Residents' attitudes toward tourism development. *Annals of Tourism Research,* **29** (3), 668-688.

Travel Industry Association of America, National Geographic Traveler. (2003). *Geotourism: A New Trend in Travel*. Washington DC: Travel Industry of America.

Uriely, N., Israeli, A.A., and A. Reichel. (2002). Heritage proximity and resident attitudes toward tourism development. *Annals of Tourism Research,* **29** (3), 859-862.

Waldman, H. (1994, June). *New Life for a Forgotten People, Return of the Natives—A Hartford Courant Reprint*, pp. 3-5.

Walpole, M.J., and H.J. Goodwin. (2000). Local economic impacts of dragon tourism in Indonesia. *Annals of Tourism Research,* **27** (3), 559-576.

World Tourism Organization (WTO). (1998). *Guide for Local Authorities on Developing Sustainable Tourism*. Madrid: World Tourism Organization.

World Tourism Organization. *http://www.world-tourism.org/quality/E/standards.htm. 2003*, accessed 11/25/03.

Zaslowsky, D., and T.H. Watkins. (1994). *These American Lands*. Washington, DC: Island Press.

11

The Distribution of Tourism Benefits

Claudia Jurowski
Margaret J. Daniels
Lori Pennington-Gray

Tourism is most often promoted as an economic development strategy, with the expectation that a growing economy will result in a higher quality of life. However, as discussed in Chapter Eight, growth of the tourism industry does not necessarily result in a higher quality of life for the residents and may detract from the quality of the tourists' experience. Barkley (1991) provides a useful distinction between economic growth and economic development that can be applied to tourism initiatives:

To economists, economic growth and economic development are related but distinct phenomena. "Economic growth" is a quantitative measure of changes in the size of the local economy. Growth is generally represented by changes in population, employment, production of goods and services, housing stock, etc. Alternatively, "economic development" is a qualitative measure in variations of local quality of life. Variables used to reflect these changes include poverty and infant mortality rates, level of education, mean family income, and quality of the housing stock" (p. 15).

Unfortunately, what policymakers term as economic development is often more concerned with growth and therefore does not systematically consider the welfare and quality of life of residents. As emphasized by Courant (1994), "What we should seek to measure in our assessments of local economic development policies is changes in the level and distribution of economic welfare" (p. 863).

This chapter discusses tourism development as it relates to economic growth and economic development evidenced through the distribution of benefits and costs to both residents and tourists and linked to quality tourism experiences. First, economic efficiency and equity will be defined and the distribution of costs and benefits in terms of employment, space, and time will be considered. Second, social exchange theory will be discussed as a useful basis for evaluating the costs and benefits of tourism experienced by the residents of tourist destinations. Finally, a case study will demonstrate how the social exchange theory is useful for evaluating equity issues related to tourism development. When residents perceive that the costs of the tourism exchange do not exceed the benefits, they perceive an equitable exchange. However, when residents perceive that the costs are greater, the equity of the exchange is questioned. An assessment of residents' perceptions is important in determining when continued economic growth through tourism is no longer in the best interests of the community.

Efficiency and Equity

Galston and Baehler (1995) argue that a defining element of acceptable development is equity, emphasizing that "growth strategies that unfairly impact on the least advantaged members of the community cannot be justified and should not be implemented" (p. 27). Equity addresses the distribution of benefits and costs among individuals and groups, whereas efficiency is the net benefits a program provides society (Barkley, 1991). Thus, an efficient program is not necessarily equitable and an equitable program is not necessarily efficient. Further, it is possible to achieve one, both, or neither, depending on how economic policies are determined and implemented (Page, 1997).

Three principles of equity are discussed by Galston and Baehler (1995): (1) the no-harm principle, (2) the maximin principle, and (3) the equalization principle. First, the no-harm principle, where efficiency is the goal, states that economic growth cannot result in a decrease in well-being for the members of a target community who are currently the least advantaged. The implication of the no-harm principle is that the well-being of this group will not necessarily increase, either. Second, the maximin principle states that, when choosing among development programs, the program that is most likely to improve the well-being of the least advantaged individuals should be chosen. Accordingly, the maximin principle emphasizes equity over efficiency. Third, the most stringent of the three principles, the equalization policy, strives for a balance between efficiency and equity. It requires the selection of economic policies based on their ability to reduce the relative spread between the most and least advantaged groups in a target community. Generally speaking, an equity approach attempts to provide the most efficient program to maximize society's net benefits by compensating preferred groups (*i.e.,* members of the community who are least advantaged and/or most negatively affected by the program) for their losses when an economic policy results in considerable overall welfare loss to society (*e.g.,* Lindberg et al., 2001).

An important component of economic development is a change in employment. The most common measure of economic development in relation to employment is the number of new jobs created. However, this measurement fails to consider the type of jobs and the wages paid (Bloomquist and Summers, 1988). This point is particularly relevant to tourism employment opportunities that suffer, sometimes justly, from a reputation of being low paid. Further, increased employment opportunities due to the addition of new, competing establishments may disrupt employment in existing enterprises or economic sector (Fleisher and Felsenstein, 2000). Employment growth for one tourism firm may result in employment loss for another.

Even in situations of employment growth, counting jobs can be misleading in terms of suggesting improved social welfare. For example, whereas governments often point to predicted increases in output and employment when providing capital subsidies, Courant (1994) clearly illustrates that, in many cases, the costs of this policy often far outweigh the benefits. He explains that "output and employment are easy to point to, where the costs of the subsidy may be widely dispersed throughout the local economy. . . . The policies may well affect economic variables, but their certain costs exceed their maximum potential benefits" (p. 869). Thus, subsidies for hotels and other large tourism-related projects in the name of output and employment may result in outcomes that are neither equitable nor efficient. As pointed out in Chapter Nine, employment status and change due to development results in both winners and losers.

Further understanding of equity and efficiency can be gained through the application of the spread-backwash concept. The spread-backwash concept explains the spatial distribution of costs and benefits of growth on an economy. In his thorough analysis of the classical spread-backwash literature, Gaile (1980) explains, "Spread-backwash processes attempt to explain the developmental change of peripheral areas spatially-related to core areas" (p. 24). Broadly considered, spread effects are gains to a whole region that are evidenced through growth of the core, whereas backwash effects represent unfavorable outcomes to the region due to growth of the nodal center (Gaile, 1980). Gaile highlights structural factors that influence spread-backwash effects, including the distribution of power, an area's distance from the core, the spatial distribution of development, the size and growth rate of the core, the transportation network, and the communication network. For those living in peripheral areas, the prospect of spread impacts being greater than backwash impacts is bleak, in that "spread impacts are weak beyond the commuting range, especially in less developed countries. Further, given the distance decay form of spread impacts, any nodal, spatial investment strategy will exacerbate intra-regional developmental inequalities" (p. 24).

Resource distribution over time is another consideration of efficiency and equity. Using a time concept when explaining tourism development and sustainability, Piga (2003) emphasizes the need to consider efficiency in light of intra-generational and inter-generational equity:

Applying the notion of weak sustainability is possible if it is assumed that natural and physical capital are substitutable, or when changes to the natural asset are reversible. This implies that under the weak sustainability paradigm, intra-generational equity is obtained through the distribution of efficiency gains arising from the implementation of development projects, while future generations are compensated for the loss of natural assets by inheriting a stock of physical capital. However, even advocates of weak sustainability acknowledge that under certain circumstances (such as when the physical capital is a poor substitute for the natural resource), efficiency considerations ought not occupy a central role. (p. 888)

The point being reinforced here is that some tourism resources, such as preservation of the local culture, are not substitutable and must be preserved for future generations. Howe (1997) explains that inter-generational transfers may be conventional goods and services or natural systems that provide environmental amenities. In cases of irreplaceable natural or social transfers, equity must override efficiency to gain the support of the host population.

Social equity suggests that each citizen, regardless of economic resources or personal traits, deserves and has a right to be given equal treatment by the political system. The principles of equity form the foundation for quality tourism experiences for tourists and quality-of-life experiences for local residents. The reader is referred to Chapter Eight for a discussion of the link between quality tourism experiences for tourists and quality of life for residents. Chapter Twelve includes a discussion of the critical role participation by local residents and tourists plays in defining quality experiences.

Economic development programs that fail to serve the needs of the local people equitably may create an unfriendly host population, establishing a situation that jeopardizes the quality of tourism experiences for both the residents and tourists. Consequently, the creation of quality tourism experiences requires continuous monitoring of the willingness of the host population to exchange their resources for the benefits of economic growth through tourism. The social exchange theory affords a suitable underpinning for evaluating the equity of tourism as an economic development tool.

Social Exchange Theory

Issues of equity form the basis of the social exchange theory that suggests individuals will engage in exchanges if (1) the resulting rewards are valued, (2) they believe the exchange is likely to produce valued rewards, and (3) perceived costs do not exceed perceived rewards (Skidmore, 1975). The theory assumes that individuals select exchanges after having assessed the costs and benefits and that inequitable exchanges will not be favored (Homans, 1961). In relation to quality tourism experiences, residents who view tourism as potentially or actually valuable and believe that the costs do not exceed the benefits favor the exchange and are supportive of development efforts (Turner, 1986). However, when the cost of tourism is seen to exceed the benefits, residents oppose its growth and/or development.

The basic precepts of the social exchange theory are implied in considerable research related to residents' experiences with tourism development (Ap, 1992; Gursoy et al., 2002; Jurowski, 1994; Lindberg and Johnson, 1997; Perdue et al., 1990). The relationships between and among perceived benefits, perceived costs, perceived impacts, and support for tourism are the basis for much of the resident attitude research (Pizam, 1978; Tyrrell and Spaudling, 1984). Tourism literature is replete with resident attitude studies that ask residents to evaluate the effects (commonly referred to as impacts) of tourism, to render an opinion about tourism, and to describe the degree to which they support its development (Gee et al., 1989; Gursoy et al., 2000; Milman and Pizam, 1988; Perdue et al., 1990). The reader is referred to Chapter Eight for a discussion of the impacts commonly measured in tourism studies. Favorable impacts are considered *benefits;* unfavorable impacts are *costs.*

There is clear evidence that residents perceive both costs and benefits of tourism and that perceived costs are negatively related to residents' reaction to its development (Gursoy et al., 2000; Jurowski et al.,1997; Keogh, 1990; Lee and Back, 2003; Long et al., 1990; Milman and Pizam, 1988; Prentice, 1993; Ritchie, 1988). However, all residents do not evaluate costs and benefits in the same manner. Studies have identified a variation in residents' evaluations of costs and benefits of tourism based on differences in the following: participation in recreation (Keogh, 1990; Perdue et al., 1987); attachment to the community or length of residence (Um and Crompton, 1987); knowledge about the industry (Davis et al., 1988); proximity to its business zone, or contact with tourists (Belisle and Hoy, 1980;

Jurowski and Gursoy, 2003; Sheldon and Var, 1984); sociodemographic character-istics (Brougham and Butler, 1981; Ritchie, 1988); political and demographic position in society (Mansfeld, 1992; Thomason et al., 1979); type and form of tourism (Murphy, 1981; Ritchie, 1988); and economic benefits derived from the industry (Ap, 1992; Liu and Var, 1986; Pizam, 1978; Prentice, 1993). As intro-duced in Chapter Ten, the level of involvement and input from various planning and development sectors (*i.e.,* businesses, nonprofit organizations, and govern-ment agencies), as well as the inclusion of residents in the planning process, can greatly influence the perception of quality and the balance of costs and benefits (Gunn and Var, 2002).

Several models based on the social exchange theory have proposed explanations for the variations in resident attitudes (Ap, 1992; Gursoy et al., 2002; Jurowski, 1994; Jurowski et al., 1997; Lee and Back, 2003; Lindberg and Johnson, 1997). The Jurowski (1994) model demonstrates that attitudes toward tourism are influ-enced by residents' perceptions of economic, social, and environmental impacts (*e.g.,* tax revenues and traffic congestion), and that these perceptions are influ-enced by perceived economic gain, the level of use of the recreation resource, and attitudes about humankind's role in the preservation of the natural environment. Gursoy and colleagues (2002) modified the Jurowski (1994) model by segregating the variables in the economic, social, and environmental-impacts constructs into costs and benefits to examine the influence of the perceptions of costs and bene-fits on support. These two structural models provide evidence of a relationship between the evaluation of costs and benefits and support for tourism. Several fac-tors affect the way residents evaluate rewards in relation to costs. The expectations of economic benefits have the largest positive effect on support by local residents. Residents who received the greatest economic benefits favor tourism more than those who receive fewer or no benefits (Akis et al., 1996; Perdue et al.,1990; Ritchie, 1988). In like manner, there is a direct relationship between the positive evaluation of social and cultural impacts and support (Besculides et al., 2002; Brunt and Courtney, 1999; Lankford and Howard, 1994; Madrigal, 1993, 1995). Residents who fear that tourism development will destroy or damage the environ-ment are opposed, whereas those who see tourism as an incentive to preserve and protect the natural environment are supportive (Butler, 1980; Hillery et al., 2001; Martin and Uysal, 1990; Liu and Var, 1986). The studies confirm differences in residents' perceptions of the costs and benefits of tourism and the direct relation-ship between a positive evaluation of benefits versus costs and support for tourism development.

Differences in residents' perceptions of benefits and costs are generated by a number of factors. Long-time residents and those who feel an emotional bond to the community use different criteria to evaluate the impacts than those who do not develop strong bonds or feelings of attachment to their community (Allen et al., 1988; Gursoy et al., 2002; Jurowski, 1994; Lankford, 1994; McCool and Martin, 1994). Residents who use the recreation resource that attracts tourists may be more concerned about overcrowding and may have a greater desire for infrastructure improvements. Consequently, the recreation base users will have a different per-spective than those residents who do not use the recreation base (Jurowski, 1994; Keogh, 1990; Lankford et al., 1997). Residents who are more knowledgeable about tourism and those who are most concerned about the local economy will use a dif-ferent set of criteria to evaluate the impacts of tourism than those who know little about the industry or the local economy (Davis et al., 1988; Gursoy et al., 2002; Lankford, 1994). In addition, studies have demonstrated that evaluation of costs and benefits varies with sociodemographic characteristics (Ritchie, 1988; Williams and Lawson, 2001); political and demographic position in society (Mansfeld, 1992; Thomason et al., 1979); level of contact with tourists (Akis et al., 1996; Brougham and Butler, 1981; Lankford, 1994); environmental attitudes (Gursoy et al., 2002; Jurowski et al., 1997); and type of tourism (Gursoy et al., 2002; Jurowski, 1994; Murphy, 1981; Ritchie, 1988).

The case study that follows adds to existing knowledge by directly linking support for tourism development strategies to beliefs about whether the benefits of tourism are greater or less than the costs. It demonstrates that residents who perceive the benefits to be greater than the costs support tourism, while those who believe the costs exceed the benefit oppose tourism development, thereby validating the social exchange theory's usefulness in explaining resident attitudes toward tourism development.

Case Study: Daytona Beach, Florida

Data for this study were gathered in Daytona Beach and Ormond Beach, which are located on the east Atlantic coast of Florida, northeast of Orlando. The sample was comprised of individuals 18 years of age and older whose names appeared on the Volusia County tax roles. The Volusia County tax role included residents, businesses, and primary landowners (tenants were excluded).

For each town, 500 residents were selected. Therefore, for Ormond Beach, every 66th name from the list of 33,000 was chosen, and for Daytona Beach, every 88th name from the list of 44,000 was chosen. In the event a resident was selected previously or the selection was a place of business, it was subsequently skipped, until a resident could be chosen. A combined total of 1,000 residents from Ormond Beach and Daytona Beach, Florida, were selected.

The primary means of data collection was a mail survey questionnaire using a modified total design method (Dillman, 2000). The first mail-out was sent on October 1, 2001. Nonrespondents were sent a letter and a second survey. A response of 152 was achieved. A total of 12 surveys had to be discarded. Therefore, a final response rate of 14% (n = 140) was achieved. Due to a low sample size (probably due to the events of 9/11 and the anthrax scare), an alternative method of data collection was appropriate. Therefore, face-to-face interviews were conducted for three weeks in December 2001. Interviews were conducted at three sites: two shopping malls and the beach. Approximately 36 people refused to fill out the questionnaire. Residents of Volusia County completed a total of 100 face-to-face interviews. T-tests were run on the demographics of respondents from both data collection methods. No statistical differences in demographics were revealed.

Respondents were asked for their level of agreement with the following statement: "Overall, the benefits of tourism are greater than the costs to the people of the area." The mean score on this variable was 4.10 on a 7-point scale, which could be interpreted either as a neutral feeling about the costs and benefits or as a division in the opinions of the respondents. To identify the appropriate interpretation of the mean score, respondents were grouped into those who believed that costs outweighed benefits for tourism, those who believed benefits outweighed costs of

Source: VISIT FLORIDA

Daytona Beach, Florida

tourism, and those who were neutral in their belief. Respondents who disagreed with the statement (scored 3 or less) were labeled *costs-greater,* whereas those who scored 5 to 7 were called *benefits-greater.* Of the 240 respondents 111 (46.3%) were classified as *benefits-greater*, 85 (35.4%) were classified as *costs-greater,* and 44 (18.3%) were neutral. The differences in the mean scores of the *benefits-greater* and the *costs-greater* groups shows that, in fact, the respondents were not neutral about whether the benefits exceeded the costs or vice versa, but instead were divided on the question. The mean score on the benefits/costs greater variable of the *benefits-greater* group was 5.94 and that of *the cost-greater* group was 1.75. The division in beliefs about tourism suggests that more than one-third of the population believe the costs of tourism outweigh the benefits. Less than half of the population believes the benefits exceed the costs.

There were no significant differences between the two groups in employment, race, Hispanic origin, education, income, gender, or age. The *benefits-greater* group tended to be full-time employees (62.7%), white/Caucasian (95.5%), with some college (22.2%) or a college degree (26.9%), earning $20,000 to $40,000 each year (30.9%). The *costs-greater* group also tended to be full-time employees (60.7%), white/Caucasian (91.3%), with some college (22.6%) or a college degree (26.2%), earning between $20,000 and $60,000 (52.8%). Slightly more males comprised the *benefits-greater* group (57.3% versus 55.3%).

Analysis of the difference in the means of the *benefits-greater* group compared to the *costs-greater* group on three sets of variables revealed significant differences in the evaluation of costs and benefits and support for tourism. The *financial benefit set* asked respondents how much they personally, their company, and their community benefited financially from tourism. The *social impact set* asked respondents whether they felt seven items related to social conditions would improve or worsen if tourism were to increase. The *support set* of variables asked how much respondents would oppose or support tourism development in general and how much they would support six different tourism development strategies. The mean scores on the three sets of variables listed in Table 11-1 depict the differences in the way each group evaluated financial benefits and social impacts, and how each group differed in support of tourism development.

T-tests were performed to determine if the difference in mean scores of the *benefits-greater* and the *costs-greater* groups was significant. The results, displayed in Table 11-2, indicate that the difference in opinions of the two groups were significant at the .05 level for all variables. Compared to that of the *cost-greater* group, the mean score of the respondents in the *benefits-greater* group was higher on questions relating to how much the respondent personally benefited financially (mean = 3.30 versus 3.62); the company for whom the respondent worked benefited financially (mean = 3.74 versus 4.05); and the community benefited financially (mean = 4.70 versus 5.40). The analysis implies that those who believe the benefits outweigh the costs perceive greater financial benefits from tourism than the alternate group does. Respondents perceived that the benefits of tourism to the community (mean = 4.8) were greater than their own personal benefit (mean = 3.15) or that of the company for which they worked (mean = 3.75).

On the set of social impact variables in which respondents were asked to indicate if they felt each impact would improve or worsen if the number of tourists to the area increased, both groups agreed that opportunities to shop and recreate would improve, but traffic congestion and crime rate would worsen. However, the

199

Table 11.1   Means of Cost Benefit Variables for three groups

Variable

Benefit/Cost 1=strongly disagree; 2=moderately disagree; 3=slightly disagree; 4=neutral;
5=slightly agree; 6=moderately agree; 7=strongly agree

	All		Benefits-greater		Costs-greater	
	N	*Mean*	*N*	*Mean*	*N*	*Mean*
Overall, the benefits of tourism are greater than the costs to the people of the area	240	4.10	111	5.94	85	1.75

Financial Benefit Variables 1=not at all; 2=trivial amount; 3=slightly; 4=neutral; 5=slightly; 6=moderately; 7=extremely

How much personally have you benefited financially from tourism in the Daytona Beach area?	241	3.15	110	3.62	84	2.64
How much has the company you work for/business benefited financially from tourism in the Daytona Beach area?	232	3.75	107	4.05	80	3.33
How much has your community benefited financially from tourism to the Daytona Beach area?	237	4.80	109	5.40	84	3.79

Social Impact Variables 1=worsen tremendously; 2=worsen moderately; 3=worsen slightly; 4=neutral; 5=improve slightly; 6=improve moderately; 7=improve tremendously

	All		Benefits-greater		Costs-greater	
	N	Mean	N	Mean	N	Mean
Opportunities for shopping	243	4.99	110	5.47	84	4.42
Opportunities for recreation	244	4.93	110	5.46	84	4.24
Traffic congestion	245	2.71	111	3.30	84	1.92
Crime rate	244	3.12	110	3.63	84	2.64
Local services (police and fire protection)	244	4.03	111	4.32	84	3.49
Preservation of the local culture	244	3.75	111	4.16	83	3.10
Relationships between residents and tourists	244	3.72	111	4.10	84	3.70

Support Variables How much do you support? 1=not at all; 2=moderately oppose; 3=slightly oppose; 4=neutral; 5=slightly; 6=moderately support; 7=extremely

	All		Benefits-greater		Costs-greater	
	N	Mean	N	Mean	N	Mean
Tourism development (new attraction, new hotels/resorts)	244	4.56	111	5.36	85	3.59
Attractions designed for large numbers of tourists (theme parks/large resorts)	244	4.06	111	4.62	85	3.26
Visitor services (hotels and restaurants)	234	4.74	111	5.37	85	3.95
Small and independent businesses (gift shops, guide services)	243	4.75	111	5.31	85	3.99
Outdoor recreation programs (such as organized hikes, company events)	242	5.18	110	5.52	85	4.62
Tourism programs (such as events or festivals)	243	5.03	111	5.65	85	4.11
Promotion of the area as a tourist destination (TV/advertisements/brochures)	242	4.95	111	5.61	85	4.11

Table 11.2 Results of t-test comparison of means: benefits–greater versus costs–greater

Variable	F Value	Significance
Overall, the benefits of tourism are greater than the costs to the people of the area	1335.961	.000
How much personally have you benefited financially from tourism in the Daytona Beach area?	9.985	.002
How much has the company you work for/ business benefited financially from tourism in the Daytona Beach area?	3.910	.049
How much has your community benefited financially from tourism to the Daytona Beach area?	34.358	.000
Opportunities for shopping	24.177	.000
Opportunities for recreation	30.482	.000
Traffic congestion	28.390	.000
Crime rate	28.344	.000
Local services (police and fire protection)	13.750	.000
Preservation of the local culture	25.119	.000
Relationships between residents and tourists	19.980	.000
Tourism development (new attraction, new hotels/resorts)	48.359	.000
Attractions designed for large numbers of tourists (theme parks/ large resorts)	23.681	.000
Visitor services (hotels and restaurants)	34.211	.000
Small and independent businesses (gift shops, guide services)	27.472	.000
Outdoor recreation programs (such as organized hikes, company events)	27.472	.000
Tourism programs (such as events or festivals)	12.740	.000
Promotion of the area as a tourist destination (TV/advertisements/brochures)	37.698	.000

extent to which the conditions would improve or worsen was significantly different (p = .05). Scores hovered around the neutral mark (4.0) on local services (3.96
versus 4.32), preservation of the local culture (3.71 verses 4.16), and relationships
between residents and tourists (3.70 versus 4.10). The *benefits-greater* group
scored significantly (p = .05) higher than the *costs-greater* group on all three of
these variables.

Results were similar on the set of questions related to whether the respondents
would support or oppose tourism development and tourism promotion. The *benefits-greater* group supported (supported = mean > 5) all development strategies
except for attractions designed for large number of tourists, such as theme parks
and large resorts. *The costs-greater* group was neutral (neutral = mean < 4.5 and >
3.99) about promotion and the development of programs, such as events or festivals, visitor services, and small and independent businesses. They appeared to be
slightly opposed to tourism development in general (mean = 3.59) and attractions
designed for large numbers of tourists (mean = 3.26). However, they had a more

favorable attitude toward outdoor recreation programs, such as organized hikes and company events (mean = 4.62).

In this study residents were willing to support tourism when they felt the benefits were greater than the costs, suggesting that the principles of the social exchange theory can be applied in the study of resident reactions to tourism. To determine the extent to which the principles of the social exchange theory were validated by this study, a regression analysis was conducted. Seven regression equations were analyzed in which the dependent variable was one of the support variables in each equation. Figure 11-1 provides a list of the support variables. The predictor variables were the nine impact variables displayed in Figure 11-2. All independent variables were entered into each of the regression equations using the step-wise method. Table 11-3 displays the results of the seven multiple regression analyses. The most important finding was that the *benefits outweigh the costs* variable was a significant predictor of support for tourism development and for each of the strategies except for outdoor recreation programs (organized hikes, company events, etc.). Two other variables were consistently identified as predictors of the dependent variables: *the relationship between residents and tourists* and *opportunities for shopping*.

Two new predictors—opportunities for recreation and improved local services (police and fire protection)—entered into the equation when outdoor recreation

Tourism development (new attractions, new hotels/resorts)
Attractions designed for large numbers of tourists (theme parks/large resorts)
Visitor services (hotels and restaurants)
Small and independent businesses (gift shops, guide services)
Outdoor recreation programs (such as organized hikes, company events)
Tourism programs (such as events or festivals)
Promotion of the area as a tourist destination (TV/ advertisements/ brochures).

Figure 11.1   Support Variables.

How much personally have you benefited financially from tourism in the Daytona Beach area?
How much has the company you work for/business benefited financially from tourism in the Daytona Beach area?
How much has your community benefited financially from tourism to the Daytona Beach area?
How much do you perceive each statement to either worsen or improve, based on increased tourism:
   Opportunities for shopping
   Opportunities for recreation
   Traffic congestion
   Crime rate
   Local services (police and fire protection)
   Preservation of local culture
   Relationships between residents and tourists

Figure 11.2   Predictor Variables.

Table 11.3 Regression Statistics

Predictor variable	Tourism Development		Attractions		Visitor Services		Small Business		Outdoor Recreation		Tourism Programs		Promotion	
	β	Sig	β	Sig	β	Sig	β	Sig	β	Sig	β	Sig	β	Sig
Benefits greater than costs to people	.283	.000	.138	.032	.213	.000	.188	.003			.241	.000	.249	.000
Opportunities to shop	.257	.000	.405	.000	.328	.000	.223	.001			.288	.000	.254	.000
Preservation of local culture	.209	.001					.247	.000						
Relationship between residents and tourists			.207	.002	.227	.000			.163	.005	.213	.001	.264	.000
Opportunities for recreation									.205	.005				
Local services									.175	.025				
Personal benefits														
F value	33.766		21.659		37.328		23.883		18.117		33.012		36.121	
P		.000		.000		.000		.000		.000		.000		.000
R²		.316		.229		.338		.247		.199		.311		.332
Adjusted R²		.307		.218		.329		.236		.188		.302		.323

was the dependent variable. *Benefits greater than costs* and *opportunities for shopping* were not significant predictors of support for outdoor recreation. It is possible that the cause of the anomaly is that residents may not have associated the examples of outdoor recreation with tourism and/or those who do not support tourism support the development of outdoor recreation opportunities. The model's r^2 (.199) was lower than that of all the other equations, indicating the weaker predictive ability of the model. The three significant predictors for support for tourism development, *benefits greater than costs to the people* ($\beta = .283$), *opportunities for shopping* ($\beta = .257$), and *preservation of the local culture* ($\beta = .209$) explained more than 30% of the variance ($r^2 = .316$).

When the same variables were regressed against the *attractions designed for large numbers of tourists* variable, the model was able to explain 22.9% of the variance. *Opportunities for shopping* had the highest beta ($\beta = . 280$), followed by *relationships between residents and tourists* ($\beta = .207$). *Benefits greater than costs to the people* was a significant predictor with less weight than in the support for tourism equation ($\beta = .138$). The same variables were found to be predictors of *support for visitor services* (hotels and restaurants) ($r^2 = .338$). Only small variances with the other models were observed when the dependent variables were *support for small and independent businesses* and *promotion of the area as a tourist destination*.

Of interest is the strength of the *opportunities for shopping* variable on *support for attractions* (such as theme parks, large resorts, hotels, and restaurants) and for *tourism programs* (such as special events and promotions). *Shopping opportunities* is a significant predictor ($p < .05$) of support for all strategies except for outdoor recreation. Variables that failed to predict support for tourism in general and support for the specified strategies included the three financial benefits of variables, traffic congestion, and crime rate.

Implications

The results of this study support the three propositions of the social exchange theory—that is, individuals will engage in exchanges if (1) the resulting rewards are valued, (2) they believe the exchange is likely to produce valued rewards, and (3) perceived costs do not exceed perceived rewards. Tourism experiences related to improved shopping opportunities as well as opportunities to interact with tourists appear to be valued benefits for residents who believe tourism experiences produce the reward they value. Most importantly, the study implies that these residents perceive tourism can produce a valued reward and they support tourism development (*i.e.*, are willing to exchange their resources for the benefits of tourism). On the other hand, residents who judged tourism experiences to result in greater costs than benefits are unwilling to exchange what they value for the potential rewards of tourism development.

Measuring the equity of the exchanges related to tourism experiences is critical to the production of quality tourism experiences for both residents and tourists. Information that helps public planners and policymakers identify that which residents are willing to exchange for the benefits of tourism can be used to design economic development strategies that improve community quality of life rather than strategies that result in inequitable economic growth. The social exchange theory provides an appropriate underpinning for the tourism quality of Life (TQOL) index discussed in Chapter Eight. The index identifies the costs and benefits that residents are willing to exchange, but more importantly it indicates how consequential each factor is in determining community quality of life as well as to what extent tourism can be held responsible for the cost or benefit. This is a critical point in the creation and maintenance of quality tourism experiences for both residents and tourists. Once residents begin to feel that the exchange is inequitable or unfavorable, they are likely to resent the presence and activities of the tourists creating an unpleasant atmosphere that reduces the quality of tourism experiences. The ability to identify the specific aspect of tourism that reduces the quality of the tourism experience is important for policymakers who have the power to make adjustments to reduce the irritant that diminishes the residents' quality of life and thereby the quality of the tourism experience for both parties in the exchange process.

References

Akis, S., Peristianis, N., and J. Warner. (1996). Residents' attitudes to tourism development: The case of Cyprus. *Tourism Management,* **17,** 481-494.

Allen, L.R., Long, P.T., Perdue, R.R. and S. Kieselbach. (1988). The impact of tourism development on residents' perceptions of community life. *Journal of Travel Research,* **27** (1), 16-21.

Ap, J. (1992). *Understanding Host Residents' Perceptions of the Impacts of Tourism through Social Exchange Theory.* Dissertation Abstracts International. Ann Arbor MI: UMI Dissertation Services.

Barkley, D.L. (1991). *Job Generation Strategies for Small Towns: An Overview of Problems and Potentials.* Clemson, SC: Regional Economic Development Research Laboratory at Clemson University.

Belisle, F.J., and D.R. Hoy. (1980). The perceived impact of tourism by residents: A case study in Santa Marta Columbia. *Annals of Tourism Research,* **7,** 83-101.

Besculides, A., Lee, M., and P.McCormick. (2002). Residents' perceptions of the cultural benefits of tourism. *Annals of Tourism Research,* **29,** 303-319.

Bloomquist, L.E., and G.F. Summers. (1988). Employment growth and income inequality. In G.F. Summers (Ed.), *Community Economic Vitality* (pp. 69-76). Ames, IA: North Central Regional Center for Rural Development.

Brougham, J., and R.W. Butler. (1981). A segmentation analysis of resident attitudes to the social impact of tourism. *Annals of Tourism Research,* **8,** 569-590.

Brunt, P., and P. Courtney. (1999). Host perceptions of sociocultural impacts. *Annals of Tourism Research,* **26,** 493-515.

Butler, R. (1980). The concept of a tourist area cycle of evolution: Implications for management of resources. *Canadian Geographer,* **24,** 5-12.

Courant, P.N. (1994). How would you know a good economic development policy if you tripped over one? Hint: Don't just count jobs. *National Tax Journal,* **47** (4), 863-881.

Davis, D., Allen, J., and R.M. Cosenza. (1988). Segmenting local residents by their attitudes, interest, and opinions toward tourism. *Journal of Travel Research,* **27,** 2-8.

Dillman, D.A. (2000). *Mail and Internet Surveys: The Tailored Design Method* (2nd ed.). New York: John Wiley and Sons.

Fleisher, A., and D. Felsenstein. (2000). Support for rural tourism: Does it make a difference? *Annals of Tourism Research,* **27** (4) 1007-1024.

Gaile, G.L. (1980). The spread-backwash concept. *Regional Studies,* **14,** 15-25.

Galston, W.A., and K.J. Baehler. (1995). *Rural Development in the United States: Connecting Theory, Practice, and Possibilities.* Washington, DC: Island Press.

Gee, C., Mackens, J., and D. Choy. (1989). *The Travel Industry.* New York: Van Nostrand Reinhold.

Gunn, C.A., and T. Var. (2002). *Tourism planning* (4th ed.). New York: Routledge.

Gursoy, D., Chen, J., and Y. Yoon. (2000, June 11-14). Using structural equation modeling to assess the effects of tourism impact factors and local residents support for tourism development. *Thirty-first Annual Travel and Tourism Research Association Conference Proceedings* (pp. 243-250). San Fernando Valley, CA.

Gursoy, D., Jurowski, C., and M. Uysal. (2002). Resident attitudes: A structural modeling approach. *Annals of Tourism Research,* **29,** 79-105.

Hillery, M., Nancarrow, B., Griffin, G., and G. Syme. (2001). Tourist perception of environmental impact. *Annals of Tourism Research,* **28,** 853-867.

Homans, G. (1961). *Social Behavior in Elementary Forms.* New York: Harcourt Brace Jovanovich.

Howe, C. W. (1997). Dimensions of sustainability: Geographical, temporal, institutional and psychological. *Land Economics,* **73** (4), 597-607.

Jurowski, C. (1994). *The Interplay of Elements Affecting Host Community Resident Attitudes toward Tourism: A Path Analytic Approach.* PhD dissertation. Virginia Polytechnic Institute and State University.

Jurowski, C., and D. Gursoy. (2003). Distance affects resident attitudes. *Annals of Tourism Research,* **31** (2), 296-312.

Jurowski, C., Uysal, M., and R.D. Williams. (1997). A theoretical analysis of host community resident reactions to tourism. *Journal of Travel Research,* **36** (2), 3-11.

Keogh, B. (1990). Resident recreationists' perceptions and attitudes with respect to tourism development. *Journal of Applied Recreation Research,* **15** (2), 71-83.

Lankford, S. (1994). Attitudes and perceptions toward tourism and rural regional development. *Journal of Travel Research,* **24** (3), 35-44.

Lankford, S. (1996). Crime and tourism: A study of perceptions in the Pacific Northwest. In A. Pizam and Y. Mansfeld (Eds.), *Tourism, Crime and International Security Issues* (pp. 51–58). Chichester: Wiley.

Lankford, S., and D. Howard. (1994). Developing a tourism attitude impact scale. *Annals of Tourism Research,* **24,** 121-139.

Lankford, S., Williams, A., and J. Lankford. (1997). Perceptions of outdoor recreation opportunities and support for tourism development. *Journal of Travel Research,* **35** (3), 65-60.

Lee, C.K., and K.J. Back. (2003). Pre- and post-casino impact of residents' perception. *Annals of Tourism Research,* **30** (4), 868-885.

Lindberg, K., Andersson, T.D., and Dellaert, B.G.C. (2001). Tourism development: Assessing social gains and losses. *Annals of Tourism Research,* **28** (4), 1010-1030.

Lindberg, K., and Johnson, R. (1997). Modeling resident attitudes toward tourism. *Annals of Tourism Research,* **24,** 402-424.

Liu, J., Sheldon, P.J., and T. Var. (1987). Resident perception of the environmental impacts of tourism. *Annals of Tourism Research,* **14,** 17-37.

Liu, J., and T. Var. (1986). Resident attitudes toward tourism impacts in Hawaii. *Annals of Tourism Research,* **13,** 193-214.

Long, P.T., Perdue, R.R., and L. Allen. (1990). Rural resident tourism perceptions and attitudes by community level of tourism. *Journal of Travel Research,* **28** (3), 3-9.

Madrigal, R. (1993). A tale of tourism in two cities. *Annals of Tourism Research,* **20,** 336-353.

Madrigal, R. (1995). Residents' perceptions and the role of government. *Annals of Tourism Research,* **22** (1), 86-102.

Mansfeld, Y. (1992). Group-differentiated perceptions of social impacts related to tourism development. *Professional Geographer,* **44,** 377-392.

Martin, B., and M. Uysal. (1990). An examination of the relationship between carrying capacity and the tourism lifecycle: Management and policy implications. *Journal of Environmental Management,* **31,** 327-332.

McCool, S., and S.R. Martin. (1994). Community attachment and attitudes toward tourism development. *Journal of Travel Research,* **32** (3), 29-34.

Milman, A., and A. Pizam. (1988). Social impact of tourism on Central Florida. *Annals of Tourism Research,* **15,** 91-204.

Murphy, P.E. (1981). Community attitudes to tourism: A comparative analysis. *Tourism Management,* **2,** 188-195.

Page, T. (1997). On the problem of achieving efficiency and equity, intergenerationally. *Land Economics,* **73** (4), 580-596.

Perdue, R., Long, P., and L. Allen. (1987). Rural resident tourism perceptions and attitudes. *Annals of Tourism Research,* **14,** 420-429.

Perdue, R., Long, P., and L. Allen. (1990). Resident support for tourism development. *Annals of Tourism Research,* **17,** 586-599.

Piga, C.A.G. (2003). Territorial planning and tourism development tax. *Annals of Tourism Research,* **30** (4), 886-905.

Pizam, A. (1978). Tourism's impacts: The social costs to the destination community as perceived by its residents. *Journal of Travel Research* **16** (4), 8-12.

Prentice, R. (1993). Community-driven tourism planning and residents' preferences. *Tourism Management,* **14,** 218-227.

Ritchie, J. (1988). Consensus policy formulation in tourism. *Tourism Management,* **9,** 99-216.

Sheldon, P.J., and T. Var. (1984). Resident attitudes to tourism in North Wales. *Tourism Management,* **5,** 40-47.

Skidmore, W. (1975). *Theoretical Thinking in Sociology.* New York/London: Cambridge University Press.

Thomason, P., Crompton, J., and B. Dan Kamp. (1979). A study of the attitudes of impacted groups within a host community toward prolonged stay tourist visitors. *Journal of Travel Research,* **17** (4), 2-6.

Turner, J.H. (1986). *The Structure of Sociological Theory.* Chicago: Dorsey Press.

Tyrrell, T., and P. Spaulding. (1984). A survey of attitudes toward tourism growth in Rhode Island. *Hospitality Education and Research Journal,* **8,** 22-23.

Um, S., and J.L. Crompton, (1987). Measuring resident's attachment levels in a host community. *Journal of Travel Research,* **26** (2), 27-29.

Williams, J., and R. Lawson. (2001). Community issues and resident opinions of tourism. *Annals of Tourism Research,* **28,** 269-290.

12

Political-Economic Construction of Quality Tourism Experiences

Lori Pennington-Gray
Barbara A. Carmichael

As seen in the previous chapters, especially Chapter Eight, the link between politics and tourism is fervent. According to Holupka and Shlay (1993) tourism "decision making processes tend to be undemocratic; critical decisions are typically hidden from the public view and the public serves to legitimize decisions rather than to play a material role in making them" (p. 178). Traditional tourism development has employed "top-down" strategies of decision making whereby networks of social relations are unequal in power (Belsky, 1999). The inherent implication of top-down tourism development is an inaccurate interpretation of "quality tourism experiences." Top-down tourism development tends to avoid inclusion of opinions and values of key stakeholders in tourism. Success or failure of the tourism industry is based on accurate interpretation of quality tourism experiences. Key to this interpretation is the inclusion of local residents through participation in the decision making process (Lankford, 1994).

The purpose of this chapter is, first, to examine the political nature of tourism decision making. A model of planning and development of tourism will be presented within this chapter. Second, sustainable tourism planning will be discussed and three tenets of sustainability will be addressed. Third, social equity and democratic decision making will be discussed. Fourth, a revised model of tourism planning and development is presented, and, finally, two case studies will be used to illustrate the underlying democratic or undemocratic nature of the tourism planning and development process.

Model of Tourism Planning and Development

Historically, tourism planning has involved "elite players" who make decisions on behalf of others in the community (see Chapter Ten). According to Middleton and

Hawkins (1998), tourism planning and development involves four main groups of "players" (see Figure 12-1). In their model, the visitor activities and products are at the hub. The wheel in Middleton and Hawkins' model is divided horizontally, with the upper half designated as visitor demand and the lower half as the resource side. The ten spokes are then divided into the four groups of players: (1) residents, (2) elected representatives and appointed officials, (3) businesses, and (4) visitors. Ultimately, it is a combination of these players that comprise the development team for a destination. Traditional tourism planning and development strategies have employed a top-down approach with minimal players at the table. However, more recent paradigms of development are bottom up and include as many representatives as possible.

According to Sharpley (2002), the evolution of development thought has become increasingly complex over time. It has moved from being prescriptive to analytical in focus. Impact assessments of development policies are becoming more important as they relate not only to changes in the environment but also to changes to local communities. The linkages to the local community and its role in development decision making are becoming more essential as development policies start to operate under the paradigm of sustainability (p. 5). Clearly, one of the main tenets of sustainable tourism is local community input and involvement in decision making.

Sustainability and Tourism Planning: The Three Tenets of Sustainability

The concept of sustainable development can be traced to the World Commission on Environment and Development (1987, p. 5), also known as the Brundtland Commission. The 1992 Earth Summit brought the issues of sustainable development to the forefront. Sustainable development is "development that meets the needs of the present without compromising the ability of future generations to

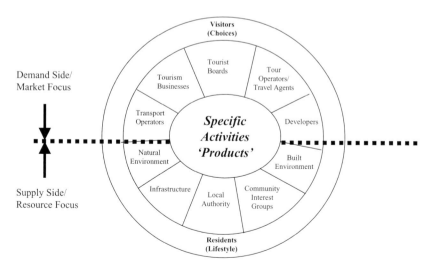

Figure 12.1   Model of Tourism Planning and Development (Middleton and Hawkins, 1998).
© Butterworth-Heinemann, 2003. Reproduced with permission.

meet their own needs" (World Commission on Environment and Development, 1987, p. 7). Sustainable development proponents argue that problems in the economy, environment, and society are interrelated and global in content (Flint and Danner, 2001). Sustainable economic development encompasses three main tenets: economic vitality, ecologic integrity, and social equity (Figure 12-2).

According to their model, "the overlapping circles demonstrate the interconnectedness of a community's economic social and ecological dimensions" (Flint and Danner, 2001, p. 6). They recommend looking at sustainable development as a three-legged stool, where each leg represents one of the basic tenets. If one of the legs is removed, the stool collapses.

First, economic vitality is "a healthy economy that grows sufficiently to create meaningful jobs, reduce poverty, and provide the opportunity for a high quality of life for all in an increasingly competitive world" (The President's Council on Sustainable Development 1996, p. 15; Anderson and Lash, 1999, p. iii). Government policies put in place by politicians combine with existing market forces to assure a healthy economy (Jacobs, 2000).

Second, ecological integrity (presented as a concept in Chapter Ten and Eleven) is a core element of sustainable development. Preservation of the natural resource and elimination of toxic waste and pollutants are all part of ecological integrity. Clean air and clean water are at the foundation of the community. Members of the community must be involved with promoting and ensuring ecological integrity.

Third, social equity refers to the fairness among community members. Sustainable development requires equal distribution of benefits and equal input into decisions regarding the direction for tourism development in the community. At the core of sustainable development is social equity or ethical decision making.

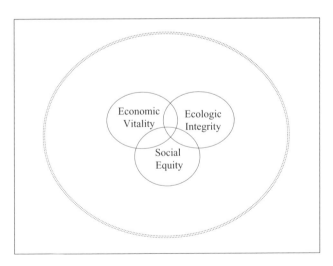

Figure 12.2 Sustainability Model from Flint and Danner.
Sustainability model of overlapping circles suggesting the interrelatedness of community sectors
Source: Flint and Danner, 2001.

Social Equity at the Core of Decision Making

Advocates for the inclusion of local community participation in tourism planning and development have used ethic-based frameworks (Hughes, 1995). The capacity with which players can participate in tourism development projects of any type depends on social infrastructure and social and economic capital. According to Flora and colleagues (1997), the community's ability and willingness to resolve internal and external issues concerning the inequitable distribution of wealth and power are central to participation.

Social equity encompasses two main thoughts: (1) fair share and (2) fair play. Fair share focuses on access to resources. This access is necessary for equality as "a reasonable share of society's resources, sufficient to sustain life at a decent standard of humanity" (Ryan, 1981, p. 8) to sustain equity among human beings. Fair play "stresses the individual's right to pursue happiness and obtain resources" (p. 8). Thus, according to Ryan, fair share precedes and leads to fair play.

According to Walsh and associates (2001), "Social equity has not appeared or been identified in the sustainable tourism literature by name, however it has been discussed implicitly" (p. 201). These authors then go on to suggest that stakeholder involvement is one approach that increases social equity. Interestingly, King and Stewart (1996) argue that local players need help from political powers with regard to skills, resources, and capital to develop facilities. This relationship is then symbiotic in nature, where the need for local player involvement is critical, but local involvement rarely can exist without political power involvement. Therefore, communities, which are marketing themselves as tourism destinations, must find a way to increase social equity of all tourism stakeholders (Hunter, 1997). Without this balance of power, any decision making related to sustainable development is merely a façade (Hunter, 1997). A social equity paradigm allows for individuals affected by decisions and policies to become involved with the decision making process.

One of the main implications of ethical decision making is the long-term sustainability of a destination. Tied to this sustainability is the notion of quality tourism experiences. Quality tourism experiences can be interpreted from the perspectives of both the host and the guest. The host must view tourism as an enhancement to quality of life (*e.g.,* more economic benefits, minimal negative impacts, more opportunities for recreation; see Chapters Seven, Eight, and Eleven). In order for tourism to result in quality experiences, local players must make decisions that promote the benefits of tourism. On the other side of the coin, the guests must view their experience as quality. They must be welcomed into the community, have positive customer service experiences, and feel an overall enjoyment of their experiences. As a result, decision making by the local players must plan for quality guest experiences. Overall, more local involvement should lead to more self-determined choices for tourism development, thus allowing for higher-quality experiences on both sides.

Revised Model of Tourism Planning and Development

Building on the original model presented earlier, the revised model changes the "core" of the model to focus on quality tourism experiences rather than merely the activities and products available in the destination (Figure 12-3). The focus on quality tourism experiences forces local players to consider both supply side and demand side issues related to tourism development in the community. All decisions regarding tourism planning and development will focus on the interpretation of quality. This obviously involves the tourist. As one of the main "players," feedback from the tourist is required as part of the decision making process. Not only will the tourist provide feedback with his or her money, but there must be continuous research conducted that measures quality experiences.

The following section identifies two case studies that provide examples of political-economic construction of quality tourism experiences. Case Study #1 looks at government labeling in one province in Canada; Case Study #2 looks at local-level tourism that plans for quality tourism experiences.

Case Study #1
Government Labeling of a Quality Tourism Experience:
An Example from Ontario, Canada: Is the Process Democratic?

According to the modified model, tourism experiences are the result of the interaction of tourism demand and tourism supply. Research into tourism conducted by government and industry is more often geared toward understanding tourists and the demands for tourism rather than the tourism product itself (Hall et al., 1997). This case study focuses on an example of the Ontario provincial government in Canada's initiative in regional tourism planning that was developed to measure the "quality" of a tourism destination with a focus more on the supply

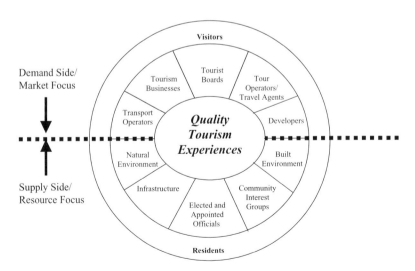

Adapted from Middleton and Hawkins, 1998

Figure 12.3 A model for Quality Tourism Experiences.

rather than purely the demand side. However, supply, demand, and future dimensions of quality tourism experiences are incorporated into the measurement process in a novel and, to a certain extent, democratic way.

In 2001, the Ontario Ministry of Tourism, Culture and Recreation (MTCR), now called the Ministry of Tourism and Recreation (MTR), commissioned a study through its Investment and Development Office to create a framework that captures the attributes, factors, and conditions that make up a "premier-ranked tourist destination" (Malone, Given and Parsons Ltd., 2001). This is an example of a top-down initiative that was designed to create a self-guided workbook for "use by any destination area, rather than for individual attractions and is relevant to destinations of any size and with any degree of current marketing success" (Malone, Given and Parsons Ltd., 2001). The process involves working through seven steps in the workbook, either as a group as a whole or by individuals or groups in a coordinated team process. The seven steps are (1) complete the resource audit, (2) measure the destination product, (3) measure the destination performance, (4) measure the destination futurity, (5) complete the destination performance summary, (6) determine whether the destination is among the premier ranked, and (7) determine the next step in tourism development for the destination.

The workbook suggests that the group composition could include members from the destination marketing organization (DMO), other suppliers, the municipality (particularly representing the economic development and planning functions), and other agencies managing key resources (*i.e.,* Ministry of Natural Resources). Ex-officio members could be local consultants, for example, with the Ministry of Tourism and Recreation or Northern Development and Mines. This process builds on existing partnerships and facilitates the creation of new ones. Local actors have an input into data gathering for tourism planning and marketing and have the opportunity to engage in team building and visioning. *Visioning* is the process whereby local actors come together to discuss a "vision" for tourism in the community. Participating in this process may well be as valuable as the final rating of the attractions within the destination region.

To be a "premier-ranked" tourism destination, the region must demonstrate well above average performance along dimensions that capture destination attractiveness, quality of tourism experience, and market success. These dimensions are comprised of product, performance, and futurity, as shown in Table 12-1. The three dimensions are comprised of questions for 11 elements (A-E) that in turn are described by 37 criteria composed of 107 measures that in all provide a very detailed resource inventory of the tourism product, integrated with data on tourist numbers and future potential. Framework details are illustrated in Figure 12-4 and show a well-organized system for measuring the quality of tourism experiences. One drawback, however, may be access to data at the regional scale and at a high enough level of detail to make it operational.

The futurity dimension is used as an example of the complexity of data needed for the implementation of the framework. According to Genest and Legg (2001), the framework can provide a measure of performance and balance across and within key dimensions that address economic and environmental sustainability. The futurity dimension recognizes that, in order for quality and success to be maintained, limits of growth and sustainability issues should be managed and planned for. Element K of the inventory addresses the need to manage within carrying

Table 12.1   Dimensions for a premier ranked tourism destination

The Product Dimension	A premier ranked tourism destination provides a high quality tourism experience, enabled through the destination's offering of: A. Distinctive Core Attractions B. Quality and Critical Mass C. Satisfaction and Value D. Accessibility; and E. An Accommodations Base
The Performance Dimension	The quality of the tourist experience and the destination's success in providing it is validated by: F. Visitation G. Occupancy and Yield; and H. Critical Acclaim
The Futurity Dimension	And sustained by: I. Destination Marketing J. Product Renewal K. Managing within Carrying Capacities

Source: Genest and Legg, 2001, p. 106; Malone, Given and Parsons (2001); Investment and Development Offce (2003)

capacities, and the seven criteria and their detailed measures listed in Table 12-2 illustrate the in-depth nature of this inventory tool. Figure 12-4 shows different ways in which destination communities can measure and understand capacity thresholds in the local economy, ecosystems, guest satisfaction levels, services infrastructure, and administrative systems.

The Investment and Development Office that commissioned the workbook and assisted with its implementation is dedicated to helping the tourism industry increase its competitiveness by supporting new product development and investment in Ontario. As such, there is the assumption that growth is good because of the potential for economic benefits. Its mandate is to provide support to improve the investment climate and increase investment in Ontario. The supply inventory framework provides information to the tourism region about its strengths, weaknesses, and destination ranking according to a "premier" yardstick. This information can be used for marketing and planning and for identifying gaps in performance as well as knowledge. However, it also directs the attention of potential investors and developers to existing successful tourism communities. This process may act to concentrate investment into current growth poles, while communities with lesser attractions are disadvantaged. Furthermore, the steps in the workbook need in-depth knowledge of the regional product. Such statistics may not exist for smaller destinations so they cannot be accurately reflected in the inventory.

The workbook was used in January 2001 in a test case in the South Georgia Bay region and towns within the region were identified according to the ranking criteria. The town of Collingwood was identified as a premier-ranked destination. This was not surprising, however, because, by 2001, the major ski company Intrawest had already chosen Collingwood for expansion into a four-season destination resort and the area was experiencing very rapid tourism growth. It is interesting that Niagara Falls has not used the system yet. Perhaps it already recognizes that it has a world attraction. However, lesser cities are using the inventory, perhaps to validate their attractiveness for investors and their tourism competitiveness, much

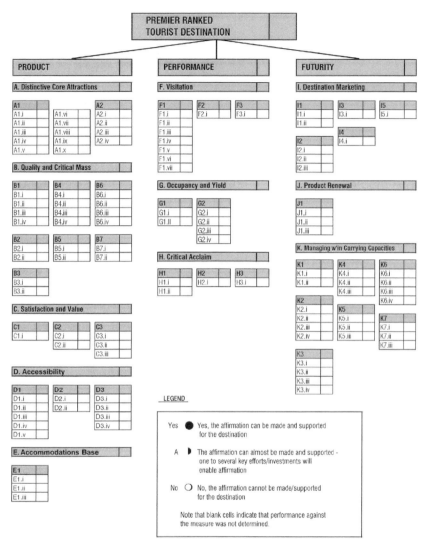

Figure 12.4 Framework Used in the Premier Ranking Destination Measurement Process. Source: Investment and Development Office (2003), *www.tourism.gov.on.ca/english/ido/prtd-workbook.pdf* (pp. 82, 83, 85). © Queen's Printer for Ontario, 2003. Reproduced with permission.

as cities today compete to be recognized as global cities. As the ranking process unfolds, some of the problems are with data availability and funding, especially for less successful rural regions. This is an innovative initiative, but, unfortunately, as with any superior designation system (World Heritage Attractions, Area of Outstanding Scenic Beauty, National Parks), it works strongly in the favor of the established and well known in attracting interest from tourists and entrepreneurs and against the struggling newcomers. Simply being labeled as a premier destination will add to the attractiveness of the area.

Table 12.2   Criteria and Measures used in Assessing Element K: Managing within Carrying Capacities

K1 Destination visitation generates economic benefits to the host community.
i)   Guest visits and expenditures make a net positive contribution to the local economy.
ii) Benefits and costs are balanced equitably across municipal boundaries.

K2 Visitation does not consume local resources or increase their values to an extent that the local population is negatively affected.
i)   Attractiveness of the destination to recreational and retirement home or investment markets has not bid up the cost of housing to the extent that it is unaffordable to the locally employed population.
ii) Where housing impacts are occurring, a response plan is being implemented.
iii) Servicing guest visitation, or the investment to attract and accommodate it, does not consume labor or materials to the extent that their cost or availability to other sectors is impairing those sectors' profitability.
iv) Where resource cost or availability impacts are occurring, a response plan is being implemented.

K3 Trained labor is available to serve visitation demands at a level that maintains guest satisfaction.
i)   There is a labor pool sufficient to accommodate projected levels of visitation.
ii) Where labor pool constraints are occurring, a response plan is being implemented.
iii) Guest surveys confirm satisfaction with hospitality and service.
iv) Where dissatisfaction has been identified, a response plan is being implemented.

K4 Carrying capacity of the natural systems that sustain local ecosystems and quality of life are not overwhelmed by destination visitation.
i)   There is an environmental monitoring program in place that provides early warning of capacity thresholds being approached.
ii) There is a "wellness" monitoring program in place that provides early warning of whether quality of life impact thresholds are being approached.
iii) Evidence from formal monitoring programs or informal observations indicates that no capacity/thresholds are being exceeded.

K5 Growth in visitation to the destination is not exceeding the carrying capacity threshold of enjoyment to the dissatisfaction of the guests.
i)   Overcrowding, overuse, diminished quality of the environment or diminished quality of the guest experience are not being raised by guest surveys or by managers of facilities and resources.
ii) If issues are raised, they relate to one or two peak weekends only.
iii) A response to identified issues has been defined and is being implemented.

K6 Infrastructure is available to accommodate current or projected levels of demand without exceeding carrying capacities
i)   There is current/planned water treatment and delivery capacity to accommodate current and projected levels of visitation.
ii) There is current/planned sewage treatment and trunk capacity to accommodate current and projected levels of visitation.
iii) There is current/planned road transit, parking, and trail capacity to accommodate current and projected levels of visitation.
iv) Assessment of the environmental effects of infrastructure expansion have been completed, with effects considered mitigable and acceptable.

K7 Municipal entities with approval authority are able to address development applications in a timely manner.
i)   Local and upper tier (where present) Official Plans have tourism-related objectives and policies in place.
ii) There is political will to move forward with those projects considered to further the objectives expressed in the official plan.
iii) There are sufficient administrative resources in place to efficiently manage, review approvals, and permit processes.

Source: Malone, Given Parsons (2001) Investment and Development Office (2003) © Queen's Printer for Ontario, 2003. Reproduced with permission.

The process of creating a mechanism for understanding a region's resource base illustrates the government's role of assisting communities in gaining knowledge about their existing products as well as facilitating product planning. As mentioned earlier, local players need help from political powers with regard to skills, resources, and capital. Tourism planning consultants who work for the IDO in this case are available to help with the implementation of the inventory process. However, as in other regions, quite often the necessary data for resource inventories may not exist or are not available in a fashion suited to the needs of tourism or other land use decision makers (Williams et al., 1996).

The usefulness of inventory systems depends on a variety of factors, for example, (1) how rigorously and credibly they reflect the relative importance that tourists and tourism operators place on an area's natural, cultural, and heritage attribute and (2) how effectively they support resource planning and management decision making (Pigram, 1983).

Decision making for tourism may involve spatial differentiation. For instance, it may be necessary to determine priorities for development among a given range of sites, or general evaluations for regional or national planning may require the identification and delimitation of those areas most suitable for one or more forms of tourism development (Pearce, 1991). Furthermore, how the criteria are chosen, combined, and weighted to derive an overall measure of attractiveness is an issue in assessing an inventory's validity and usefulness. For practical purposes, most writers have limited themselves to 10 to 20 factors or have reduced a larger number of factors to a common index (Pearce, 1991). Weighting procedures may be based on visitor surveys or expert evaluation, or they may be arbitrarily assigned. Maps produced from combining the factors provide a description of the spatial patterns of resource attributes. Early studies by Gunn (1979) used computer mapping, incorporating the arbitrarily assigned weighting of different factors and their aggregation into composite scores. More recent work uses Geographic Information Systems to produce resource inventory maps that indicate overall suitability for development—for example, Williams and colleagues (1996) in the case of coastal tourism, and Boyd and colleagues (1994) in the case of ecotourism. A further consideration in regional tourism resource analysis is the definition of the size and shape of the region and its effect on resource inventory measurement (Smith, 1995).

In the development of the criteria for a premier-ranked tourism destination, Genest and Legg (2001) reported that they consulted academic literature sources (Gee et al., 1989; Godfrey and Clarke, 2000; Goeldner et al., 2000; Gunn, 1997; Heath and Wall, 1992; Pine and Gilmore, 1999) as well as conducted key informant interviews from the tourism industry. This research established that a premier-ranked tourism destination must offer better than average opportunity to find a high-quality travel experience and that a significant part of this opportunity arises from the quality of the activities and services available to the tourist. Further, what is relevant or distinctive about a destination's offerings must address the wants and needs of tourist markets and the offerings of competitive destinations. The natural resource base or setting is also deemed to be very important in the quality tourism experience (Genest and Legg, 2001).

In implementing the workbook (described in this case study), the three overall quality dimensions were combined in an aggregate score. There was no attempt to weight the variables in any systematic way. If there were conflicting responses at the lower measures level, the team could make judgments for the overall evaluation of criterion levels; similarly, criterion evaluations build up to produce element evaluations that, in turn, build up to produce dimension evaluations. However, minimum thresholds of performance on the dimensions had to be met. To be designated as a "premier-ranked" destination, a "yes" response had to be achieved on all three dimensions. The threshold for a "yes" for the product dimension required "yes" for A, B, and C elements; for the performance dimension, it required a "yes" for F and H elements; and for futurity, it required a "yes" for I, J, and K elements. At each stage, the project team made a number of discretionary decisions. The product of this inventory process is more than just a determination of whether or not a destination is premier-ranked. It shows destinations where their product gaps are and raises the questions of sustainability from an environmental and cultural as well as an economic perspective. Overall, although the process is top down in its origin and design, it is also to a large extent democratic. Community stakeholders are involved in assessment decisions both in terms of current resources and markets as well as for future development potential. Although the process may be critiqued on the detail of its measurements and lack of weighting of criteria, it does show one way of trying to measure the elusive concept of quality tourism experiences.

Case Study #2
Political-Economic Construction of Quality Tourism Experiences in a Medium-Sized County in Florida: How to Do It Right

As per the modified model of Middleton and Hawkins (see Figure 12-3), quality tourism experiences are facilitated by four "players." Typically, tourism has employed a top-down decision making strategy. This case study demonstrates how one county in Florida has worked hard to involve all four groups and create policy that results in "quality" tourism experiences.

At the core of tourism development in the state of Florida is a nine-member board called the Tourism Development Council. The TDC is present in 47 of Florida's 63 counties. The 47 TDCs are tied to county-lines due in part to the collection of the tourism development tax, better known as the "bed tax." The Tourism Development Council is responsible for making decisions about tourism planning and development within the county. Florida State Statute guides the composition of the board and dictates that the Council must consist of one County Commissioner, one commissioner from the largest municipality, one commissioner from another municipality, three citizens-at-large, and three owner/operators in the lodging sector. Interested citizens can become involved through an application process. The Board of County Commissioners (BOCC) in the county appoints the nine TDC members. The BOCC typically appoints individuals with a vested interest in tourism. Members are appointed for a three-year term and rely heavily on citizen input on tourism decisions.

Many counties in Florida use a strategic marketing plan to guide development decisions. The Visioning Process (see Chapter Nine Case Study) is the initial step in community involvement in tourism planning and development. The Visioning Process brings the four players (residents, elected representatives and appointed officials, business merchants, and visitors) together to outline a vision for tourism in the county. As Lea (1993) suggests, decisions regarding local ownership and control and use of local resources and amenities are critical to sustainable tourism development. The strategy enables "fair share and fair play" by the players. According to our proposed model, social equity is critical to sustainable tourism planning.

Social Equity in Alachua County Tourism Planning

Extending the discussion from Chapter Nine regarding the process of the TDC, this section provides detailed information on the distribution of equity within the county. First, money from the destination development tax (or bed tax) is redistributed in three main areas in order to develop tourism. The three "pots" of money are distributed in the form of grants. The first grant is a meetings/conventions grant, the second is a special projects grant, and the third grant is called "Destination Enhancement." With all three "pots" of money, the four "players" are given opportunities to participate and provide input into any decisions. Residents, visitors, elected representatives, and businesses are given equal chances at involvement in the process.

On the supply side, the major opportunity for social equity is through attending the monthly TDC meetings. A state law, called the "Sunshine Law," maintains that all public meetings must be announced prior to when the meetings take place. In this county, notification of upcoming meetings is given in two forms: e-mail and newspaper. Notification does not ensure participation; however, it does facilitate participation by interested parties. During the TDC meetings, residents are given the opportunity for input regarding use of the bed tax. Business owners/operators (especially those dependent on tourism) are invited to participate in the meetings and provide input regarding decisions. In addition, many times the businesses are the applicants applying for money from one of the three "pots." Finally, the involvement of the elected representatives and appointed officials is evident. The TDC makes recommendations to the BOCC for final approval. Decisions that have not involved residents, businesses, and visitors are not likely to receive support.

Another demonstration of social equity in the county is related to distribution of the Destination Enhancement Grant. This grant is available to support the arts, heritage, culture, and nature. After years of quarreling among the different parties about the distribution of dollars, the BOCC ruled to allow the actual players to determine who would get destination enhancement money. The destination enhancement category was divided into three groups: (1) professional arts alliance (this is exclusive to four members as identified by whether they are "professional" arts performing groups); (2) arts groups (all other arts organizations not identified as professional); and (3) eco-heritage groups (all sites identified by themselves as eco-tourism or heritage tourism sites). Membership in the two later groups is voluntary. Groups must identify themselves as willing participants to be included in funding efforts. A formula based on number of participants, overall budget, and number of visitors determines how much money each group is eligible for within their category. A category leader asks for proposals each year that outline how the group will use its portion of the money and how the group's proposal conforms to the State Statute. The formula is ratio based on the projected bed tax allocated to each category within the

Destination Enhancement Grant. All players have an opportunity to take advantage of tourism development dollars. One can argue that this is truly a democratic process. In all, this county has worked very hard at identifying and including the three tenets (ecological integrity, economic vitality, and social equity) of sustainability in the redistribution of the destination enhancement tax.

On the demand side, social equity is monitored via visitor satisfaction surveys. Tourism decisions take into consideration the voice of the visitor. For example, recently there has been a thrust to make the county more visitor-friendly to opposing sports teams' fans. Many destinations throughout the country are developing a bad reputation for not welcoming visitors from opposing teams. This county has implemented programs to welcome the opposing team and its fans and even provides parties targeted at the fans of the opposing team.

Economic Vitality in Alachua County Tourism Planning

As suggested by the section "Sustainability and Tourism Planning: The Three Tenets of Sustainability," tourism planning should incorporate economic vitality. With the first two grants (meetings/conventions and special projects grant), successful grants pay out money based on the amount of 'heads in beds' that are generated. For example, in the meetings/convention grant, the proposal receives more points based on participation in multiple venues within the community. Likewise, for the special projects grant, the proposal receives more points for including opportunities for residents to participate in the project (*i.e.,* a festival).

Ecological Integrity in Alachua County Tourism Planning

With regard to tourism planning and ecological integrity, the county has tried to reward applications to two of the grants by incorporating sustainable management techniques. Those that do incorporate sustainable management techniques (ecological integrity) related to tourism are rewarded more favorably. In general, applications are graded based on evidence of environmental sustainability. For example, with the meetings/conventions grant, those applicants who include recycling, recycled materials, or book at a "green hotel" would receive more points than an applicant who did not do these things. This translates into more points, which usually means more grant money to fund the conference/convention or meeting. This particular Florida county has provided the opportunity for local players to become involved in the process, and they have shifted to a bottom-up approach for managing quality tourism experiences.

Implications

The implications for this chapter are vast. The first half of the chapter outlines the theory that decision making processes tend to be undemocratic, critical decisions are typically hidden from the public view, and the public serves to legitimize decisions rather than playing a material role in making them (Holupka and Shlay, 1993). Based on Holupka and Shlay's notion that tourism processes tend to be undemocratic is the notion that tourism planning and development is shifting from top–down to bottom–up decision making. The two cases illustrate different levels of government control over decision making, different levels of consultation and facilitation of the four players, and different notions of fair share and fair play (the two underpinnings of social equity).

With the first case, Government Labeling of a Quality Tourism Experience: An Example from Ontario, decision making is facilitated by the Ontario government. A workbook is provided to educate and assist destination management knowledge needs. This is an initiative that involves local actors as part of the information-gathering process. Furthermore, the tenets of sustainability are included in the futurity aspects of the framework and draw attention to long-term effects. Destination management involves detailed knowledge of the tourism product; how it is perceived by the tourists in terms of meeting their needs for quality, satisfaction, and value; and how it is performing in terms of capacity limits. This case study has presented a tool for assessing the quality of a tourism destination in terms of its resource attributes and ability to meet customer needs for a quality experience. Regional stakeholders in the tourism industry working in partnership are able to use the assessment tool by using a workbook. This allows the team members to understand and identify gaps in the products they are offering. Ideas on long-term sustainability of tourism in the region are also identified. Stakeholders have no input into the design of the workbook format or the criteria for what defines a "premier-ranked" tourism destination. Those decisions are already made by the consultants working for the Province of Ontario. However, this is necessary to ensure consistency and reliability of the measurement tool. Furthermore, it would be beyond the financial resources of many DMOs to design this for themselves. The tool is now an easily available resource for assessment and planning that can be applied by non-experts. It is available for downloading from the Ontario Ministry of Tourism and Recreation website. The ongoing drawback at present may be in the lack of data to implement the process at the regional level.

This case study has illustrated the provincial government's role as a facilitator for knowledge dispersal in the form of how to assess a destination region in terms of quality. Such knowledge will assist in decision making in tourism planning and marketing at the regional level. It will also identify areas for entrepreneurial investment, as under the mandate of the Industrial Development office. Such frameworks, despite being top down, are useful and cost saving to the regions.

In contrast, the second case, Political-Economic Construction of Quality Tourism Experiences in Medium-Sized County in Florida: How to Do It Right, demonstrates how one county has tried to provide a foundation for quality tourism experiences. At the heart of this is the three tenets of sustainability, and tied to that is social equity. Decision making is guided by player involvement in tourism planning and development. The Board of County Commission is a political stamp on the plan rather than a decider of the plan. Players are given the opportunity to become involved on many levels. The vision for where the county is headed is not merely the vision of the politicians but rather one of the citizens. Social equity is critical to planning for quality tourism experiences.

Providing for social equity and citizen involvement related to tourism planning is critical to the production of quality tourism experiences for both residents and tourists. Incorporating citizens' opinions and including citizens in decisions is critical to policy formation. Elected officials need to find ways to foster positive experiences for citizens to become involved in tourism planning. In addition, distributions of the benefits of tourism (mainly bed tax dollars) need to be equitably administered. The two case studies provided in this chapter provide glimpses into ways governments have come together to allow for citizen involvement and socially equitable distribution of benefits.

References

Anderson, R., and J. Lash. (1999). *Towards a Sustainable America: Advancing Prosperity, Opportunity and a Health Environment for the 21ˢᵗ Century* (158 pages). (*www.whitehouse.gov//PCSD, retrieved* 10/2/03). Washington, DC: The President's Council on Sustainable Development Publications.

Belsky, J.M. (1999). Misrepresenting communities: The politics of community based rural ecotourism in Gales Point Manatee, Belize. *Rural Sociology,* **64** (4), 641-666.

Boyd, S., Butler, R.W., Haider, W., and A. Perera. (1994). Identifying areas for ecotourism in Northern Ontario: Application of a geographic information system methodology. *Journal of Applied Recreation Research,* **19** (1), 44-66.

Flint, W.R., and M.J.E. Danner. (2001). The Nexus of sustainability and social equity: Virginia's Eastern Shore (USA) as a Local Example of Global Issues. *International Journal of Economic Development,* **3** (2), 1-30.

Flora, J.L., Sharp, J., Flora, C., and Newlon, B. (1997). Entrepreneurial social infrastructure and locally initiated economic development in the non–metropolitan United States. *Sociological Quarterly,* **38**, 623-645.

Gee, C.Y., Makens, J.C., and D. Choy. (1989). *The Travel Industry* (2nd ed.). New York: Van Nostrand Reinhold.

Genest, J., and D. Legg. (2001). The premier-ranked tourism destinations workbook: One measure of optimization. In M. Joppe, *TTRA-Canada Conference Proceedings* (pp. 105-113). Toronto, Canada: Ryerson University.

Godfrey, K., and J. Clarke. (2000). *The Tourism Development Handbook.* New York: Cassell.

Goeldner, C., Ritchie, J.R., and R.W. McIntosh. (2000). *Tourism: Principles, Practices, Philosophies* (8th ed.). Toronto: John Wiley and Sons.

Gunn, C.A. (1979). *Tourism Planning.* Washington, DC: Taylor and Francis.

Gunn, C.A. (1994). *Tourism Planning* (3rd ed.). Bristol, PA: Taylor and Francis.

Gunn, C.A. (1997). *Vacationscape: Developing Tourist Areas* (3rd ed.). Washington, DC: Taylor and Francis.

Hall, C.M., Jenkins, J., and G. Kearsley. (1997). *Tourism, Planning and Policy.* Sydney, Australia: McGraw Hill.

Heath, E., and G. Wall. (1992). *Marketing Tourism Destinations: A Strategic Planning Approach.* Toronto: John Wiley and Sons.

Holupka, C.S., and A.B. Shlay. (1993). Political economy and urban development. In R.D. Bingham and R. Mier (Eds.), *Theories of Local Economic Development: Perspectives from Across the Disciplines* (pp. 175-190). Newbury Park, CA. Sage.

Horoschowski, K., and R.N. Moisey. (2001). Sustainable tourism: The effect of local participation in Honduran ecotourism development. In McCool and Moisey (Eds.), *Tourism, Recreation and Sustainability: Linking Culture and the Environment* (pp. 163-175). Oxon, UK: CABI Publishing.

Hughes, G. (1995). The cultural construction of sustainable tourism, *Tourism Management,* **16** (1), 49-59.

Hunter, C. (1997). Sustainable tourism as an adaptive paradigm. *Annals of Tourism Research,* **24** (2), 850-867.

Investment and Development Office. (2003). *Premier-Ranked Tourist Destinations: A Self-Guided Workbook* (2nd ed.). Toronto, Ontario: Ministry of Tourism and Recreation, p. 82 of 85. Downloaded 12 June 2005. [*www.tourism.gov.on.ca/english/ido/prtd-workbook.pdf*].

Jacobs, J. (2000). *The Nature of Economies.* New York: The Modern Library.

King, D.A., and W.P. Stewart. (1996), Ecotourism and commodification: Protecting people and places. *Biodiversity and Conservation,* **5,** 293-305.

Lankford, S. (1994). Attitudes and perceptions toward tourism and rural regional development. *Journal of Travel Research,* **33,** 35-43.

Lea, J. P. (1993). Tourism development ethics in the third world. *Annals of Tourism Research,* **20,** 701-715.

Malone, Given and Parsons, Ltd. (2001). *Premier-Ranked Tourist Destinations: A Self-Guided Workbook.* Toronto, Ontario: Ministry of Tourism, Culture and Recreation, Industrial Development Office.

Middleton, V.T.C., and R. Hawkins. (1998). *Sustainable Tourism, A Marketing Perspective.* Oxford: Butterworth-Heinemann.

Pearce, D. (1991). *Tourism Development.* London: Longman.

Pigram, J.J. (1983). *Outdoor Recreation and Resource Management.* Beckenham: Croom Helm.

Pine, J., and J. Gilmore. (1999). *The Experience Economy: Work is Theatre and Everyday Business a Stage.* Boston: Harvard Business School Press.

President's Council on Sustainable Development (PCSD). (1996). *Sustainable America: A New Consensus for Prosperity, Opportunity and a Healthy Environment for the Future.* Washington, DC: U.S. Government Printing Office.

Ryan, W. (1981). *Equality.* New York: Pantheon.

Sharpley, R. (2002). Tourism: A vehicle for development? In Sharpley and Telfer (Eds.), *Tourism and Development: Concepts and Issues* (pp. 11-34). Clevedon, UK: Channel View Publications.

Smith, S.L.J. (1995) *Tourism Analysis* (2nd ed.). Harlow, UK: Longman.

Walsh, J.A., Jamrozy, U., and S.W. Burr. (2001). Sense of place as a component of sustainable tourism marketing. In McCool and Moisey (Eds.), *Tourism, Recreation and Sustainability: Linking Culture and the Environment* (pp. 195-216). Oxon, UK: CABI Publishing.

Wheeler, B. (1994). Egotourism, sustainable tourism and the environment—A symbiotic, symbolic, or shambolic relationship. In A.V. Seaton (Ed.), *Tourism: The State of the Art* (pp. 647-654). Toronto: John Wiley and Sons.

Williams, P.W., Paul, J., and D.H. Hainsworth. (1996). Keeping track of what really counts: Tourism resource inventories in British Columbia. In L.C. Harrison and W. Husbands (Eds.), *Practicing Responsible Tourism* (pp. 401-421). New York: Wiley and Sons.

World Commission on Environment and Development. (1987). *Our common future* (pp. 43). Oxford, UK: Oxford University Press (Known as the Brundtland Commission).

VI

Towards a Conclusion

The overall premise of *Quality Tourism Experiences* has been that there is no one definition of quality tourism experiences. Given the nature of tourism and its complexity and multiplicity of participants and resultant interactions and connectivity, the varying expectations, attitudes, and profiles of participants—the notion of quality will vary. In the preceding sections of *Quality Tourism Experiences,* authors have explored the *Social Construction of Quality Tourism Experiences, Mediating Meaning*, the *Interpretation of Meaning and Place, Quality of Life and Interpretation of Quality Tourism Experiences*, the *Political-Economic Construction of Quality Tourism*

Experiences, and now we move *Towards a Conclusion*. As the title of this Section suggests, this is but one conclusion; readers no doubt will draw their own conclusions based on their own experiences, constructions, interpretations, and mediations.

In Chapter Thirteen, Norma Polovitz Nickerson provides some reflections on quality tourism experiences using her interpretation of a number of the constructions presented within the previous chapters of *Quality Tourism Experiences*. In keeping with the premise of this book, the reflective reconstructions are not intended to be nomothetic or representative, since the book argues that interpretations of "quality tourism experiences" are complex and manifold. The chapter concludes by posing a number of questions to stimulate additional research in regard to developing our understandings of *Quality Tourism Experiences*. As she notes, readers will also make their own interpretations and constructions in regard to what constitutes *Quality Tourism Experiences*.

Following Chapter Thirteen, a summary of various research agendas presented throughout *Quality Tourism Experiences* are compiled. The agendas are based on the writings of Gayle Jennings, Sue Beeton, Heather E. Bowen, Carla Almeida Santos, Betty Weiler, Kathleen Andereck, Kelly S. Bricker, Deborah Kerstetter, Norma Polovitz Nickerson, Barbara A. Carmichael, Claudia Jurowski, Margaret J. Daniels, and Lori Pennington-Gray.

13

Some Reflections on Quality Tourism Experiences

Norma Polovitz Nickerson

Postpositivism, social construction, critical theory, and a postmodern paradigm have all been part of the views within this book. Through these approaches, quality tourism experiences, the concept, has been expressed through the visitor, the broker, the product, the media, and the local community. The tie that brings this book together is the complexity of the concept of *quality* and its relationship to tourism.

The purpose of this final chapter is to reflect on some of the concepts and ideas presented in various chapters of this book. The multiplicity of interpretations throughout this book makes it impossible to simplify quality tourism experiences. As stated in Chapter One, quality is a socially constructed term with a variety of meanings. With this in mind, and for the sake of further understanding and research, a diagram based on writings within this book has been developed (see Figure 13-1). The diagram visually illustrates topics discussed in the chapters. It cannot be an all-encompassing diagram because the book did not present all possible influences on quality tourism experiences; however, it provides the reader with a synthesized visual of the chapters. The topics within the diagram originate from multiple perspectives and are a collaboration of interdisciplinary views. The authors who contributed to this book hail from Australia, Canada, England, Portugal, and the United States. These individuals have traveled on every continent (excluding Antarctica), lived in countries other than their birth country, and come from diverse economic backgrounds. The authors' social construction of the world, their lives, and their personal tourism experiences have shaped the views within this book and ultimately the perspective presented in this chapter. This final chapter offers some reflections of quality tourism experiences that highlight the complicated nature of the multiple perspectives presented from interdisciplinary views.

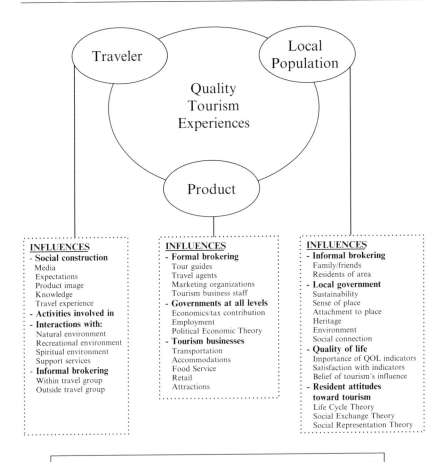

INFLUENCES
- **Social construction**
  Media
  Expectations
  Product image
  Knowledge
  Travel experience
- **Activities involved in**
- **Interactions with:**
  Natural environment
  Recreational environment
  Spiritual environment
  Support services
- **Informal brokering**
  Within travel group
  Outside travel group

INFLUENCES
- **Formal brokering**
  Tour guides
  Travel agents
  Marketing organizations
  Tourism business staff
- **Governments at all levels**
  Economics/tax contribution
  Employment
  Political Economic Theory
- **Tourism businesses**
  Transportation
  Accommodations
  Food Service
  Retail
  Attractions

INFLUENCES
- **Informal brokering**
  Family/friends
  Residents of area
- **Local government**
  Sustainability
  Sense of place
  Attachment to place
  Heritage
  Environment
  Social connection
- **Quality of life**
  Importance of QOL indicators
  Satisfaction with indicators
  Belief of tourism's influence
- **Resident attitudes**
  toward tourism
  Life Cycle Theory
  Social Exchange Theory
  Social Representation Theory

The *Traveler*, the *Product*, and the *Local Population* influence and are influenced by multiple variables which ultimately affect the quality of the tourism experience.

Figure 13.1 Various Influences on Quality Tourism Experiences.

Influences on Quality Tourism Experiences

The Quality Tourism Experiences Influences diagram (Figure 13-1) presents a view of tourism and the resulting experiences tourists take from their travels. These influences engage the political-economic perspective, social construction, mediation of meaning, interpretation of meaning and place, and quality-of-life interpretations into three segments: the traveler, the local population, and the product. Each segment has multiple influences within it, and each is interwoven with the other two. For example, the local government has a direct impact on the local population, and all levels of government have an impact or influence on tourism products offered. All of these influences have an effect on the tenet of this book, hence the title *Quality Tourism Experiences* rather than *The Quality Tourism Experience*. It signifies the complexity of understanding quality and tourism together.

In this book the influences on quality are presented through the traveler, the product, and the local population. Quality is a subjective concept. It refers to excellence, superiority, class, eminence, value, and worth, but what is quality for one person may not be quality for the next. The concept of quality, therefore, has many influences, as presented in the diagram.

The Traveler

The complexity of quality tourism experiences stems from the basic theory of social construction (Chapter Two). Each traveler comes to the destination with a variety of influences. For example, before individuals become travelers, their social construction of a given destination is influenced by the media, which results in expectations and a preconceived image of the destination. Travelers' knowledge of the area and their previous travel experience also influence their interpretations of a quality experience. The influences that media has on quality tourism can depict destination expectations (Chapter Three) that may or may not pan out while the traveler is visiting. If expectations are not met, it is less likely that the traveler will say a quality tourism experience occurred.

Another influence on quality tourism experiences is the specific activities in which the traveler participates. The choice of activities while on a trip can be a predictor of satisfaction and possibly quality experiences. The findings reported in Chapter Five illustrated that "activities engaged in" are frequently reported as the highlights of a travel experience. When travelers talked about their tourism experience, their activities were mentioned as the experience itself. Importantly, the activities were intricately connected to the environment in which the activity took place. For example, although horseback riding can be experienced in one's local area, horseback riding in the mountains of the western United States makes the experience much more memorable and suggestive of a quality experience. In this instance, then, removing oneself from a familiar environment and engaging in that activity in a new environment might induce the feeling of quality because it "feels" like a new activity and engages many senses of the body (the smells, views, and sounds are all different from home). Theoretically, activity within a particular or new "setting" is a conduit for quality tourism experiences. More discussion and research related to where activities take place and the resultant perception of quality are necessary for illustrating connections from "quality" to "activity."

Influence on quality tourism experiences for the traveler also relates to the multitude of interactions the traveler has with other people, the natural environment, the recreation environment, and the spiritual environment. As one form of informal brokering, travelers typically listen to other travelers since other travellers are not viewed as walking billboards or paid agents. Since most travelers are genuinely seeking quality, it behooves them to listen to those who said they had a positive experience. The other form of informal brokering lies within the local population, as addressed later. The natural environment can also be an influence on quality tourism experiences. Chapter Five offered examples of travelers' expressions of fulfillment when viewing the natural environment around them in their travels. The scenery provided a quality experience for them, often because it was different from what they had at home. In addition, the natural environment was the conduit for a spiritual connection, which in turn provided a quality tourism experience. The built environment, as in city tourism, can also be a conduit of quality experience. An outstanding symphony performance followed by a glass of wine overlooking the river can provide the environment for quality. The theory and question that stem from this discussion are whether or not distance and uniqueness enhance quality. Further study in this field is needed.

Not surprisingly, other people affect the quality of tourism experiences, which is the case with both the travel group and those with whom travelers interact outside their travel group. If a traveler receives poor service while on vacation, it could change a quality experience into a bad one. However, the opposite is also true in that good service could be the conduit for a quality experience. As discussed in Chapter Three, media outlets such as the Travel Channel presume that quality is related to personal service whenever the traveler wants service. The traveler may expect this construction of a quality experience, but the service may not occur. Hence, a quality tourism experience is not achieved.

In summary, the traveler, as depicted in Figure 13-1, is subject to many influences that ultimately help define a quality tourism experience. All of these factors come together for an understanding of the experience. However, these influences on the traveler are generally within the consumer (expectations, social construction, media exposure, and interactions with environments) and are one segment of what helps determine a quality experience. The product and the local population also contribute to the experience.

The Product

As highlighted throughout this text, a tourism experience includes the traveler's interpretation, the atmosphere created by the local population, and the brokering, businesses, and governments. In Figure 13-1 the product influence refers to formal brokering, tourism businesses, and governments. Each of these segments will influence the type of experience a traveler will have.

Formal brokering, as discussed in Chapter Four, refers to the influence of tour guides, travel agents, marketing organizations, government, and other stakeholders, as well as staffs with whom tourists interact. Chapter Four draws on the social construction of meaning as the lens to understand the role of both formal and informal mediation and brokering and the resulting impacts on tourism experiences. It also notes that the social construction of meaning may result in negative tourist experiences that are somewhat lacking in quality. The purpose behind formal brokering is to provide a quality tourism experience or expectation of the experience. Either through interpretation or through the delivery of a tour, formal brokering is a mechanism with which to influence the perception of quality tourism experiences. Each person involved in formal brokering is deemed the "expert" by the traveler. These experts may guide the tourist from the planning stages through the actual experience. Sometimes these brokers are poorly trained, front-line employees who do not treat the traveler with the respect or concern desired, which in turn changes a good experience into a bad one, as mentioned in the Arizona example (Chapter Five). Other times the broker, such as a travel agent, arranges a trip that runs so smoothly that the traveler can relax and truly enjoy the experience. The challenge with brokering is the inconsistency in delivery of services as well as how the visitor reconstructs the experience based on previous knowledge, skill level, expectations, and degree of engagement with the broker. Some brokers are first-class; others are bad. How do travel agents select those products that exemplify quality versus those that are questionable? What are the factors that separate the good from the bad? Research is needed to understand these factors and to help reduce the risk of a poor quality experience.

Governmental influences on quality tourism experiences occur at all levels—local, state/provincial, and national. In Chapter Nine, the authors present the political-economic theory that suggests a context in which short-sighted developers, undemocratic decision making, and a small number of people reaping the benefits of tourism can create a situation in which there is little support from the local people. With a lack of support, the opportunity for a quality tourism experience diminishes. The challenge for governments is to realistically assess whether or not tourism can truly be an economic driver within their community. When it works, employment in the basic tourism sectors increases, which in turn creates an increased demand for products and services by tourism employees. This sets the stage for the economic engine to further develop. When it doesn't work, property taxes increase on a population that is underemployed. The example of Alachua County, Florida (Chapter Nine) illustrates how one area's government was able to include residents in their decision making, which resulted in a community-accepted tourism plan related to eco-heritage. By valuing what was in their area, the residents and the government entities involved were able to include tourism planning in their Smart Growth plan. The emphasis on how the government affects quality tourism experiences is stressed because every community has different players coming to the table with different agendas. Politics and policy affect the ultimate experience of the traveler, either explicitly or implicitly. More case studies regarding how tourism is discussed and planned at the governmental level are needed for furthering the knowledge base of the influence of government on quality tourism experiences.

Tourism sectors such as transportation, accommodations, food service, retail, and attractions are often the conduit to a good or bad quality tourism experience. These are products involved in the experience and may or may not be sought after as part of the experience. For example, a traveler visiting London may simply want an accommodation close to the hustle and bustle of the city center, not necessarily an "experience" with the hotel. On the other hand, a traveler may choose to stay in a nearby bed and breakfast because of the experience. How the room and food are presented can make a major difference between a quality experience and a bad experience. The common denominator of the tourism businesses, however, is the people. As discussed under formal brokering, the traveler takes a risk when he or she is dependent on the people who are involved in the traveler's experience. Likewise, if the tourism business takes pride in customer service, more than likely the traveler will experience something positive. Everywhere the traveler turns there is a front-line person who can affect the experience. Granted, one should not allow a poor waiter to affect an entire trip experience; however, repeated negative encounters will taint any travel experience. Research regarding the effect of one-on-one interaction between visitors and suppliers would be useful in determining how quality becomes part of the experience. In addition, research is needed to look further into how the visitor interprets quality as it relates to government policy and business practices.

Local Population

In the diagram, the local population is the third leg influencing quality tourism experiences. Informal brokering, a sense of place, quality of life, local governments, and residents' attitude toward tourism all influence the prospect of a quality experience.

Informal brokering refers to influences that other travelers, friends and family, and the local person walking the street can have on the tourism experience (Chapter Four). This area of limited research requires further attention, and it would be particularly useful to learn the effectiveness of this type of brokering from a tourist's perspective. Informal brokering may be engaged in by travelers, those in the industry, and those outside the industry. The role of those not employed in the industry (such as local residents) is particularly under-researched. Residents of the area can portray friendliness or indifference towards visitors. These encounters occur anywhere, such as when a visitor requests directions or when standing in line at the local market. How the resident treats the visitor puts a "feeling" into the experience. In some instances, a reaction by a resident when asked what there is to do in the area is, "Oh, there's nothing to do here!" In developing nations the resentment toward outside tourism corporations and trinketization can create indifference to the visitor. On the other hand, many locals will often share their special biking trail, cozy restaurant, or favorite marketplace with the traveler. These types of interactions with the residents add to or take away from the quality of the experience travelers have on their trip.

As presented in Chapter Six, sense of place can have a dramatic effect on quality experiences by travelers. If the local population is tied to their area by culture, heritage, or simply a sense that the place feels like home, they are more likely to respond to pressures that might change their community in a negative way. These special places can maintain their unique features only if tourism is conducted in a sustainable manner, assuming that the local population and government strive to protect these special features. Communities that work together for a common good are more prepared to provide an atmosphere for quality experiences for residents and visitors. Chapter Ten further discusses quality tourism as it relates to development and planning in a community. When power elites of a community ignore the rest of the population, long-term sustainability is questionable. However, when sustainability is addressed, the local population maintains their culture, their environment, and their peace of mind. Travelers who happen upon places like these can easily feel that a quality experience is occurring because it is "real," not "contrived."

Another component affecting quality tourism experiences within a community relates to the political nature of tourism decision making, as described in Chapter Twelve. Two case studies demonstrate that stakeholders, including government, can be instrumental in providing for quality tourism experiences. From an assessment workbook to an integrated working group deciding on what is best or works well within the community, the decision making process is inclusive and decisive. It indicates that quality tourism experiences can be represented through various levels of government and types of stakeholders.

Along with the concept of sense of place and decision making, falls the idea of quality of life. In Chapters Seven, Eight, and Eleven, quality of life and how it relates to quality tourism experiences are discussed in regard to residents' attitudes toward tourism. This area of tourism has received ample attention from researchers over the years, as individuals generally seek a life of quality, and tourism may affect that quality. For example, how an area is developed may restrict local use, whereas previous access was available. Residents connect the tourism development to a "taking" of one aspect of why they live there, hence a reduction in their quality of life. In most studies conducted about quality of life and tourism, a split in the costs and benefits generally comes to the surface. Residents perceive tourism to be an economic benefit but believe this comes with a higher cost of living. Chapter Nine presents "winners" and "losers" as a result of development. Where the distribution of tourism benefits is costly to the individual, support for tourism decreases, and vice versa. Figure 13-1 shows that quality tourism experiences can be affected by the perceived quality of life of residents.

In summary, the local population has a direct line to quality tourism experiences. Informal resident-visitor contact can support a quality experience, depending on how each side is treated by the other. The type of interaction between residents and visitors is a result of how the local government develops tourism and distributes the benefits to the residents. If benefits are perceived to improve quality of life, the resident is more likely to assist in providing a quality tourism experience either through direct contact with the visitor or through support of government policy.

Future Directions

When one travels on vacation, one usually seeks the best experience possible. How quality is attained depends on the traveler, the product and its presentation, government, other industry-related stakeholders, environmental influences, and the local population. All of these influences are part of determining if a quality experience will occur. The question, then, is: Where do we go from here?

Referring to the diagram (Figure 13-1), a number of directions can be suggested. First and foremost, however, is the acknowledgment of the variety of influences that affect quality tourism experiences. In reviewing all the influences in the diagram, each one has a substantial stake in the outcome of a tourism experience.

One interpretation of quality tourism experiences, therefore, stems from the product. Obviously, without the product, there is no tourism. The large and small tourism business owner and the government agencies overseeing land areas where tourism and recreation occur are the beginning stages of the entire tourism system. How these individuals and agencies assume their roles in tourism industry sectors will ultimately direct the experiences of quality, yet we have little information about the interactions, decisions, and management of these owners and agencies in relationship to the overall role of providing quality tourism experiences. Studies need to be conducted to examine these roles to further understand how tourism is developed and sustained as well as where improvements in the process can be made. For example, studies that reveal the role entrepreneurs play in formulating government policy on environmental or planning issues would be paramount. However, simply documenting where tourism discussions occur or do not occur in everyday government planning sessions will provide ample information on why some areas have quality tourism experiences and others do not.

From a quality tourism experience perspective, there is a need to understand the extent to which short-term and long-range thinking affect business and government decisions as related to the tourism product. Tourism business owners might look at their business as short term, and therefore not spend the energy in hospitality training and community planning for tourism. If their objective is to succeed quickly in a short amount of time, it doesn't matter to them what legacy they leave behind. The challenge, then, is to further understand the mindset of the tourism business owner who is providing the product for the visitor. Hence, from this perspective, the decision making process of the business owner and the government regulators needs to be analyzed and presented as a means to improve tourism experiences.

Another perspective suggests that local population and the influence the product has on that population leads us to believe that the responsibility of the product (business owners, government agencies, etc.) is to work within the community in roles of influence. If people who have control over the product are not involved in the sustainability of their product, and hence their community, they are ultimately a detriment to tourism development and the quality of life within that community. These business and government leaders should be represented on boards and committees. When board members have the mindset of improving and maintaining a good quality of life as a goal through the tourism industry, then the community benefits, residents will support tourism, and the business owner is likely to be successful. In the end, the visitor is rewarded with a quality experience. It is this roundabout way of providing a quality experience for the visitor that reaps many benefits. To put it in perspective, travelers visit areas because they like what is there. People generally live in an area because they like what is there. Common sense dictates that if both parties like the same thing, everyone should strive to maintain it. In most communities, tourism is part of everyone's life, whether they realize it or not. Residents and visitors appreciate what tourism typically provides—cultural activities, escape from home, a pleasant atmosphere, and an opportunity to do something different. If the tourism landscape is not maintained to the residents' desires, quality of life for the residents and a quality experience for the visitors will be diminished.

We have discussed at length the local population and the products' influence on quality tourism experiences. However, as Figure 13-1 indicates, the traveler also has a large role. The traveler makes judgments based on numerous inputs and ultimately determines if a quality experience has occurred. What we really don't know is how an individual tourist would define a quality experience. Certain expectations, of course, are made in advance of the experience, but how do we measure if a quality experience has occurred? Can we simply ask the visitor? Who is the judge of quality and how do we find out about quality experiences? Is it as simple as satisfaction? Does traveler satisfaction convert to quality? Were expectations met? If yes, does that convert to a quality experience? Researchers need to consider the visitors in more depth, with direct questions about what makes a quality tourism experience for them. As suggested earlier, the relationship between distance from home and uniqueness (environment) should be explored as a possible predictor of quality tourism experiences.

In review, this chapter synthesized a number of ideas presented throughout the book, which are represented in Figure 1-1. Additionally, suggestions were made regarding where we need to go to further understand quality and tourism experiences. This book demonstrates that multiple theoretical lenses can create a better understanding of a quality tourism experience, but no one definition of quality tourism experiences exists. Figure 1-1 reflects a perspective of many of the influences on quality tourism experiences expressed in this book. The complexity of this topic has been highlighted throughout the book, and the interaction between tourists, the local populations, and the product provides one possible construction of quality tourism experiences.

Appendix

Quality Tourism Experiences: Summary of Implications for Research

Kathleen Andereck, Sue Beeton, Heather E. Bowen, Kelly S. Bricker, Barbara A. Carmichael, Margaret J. Daniels, Lori Pennington-Gray, Gayle Jennings, Claudia Jurowski, Deborah Kerstetter, Norma Polovitz Nickerson, Carla Almeida Santos, and Betty Weiler

In each of the chapters of *Quality Tourism Experiences* the contributors have provided a number of implications for research based on the thematic content presented in each chapter. The various implications are collated here to assist readers in accessing a complete overview in one location.

Chapter 1: Perspectives on Quality Tourism Experiences: An Introduction

Gayle Jennings

Tourism researchers need to engage in and/or utilize:

- Holistic research
- Suite of research paradigms
- Quantitative, qualitative, indigenous methodologies and mixed methods
- Emic and etic approaches
- Interdisciplinary research projects (and multidisciplinary approaches)
- Team-skilled projects
- Studies across spaces
- Collaborations (See p. 14)

Section One: Social Construction of Quality Tourism Experiences

Chapter 2: State of Knowledge: Mass Media and Its Relationship to Perceptions of Quality

Sue Beeton, Heather E. Bowen, and Carla Almeida Santos

The implications of bringing the social construction and media theories into the realm of tourism are significant. Through applying these theories we are providing another way in which to view social construction in terms of tourism and mass media. This opens up possibilities for:

- Improved in-depth research into tourist motivation
- Examining the expectations of quality and satisfaction
- Introducing theories and models from other disciplines
- Developing new models and theories specific to tourism (See p. 35)

Chapter 3: Constructing Quality, Constructing Reality

Heather E. Bowen and Carla Almeida Santos

In the past, the individual consumer has been used as the measurement for studies into quality tourism experiences ... In Chapter Three, however, we argue that notions of quality tourism experiences must be investigated from a mass-mediated perspective, allowing us to understand how the construction of quality occurs in the first place.

We propose that:

- A social constructivist perspective provides insight into mass-mediated travel narratives by questioning the representations utilized to promote notions of what constitutes quality tourism experiences.
- By examining mass-mediated approaches to tourism, we are able to identify what is socially regarded as relevant and important in a tourism experience.
- This allows for discussion about the manner in which notions of quality tourism experiences introduced by mass media come to be taken for granted and accepted as natural and are therefore rarely questioned. (See p. 39)

Section Two: Mediating Meaning

Chapter 4: Mediating Meaning: Perspectives on Brokering Quality Tourist Experiences

Gayle Jennings and Betty Weiler

We offer the following research questions as starting points for exploring how mediation by formal and informal brokers relates or contributes to a quality tourist experience:

- What are the key attributes and characteristics of an effective mediator/broker?
- How and when do different types of brokers contribute to a quality tourist experience?
- What are the relative roles of informal and formal brokers in the experience?
- What processes can be used to better match tourist requirements in regard to brokering (*e.g.,* differing tourist types) in respect to quantity and quality of 'access' and therefore subsequent influence on the quality of tourist experiences?
- Can interactions with formal and informal mediators and brokers be planned and managed to result in a higher quality tourist experience?
- How is the role of the mediator/broker changing in relation to changing visitor profiles, including growth in independent travel by relatively inexperienced travelers?
- How can the industry better respond (*e.g.,* recruitment, training, accreditation, reward systems) to improve the effectiveness of mediators/brokers?
- How can mediators/brokers respond to increasing demand for more travel options, specialization and flexibility in travel, destinations, tours, and products? (See p. 75)

Section Three: Interpretation of Meaning and Place

Chapter 5:   Connecting Experiences to Quality: Understanding the Meanings Behind Visitors' Experiences

Kathleen Andereck, Kelly S. Bricker, Deborah Kerstetter, and Norma Polovitz Nickerson

Experience can be documented at a multitude of levels and through different methodological approaches. However, understanding what those experiences mean is difficult, if not impossible, using quantitative methods (*i.e.,* satisfaction approaches, benefits-based approaches). (See p. 84)

Research implications:

- Only after deeper discussion (*i.e.,* in-depth interview) or total emergence (*i.e.,* participant observation) is the researcher able to elicit life-enriching stories told by participants. (See p. 84)
- Travel and tourism providers need to be conscious (as much as possible) of the expectations tourists bring to their site.
- If managers understand the types of experiences expected and valued by their customers, they will be able to develop more effective strategic initiatives, including communication (*e.g.,* advertising, publicity, or public relations), a cornerstone of an effective marketing campaign. (See p. 96)

Chapter 6:   Saravanua ni vanua: Exploring Sense of Place in the Rural Highlands of Fiji

Kelly S. Bricker and Deborah Kerstetter

Developing quality tourism experiences while keeping in mind the culture, including sense of place, of a travel destination is challenging, but feasible.

Research implications:

- The importance of engaging in tourism research from the emic, or "insiders,'" perspective.
- Chapter Six highlights one technique using an emic perspective and the importance of engaging stakeholders when commencing the development of a quality tourism experience.
- Accuracy in representation of community identities. The results of Chapter Six demonstrate that adopting the emic perspective allows tourism operators to adjust elements of the operation–such as guide selection, visitation, and rules for visiting the village–in response to villagers' concerns for conservation and thereby represent the identities of a community accurately. (See pp. 107 and 108)

Section Four: Quality of Life and Interpretation of Quality Tourism Experiences

Chapter 7: Linking Quality Tourism Experiences, Residents' Quality of Life, and Quality Experiences for Tourists

Barbara A. Carmichael

The theme of Chapter Seven was the linkage between quality of life for local residents in a tourism region and quality of life for tourists. . . . there are a number of gaps in theory development that need to be addressed, such as:

- The type of tourist and the type of resident in the context of different levels of social interaction.
- The desired levels of social interaction of both residents and visitors, whether or not those desired levels of interaction are achieved, and how that relates to quality.
- Does quality mean being comfortable and relaxed with the level and type of social interaction accepted and nonthreatened but at the same time stimulated?

There is the potential to use the theory developed for understanding resident attitudes and apply this theory to tourists.

- The quality tourism experience could be framed in life-cycle concepts and an "Irridex" scale for tourists, conceptualized in a similar manner to models posed in the culture shock literature.
- Social exchange theory offers a framework for understanding tourists' attitudes toward residents and the resulting impact on quality tourism experiences. Such a framework would be based on perceived benefits and costs for the tourist.
- Similarly, social representations and tourist values research may help explain how different types of tourists perceive the quality of their tourism experiences and form images of residents. Perhaps an application of such theory could be used to explore tourist and guide interaction and its effect on perceptions of quality.
- Perceptions of tourists and their attitudes toward host communities remains an area about which we know relatively little and which offers potential for theory development.

■ The dynamic situation between quality of life for residents and quality tourism experiences and that the life-cycle trajectory of the resort cycle will mean that these relationships need to be investigated over time.

Furthermore, practitioners and destination marketing organizations would benefit from knowing how locals are perceived and how they may, or may not, contribute to quality tourism experiences. (See pp. 129-130)

Chapter 8:   Tourism and Quality of Life

Kathleen Andereck and Claudia Jurowski

Residents' quality of life is both positively and negatively affected by tourism experiences.
    Research implications:

■ The Tourism Quality of Life Index (TQOL) can be a valuable tool . . . because of its ability to identify elements the tourism industry affects that are valued by the residents.
■ It is uncommon to find a relationship between demographic characteristics and tourism attitudes; however, the Arizona study presented in Chapter Eight shows that demographic characteristics influence residents' perceptions of how tourism impacts their quality of life. . . . Additional research is needed to discover the reason for the differences, including
    ▪ Does tourism improve the quality of life of these groups more than others?
    ▪ Is the perception based on a greater need for economic growth?
    ▪ Is the difference the result of experiences with tourism?
    ▪ Are some groups less likely to attribute negative consequences within their communities to tourism?

Most important, the newly developed TQOL index:

■ Is an effective and valuable instrument for monitoring residents' tourism experiences.
■ Responds to the recommendations of economists that advocate non-economic measures to justify the benefits and the costs of growth.
■ Can be as effective in determining when increased income from tourism is reducing rather than improving the community quality of life. (See pp. 150-151)

Section Five: Political-Economic Construction of Quality Tourism Experiences

Chapter 9:   Introduction to Political-Economic Construction of Quality Tourism Experiences

Margaret J. Daniels and Lori Pennington-Gray

While tourism, economic, and political research abounds, there is a lack of literature that deliberately and clearly illustrates the linkages between the three areas within the context of quality tourism planning and development. Use of the premises of Political Economic Theory enables such linkages to be examined, particularly:

- How powerful political actors influence tourism development and planning?
- How the distribution of benefits from tourism development is highly skewed?
- How tourism decision making tends to be undemocratic?
- How tourism development is often guided by political and economic principles and practices that can either uphold or degrade quality tourism experiences? (See p.168)

Chapter 10:   Quality Tourism Development and Planning

Kelly S. Bricker, Margaret J. Daniels, and Barbara A. Carmichael

Tourism development decisions are usually made by powerful elites. Such decisions may be motivated by short-term gain rather than long-term sustainability in terms of quality of life for local residents.
Research implications:

- Are overall benefits perceived to be outweighing overall costs?
- Perceived impacts are often more important than actual impacts of tourism development in influencing quality of life.
In relation to this, Chapter Ten presented two case studies:
- One that used a meta-analysis of biodiversity and tourism studies to reveal that there are many barriers to the realization of the sustainable development of tourism.
- A second one that linked issues of power, quality, land use, and tourist development within the context of Native Americans and their recent ventures in economic development through tourism and casino gaming. (See p. 189)

Chapter 11:   The Distribution of Tourism Benefits

Claudia Jurowski, Margaret J. Daniels, and Lori Pennington-Gray

Measuring the equity of the exchanges related to tourism experiences is critical to the production of quality tourism experiences for both residents and tourists.
Research implications:

- The Tourism Quality of Life (TQOL) index ... identifies the costs and benefits residents are willing to exchange. It also:
  - indicates how consequential each factor is in determining community quality of life, and
  - to what extent tourism can be held responsible for the cost or benefit.
- The ability to identify the specific aspect of tourism that reduces the quality of the tourism experience is important for policy makers who have the power to make adjustments to reduce the irritant that diminishes the residents' quality of life and thereby the quality of the tourism experience for both parties in the exchange process. (See p. 204)

Chapter 12: Political-Economic Construction of Quality Tourism Experiences

Lori Pennington-Gray and Barbara A. Carmichael

Traditional tourism development has employed "top-down'" strategies of decision making based on unequal power relations. The inherent implication of top-down tourism development is an inaccurate interpretation of "quality tourism experiences."

A focus on quality tourism experiences forces local players to consider:

- Both supply side and demand side issues related to tourism development in the community.
- The interpretation of quality . . . but there must be continuous research conducted that measures quality experiences.

Chapter Twelve presents a revised model of tourism planning and development as an additional tool in regard to ethical decision making in tourism planning and development. (See p. 208 and 212)

Section Six: Towards a Conclusion

Chapter 13: Some Reflections on Quality Tourism Experiences

Norma Polovitz Nickerson

Research needs to be conducted in regard to quality and product:

- The interactions, decisions, and management of large and small tourism business owner and the government agencies overseeing land areas where tourism and recreation occur in relationship to the overall role of providing quality tourism experiences.
- Studies need to be conducted to examine these roles to further understand how tourism is developed and sustained as well as where improvements in the process can be made. For example, studies that reveal the role entrepreneurs play in formulating government policy on environmental or planning issues would be paramount.
- There is a need to understand the extent to which short-term and long-range thinking affect business and government decisions as related to the tourism product.

Research needs to be conducted in regard to quality and local population:

- Their involvement in decision making
- Influences on quality tourism experiences

Research needs to be conducted in regard to quality and traveler, for example:

- How does an individual tourist define a quality experience?
- What are the linkages between expectations, satisfaction, and quality?
- Is there a relationship between distance from home and uniqueness (environment) as a possible predictor of quality tourism experiences? (See pp. 233-234)

Conclusion

The preceding summaries provide interpretations, suggestions, and directions for readers to (re)construct their own research agendas in regard to "quality tourism experiences." They are by no means a definitive listing; the summaries do, however, provide a starting point upon which readers may reflect.

Index

A

A River Runs Through It, 88

Accommodation/s, 32, 40, 43, 44, 48, 50-53, 63, 85, 87, 160, 172, 214, 228

Activities, 5, 8, 9, 20, 31, 41, 43, 49, 50, 51, 59, 84-90, 92-93, 95, 119, 142, 150, 160, 161, 162, 163, 175, 176, 178, 183, 204, 209, 212, 228, 229, 234

Advertising, 33, 34, 36, 37, 41, 53, 54, 96

African Conservation Corp-Kenya, 175

Agua Caliente, 86

Animal, 85, 89, 101

Arizona, 80, 84-87, 93-96, 142-143, 149, 151-154

Aspirations, 100, 153

Atlantic Forest, 177

Attachment, 99, 111, 124, 141, 142, 153, 154, 195, 196, 206, 207, 228

Attraction/s, 14, 30, 40, 60, 83, 84, 85, 86, 87, 93, 101, 122, 126, 163, 167, 168, 184, 186, 200, 201, 202, 203, 204, 213, 214, 215, 228, 231

Attractions and activities, 84-86

Australia, 13, 26, 27, 36, 63, 66, 68, 76, 99, 110, 161, 169, 177, 227

Authenticity, 2, 11-13, 16, 18-19, 26, 33-35, 37, 42, 59, 70, 77, 98, 102, 174, 175,186

Automobile, 80, 84

B

Badlands, 88

Basic and nonbasic activities, 162-163

Beliefs, 28, 29, 41, 51, 101, 116, 121, 123, 125, 130, 132, 138, 140

Benefits, 5, 6, 9, 21, 39, 62, 65, 67, 68, 84, 98, 101, 102, 120, 121, 122, 125, 126, 127, 128, 129, 136-142, 147-148, 180-181, 156, 163-166, 168, 169, 170, 171, 173-174, 16-178, 180, 182-183, 186, 187, 192-197, 199-205, 207, 210, 211, 214, 216, 222, 231, 233, 234

Benefits-based approaches, 80, 83-84

Benefits-greater, 199-201

Biodiversity, 109, 156, 166, 123, 177, 174-178, 180, 182-183, 189-190

Birding, 88

Bottom up planning, 209, 220-221

Brazil, 174, 189

Brazilian Cerrado, 177

Broker/mediator, 58-59

Brokering, 4, 13, 34, 56-62, 65-69, 71-73, 75, 77, 129, 228-232

Business/businesses, 5, 7, 19, 30, 36, 40, 47, 61, 63, 68, 74, 81-82, 95, 97-98, 101, 108, 117, 125, 139, 160, 164, 166, 168, 173, 195, 196, 197, 200-204, 209, 212, 219, 223, 228, 230-233, 234

C

California Floristic Province, 177

California, 84, 88, 90-94

Campaign, 96

Camping, 88

Canary Islands, 172, 190

Cape Floristic Region, 177, 179, 181
Capitalism, 92
Caribbean, 177, 179, 181
Caring, 99
Case study/case studies, 3, 13, 19, 20, 75, 80, 84, 93, 96, 109, 114, 118, 124, 130, 152, 156, 157, 159, 165-168, 170, 171, 174-183, 184-188, 189, 192, 197-204, 205, 208, 212, 212-218, 218-220, 222, 231, 231
Casino, 101, 119, 121, 124, 125, 132, 133, 134, 156, 171, 183-190, 206
Catechist, 103
Caucasus, 177
Central Chile, 177
Certification, 17, 100-101, 109
Challenge/s, 10, 16, 59, 72, 91-92, 101,102, 109, 111, 156, 187
Character, 82-83, 140
Characteristics, 29, 39-40, 42-44, 48, 52, 53, 75, 102, 109, 118, 119, 127, 142, 151
Chief, 103
Choco-Darien-Western Ecuador, 177
Clark, 89-90
Coastal, 5, 17, 99, 177, 181, 217
Colorado, 88
Commodification, 12, 13, 173, 223
Commoditization, 187
Commodity/commodities, 9, 34, 71, 104, 107, 160, 163
Communication theory, 4, 24, 37, 54, 56-57, 74
Communication, 100, 109
Community attachment, 141-142, 153
Community connection, 146-148, 150
Community relationships, 134, 151
Community residents, 117, 128, 134, 138, 156, 165
Community well-being, 136, 146-148, 150-151
Community/communities, 4, 5, 6, 11, 13, 14, 16, 17, 27, 29, 35, 52, 56, 57, 60, 62, 63, 65, 66, 67, 69, 71, 72, 74, 80, 83, 93, 100-102, 107-109, 111, 116, 117-125, 127-128, 130-135, 136-154, 156-169, 171-174, 176, 178, 180, 183-184, 189, 190, 193, 195-196, 199, 201, 202, 204, 205, 206, 207, 208-214, 216-215, 220, 222, 227, 231-232, 234
Connecticut, 183-188, 190
Conservation International, 175, 177, 189-190

Conservation, 17, 19, 80, 97, 107-109, 110, 111, 156, 166, 171, 174-183, 189-190, 223
Conserve, 104-107, 166
Constituency building, 171, 174, 176, 178-179
Constructed notions of quality tourism, 33, 44-49, 49-51
Construction of quality tourism, 24, 29, 34, 40, 52, 56, 157, 212, 221, 226, 235
Consumer, 8, 19, 36, 39, 53, 54, 81-83, 94-96, 162, 174, 230
Contact with tourists, 65, 119, 124, 141, 147, 150, 195,197
Contested spaces, 124, 156, 171, 184, 186
Corridor, 92-93
Costs, 48, 67, 120, 121, 122, 126, 129, 131, 137, 138, 140, 141, 142, 151, 156, 163, 164, 166, 172, 176, 187, 188, 189, 192-197, 199-204, 207, 216, 233
Costs-greater, 199-201
Cottonwoods, 92
Crater, 86, 94
Crime, 138, 140, 144, 146-149
Critical theory, 2-3, 80, 156, 227
Cultural awareness and amenities, 145, 147-148, 150
Cultural brokers/brokering/brokerage, 4, 34, 56, 58
Cultural heritage, 92, 93, 139, 144, 145, 150, 151
Cultural impacts, 110, 152, 196, 205
Cultural politics, 184, 188-190
Cultural, 99-102, 104, 110-111
Culture shock, 128-129, 134
Culture /s, 5, 13, 16, 17, 20, 25, 26, 29, 35, 36, 37, 52, 53, 58, 69, 75, 83, 96, 98-102, 107, 110, 119, 128, 129, 140, 144-5, 166-168, 169, 172, 182, 185, 189, 194, 200, 201, 202, 203, 213, 219, 222, 223, 232
Customs, 66, 101-102, 182

D

Decision making, 10, 13, 37, 67, 74, 108, 119, 124, 141, 147, 156, 157, 164, 165, 168, 174, 208-212, 217, 218, 220, 221, 231, 232, 233, 234
Degradation, 6, 7, 102, 137, 165, 172, 176
Dehumanizing, 101

Demographic, 99, 117, 119, 142, 147, 150, 151, 196, 197

Desire/s, 18, 30, 31, 33, 40, 45, 58, 68, 71, 72, 73, 74, 80, 96, 100, 117, 129, 196, 230, 234

Destination/s, 31, 32, 33, 34, 35, 39, 40, 47, 54, 62, 71, 75, 76, 83, 85, 88, 95, 98, 107-109, 117, 119, 120, 128, 130, 134, 135, 136, 138, 159, 165, 168, 180, 183, 200, 201, 202, 204, 207, 209, 211, 212, 213, 214, 215, 216, 217, 218, 219, 220, 221, 229

Developer/s, 100-101, 107-109, 122, 124, 131, 134, 163, 184, 209, 212, 214, 231

Development, 1, 4, 6, 10, 16, 17, 18, 19, 26, 27, 30, 37, 46, 56, 70 76, 80, 88, 92, 94, 96, 99-103, 107-111,114, 116, 118, 119-135, 136, 136-137, 140-142, 151, 152-154, 156-157, 159, 161-168, 169, 171-189, 190, 191, 192-197, 199, 200-204, 205-207, 208-214, 216-222, 223, 232, 233, 234

Diary, 80, 84, 87, 93-95

Dimension, 9, 57, 63, 66, 82, 88, 90-93, 104, 117, 125, 127, 137, 138, 213, 214, 218

Disney world, 89

Distance from the core, 194

Distribution of economic gains, 192-194

Distribution of power, 194

Dramaturgical references, 70

Dry suits, 92

Dynamic, 73, 82, 84, 93, 96-97, 124, 130

E

Earth, 89, 99, 209

Eastern Arc Mountains & Coastal Forests, 177, 179-181

Ecological integrity, 157, 210, 220

Economic base theory, 4, 159, 161-163

Economic benefits, 6, 101, 127, 136, 138, 140, 151, 156, 165, 170, 171, 174, 180-182, 186, 196, 211, 214, 216

Economic growth, 137, 151, 153, 156, 162, 184, 188, 192-193, 195, 204

Economic impacts, 118, 140, 147, 191

Economic strength, 146-149

Economic vitality, 10, 157, 205, 210, 220

Economics, 136, 137, 156, 159, 161, 167, 169, 172, 228

Ecotourism, 15, 17, 20, 77, 100, 102, 109-111, 176, 189-191, 217, 222, 223

Educate, 102, 221

Education, 40, 73, 101, 103, 147, 148, 150, 166, 174, 178, 180, 192, 199

Effects of tourism, 118, 123, 140, 143, 147, 149, 154, 163, 205

Efficiency, 16, 136, 156, 166, 167, 192-194, 207

El Dorado, 90, 92

Elders, 103, 108

Elected officials, 221

Elites, 156, 173, 178, 183, 189, 232

Emic/Emic perspective, 59, 108

Employment, 101, 138, 139, 142, 147, 161, 164, 169, 176, 178, 180, 186, 192-194, 199, 205, 228, 231

Engagement, 24, 82, 84, 231

Environment, 5, 15, 19, 36, 58, 67, 71, 72, 80, 82, 84, 86, 85, 89, 90, 91, 93, 94, 95, 100, 104, 105, 106, 107, 108, 109, 110, 111, 117, 118, 122, 128, 136, 140, 141, 144, 146, 152, 156, 160, 163, 165, 166, 167, 173, 174, 175, 177, 178, 180, 187, 196, 209, 210, 212, 216, 222, 223, 228-230, 232-234

Environmental education, 178

Environmental impacts, 102, 114, 141, 153, 176, 183, 187, 196, 206

Equalization principle, 193

Equity, 10, 17, 136, 156-157, 166, 173, 182, 192-195, 204, 207, 208, 21-211, 219-221, 222

Etic/Etic perspective 14, 70, 73

Events, 28, 31, 40, 44, 62, 73, 82-83, 85, 95, 110, 119, 125, 132, 140, 163, 165, 168, 169, 170 197, 200-202, 204

Evolution, 96, 83, 131, 205, 209

Experience-based approaches, 80

Experiential, 8, 9, 56, 59, 84, 96, 117

Extinction, 171

F

Factor analysis, 125, 126, 145-146

Fair play, 211, 219, 221

Fair share, 211, 219, 221

Family, 31, 43, 52, 62, 63, 66, 85, 87, 91, 92, 99, 104-106, 108, 117, 126, 137, 141, 168, 192, 228, 232

Feelings, 31, 74, 80, 82-84, 87, 93, 94, 120, 126, 137, 138, 141, 196

Fellowship, 100

Fiji Ecotourism Association, 102

Fiji, 80, 99-103, 105, 107, 109, 111

Fishing, 20, 87-89, 91, 107, 135, 140, 141, 176, 178
Formal brokers, 61, 63, 67, 71, 75
Foxwoods Resort Casino, 134, 184-185, 190
Framing, 26, 37, 41, 44, 54
Friends, 62, 66, 85, 87, 91-92, 228

G

Gathering place, 91-92
Gaze, 9, 12, 20, 26, 27, 31, 36, 37, 77, 82
Genuine Progress Indicator, 137, 153
Ghana, 174
Glacier, 88
God, 81, 89-90
Gold Rush, 90
Government, 5, 6, 13, 14, 24, 60, 62, 65, 66, 117, 134, 139, 144, 146, 159, 160, 161, 162, 163, 168, 172, 173, 178, 180, 196, 206, 210, 212, 221, 223, 228, 230-234
Grand Canyon, 84, 86-87, 94
Great Britain, 63, 74
Green Globe, 100-101, 110
Gross Domestic Product, 136
Growth, see also regional growth, tourism growth and Smart Growth plan, 17, 20, 26, 31, 75, 91, 92, 119, 124, 134, 136, 137, 140, 144, 146, 151, 153159, 161, 162, 164, 165, 166, 167, 168, 170, 172, 173, 176, 184, 186, 189, 192-195, 204-205, 207, 213, 214, 216, 231
Guinean Forests of West Africa, 177

H

Habitat/s, 171, 175-176
Harmony, 101, 108
Hawaii, 99
Headman, 103
Health, 44, 60, 101, 104, 166, 222
Heritage, 6, 7, 12, 13, 16, 17, 18, 19, 33, 47, 78, 83, 90-93, 98, 104, 107, 139, 144, 145, 150, 151, 167, 168, 172, 174, 185, 191, 215, 217, 219, 228, 231, 232
Heritage-Environmental, 90-92
Highlands, 99, 101-103, 105, 107, 109, 111
Highway, 85
Hiking, 88-89
Hispanic, 142, 148-149, 154, 199
History, 101
Holistic, 14, 73, 178, 99
Home, 63, 65, 76, 81, 89, 92, 108, 109, 119, 128, 140, 152, 160, 161, 166, 168, 216, 229, 230, 232, 234

Homolovi Ruins State Park, 85
Horseback riding, 88
Host, 6, 7, 42, 45, 63, 66, 69, 76, 83, 100, 85, 121, 125, 128, 1131, 159, 165, 205, 211
Host community, 5, 14, 60, 62, 65, 66, 67, 69, 71, 72, 80, 83, 100, 116, 117, 127, 128, 130, 132, 133, 134, 153, 172, 180, 184, 190 206 207, 216
Host culture, 69, 119
Host perceptions, 125, 131, 152, 154, 205
Host population, 83, 136, 163, 175, 194, 195
Hotspot, 171, 174-177, 179, 181, 183, 190
Human Development Index, 137
Human, 15, 17, 28, 29, 37, 39, 44, 46, 57, 73, 82, 86, 90, 92, 93, 101, 102, 109, 110, 131, 132, 137, 154, 171, 172, 174, 175, 180, 211, 82, 86
Human-Recreation, 90-92

I

Images and advertising, 40-41
Images of "others", 26, 34
Images of quality tourism, 38-39, 43, 45, 48, 52-53
Impacts, see also cultural impacts, economic impacts, environmental impacts, perceived impacts, social impacts and tourism impacts, 4, 6, 7, 65, 66, 72, 76, 80, 86 93, 100, 109, 110, 114, 115, 116, 117-118, 119, 122, 123, 125, 126, 127, 128, 130 132, 133, 138, 141, 142, 145, 147, 149, 151, 152, 153, 154, 165, 166, 168, 172, 175, 180, 187, 189, 191, 194, 195, 196, 205, 211, 216, 230
Importance scales, 143
Income, 31, 53, 101-102, 108, 136, 137, 147, 151, 161, 163, 165, 176, 178, 180, 183, 192, 199, 205
In-depth interview, 84, 93-94
Indians, 16, 90, 187, 188
Indicators, 53, 118, 125, 138, 144, 145, 149, 151, 152-154, 172, 175, 228
Indigenous, 10, 14, 57, 65, 76, 100, 102, 109-110, 124, 127, 172, 173, 178, 190
Indo Burma, 176-177, 179, 181
Industry See Chapters 1-13
Informal brokers, 63, 66-67, 71-72, 74, 228, 229, 232
Informants, 103, 107, 217
Infrastructure, 102, 117, 118, 120, 123, 137, 163, 180, 183, 186, 196, 209, 211, 212, 214, 216

Interaction, 5, 6, 14, 26, 32, 34, 44, 54, 58, 65, 82, 83, 85, 87, 90, 93, 94, 114, 116, 119, 124, 128, 129, 130, 131, 133, 185, 212, 231, 233, 235
International Institute for Environment and Development, 175
International travel, 30-31, 39
Involvement, 13, 17, 81, 90, 98, 119, 141, 142, 147, 165, 167, 172, 173, 176, 178, 183, 196, 209, 211, 218, 219, 221, 222
Islands, 100, 110

J
Jerome, 86

K
Kava, 103
Komodo National Park, 173

L
Land, 99, 101-102, 107, 110
Landscape/s, 32-34, 46, 84-86, 93, 111, 184-185
Legacy, 104, 107
Leisure, 8, 17, 18, 19, 20, 26, 30, 31, 33, 36, 37, 53, 63, 77, 83, 109, 111, 116, 126, 135, 160, 161, 168, 180
Lewis, 89-90
Life cycle theory/model(s), 4, 114, 119, 120, 123, 124, 129, 130, 228
Local population, 5, 58, 151, 216, 228-230, 232-235
Logging, 107, 110

M
Madagascar and Indian Ocean Islands, 177, 179, 181
Marginality theories, 149
Marketers, 31, 95, 100, 129
Marketing, 11, 12, 13, 15, 18, 19, 21, 36, 39, 54, 62, 74,78, 88, 95, 96, 98, 116, 117, 128, 130, 133, 134, 135, 160, 170, 173, 211, 213, 214, 218, 221, 222, 223, 228, 230
Mashentucket Pequot Tribe, 184-186, 188
Mass entertainment, 24, 30
Mass media and social construction p. 27-30
Mass media and social reality, 30, 32-34
Matagali, 102-103, 107-108

Mauritius, 173, 190
Maximin principle, 193
Meaning/s, 5, 7, 9, 13, 14, 16, 24, 25, 28 29, 31, 40, 59, 80-84, 87-88, 90-97, 99, 101-104, 106, 184, 226, 227, 228, 230
Meanings-based approaches, 80, 83
Mean/s, 106, 145-146, 149, 150, 192, 197, 199-201
Measurement scales, 124, 130
Media and images of the "real" world, 40-41
Mediascapes, 24, 32-33
Mediation, 4, 11, 24, 26, 29, 31, 56-59, 61-63, 65-68, 70-75, 78, 226, 228, 230
Mediterranean, 172, 177, 179, 181
Mediterranean Basin, 177, 179, 181
Memory, 18, 82
Mesoamerica, 176-177, 179, 181
Meta-analysis, 156, 174-176, 183, 189
Meteor Crater, 86
Methodologies, 2, 3, 14, 42, 82, 120, 124, 132, 222
Methodological, 49, 80, 83, 84, 114, 115, 118, 124
Mexico, 173
Migration, 102-102, 162
Missouri River, 89
Mohegan Sun Casino, 125, 184, 186
Mohegan Tribe, 184
Money, 28, 33, 48, 59, 67, 71, 72, 104-106, 108, 128, 161, 176, 188, 212, 219, 220
Montana, 80, 84, 88-90, 93-94, 97-98
Mood states, 82

N
Nabukelevu, 99, 103-104, 106-108
Nakavika, 99, 103-104, 106-108
Namosi, 99-100, 102-103
National Geographic Traveler, 94, 180, 183, 191
National parks, 88, 171, 175, 190
Native American/s, 86, 90, 101, 110, 124, 156, 171, 183-185, 188, 190-191
Natural environment/s, 107, 109, 136, 140, 141, 173-175, 180, 196, 209, 212, 228, 229, 230
Natural/cultural preservation, 146-148, 150
Nature, 37, 46, 80-82, 84, 86, 88-89, 91-93, 96-100, 102, 109, 110, 166, 167, 175, 180, 189, 219
NEAP, 100-101, 111

NEVP, 102
New Caledonia, 177
New Zealand, 177, 179, 181
Nez Perce Trail, 90
No-growth and smart growth initiatives
    p. 159, 165-168
No-harm principle, 193
N-Vivo, 88

O

Oaxaca, 173
Operators, 10, 19, 47, 61, 62, 66, 67, 71, 72,
    100, 102, 108, 160, 167, 209, 212, 217,
    218, 219

P

Pacific Northwest, 171
Parks, 20, 60, 71, 88, 141, 171, 175, 180, 190,
    200, 201, 202, 204, 215
Partnership/s, 10, 172, 174, 186, 213, 221
Peace, 89, 141, 144, 146, 108, 232
Perceived impacts of tourism, 115-119,
    126-127, 132, 152, 153, 165, 187-188,
    195
Performing, 29, 81, 102, 219
Personal benefits, 125, 147, 150, 203
Personal Construct Theory, 4, 82, 97
Petrified Forest, 86
Phenomenon, 13, 14, 27, 29, 32, 75, 80, 82,
    134, 141, 156, 161
Philippines, 177
Photography, 26, 33, 88
Pilgrimage, 76, 83
Pioneers, 88-89
Place/s (including sense of place), 1, 4, 6, 7,
    11, 12, 13, 15, 16, 18, 21, 25 31, 32, 34,
    36, 46 ,47, 50, 51, 52, 53, 56, 63, 65, 71,
    73, 74, 76, 80, 84, 85, 87-96, 98, 99,
    101-102, 110, 114, 118-121, 123, 124,
    126, 127, 128, 129, 134, 149, 152, 156,
    161, 184, 187, 188, 190, 223, 226, 228,
    229, 232, 233
Plains, 88
Planners, 100, 125, 131, 137, 161,
    163, 204
Political economic theory, 4, 156, 159,
    163-164, 168, 183, 228, 231
Politics, 4, 12, 15, 19, 24, 30 35, 36 37, 56,
    74, 156, 157, 159, 184, 188, 189, 190,
    208, 222, 231
Politicians, 172, 210, 221

Polynesia and Micronesia, 177
Polypro, 92
Population (see also local population), 25, 83,
    99, 117, 118, 119, 122, 123, 124, 136,
    140, 142, 146, 151, 163, 172, 175, 185,
    192, 194, 195, 199, 216, 231, 232, 234
Postmodern, 3, 11-12, 19, 24, 25, 26, 40, 53,
    56, 59, 71, 73, 227
Postmodernism, 2
Postpositivism, 2-3, 80, 156, 227
Poverty, 102, 117, 166, 174, 183, 187, 192,
    210
Power relations/relationships, 122, 124, 173,
    174, 183-186, 188
Predictors of resident attitudes, 195-196, 205-
    207
Preservation, 92, 144, 146, 147, 148, 150,
    151, 168, 172, 194, 196, 200-203, 210
Preserves, 101, 108
Pride, 102, 144, 146, 150, 186, 231
Product/s, 6, 7, 8, 13, 31, 33, 38, 40, 41, 59,
    72, 95, 100-102, 107-110, 117, 120, 134,
    138, 163, 174, 189, 212, 227-231,
    233-235
Protected areas, 60, 172, 175-176, 178, 180,
    182
Provocative, 82
Psychological, 16, 97, 99, 127, 140, 206
Public, 5, 6, 8, 28, 30, 31, 38, 41, 51, 60, 66,
    85, 87, 95, 96, 123, 133, 141, 144, 146,
    147, 150, 153, 160, 163-166, 170, 171-
    172, 176, 204, 208, 219, 220
Public facilities, 85, 87, 141
Public lands, 95, 96, 171-172
Public relations, 96
Pull factor/s, 33, 84-85, 86
Push factors, 33
Push and pull factors, 33

Q

Quality of Life Index, 118, 138
Quality of life indicators, 118, 138, 143
Quality of life measures, 4, 136
Quality of life, 4, 6, 7, 10, 19, 56, 80,
    113-121, 123-127, 129-143, 145, 147,
    149-154, 156, 157, 165, 168, 171,
    183-184, 186-190, 192, 194-195, 204,
    210, 211, 216, 226, 228, 232-234
Quality tourism-ability to pay, 40, 44,
    52-53
Quality tourist experience, 38, 51, 58, 59, 68,
    73, 75

Quality-based experiences, 82
Quality-of-life dimensions, 137-138
Quantitative methods, 2, 83-84
Questionnaire, 80, 84, 90, 93, 142-143, 197

R

Rafting, 67, 84, 88, 90, 100, 102
Rawness, 88
Real world versus mediated world, 39-41
Recreation-Environmental, 90-91
Recreationists, 16, 90, 92, 96, 109, 206
Reflections, 3, 56, 82, 226, 227
Regional development, 153, 161-163, 169,
     170, 206, 223
Regional income, 162-163, 165
Regression analysis, 126, 142, 147-148, 187,
     202
Relationship building, 72-74
Relationships, see also community
     relationships, 34, 63, 66, 69, 72, 73, 74,
     76, 81, 107, 114, 119, 124, 130, 134,
     142, 151, 152, 162, 173-177, 180, 186,
     187, 189, 195, 200, 201, 202, 203
Remote, 99
Reproduction, 100
Research agenda, 14, 73-75
Residence, 76, 99, 106, 119, 160, 195
Resident attitudes, 115-121, 123-124, 126,
     129-135, 138, 141, 152, 153, 188,
     190-191, 196-197, 205-207, 228
Resident reactions, 127, 133
Residents, 99, 102-104, 106-109, 138-142,
     144-147, 149-154, 156, 157, 159, 165,
     166, 168, 182, 184-189, 191, 192-207,
     208, 209, 210, 212, 218, 219, 220, 221,
     228, 231-234
Resource sustainability, 156-157, 166
Resources, 51, 71, 93, 104-107, 124, 131,
     133, 137, 147, 150, 161, 162-168,
     171-172, 180, 182, 183, 185, 194, 195,
     204, 205, 211, 213, 216-219, 221
Reward/ing, 81-83
Rights, 100-102, 109
Ritual, 100, 102
River, 84, 87-94, 96-98
Rivers Fiji, 102
Road, 85, 87, 95
Rocks, 86-87
Rocky Mountains, 89
Rootedness, 81, 104, 107
Rugby, 103
Rural, 99, 101-103, 105, 107-109, 111

S

Salience, 104
Sampling methods, 84, 90
San Xavier del Bac Mission, 86
Saravanua ni vanua, 99
Satisfaction approaches, 80, 84
Satisfaction scales, 143
Scenery, 32, 83-87, 180, 229
Semiotic analysis, 35, 43
Sensations, 83
Sense of place, 12, 18, 80, 99-100, 103-104,
     106-107, 109-111, 228, 232, 233
Serua, 99, 102-103
Services marketing triangle, 116-117
Sevu Sevu, 103, 108
Snapshot, 6, 82
Social construction, 4, 8, 15, 21, 23-24,
     27-31, 33-37, 39, 49, 52, 56, 59, 69, 73,
     75, 77, 83, 129, 226-230
Social constructivism, 2-3, 24, 56, 156
Social disruption hypothesis, 120
Social equity, 10, 17, 157, 194, 208,
     210-211, 219-222
Social exchange theory, 4, 114, 120-121, 123,
     128-129, 141-142, 156, 157, 192, 195-
     197, 202, 204-205, 228
Social representation/s, 4, 114, 119, 121-123,
     129-131, 134, 183, 187-188, 228
Social representation theory 4, 114, 119, 121,
     123, 129, 228
Social impacts, 6, 118, 125, 131, 134, 135,
     153, 154, 164, 165, 199, 206
Socialization, 28, 39, 52
Socially constructed notions of tourism,
     49
Socio-cultural, 31, 57, 59, 66, 69, 102, 110,
     114, 131, 132, 139, 140-141, 142, 152,
     176, 205
Socioeconomic, 166, 172
Socioscapes, 32-34
Solidarity, 37,
South Central China, 177
South Fork of the American, 90, 96
Southwest Australia, 177
Spatial distribution of development, 194
Special place, 16, 90-92, 96, 98, 232
Species, 171, 175
Spirituality, 81, 88-90, 94
Spokesperson, 103
Sprawl, 88, 94
Spread-backwash, 194, 205
Stages, 32, 59, 60, 71,82, 120, 123, 128, 230,
     233

Stakeholders, 11, 13, 24, 56, 57, 61, 65, 66, 67, 74, 103, 108, 173, 208, 211, 218, 221, 230, 232, 233
Stock of knowledge, 27-28
Strategies, 97, 98, 100, 109, 125, 126-128, 131, 152, 161, 170, 188, 193, 197, 199, 201, 202, 204, 205, 208, 209
Structural models, 196
Suburban, 88
Succulent Karoo, 177, 179, 181
Sundaland, 177
Sunset Crater, 86
Survey, mail, 142-143, 197
Survey, telephone, 142
Survival, 102, 110-111, 133
Sustainability, 2, 6-7, 10-11, 17, 108, 124, 128, 152, 153, 156, 157, 167, 175, 180, 186-187, 189, 194, 206, 208-211, 213, 218, 220-223, 228, 232, 234
Sustainable development, 109, 166, 177, 182-183, 209-211, 222-223
Sustainable Net Benefit Index, 137
Sustainable, 10, 80, 99-100, 103, 108-110, 137, 152, 153, 165-167, 171, 175-177, 178, 182, 183, 189, 190, 191, 208-211, 219-220, 222-223, 232
Symbolic interaction, 4, 24
Symbolic interactionism/ist, 43-44
Symbolism, 31, 44

T

Tangible, 44, 82, 95
Technology, 40, 47, 95, 161
Television and construction of quality tourism, 39-41, 51-52
Tenor, 94
Tenure, 102, 182, 184
The Australian, 40, 49, 51, 53
The Horse Whisperer, 88
Themes, 2, 3, 4, 7, 12, 31, 35, 49, 73, 104, 107, 183, 189
Top down tourism development, 208
Tour/s, 19, 21, 29, 47, 58, 60-63, 66, 67, 68, 71, 75, 77, 78, 87, 101, 108, 108, 128, 129, 160, 178, 209, 212, 228, 228, 230
Tour guides, 29, 58, 60-62, 66-68, 71, 77-78, 129, 178, 228, 230
Tour operators, 66, 160, 209, 212
Tourism and Quality of Life Index, 118, 138
Tourism and regional development p. 161-163, 169-170
Tourism as an export, 161-163

Tourism benefits p 148, 150, 156, 173 177, 192-207, 233
Tourism destination/s, 10, 18, 30, 35, 62, 95, 108, 109, 117, 119, 130, 142, 151, 211, 212, 213, 214, 217, 221 222
Tourism development, 10, 17, 18, 19, 56, 80, 99, 101-109, 111, 116, 171-185, 187, 189-191, 192-197, 199-207, 208, 210, 211-213, 217, 218-220, 222-223, 233, 234
Tourism economics, 170
Tourism experiences and quality of life p. 142
Tourism imaging p .24, 30, 32, 38
Tourism impacts, 17, 114, 123, 125, 131, 138-139, 151-153, 206
Tourism growth, 20, 165, 172, 176, 189, 207, 214
Tourism perceptions, 133, 145, 206, 207
Tourism planning, 4, 133, 153, 168, 169, 172, 205, 207, 208-209, 211-213, 217-222, 231
Tourism policy, 6, 102, 109, 133, 153, 159, 162, 165-168, 169, 173, 179, 187, 190, 193, 194, 206, 207, 218, 221, 222, 231, 232, 233,
Tourism quality of life (TQOL) index, 114, 138, 143-147, 149-151, 157, 204
Tourism sector/s, 31, 190, 231
Tourist and host roles, 42, 44-46, 51
Tourist gaze, 9, 20, 26, 37, 77
Tourist gaze and westernized representation p. 26-27
Tourist/tourism settings, 37, 58, 68, 70, 77
Tourist types See Chapters 1 - 13
Tourist/s, 80-83, 85-88, 90, 93-97, 172-176, 178, 180, 182-184, 189
Traditions, 16, 20, 80, 98, 101, 104-106, 108, 122, 127, 140
Traffic, 85, 95, 120, 137, 141, 144, 145, 146, 149, 196, 199, 200, 201, 202, 204
Training, 61, 63, 73, 75, 95, 101, 180, 182, 234
Travel experience, 8-9, 16-17, 39, 60, 69, 71, 73, 76, 80, 83, 85, 217, 228-229, 231
Travel Industry Association of America, 180, 191
Travel narratives, 31, 33, 30
Traveler typologies, 4, 56
Traveler, 4, 33, 56, 63, 69, 73, 94, 134, 180, 183, 191, 228-234
Tropical Andes, 177
T-test, 106, 197, 199, 201
Turkey, 172, 190
Turkey vultures, 92

Types of brokers, 57, 60, 75
Typifications, 28

U

United Nations Environment Program, 175
United States, 26, 44, 45, 49, 71, 88, 90, 169,
    177, 183, 191, 205, 227, 229
Upper Navua Conservation Area, 108
Upper Navua River, 107-108
Upper Stretch, 92
Urban, 15, 16, 19, 20, 94, 102, 117, 120, 132,
    135 144, 146 147, 148, 149, 169, 172,
    190, 222
Urban environment, 172
Urban issues, 146-148

V

Vacation experience, 9, 88, 94, 98
Value/valued, 82-83, 94-96
Values, 3, 27, 31, 41, 72, 99-101, 121, 123,
    124, 129, 140, 164, 166, 167, 168, 187,
    208, 216
Values-based approach, 123
Vanua, 99, 101, 103
Vegetation, 101, 140, 175
Velvet, 88
Venice, 172
Village, 49, 87, 99, 102-108
Visitation, 108, 172, 183, 214, 216
Visitor impact management, 172
Visitor/s, 18, 37, 61, 66, 73, 74, 75, 80-81,
    83-84, 88-90, 92-97, 124, 128, 130, 132,
    133, 167, 172, 182, 183, 200, 201, 202,
    203, 204, 209, 217, 220, 227, 231,
    232-233, 234

Viti Levu, 99, 108

W

Way of life, 138, 144, 146-148
Wealth Accounting System, 137
Weather, 50, 85-87, 89, 95
West Africa, 177
West Virginia University, 175, 189
Western Frontie, 88-89
Western Ghats and Sri Lanka, 177
Wetlands, 140, 171
Whitewater, 16, 90-92, 96, 102, 109
Wilderness, 15, 16, 20, 75, 81, 91, 96-98,
    171, 176, 191
Wildlife refuges, 171
Wildlife, 65, 83, 85, 92, 109, 139, 140, 144,
    146, 171, 176, 178, 191
World Conservation Monitoring Center
    p. 175
World Tourism Organization, 174-175,
    191
World, 83-84, 89, 91, 94
World's Best, 39, 41-44, 47, 49, 52-54
Wupatki National Monument, 86

Y

Yavusa, 103
Yellowstone, 88, 97